José A. Valciukas, PhD

Forensic Neuropsychology: Conceptual Foundations and Clinical Practice

Pre-publication
REVIEW

"**F** ORENSIC NEUROPSYCHOLOGY IS A REMARKABLE ACHIEVEMENT and a much-needed contribution to the forensic sciences literature. Essential reading for mental health professionals who perform evaluations for the courts, as well as consumers of their evaluation reports such as court officers, judges, and attorneys, the book will also prove valuable for advanced graduate study and continuing education purposes. Having produced a volume that is nearly encyclopedic in scope, Dr. Valciukas succeeds masterfully in enlivening his subject through his inclusion of numerous case vignettes drawn from his vast experience at a major urban forensic psychiatry clinic. The questions for review and further discussion which follow the case illustrations are sure to stimulate not only graduate seminars but peer discussions among veterans in this challenging field.

Few books attempt to navigate as wide a terrain as Dr. Valciukas has set out to do in this ambitious volume, and fewer still succeed as he has done. While Dr. Valciukas' stated emphasis is on criminal court cases, the book's treatment of civil legal situations will be useful to those whose practice involves them primarily with civil legal matters. Dr. Valciukas has produced an outstanding book which deserves to become the standard against which other contributions to the forensic neuropsychology literature are measured."

Steven M. Sichel, PhD
Adjunct Assistant Professor,
Manhattanville College,
Purchase, NY

FORENSIC NEUROPSYCHOLOGY

CONCEPTUAL FOUNDATIONS AND CLINICAL PRACTICE

FORENSIC NEUROPSYCHOLOGY

CONCEPTUAL FOUNDATIONS AND CLINICAL PRACTICE

JOSÉ A. VALCIUKAS

LINCOLN MEDICAL AND MENTAL HEALTH CENTER AND NEW YORK MEDICAL COLLEGE

FOREWORD BY NATHANIEL J. PALLONE, RUTGERS UNIVERSITY

THE HAWORTH PRESS, INC.

NEW YORK - LONDON

1995

The Haworth Press, Inc., 10 Alice Street, Binghamton, NY 13904-1580

Library of Congress Cataloging-in-Publication Data

Valciukas, José A.
    Forensic neuropsychology : conceptual foundations and clinical practice / José A. Valciukas.
       p.   cm.
    Includes bibliographical references and index.
    ISBN 1–56024-402-X (alk. paper)
    1. Forensic neuropsychology. I. Title.
    [DNLM: 1. Forensic Psychiatry. 2. Neuropsychology. W 740 V141 1994]
RA1147.5.F66   1994
614'.1–dc20
DNLM/DLC
for Library of Congress
                                         94-20581
                                              CIP

To Drs. Pedro and Tauba Pasik, my mentors when I trained in New York City in the 1960s in experimental neurology. I continue to honor their influence and their friendship.

— José A Valciukas

ABOUT THE AUTHOR

José A Valciukas is Senior Psychologist at the Outpatient Division of the Department of Psychiatry, Associate Professor of Psychiatry, New York Medical College, Lincoln Hospital Affiliation, and Director of the Psychology Internship Program at Lincoln Hospital, Bronx, New York. He is also a Senior Psychologist at the Communicable Diseases Unit of the Mental Health Services, Montefiore Hospital at Rikers Island. He was Senior Psychologist at the Forensic Psychiatric Clinic for the Criminal and Supreme Courts of New York State, New York City District (1988-1992) and also Associate Professor for the Environmental and Occupational Medicine Division, Department of Community Medicine (1976-1988). While at Mount Sinai, Dr Valciukas was Head of the Environmental Neurotoxicology Unit of the Environmental Research Laboratory, Managing Editor of *Environmental Research*, and Associate Editor of the *American Journal of Occupational Medicine.*

Dr Valciukas has published numerous research papers on environmental and occupational neurotoxicology and is the author of *Foundations of Environmental and Occupational Neurotoxicology,* published in 1991.

CONTENTS

FOREWORD

In the final chapter of this masterful volume, Dr. José Valciukas quite correctly observes that "Scientific research at the interface between neuropsychology and criminal law has barely begun." That the statement is unerringly accurate is unquestionable; that it need not have been thus is a lamentable historical reality. There is strong evidence that, indeed, the first historically-documented "expert witness" in a British courtroom (or perhaps in any courtroom anywhere) to offer scientifically-anchored testimony on the mental condition of a defendant relied on grounds that were frankly neuropsychological — and at a time that preceded by three generations psychiatry's and psychology's descent into the murky world of id, ego, and superego.

In his resourceful 1968 treatise *Crime and Insanity in England: The Historical Perspective,* the distinguished Oxford criminologist Nigel Walker traces the remote antecedents for the principles announced at M'Naghten's trial of 1843 to Saxon jurisprudence, well before the Norman conquest — and, indeed, opines that even earlier sources may be found in the laws of Rome applied during the Roman occupation of Britain in the first century. Certain provisions of the Roman code, Walker believes, were preserved orally and were thus incorporated into the first written laws for what was to become modern Britain. Thus, as Walker observes (pp. 16-20), the "Penitentials" of Egbert, the eighth-century Saxon archbishop of York, contained provisions for exculpation for murder for "a man who hath fallen out of his senses or wits, and it come to pass that he kill someone." Similarly, the laws of the Saxon king Ethelred prescribed leniency (but not exculpation) "if anyone does anything unintentionally" or "when a man is an involuntary agent [because] he acted as he did from compulsion."

Walker (p. 67) cites some 222 trials at one British court alone — albeit, London's central criminal court (the celebrated "Old Bailey") — in the century preceding M'Naghten at which either the matter of the accused's mental state at the time of the criminal act *or* his or her mental fitness to stand trial was raised. By Walker's count, the pleading of incompetence to stand trial prevailed in 83% of the cases in which it was raised, while what amounts to an insanity defense prevailed in 45% of the cases in which it was raised. For the United Kingdom as a whole, there were perhaps four times as many insanity defenses during that period (p. 72). Thus, Walker contends (p. 74), "Successful defences of insanity had been a regular feature of Old Bailey trials" well before the M'Naghten case, including even the empaneling of physicians to offer what we would today call "expert witness" testimony as to the defendant's state of mind at the time of his or her allegedly criminal behavior.

Of those cases tried in the Old Bailey in the century before M'Naghten, certainly the most significant to the central tenets of Dr. Valciukas' volume is the Hadfield trial of 1800 (Walker, pp. 73-83). In May of that year, Hadfield fired a pistol at George III as the King entered the Royal Box at the Drury Lane Theatre. Though the shot went a foot wide of its mark and landed harmlessly in the orchestra pit, the event amounted to attempted homicide; and an attempt to kill the King itself constitutes treason, then as now a capital offense.

For that reason, Hadfield was permitted greater latitude in the preparation and presentation of a defense than was the custom in ordinary criminal matters. A jurist named Erskine, whom Walker (p. 75) describes as "at the peak of his career" and as having "mastered the literature of his subject," appeared for the defense. To examine the defendant, Erskine engaged "Sir Alexander Crichton, whose recently published *Inquiry into the Nature and Origin of Mental Derangement* included discussions of insane motives for murder" and who later became personal physician to Czar Alexander I and, in that position, organized the first department of health for Imperial Russia.

According to Walker, those physicians who had testified in earlier trials had typically known the defendant personally for some time, either as patient or as a member of the community whose "peculiarities" had become common knowledge. But Crichton did not meet or examine Hadfield until well after the attempt on the King's life, so that Walker construes his activity as the precursor for the role and function of today's "expert witness" in mental health.

But the capital issue is that — and, as a consequence of the knowledge explosion in the neurosciences of the past three decades, this point is more significant today than it was when Walker composed his treatise — the pivot for Hadfield's madness was not primarily psychological, but rather *neuro*psychological: Hadfield "had obvious and disfiguring wounds in the head, acquired in the service of his King in action against the French six years before. One of these had penetrated the skull, so that Erskine was able to invite the jury to inspect the membrane of the brain itself [and] The regimental surgeon [testified] how he had been compelled to have Hadfield tied to a bed for a fortnight . . . incoherent, with 'manifest symptoms of derangement.' Crichton's evidence was to the effect that the prisoner's madness was probably the result of his wounds" (pp. 76-77).

Both the jury and the Lord High Justices were persuaded by Crichton's testimony — which had very clearly designated a *neurological* basis for Hadfield's mental condition, and thus stands as the originating point for forensic neuropsychiatry. But Hadfield had made an attempt at the life of the monarch, an act that might have gained him popularity among the American colonists who had fought a revolution against the same monarch; and, from Crichton's testimony, it was clear that Hadfield might, at any moment and without warning, emit what we might today describe as impulsive neurogenic violence.

Yet the state of the law at that time contained no provision for the confinement even of dangerous persons who had been found not culpable on mental grounds. Very likely because the object of Hadfield's attack had been the monarch rather than a lesser personage, "a hastily drafted Bill was . . . passed by Parliament in order to provide a clear-cut and foolproof procedure for such cases . . . Whether the [Trial of Lunatics] Act of 1800 'for the safe custody of insane persons charged with offences' would have been drafted and passed with such urgency if Hadfield's target had not been a royal one . . . is doubtful" (Walker, p. 78).

The Act of 1800 made formal provision for the confinement in mental institutions of defendants found not guilty on the ground of insanity and further provided that "the only possible verdict in cases in which the jury was satisfied that the accused was insane at the time of his crime was to be the special verdict [and] that the acquittal was on the ground of insanity; the alternative of plain acquittal was no longer open to them." Upon such acquittal, the defendant was "to be kept in strict custody, until His Majesty's pleasure be known." In addition, the Act provided the same disposition for persons found not competent to stand trial." The Act apparently applied only when the actual or prospective offense carried the death penalty — but at a time when "the penalty for all felonies was capital" (p. 80).

To the extent that Walker is correct in his facts and interpretations, it seems entirely clear that forensic *neuro*psychiatry and forensic *neuro*psychology long predate forensic psychiatry and forensic psychology. How very different a set of assumptions prevailed in Britain in 1843, when the hapless Daniel M'Naghten, a disappointed seeker of a political appointment in a government bureau, claimed to have received a message from God instructing him to kill the Prime Minister. Like Hadfield's, McNaghten's shot went wide of its mark — but, in this case, struck and killed the Prime Minister's secretary.

Consider the *zeitgeist* that must have prevailed at the time of McNaghten's trial to yield a conclusion in which a belief in personal communication from the Almighty rather than the hard evidence of neurological dysfunction should have become precedental throughout the English-speaking nations of the world. If one is given to analogical rumination, one might conclude that Hadfield is to M'Naghten as (approximately) science is to mythology. Alternately, that M'Naghten and not Hadfield became the very touchstone for judicial consideration of mental health testimony is perhaps no more surprising than that Freud forsook a promising career in neurology to invent the murky, mystic, mythical world of id, ego, superego. And, if we speculate even further, we might wonder whether — had the powerful investigative techniques of the neurosciences of the last half of the twentieth century been available in nineteenth century Vienna — it might not have been the case that the gigantic mind of Freud might never have experienced an intellectually compelling need for such invention.

Though scientific psychology has maintained independent perspectives at least from the time of Wundt and Fechner, clinical psychology and clinical psychiatry have emerged decisively from that mystic world only within the past three or four decades. With this volume, Dr. Valciukas, drawing upon his rich experience in neuropsychology in general and forensic neuropsychology in particular, takes a long step in liberating forensic psychology from the same murky mire.

— *Nathaniel J. Pallone, Rutgers University*

PREFACE

Many people contributed with their time and criticism in the preparation of this book. I express my gratitude especially to Dr Richard Rosner, Director of the Forensic Psychiatric Clinic for the Criminal and Supreme Courts for his constant encouragement in the preparation of this book while I was Senior Psychologist at that clinic between 1988-1992. Dr Howard Owens, from the same clinic, was a superb teacher: Almost single-handedly he trained me as a forensic psychologist, reading and sometimes editing almost all of the more than 750 reports that I wrote while at the Criminal and Supreme Courts.

At Rikers Island, I worked very closedly with Dr Raj Singh (former clinical neuropsychiatrist at the Mental Health Services, Montefiore Hospital at Rikers Island), and Dr Sonya Oquendo, currently the Director of such services. Both were inspirational in their compassion, dedication to the patients, and knowledge of the clinical and forensic issues encountered in such a large detention center.

Dr Doren Berman, former Head of the Neuropsychology Program at Queens College of the City University of New York, read the historical chapters of the book. The Introduction to this work began as an invited lecture I gave to graduate students in that program. I am also grateful to Dr Steven Sichel, a post-graduate at the Forensic Psychiatric Clinic, who read early drafts of the book.

I thank again Dr Sylvia Frank for editing this book. However, this underestimates her contributions in the many years I have known her, as she has become a good friend, something that at maturity one learns to treasure. Dr Frank has been a source of constant support during the preparation of this book.

Ms Katheryn Gleaton gave me her personal support during the sometimes difficult transition between jobs. The work benefited from the support and encouragement of many at The Haworth Press, Inc., including Bill Cohen, Bill Palmer and his staff in the book division, and Dr Nathaniel Pallone of Rutgers in his role as senior editor in criminal justice and forensic behavioral sciences for Haworth. I thank Eric Workowski of Rutgers and Jordan Leiter of Pennsylvania State University for their assistance with computerization. I especially thank Sinauer Publishing for granting me permission to reproduce the figure which appears on page 162 herein.

This manuscript was completed very soon after DSM-IV was published, following many years of preparation by the American Psychiatric Association. This work thus incorporates most of the features new to DSM-IV, with the exception of the radical elimination of the term "organic" as a descriptor of mental disorders. The DSM-IV eliminates the notion of organic on the basis that most, if not all, mental disorders have an organic basis. However, neuropsychology needs to retain the "old" terminology to emphasize the distinction between disorders that are likely to be the result of a life-long learning process where environmental factors are of paramount importance from the conditions that are clearly related to brain injury or toxic-metabolic dysfunction. Parenthetically, the World Health Organization's ICD-10 has retained the concept of "organic mental disorders."

All the vignettes that are used throughout the book depict real people that I personally observed. However, their names, demographic profiles, places of origins, and even personal circumstances have been so changed that I myself are unable to trace the original sources. None of the high profile cases in which I have been commissioned to act as an expert witness are mentioned in this book.

— _José A. Valciukas_

PART I

INTRODUCTION

1: THE SCOPE OF FORENSIC NEUROPSYCHOLOGY

PHILOSOPHERS AND CRIMINOLOGISTS HAVE LONG DRAWN THE DISTINCTION between, on the one hand, the criminal act, the offense, the charges brought against a person accused of a crime by members of society (*actus reus*) and, on the other hand, the criminal mind or the criminal intent (*mens rea*), the mind that actually intended to commit such a crime and is capable of doing so.

The criminal act (*actus reus*) — whether a crime has been committed, the nature of the crime, the standards by means of which the criminal act is evaluated, the rules of evidence, sentencing and punishment — are all questions within the province of the criminal law and are not the main focus of this book. Consequently, they are dealt with only peripherally.

Criminal law and *civil* law are separate in the US legal system. Those actions brought by government against an individual who has allegedly committed a crime are tried under the criminal law. Although neuropsychologists have been called to act as expert witnesses for either the defense or the prosecution in a large variety of criminal cases, those that typically attract public attention are murder, assault, rape, and robbery. This book inevitably reflects the author's experience in the psychological clinic serving New York's Supreme and Criminal Courts. To the court clinic are referred criminal cases in various stages of the legal proceedings including competence to stand trial, pre-pleading investigations, pre-sentence evaluations, and cases involving violation of probation or parole. Some of them are outstanding criminal cases that bring considerable public attention. However, on a typical day a psychologist-in-residence sees numerous cases that rarely bring such a degree of attention but that are equally important and sometimes even more humanly interesting.

Grillot (1983) defines a civil suit as "a dispute between private individuals involving either a breach of an agreement or a breach of a duty imposed by law." Neuropsychologists have long been recognized as expert witnesses in matters of tort law in which a person exercises his or her right to bring civil actions against another for a wrongful act or omission that causes injury (e.g., head injuries resulting from car accidents, evaluations of disability resulting from such injuries, establishing rational basis for the compensation of such individuals, etc.).

Forensic neuropsychologists are increasingly called to testify on matters of the relation between the brain and the criminal mind. Is the individual mentally retarded? Did the defendant suffer from a brain condition that predisposed him or her to commit a crime? Is the defendant truly unable to remember the events leading to his charges or is she faking lapses of memory? These are some of the questions that are the main focus of the book.

The role of psychologists in general, and that of neuropsychologists in particular, in legal procedures concerning the role of the brain in "causing" the offense needs clarification and objective consideration. There have been many attempts to discredit the contributions of psychologists in criminal forensic matters, and many slurs appear in the legal literature concerning the value of contributions of psychologists. Recent publications (most notably that of Ziskin and Faust, 1988) have been purposely written as "ammunition" pointing to weaknesses of the tools that are the daily bread of behavioral scientists. A more balanced account of the art, the technology, the science of forensic neuropsychology will be attempted in this book.

It has long been recognized that the term "criminal mind" has an implicit implication of prejudice: There is an implication that a decision has already been made that an individual is a "criminal." To avoid this prejudice — and to keep in mind the important distinction between the "offense" and the "mind" (or behavior) — the expression "state of mind" will be used throughout this book to denote *mens rea* or the criminal mind.

The Patient, the Case, the Defendant and Much, Much More

A word about terminology. In court proceedings, an individual is referred to according to the status of his or her legal proceedings. Thus, a case may represent a past decision; a suspect or a detainee is a person still not formally charged with an offense; a defendant is a person who has been indicted (charged with the offense) but is still waiting for trial or sentence; a probationer is a person who is given the opportunity of living in the community with certain restrictions and/or impositions; a parolee is a person who, after completing part of his or her sentence in jail, is eligible to spend time in the community, out of prison, often on account of his or her good behavior; an inmate is a person presently imprisoned; and a bailee is a person released in the community on bond as he or she awaits trial or sentencing. The legal status of the individual is not relevant to the argument and/or the issues to be discussed in this volume.

Thus, I will simply refer to people in the several stages of the legal proceedings as "individuals," whether men or women.

It sometimes is difficult to avoid using the style of court report writing. Whereas in journalism a woman may be referred to as a "murderer," in legal report writing she is referred to as "charged with murder." Whereas the layperson may say "she killed the man" the mental health worker writing a forensic report uses the expression "during the instant offense" or "during events dealing with Mrs Brown's charges." In the American legal system the defendant is innocent until proven guilty; mental health workers have the duty not to write anything that would lead to prejudice against the defendant.

Forensic Neuropsychology

Neuropsychology is a discipline that relates manifestations of mind and behavior to events in the nervous system, particularly to brain functions. Forensic neuropsychology is the application of the knowledge, skills, technology that has been gathered within the corpus of such discipline for legal purposes. This book is about the uses and abuses of neuropsychological concepts for forensic purposes particularly within criminal law.

Forensic is the term derived from the Latin and indicates pertaining to the court. Forensic Neuropsychology is thus the art, the technology, the science (and sometimes the ideology or pseudoscience) that is used or invoked to understand a variety of legal issues where the action of the nervous system is known or suspected. Forensic Neuropsychology is a term that has been coined only recently; unfortunately, the field was envisioned at first as concerning itself with the behavioral consequences of head injuries. The field is, in fact, much broader. One of the primary objectives of this book is to illustrate the wide range of application of neuropsychological knowledge and technological expertise to the understanding and clarification of specific issues brought to our attention by individuals who face certain aspects of legal proceedings.

NEUROPSYCHOLOGY AND THE LAW

Neuropsychology is the scientific and clinical discipline that specializes in behavioral and psychological manifestations of nervous system function, an endeavor that is well-rooted in the neurosciences. According to Kandel, Schwartz, and Jessell (1991), the goal of the neurosciences is to understand how we perceive, move, think, and remember. Until recent decades, the basic facts about brain development, brain cell communication, and modification of brain function by experience (memory) were understood in terms of facts about biology on the cell level; however, in the past two decades, the field of the neurosciences has exploded with data about the functioning of the brain at the biochemical and molecular level, leading to many new practical applications.

Although knowledge of brain-behavior relationships has been accumulating since antiquity, a branch of the behavioral sciences called *physiological psychology* appeared only at the beginning of the 19th century as a subject of scholarly inquiry and began to be formally taught in universities only in the early decades of the 20th century.

A Brief History

The historical roots of neuropsychology as a body of knowledge are difficult to identify with precision. No particular point is easily identifiable in time when a body of knowledge about the brain-mind relationship began to be accumulated. Scholars such as Boring (1950) trace the origin of the study of these relationships to the beginning of experimental science in the 17th century. However, as interest in the neurosciences continues to grow, we continue to find earlier and earlier references to the brain as the site of the human "soul" or "spirit," in at least one case, in an Egyptian papyrus dating to the seventeenth century BC (Kandel, Schwartz, and Jessell, 1991).

Second, because the "neurosciences" in general and "neuropsychology" in particular encompass such a heterogeneous body of knowledge, there are only a few historical figures who, at any given point in time, were conversant with all of the science and all of the technology associated with clinical and experimental aspects of brain research. This body of knowledge includes hands-on skill in neuroanatomy and physiology of the nervous system (often with an evolutionary and developmental perspective), brain surgery in various animal species and humans, practical knowledge of brain stimulation, knowledge of recording and techniques for data analysis, state-of-the-art imaging procedures, an interest in clinical speculations about brain-behavior relationships, techniques for the clinical assessment of individuals afflicted with brain disorders, and the knowledge of practical aspects of cognitive rehabilitation of afflicted individuals.

It is not easy to point to a particular "creator" of the scientific and professional field called neuropsychology and the precise time when the noun neuropsychology was first used. It is not that neuropsychology lacks people of achievement. Neuropsychology can claim as its own the creators of Gestalt psychology: Max Wertheimer (1880-1943), Wolfgang Köhler (1887-1967), and Kurt Koffka (1886-1941). Other prominent figures in the field include Donald O Hebb (1904-1985), Karl Spencer Lashley (1890-1958), Hans-Lukas Teuber (1916-1977), Heinrich Klüver (1897-1979), AR Luria (1902-1977), Roger Sperry (1913-1994), and Karl H Pribram (b. 1919). But neuropsychologists sometimes also claim as their own Henry Head (1861-1940), Kurt Goldstein (1878-1965), and Morris B Bender (1905-1983), who were in fact clinical neurologists. Neuropsychologists who have investigated the behavioral consequences of exposures to environmental and occupational neurotoxic agents name Bernardino Ramazzini (1633-1714) in Italy, and Alice Hamilton (1869-1970) in the United States as towering figures.

The first issue of the international journal *Neuropsychologia* appeared in January of 1964. The term *neuropsychology* was defined in that issue as "a particular area of neurology of common interest to neurologists, psychiatrists, psychologists and neurophysiologists" and traced its originators to a small meeting held by European neuropsychologists and psychologists early in the 1950s. Donald Hebb published his *The Organization of Behavior: A Neuropsychological Theory*, in 1949. An editorial that appeared in *Neuropsychologia* in 1969 indicated that "no better definition is ... available," although American psychologists in the early 1980s obviously thought of the term as applying to a particular scientific focus within psychology.

The body of knowledge concerning the biological determinants of behavior has been referred to as Biological Psychology or Biopsychology, to call attention to the fact that behavior is shaped by genetic, hormonal, and other biological systems. However, it is generally agreed that a specialized field within psychology called neuropsychology began to appear in the early 1960s; formal training programs that synthesized the neurosciences and clinical psychology began only in the late 1960s. The Epilogue of this book contains references to several other branches of knowledge that have contributed to the substance and the practice of neuropsychology in the United States.

Branches of the Law

Civil law regulates disputes between private individuals, in which the government may sometimes be a party. Criminal law brings government action against an individual for an act — the criminal offense — against society. The term *forensic* derives from forum (Latin for "the court"). Because the term is not generally recognized by the layman, the term forensic is often replaced by legal, which does not have the same meaning, particularly in this book, which focuses on the professional activity of those clinical neuropsychologists who work in the court system. At times, it would appear as if other authors have avoided the term forensic because it may connote sleuthing as depicted in popular mass media.

Forensic Psychology

The history of forensic psychology in the United States dates to the beginning of this century. It is generally agreed that the earliest contributions to the field of forensic (or legal) psychology were made by Hugo Münsterberg (1863-1916), a German psychologist who later became professor of psychology at Harvard University. A paper in the early 1900s by Münsterberg on the subject of the witness stand represents one of the early contributions to the field. A paper by Robert M Hutchins and Donald Slesinger called Legal Psychology appeared in *Psychological Review* in 1929. Hutchins, then dean of the School of Law at Yale, became long-term president of the University of Chicago and later of the Ford Foundation and ended his career as Executive Director of the Center for the Study of Democratic Institutions. Slesinger followed Hutchins to Chicago as a member of the faculty of law and later served briefly as dean of the School of Law, the first trained psychologist to serve in such a capacity.

In 1931, Lewis M Terman (1877-1956) addressed a convention of the Los Angeles Bar Association about legal psychology. However, the American Psychology-Law Society, Division 41 of the American Psychological Association, was not founded until 1961.

Psychologists began to gain formal recognition as expert witnesses in legal matters as a result of a series of landmark cases. In Jenkins v The United States, a case argued before the United States Court of Appeals in 1962, psychologists were recognized for the first time as experts who could offer opinions on matters of mental illness; until then, only a physician was permitted to offer such an opinion. In New York State, psychologists could not be called as expert witnesses about the matter of competence to stand trial until late in the 1980s. A set of ethical standards for forensic psychologists was formulated only in 1991. Also in 1991, in a landmark case (Morris et al. v Chandler Exterminators) in Georgia, upon appeal it was successfully argued that a neuropsychologist could present expert testimony on the matter of behavioral and psychological effects of exposures to neurotoxic agents; an earlier decision had denied such privilege.

The term *forensic neuropsychology* is of very recent origin and first appeared in chapters of books about clinical neuropsychology early in the 1980s (McMahon and Satz, 1981). Neuropsychology has been linked to the "law" or "lawyers" in books that appeared in the early 1990s (Sbordone, 1991; Dywan, Kaplan and Pirozzolo, 1991).

Forensic Sciences and Forensic Neuropsychology

Forensic neuropsychology is a branch of the forensic sciences, that is, one of the several disciplines applied to the law or legal proceedings. The American Academy of Forensic Sciences, with approximately 3,500 members in 1991, represents the specialties of Criminalistics, Engineering Sciences, Jurisprudence, Odontology, Pathology and Biology, Physical Anthropology, Psychiatry and Behavioral Sciences (where Forensic Neuropsychology is included), Questioned Documents, Toxicology, as well as a multidisciplinary General Section.

Forensic neuropsychology has slightly different meanings when applied to different provinces of the law. In criminal law, it is the science, the technology, the legal expertise, and the art of ascertaining whether a criminal act can or cannot be understood as the result of the dysfunction of the defendant's nervous system. Neuropsychologists sometimes evaluate the victims of criminal offenses, particularly in their capacity to function as reliable witnesses. In civil litigation, forensic neuropsychology often means the application of these skills to determine whether a defendant's wrongdoing has caused the plaintiff's brain injury or disability.

Neuropsychologists may also work in family courts, for example, in the assessment of brain damage of children physically abused by their parents. Others work in correctional facilities, addressing the multiple issues of brain disorders caused by numerous conditions including head injuries, vascular disorders, drug abuse, and/or AIDS.

Forensic neuropsychologists perform forensic investigations and write forensic evaluations. At the request of either the plaintiff, the defendant, or sometimes judges and independent agencies, they examine — using state-of-the-art techniques — the evidence for or against the presence of a neuropsychological disorder and its possible effects on behavior.

Legal Proceedings

A review of forensic neuropsychology would be incomplete without at least a cursory reference to key phases of the legal proceedings to which the written opinions are submitted.

☐ A psychiatric or psychological evaluation is often requested to determine an individual's competence to face legal proceedings against him or her. This is a team effort involving the participation of various professionals including experts in various fields of medical practice, psychiatrists, neurologists, psychologists, and sometimes psychiatric social workers; a neuropsychologist is sometimes asked to write an opinion regarding a specific point (e.g., the claim that the defendant is suffering from an amnestic syndrome, or shows cognitive and behavioral manifestations of dementia, or suffers neurological and cognitive disorders associated with in utero exposure to illegal drugs, etc.). These reports result from what are often called "fitness" examinations — or, in New York State, "a 730 examination," thus termed after Section 730.50 of the Criminal Code that explains and dictates the scope of evaluations to determine such competency.

☐ Sometimes, judges order a psychiatric or psychological report as part of pre-pleading investigation (PPI). As its name indicates, this evaluation is performed after the defendant has been formally charged with a crime but before the defendant pleads "guilty" or "not guilty." A neuropsychologist, alone or as part of a team of mental health workers, may be asked specific questions concerning the defendant's state of mind during the events leading to the charges. Sometimes these evaluations are ordered by the lawyer acting as counsel for the defendant.

☐ A neuropsychological evaluation is sometimes ordered by the judge as a result of a pre-sentence investigation (PSI) because of the seriousness of the charges brought against the convicted individual who pleaded guilty or was found guilty by a jury (e.g., in cases of either murder, assault, or rape), or because there is a need to establish whether the convicted person needs to adhere to certain rules while on probation when charged with a crime of lesser degree (e.g., for a homeless individual who is charged with petit larceny to seek treatment for a psychiatric disorder; one found to be in possession of illegal drugs to attend a drug-rehabilitation program; one charged with endangering the welfare of a child to find a job adequate for his or her limited level of intellectual function, and so on).

☐ A neuropsychological evaluation is sometimes requested "after-sentence," when the convicted is on probation or already incarcerated, facing either further mandatory incarceration, or imminent release as a result of a "split sentence" (incarceration followed by probation). In cases where the convicted person faces mandatory incarceration, a judge may be interested in determining the appropriate custody level and/or treatment, or knowing whether the individual is a good candidate for a particular sort of vocational rehabilitation program. In other cases, defendants have been asked to seek alcohol rehabilitation but did not; in fact they were found to continue to drink, neglecting their responsibilities as parents.

☐ *Probation* is time spent in the community in which the individual's behavior is monitored (e.g., by the probation officer); parole is the release into the community of an individual convicted of a crime, often, after showing good behavior. Violation of the conditions of probation or of parole are instances in which the probationer (or parolee) fails to adhere to the rules imposed when released into the community (e.g., generally, by committing additional crimes or by association with individuals who are have been charged with crimes). Because of the circumstances under which the probation or parole has been violated (e.g., failure to obey a restraining order that prohibited visiting her ex-husband, finding a random sample of urine contaminated by illegal drugs, etc.), a neuropsychological evaluation may be ordered.

When acting as expert witnesses, forensic neuropsychologists focus on single events and/or single individuals. They show, or fail to show, how nervous system dysfunction led to the events for which the defendant is charged. The forensic neuropsychologist then writes a report summarizing his or her own findings. This report is read by the conflicting parties in the court's adversary process and is often submitted to the court, thus becoming a legal document. Expert witnesses will sometimes appear in court and are challenged to defend their findings in front of a special investigative panel or a jury.

The Language of the Criminal Courts

Forensic psychologists learn a variety of languages:

- That of the law as explained by parties who sometimes, if not always, have an interest in the outcome of the case (the defendant, his or her counsel, the district attorney, the community, etc.).

- That of individuals charged with or convicted of a crime (i.e., the unique jargon defendants and inmates sometimes use, or the twisted logic and rationalizations of one who has a doctoral degree but suffers from an antisocial personality disorder).

- That of people with various professional backgrounds and training in the health professions (e.g., psychiatrists, neurologists, physicians with various specializations).

- That of the experts in other disciplines who write forensic reports concerning the offense or the offender in areas that are not necessarily the behavioral sciences (i.e., forensic toxicology including statements about blood alcohol exceeding legal standards, ballistic and engineering reports, reports dealing with environmental acoustics, textile manufacturing, etc.).

- That of professionals who work in law enforcement, prosecution, defense, probation, corrections, or as judges, because the forensic psychologist needs to be able to understand the technical language in which court documentation is written.

A comprehensive glossary defining all these concepts exceeds the scope of this book. The most common terms used in neurology, psychiatry, clinical psychology and neuropsychology are explained throughout this text. For definitions of other terms, one may consult the *Dictionary of Criminal Justice Data Terminology* published by the US Department of Justice through its now-defunct Law Enforcement Assistance Administration (1976), *Black's Law Dictionary* (1983), and *Crime Dictionary* by DeSola (1988).

THE FORMAL ASPECTS OF THIS BOOK

Forensic Neuropsychology is, then, a book concerned with state-of-the-art techniques for the assessment of brain function and behavior in a legal context; it is also the results of such an inquiry. It explains how mental health workers rely on impressions and must resist halo effects (the tendency to attribute undue significance to an outstanding piece of information or to a unique trait of the defendant's personality). It also focuses on the difficulties in obtaining basic information such as medical information and family, educational, and work-history in someone who is motivated to tell everything that is wrong with him or her, or in someone who is motivated to suggest that he is the perfect picture of health. It also concerns itself with the principles of physical examination, review of mental status, evaluation of signs and syndromes, and the identification of possible mental disorders.

Interwoven with the chapters are case histories. These case reports might be construed as "pictures" in an illustrated book. An alert reader may not fail to notice that the terminology used in the description of the cases is that of the DSM-IV (the fourth edition of the *Diagnostic and Statistical Manual of Mental Disorders,* published by the American Psychiatric Association in 1994). The "illustration" reveals not only the defendant but the evaluator in a dynamic interaction.

Target Audience

This book is written for mental health workers, students of criminology and lawyers who face issues of neurological involvement in general and brain damage in particular in the context of legal proceedings. Although many aspects of tort law are discussed throughout the book, the focus is on criminal proceedings.

Mental health workers include psychiatrists, neurologists, and psychologists who specialize in the evaluation of brain disorders, psychiatric nurses, social workers, mental retardation professionals, audiologists, speech and communication disorder specialists, professionals involved in several areas of physical rehabilitation of the brain-injured including special-education teachers, and teachers of the hearing-impaired and the blind. The book makes numerous references to issues and presents many illustrative cases of defendants who used or abused drugs; therefore professionals who work at all levels of alcohol and drug rehabilitation may benefit from this book. The author's expertise in matters of environmental and occupational health are brought to bear, particularly in Chapter 17 (Neurotoxic Agents in the Environment and the Workplace). Physicians and neuropsychologists specializing in the evaluation of workers who claim to have suffered from brain disorders as a result of occupational exposures to neurotoxic agents can also greatly benefit from this book since so few books deal with the technical and legal matters associated with both "criminal" and "toxic causation."

Approach

Neuropsychology on the one hand and the legal professions on the other are guilty of producing the most dreadful literature; most (even the best educated) stay away from such writing; only the erudite may find pleasure in reading such sources, and I am not even sure of that either. An extraordinary effort was made to make the subject matter of this book comprehensible to the layperson who is interested in the issues involved in relation to brain injuries and criminal responsibility. This includes court personnel (such as probation officers) who need to read such reports — and, in general, people who are themselves facing legal proceedings and may need to plan reasonable strategies in cognizance of their options.

PART II

THE FORENSIC NEUROPSYCHOLOGICAL EXAMINATION

2: CLINICAL EVALUATIONS

IN THE COURT CLINIC, A PROFESSIONAL OPINION IS OFTEN REQUIRED OF MENTAL health experts on a vast array of disabling and disparate conditions, such as problems resulting from normal aging, alcoholism, amputations, arthritis, birth defects, blindness or visual impairment, brain damage, cerebral palsy, deafness, alcohol and drug-abuse problems, epilepsy, facial disfigurement, hearing disorders, learning disabilities, mental and emotional disorders — including a large variety of psychotic disorders — mental retardation, multiple neurological disorders including dementia, speech and language disorders, and stroke.

In the vast majority of cases, one or another of these disabling conditions can be suspected as afflicting the individual facing legal proceedings; less often they concern other individuals mentioned in the background documentation that accompanies the defendant's case, such as his or her relatives, the victim of an attempted murder or rape, or the defendant's parents.

A mental health professional forms his or her best opinion or judgment as a result of performing a clinical examination; that opinion is written in a document called a clinical evaluation. The clinical neuropsychological examination is the systematic study of signs and symptoms associated with the normal or abnormal function of the nervous system through observation and probes. The adjective clinical indicates the use of simple observational probes and a clinical judgment. The latter is achieved after considering numerous factors such as the medical and psychiatric history, educational background, work history, and history of arrests, all of which are discussed in detail in the following chapters.

Numerous professionals participate in the evaluation of these disabling conditions, including neurologists, psychiatrists, neuropsychologists, and physical rehabilitation specialists. One needs to stress the fact that, in the forensic clinic, one often sees individuals who — at, say, age 24 — have never seen a physician. An individual who is referred for evaluation because he or she claimed to have suffered from "emotional problems" as a child, may — at the time of the referral — be discovered as having a neurological disorder. Thus, the mental health worker is often called upon to form an initial impression of a large variety of conditions for adequate referral to other mental health workers or to appropriate health care facilities according to the nature of the charges and the stage of the legal proceedings.

Examples of recommendations are, for example, that the defendant should seek psychiatric treatment; learn a skill preparatory to seeking employment or perform community work; or undertake the best treatment for a specific combination of mental disorders and/or conditions. There may be included an asssessment of whether a probationer's reasons for a delay in implementing the recommendations are well founded (Exhibit 2.1, The Ex-Cop Says He's Unable to Work in the Church).

As indicated above, the focus of the clinical neuropsychological examination depends on the legal situation that the defendant is facing. In selected cases the neuropsychologist may be called upon to testify in court about whether the offense or "criminal act" and "neuropsychological dysfunction" are "causally" related.

In addition, the settings, people who are present in, or the physical circumstances under which the clinical evaluation is performed are quite different from, say, the evaluation performed at a hospital-based clinic.

- ☐ Forensic clinicians who work in large cities at the court may lack the advanced technology normally available in a typical hospital.

- ☐ The defendant has the right to have his or her lawyer present when the information that will eventually lead to a report is gathered.

- ☐ In agreement with their clients, lawyers may impose conditions under which such information is gathered (e.g., that the events leading to the defendant's charges not be discussed).

The clinician may impose conditions of his or her own, for example, that there be no eye contact between the defendant and his lawyer during the clinical evaluation.

Of course, not all these probes provide information that have an equal bearing in understanding the individual's past history and current behavior. For example, Mr Jones had the appearance of a neurologically impaired person; there were many features of his posture, body movements and speech articulation that indicate to the trained eye that this man suffers from a condition called cerebral palsy. Through probing, it seemed likely that this condition occurred at birth as a result of brain anoxia, that is, oxygen deprivation to the brain prior to or during birth. Numerous scars on his arms were noted, said to be caused by smashing his hands into things including glass; such impulsive behavior was said to have occurred between the ages of 9 and 19 (Exhibit 5.1, New York City Child Learns to Walk by Himself). These observations are key to evaluating the individual and are more critical than other factors in arriving at professional decisions about the defendant and recommendations for his or her rehabilitation. In the next chapters, we review the components of the clinical examination performed for forensic purposes.

☐ EXHIBIT 2.1

The Ex-Cop Says He's Unable to Work in the Church

Mr Andrews was a Caucasian male of 40 with high school education who used to be a policeman; he was originally charged with stealing property recovered from burglaries stored at his precinct; he was about to receive a sentence for violation of his probation because he did not complete community work as required; the probationer indicated that he could not complete community work because of a variety of problems. He has recently come to realize that he could not adequately explain why he had been unable to complete 1000 hours of community work imposed about eight years earlier. The probationer was experiencing a mild form of adjustment disorder with anxiety.

Mr Andrews was once a member of an Olympic bicycle team and, although he suffered a car accident in which he claimed that his right lung was injured, he appeared to be in excellent physical condition.

He was under financial stress. The probationer said that he was paying alimony to his first wife, and — in order to meet his financial obligations — he had to have three different jobs. The probationer had no or minimal symptoms; the few present were transient and predictable reactions to his stressors (e.g., anxiety as a result of being found to have violated his probation and thus facing a new sentence).

The neuropsychologist was required to write an update of existing conditions and recommendations. The report covered these issues.

Community work at the church. Mr Andrews discussed the reasons why he could not complete his work at the church. He indicated that — as a heterosexual male — he felt uncomfortable being in a church serving homosexuals living in Greenwich Village; he said that sometimes people pinched his "rear end" and made remarks about his being there. However, the probationer appeared to be unable to substantiate claims that he was sexually harassed or mistreated in any way. His job was essentially that of a "jack-of-all-trades," repairing things that needed to be repaired around the church. The probationer admitted a feeling of humiliation when receiving instructions from a person of "inferior standing." He admitted that nobody was trying to push a "bitter medicine" by forcing a heterosexual male to perform community duties in a mixed homosexual neighborhood; he also recognized that the selection of that particular church was a matter of convenience, as it was the closest place to his home where he could fulfill his community service.

Alternative places where he could perform community work. Mr Andrews recognized that at any time during the course of his probation, he could have discussed the possibility of performing his required community work in places other than the church. He also understood that he had many abilities that could be used for the good of the community (sports training, reading to children). The probationer could not explain why he did not write a letter to his Probation Officer or discuss with her these alternative possibilities. The probationer appeared to think that, as time elapsed, the requirement relating to his probation would be forgotten.

Possible medical reasons. At some point, Mr Andrews appeared to argue the point that there was a medical reason that prevented him from completing his community work. He said that he suffered a car accident after which his right lung collapsed and "functioned at 50 percent capacity." When asked whether this figure (50 percent) resulted from some objective testing — such as the results of a pulmonary function test (sometimes called "vital capacity test") — he replied that they did not, but he "felt 50 percent of his lung capacity was gone." Inconsistently with these complains, the probationer described a life of sports, enjoying bicycling outdoors.

Possible financial reasons. Mr Andrews also argued the point that an hour to earn a salary was "lost" for every hour of community work. As a result, he could not accomplish one thing without jeopardizing the other. He said that he currently worked as a bartender 22 hours a week where he earned $240; he also worked as a porter in one place where he worked 30 hours a week and earned about $100; and that he also worked as a porter in another place where he worked 20 hours a week and where he earned $90 dollars. The income of his current wife was stated to be about $300 a week. The probationer still paid alimony to his former wife.

Reasons of mental health. A screening battery of probes that included examination of posture, gait, whole-body balance, muscle strength, tremor at rest, intentional tremor, motor coordination, general appearance of the eyes, eye movements and reaction of the eyes to light was administrated; the results were all within normal limits. In addition, signs and/or symptoms possibly indicative of neurological or mental disorders were probed and Mr Andrews was asked whether he had ever experienced them, and, if so, to give examples. He denied ever having experienced these signs or symptoms. Paranoid ideation, delusions and hallucinations were denied.

Scales from the Wechsler Adult Intelligence Scale — Revised (also called WAIS-R) were administered. These included Information, Picture Completion, Picture Arrangement, and Digit Symbol. Mr Andrews' IQ was estimated to be about 120, a level generally considered to be a bright normal level of intellectual functioning.

Mr Andrews was asked to read the following: "The crown and glory of a useful life is character. It is the noblest possession of man. It forms a rank in itself, an estate in the general good will, dignifying every station and exhalting every position in society. It exercises a greater power than wealth, and it is a valuable means of securing honor." The probationer read the paragraph very well with an appropriate intonation.

Knowledge of the Charges and Court Proceedings. Mr Andrews was asked the meaning of probation and the consequences of violating the terms of his probation. The probationer appeared to fully understand the meaning of these terms. The probationer also acknowledged that he has a background in law and law-enforcement but he said he doubted whether anyone would be interested in these facts as he said "he violated the law when — as a policeman — he was expected to followed the highest standards."

It was concluded that Mr Andrews was unable to substantiate that there were personal problems at the church that prevented him from performing community work there. It was estimated that if the probationer had attempted to work about 10 hours a week at the church, he would have finished the terms of his probation in 1985, that is, two years after such sentence was imposed.

☐ **QUESTIONS FOR REVIEW AND DISCUSSION**

△ Why is the report on Mr Andrews a forensic report rather than merely a report of a routine psychological evaluation?

△ What is/are the legal question(s) that the neuropsychologist needs to address in a formal report?

△ Do you think that the events leading to Mr Andrews' original charges (stealing) and the reasons why he is now charged with violation of his probation are related? Explain.

△ Explain how psychological testing helps to shed light into Mr Andrews' current legal situation.

△ If you were a neuropsychologist hired by Mr Andrews' lawyer, how might you argue his case?

3: APPEARANCES AND IMPRESSIONS

THE APPEARANCE OF AN INDIVIDUAL OFTEN GIVES IMPORTANT CLUES AS TO THE nature of his or her mental problems, and — often — whether these "problems" are malingered (to pretend illness or incapacity). A good malingerer knows that he has to work on appearances.

The following is the first appearance of a person who was later found to be suffering from schizophrenia. The defendant exhibited numerous tics, that is, involuntary, sudden, rapid, and stereotyped motor movements, such as eye-blinking, non-rhythmic, sudden elevation of both eyebrows, grinning and sometimes smiling, head turning — primarily to the right and up as if he were looking for something — and smelling. He also exhibited complex motor acts such as rhythmic pressing down of his breastbone (he said he heard a "tick" there; asked whether it is the tick of the heart, he said that he heard something different from that). While sitting, he moved both arms up and down in a rhythmic manner resembling an inhibited attempt to fly; occasionally he would throw a punch in the air, to a nonexistent object.

The Problem of the Book and the Cover

The "appearance" of the defendant is his or her "outer look." Popular wisdom suggests contradictory views regarding the intrinsic relation between the external appearance of an individual and his or her mind. On the one hand, we are told that we "should never judge a book by its cover" or "all that glitters is not gold" with the obvious connotation that the appearance of an individual is not the key to his or her mind and behavior. On the other hand, we have numerous expressions in popular folklore such as "the eyes are the windows of the soul" or that "still waters run deep" or "noisy brooks are shallow" linking the external appearance to the individual's mind. In the Epilogue, I will make reference to Physiognomy — a pseudoscience that attempted the discovery of the disposition of the mind by the lineaments of the body — that was once widely accepted as a solid basis for criminology. This chapter focuses on pictures, portraits, impressions, phenomenological observations and body language. Careful observation of the appearance of the defendant can offer important clues to his or her current and/or past behavior, to what the individual is or is not telling, or to inconsistencies between what the individual tells us and what we see. Often, appearances and body language can be deceiving.

Ideally, one would like to have a still picture or to make a videotape of the defendant in order to have documentation of how he or she looked at the time of neuropsychological examination. However, this is not always possible. Inside the court clinic in New York City, for example, taking photographs may not be allowed. (However, a private expert witness who needs to work at the court sometimes may be allowed to videotape the clinical evaluation.) Therefore, a good description of how the defendant appears becomes essential. One needs to stress the fact that this description is much more than merely an anthropological account of the outer physical characteristics of the defendant. The "impression" that the individual leaves must be given in writing.

Sometimes, the impression is a single attribute or personality trait that catches one's attention. For example, "Mr Jones was a poorly developed male (5'4", 120 pounds). The defendant had a small cranium, poorly developed ears, flat, sunken nose, small-rounded eyes with unusual skin foldings, large lower lips, and unusual skin foldings in his hands" (Exhibit 9.2, The Young Man who Got No Respect).

At other times, an impression can be a complex pattern of behavior. The following is a description of a defendant afflicted with an organic personality disorder associated with long-term use of drugs.

> ☐ Mr Harris appeared disheveled, with a mild aroma of alcohol — likely to be wine — coming from his breath. He appeared restless, exhibiting numerous tics, including sudden turns of his head to the right, and often scratching his armpits as he talked. He was suspicious, with continuous and an inappropriate intense stare at the evaluator during the interview and psychological testing. Sometimes he also laughed inappropriatedly. Asked why the skin of his right hand was thicker than of his left (I suspected an occupational factor), the defendant banged his right hand very loudly over his left hand and said: "Because I like to fight!" The defendant appeared bewildered but fascinated by this question and observed his two hands placed together on the table on and off for the next two hours of the evaluative session.

☐ The defendant presented several gunshot-wounds, knife-wounds and a tattoo. He had two scars on his back, one said to be localized on the upper side of his right buttock (which was not inspected) and one on the vertebral column. He reported that a bullet was still there. In addition, he had an operation on his left hand for the removal of one bullet and two additional scars on both sides of the lower chest. When the location of these scars were drawn for him on an outline of the human figure, the defendant resented my note taking and said "I am OK!, I am OK!" The defendant also showed knife-wounds ("defensive types," that were located on the back of both his arms) and others in his head, said to be caused by frequent fights with his girl friend. Question: "What do you fight about?" Answer: "Nothing! Sometimes she asks me to go to the Bronx and I just do not want to go." The defendant suddenly went to a chair, put his jacket as though he was going to leave and then, suddenly, he sat tensely on his chair. Asked why he did that: "I am cold" (the room was hot).

Physical Evaluation

Information from the impression is carefully recorded a "physical evaluation." During "physical evaluation," a brief physical neurological evaluation is completed, to be described in more detail in Chapter 5. A wealth of information is obtained by observing and recording the defendant's appearance and behavior during this exam.

The following is an example of the defendant's explanations of various features I observed on his skin as I perform this examination: Needle marks on the inside of his left arm; numerous — rather superficial — scars from knife wounds on his left wrist said to be caused during a suicidal attempt to inspire pity as his girlfriend was threatening to abandon him; stretch marks on his back around his right shoulder (the defendant said he had grown several inches during a single year when he was a teenager); severe acne scars on his face said to have appeared after he was incarcerated at Rikers Island; scars around the area of his left eyebrow said to be produced when he was eight years old when he knocked into a coffee table while falling; scars on his left knee said to have been caused by a fallen hood of a car; and several missing lower and upper teeth.

Thus, the impression that one obtains from a physical examination gives rise to a hypothesis that can later be dismissed or confirmed; if confirmed, the impression can be linked with other observations thus creating a multidimensional picture of the defendant. From the above "impression," I already know that the defendant is a drug addict, that he was incarcerated; I also entertain the hypotheses that he was "hyperactive" or had behavioral problems as a child; that he has often been involved in physical fights as an adult; the "stretch marks" problably indicate that he physically developed very quickly and that he might have had difficulties in creating a balanced impression of himself; the presence of acne may have caused a further distortion of his body image.

Body Image

"Body image" is the awareness that we have of our own physical makeup; this "image" is actively built through the interactions with others, the comments our family members have made about ourselves; we are finally "brainwashed" into believing these remarks.

During the evaluative interview and testing, Ms Perez — who was a poorly physically developed female, 4'5", 85 pounds — appeared under the influence of intoxicants; her eyes rolled up showing only the eye's sclera (the white portion of the eye). She had to be instructed several times to stay awake to complete the interview. Her appearance was disheveled and her clothing appeared not to have been washed for a long time. She maintained poor oral hygiene. She spoke in a high-pitched voice, a form of speech often observed among people who suffer from dwarfism.

The structure and content of her speech was consistent with a serious mental disorder. At the beginning she would not talk and she would nod her head as an apparent indication of her agreement or disagreement. I had to instruct her on the need of saying "no" or "yes" to indicate her agreement or disagreement to the posed questions. The defendant often referred to herself as a child using a childish language (. . . porque yo soy una niñita chiquitita; . . . because I am a tiny little girl).

Sometimes an impression is formed by the observation of how the defendant reacts to the mere attempt of performing a physical examination. Individuals afflicted with paranoid disorder sometimes become restless; at times, some are seductive with evaluators of the opposite sex and less frequently, the same sex. One needs to be alert and careful about the depth and extent of this particular aspect of the evaluation, particularly with potentially violent people. A sense of how much of the "personal space" that surrounds each individual the defendant is willing to yield is essential. Although it is almost unavoidable at times to touch the defendant — particularly during psychological testing — I obey the rules of never touching a defendant.

Observing Reactions to Examination

Once one individual suffering from a severe paranoid disorder accused me of "touching" him when I attempted to interrupt with the hand gesture of "take it easy" (the palm of my right hand facing about 18 inches from his face); I had to interrupt his rapid firing of questions because I needed to explain his Miranda rights before interviewing. (Briefly, the "Miranda rights" are the individual's rights protecting against self-incrimination; in the forensic clinic, it is primarily a warning that the examination is not confidential).

An impression of the defendant is thus gathered from observing and asking questions about what one observes. However, the defendant needs to be reassured that we ask some questions of everybody — namely, gunshot wounds, any knife wounds or any tattoos, particularly the ones I do not see. The questions are aimed at clarifying the circumstances under which scars are produced.

☐ The following is an illustration of a case of an assaultive individual, examined in order to ascertain competence to stand trial: (1) A scar on his lips that resulted from a fight while in jail two years ago; (2) a scar on the right side of his nose originated from another fight; (3) scar said to be caused by a knife wound on the lower part of his neck (he said he does not remember under what circumstances the wound was created); (4) a scar from a gun shot on his right leg that got infected (said to have occurred four years ago but that looks more recent); (5) a tattoo on his left hand with the words MAR said to be the initials of a female after he said "it means something"; (6) an infected tattoo on the right hand (either this tattoo is recent or the defendant has recently tried to remove it vigorously); and (7) an extensive scar on his stomach said to have resulted from a gallbladder operation. Items (1) through (4) might indicate that the individual is assaultive; (5) and (6) might indicate impulsive traits (that us, the individual may act on impulse and then might regret his actions); and (7) may indicate a period of time when afflicted by health problems.

☐ The following is another example of the information obtained from probing and the resulting impression of an individual who was a severe drug abuser and was afflicted with a borderline personality disorder: (1) I note that he came to the evaluative interview and testing with a cast around his right arm and around his neck resulting from his most recent attempt to commit suicide on December 1988; (2) he suffered multiple fractures on his right arm in the area around his wrist; he also suffered a neck fracture; he was heavy on crack at that time and he jumped from a window to avoid going to jail; (3) I also note that in 1988 he cut his right foot with a knife after an argument with his mother regarding his girlfriend, who is his first cousin; (4) finally, the same year he cut his arm over an argument with her girfriend who, at that time, was trying to get an abortion. The baby was his. Item (1) indicates that the individual has suffered a major depressive episode likely to be the "crash" that follows continuous use of crack; (2) gives me a clear picture of the degree of lack of control that the individual is likely to experience during episodes of crack abuse, and that degree is obviously "extreme"; (3) and (4) are suicidal threats in an attempt to control the behavior of others, threats that are diagnostic characteristics of "borderline personality disorder."

☐ The following are the impressions resulting from probing a person who was physically abused as a child: (1) a "lump" on the back of his head about an inch in diameter said to be caused by his father when he abused the defendant during childhood; the lump seemed to be an aneurysm, i.e., an enlargement of a blood vessel in the scalp; (2) a horizontal scar about an inch and a half long above his right eye said to be caused by "a Siamese cat" when the defendant was a child; (3) a round scar on the left hand said to have been caused by his father when the defendant was eight and a half years of age [which he explained by saying that his father wanted to teach him a lesson and had burnt him on the hand with a cigarette the defendant had been smoking]; (4) another round scar on the forehead said to be caused by his father when the defendant was about the same age and for the same reason (i.e., caught while smoking cigarettes); (5) two parallel cuts on his left hand, said to have been caused by the defendant himself while in jail in 1988; and (6) the defendant bites his fingernails to the point of bleeding.

Not having the benefit of a tape recorder — which I, in fact, am not allowed to have — the results of the probing and the impressions I form depend on my ability to take notes. After the observation and probing during the physical evaluation, I sit down and tell the defendant that I will be with him or her "in a minute" and I note his or her approximate height and weight; whether the defendant is too thin or too heavy; whether he or she looks the stated chrono-logical age; whether the defendant is sickly in appearance. How is Ms Joseph dressed? Is it appropriate for her socio-economic status? I pay attention to jewelry, shoes, objects that appear to have some meaning or wording such as "Born to Die," or that might reveal gang membership. Is her clothing appro-priate for the season of the year?

An impression is the observation of a physical feature or event. The late Dr Morris B Bender (1905-1983), when he was a Professor of Neurology at Mount Sinai School of Medicine in New York City, held Phenomenological Rounds to train the staff in the art of observing and recording impressions; making clinical diagnoses assumed secondary importance during these rounds. An impression is the basis for our later conclusion that signs or symptoms of neuropsychological disorder are present. A videotape or an audio tape recorder are both accurate but we learn less about the person when the tapes have to be interpreted; the expert witness — by observing another person, preferably in direct one-to-one contact, but sometimes through tapes — is "impressed" by the "appearance" of such a person. In the evaluation of certain forms of antisocial personality disorders, experts have argued the point that sometimes these "impressions" amount to a moral judgment.

Peculiarities and Asymmetries

I often note something but I am not sure I know what it means at the time. I make a mental note to the effect that Ms Rice is a well-developed woman (5 feet, 6 inches, and 133 pounds) who appears overdressed and flashy in an outfit including a neon green shirt and tight neon orange pants. She has bejeweled, manicured hands and, when writing, tries to avoid touching the paper with her long nails; she wears open shoes showing carefully manicured and brightly painted toe nails. Whether these observations are later linked to some narcissistic traits of her personality or just an error in judgment in how to dress on the part of a person who appears in court for the first time will have to be decided later.

Choice of Clothing

Appearances are as different as individuals, and it would be misleading to expect that in a court clinic one is bound to see people reminiscent of a painting by Hieronymus Bosch, a novel by Dickens or Dumas, a story by Faulkner, or a motion picture by Fellini. A man suspected of suffering from a neuropsychological disorder can come to our office wearing a three-piece suit, a very expensive tie, and genuine leather shoes; a woman might be wearing a simple but elegant dress with subdued matching accessories.

Our personality is revealed in the way we dress, because every morning we make a choice of what to wear; what was originally a choice has now become an unconscious habit. Our personality is revealed in such a choice. This choice also applies to items that we normally carry. Significant items that the defendant brings to the evaluation room (such as books, beepers, etc.) are sometimes noted as he or she sits down for the evaluative interview and testing.

☐ For example, I noted that Mr Hill is a pleasant-looking 62-year-old man. He came to the testing room carrying a book by Malraux. The defendant often made reference to fanciful topics (like his interest in the study of rock formation in Switzerland) or figures of speech (e.g., references to the writings of the ancient Greek philosopher Plato). Reference to these topics were significant in that they were not always appropriate to illustrate a point. People afflicted with schizophrenia are likely to exhibit this type of behavior.

☐ Another example is the wearing of numerous pieces of silver jewelry by an individual, jewelry that is suspected to have symbolic meaning although denied by the defendant. One defendant wore elaborate rings — actually small silver sculptures attached to them — on each finger of his left hand. One ring showed two sirens, and two others had skulls representing death; another bore the letter "J," said to be the initial of his dead son James; a silver bracelet on the right hand had several items whose meaning was said to be "personal." Santería (a form of Caribbean religion, sometimes thought to resemble witchcraft) and/or gang membership were denied.

☐ Still another example is a Santería string held in his hands by the defendant — a 22-year-old Hispanic young man — during most of the evaluation; a close examination of the string revealed individual items that were, according to the defendant, supposed to protect him from many threats. Thus, a knife would protect him from a knife attack; a nail-of-the-Christian-cross was said to protect him from jail. (Drug dealers sometimes wear Christian crosses as a protection against sudden aggression during drug dealing). The defendant refused to explain the significance of most of the items saying that the string was a "personal matter, a gift given by his mother when he left jail for the first time."

Body Language

Many defendants understand the significance of body language, that is, the message you are sending to your interlocutor when you are not saying anything. Body language is "spoken" in the garments one wears, the items one carries, the posture one adopts, and the gestures we make with our bodies and primarily with our faces.

Our bodies often carry the history of our experiences. A broken nose, needle marks, gunshot and/or stab-wound scars, tattoos, burnings, and ear- and/or nose-piercings obviously tells us something. This is true as long as one recognizes that people who have been charged with atrocious murders can sometimes be "beautiful people," with body features intact, skins that are impeccable, and garments are that are both conservative and civilized.

I once studied the highlights of the postmortem examination to see how pathologists deduce information about an individual's lifestyle by studying the dead person's body marks. As a result of such learning experience, I now look for significant recent skin conditions such as bruises, wounds, areas of skin covered by bandages or casts. One needs to be particularly aware of the sequence of bruises, namely the coexistence of fresh, recent, and old wounds often apparent in battered and/or assaultive individuals and sometimes among people suffering from chronic alcoholism. Occasionally one sees bruises among individuals who are charged with physical abuse — that is, bruises that are caused while mistreating the victim.

Symbols of Past Injustice

Sometimes complex legal situations are unravelled when the appearance tells of past injustices. The defendant — a converted Muslim — covered his head with a piece of cloth worn by Arabs. He carried a bilingual religious book written in both English and Arabic. He also carried a towel and a pair of sandals said to be used during daily praying. The defendant reported that he was shot by police in his left eye and the bullet was surgically removed; the defendant lost his left eye. His eyelids were markedly swollen and closed without stitches and oozing pus, showing obvious signs of the beginning of an infection. The defendant said that he is not being treated for this condition. I asked the defendant to remove his head cloth and noted recent wounds on his scalp; the defendant stated that these wounds — one of which required three stitches — were caused by policemen during his apprehension a month ago.

Occupational Stigmata

The skin also reveals occupational stigmata. I pay attention to occupational stigmata, such as calluses in the palm of the hands in a person who engages in physical work or grease imbedded into the hand's skin in a person who claims to be a garage employee.

The absence of stigmata is also revealing. One defendant accused of drug dealing once told that he knows how to tell an undercover policeman from a drug abuser because the former have their nails very clean and their eyes are not bloodshot.

Jargon, Argot, and Patois

Defendants sometimes use a particular language, a mode of expression describing the circumstances under which scars occurred, that also helps to form impression.

Let's consider the following example from a person obviously suspicious and exhibiting antisocial personality traits. The defendant was alert and cooperative during the interview but in other instances he was evasive.

- ☐ Question: "How did the gunshot wound come about?" Answer: "During a shooting incident."
- ☐ Question: "But what happened?" Answer: "I was shot, that's what happened."
- ☐ Question: "But who shot you?" Answer: "You know, people sometimes get shot."
- ☐ Question: "You mean bullets just fly about until they hit you?" Answer: "If you want to put it that way . . ."
- ☐ Question: "What about the stabbing?" Answer: "I was stabbed."

Skin Sleuthing

Skin sleuthing needs to be done cautiously. There is possibly nothing more frustrating than to have believed everything the defendant has related, only later to discover that none of it is true. Sometimes, probing about the circumstances surrounding the appearance of wounds and tattoos calls attention to inconsistencies. Mr Bell — who is accused of sexually abusing his daughter — was a correction officer at the time of the events leading to the charges. A stab wound in the stomach area was said to have been inflicted in 1977 in New York City when he was a victim of robbery. (I had noted that the defendant had stated that he had been in the Marine Corps between the years of 1974 to

1979). Thus, whether the stab wound scar was caused under the circumstances the defendant claims to have occurred needed to be questioned.

Personal Hygiene

Observation of the personal hygiene of the defendant might reveal dirty clothing and malodorous individuals. I often pay attention to the constrast between the cleanliness of clothes that require simple washing — such as sport shirts — to those possibly requiring dry cleaning. I also note the excessive use of perfumes, unkempt nails, or disfiguring nail biting, and new shoes with metal points.

An impression is gained when a person "presses on" us, a professionally trained "impressionable" person and, thus far, I have described the process of forming an impression as if it were unidirectional, that is, as if the professional is the only one forming an impression. However, the individual being evaluated also forms an impression of the evaluator as the latter is far from an invisible data-gathering computer. Forensic reports almost never contain information regarding the appearance and ethnic background of the interviewer though it is a common observation that what the defendant tells an interviewer depends very much on the defendant's ability to identify with him or her.

Avoiding Biases

How does one describe the impression one individual leaves on us? The training consists, in the main, in avoiding biases. Only three of these biases are identified here: Profiling, the halo effect, and the presence of "critical events," a variation of the halo effect.

Profiling

We are familiar with the notion that if it appears to be a duck, walks like a duck, and quacks like a duck, then it is a duck. Profiling is the classification — more adequately, pigeonholing — of an individual with a set of categories. Demographic profiling is an example of simply profiling. Profiling is sometimes still used by law enforcement even when it violates an individual's rights. For example, in certain cities, all Black teenagers who arrive at a bus station by themselves in the evening are screened for possible criminal possession of controlled substances.

Primarily for no other reason than habit, the description of "appearance" by demographic profiling is widespread. Reports — including mine — often contain a statement such as that this is a 19-year-old Black man with 10th grade education born and raised in North Carolina. This simple statement contains the implicit acceptance of a person's age, ethnic background, sex, education, and origin, all important when he or she faces legal proceedings. Profiling is unavoidable, and often needed in order to keep crime statistics. It is wrong when used to reinforce "halo effects."

The Halo Effect

The "halo effect" calls attention to the human propensity to judge or assume that an individual who exhibits an outstanding personality trait possesses other — often unwarranted — capacities. For example, an outstanding football player is also thought to be an outstanding role model for the moral development of children. Reputation and beliefs affecting such judgment are often unwarranted. However, even more destructive and damaging is the fact that people attribute personality and intellectual characteristics to trivial features. Many surveys have indicated that (on the average) people who are tall and wear glasses are considered more intelligent that those who are short and do not wear glasses. At the courts, however, we often see the halo effect in reverse, of the type "give the dog a bad name . . ." Classical surveys indicate that when people are asked to recall a scene in which a white man confronts a black man with a knife, most recall the scene as if the black man were the knife-wielder.

Critical Events during the Evaluation

Finally, there are "critical events" that are bound to occur during the evaluative interview and testing; these critical events sometimes introduce biases in our judgment of an individual. I once interviewed a young male defendant who emptied the contents of his nostrils and rolled them with his two index fingers on my table. Another young man passed gas during the entire evaluative interview. I occasionally refuse to interview people such as the ones who come to the clinic with a powerful aroma of alcoholic beverages (I refuse to test them not because of the aroma but because psychological test results would probably be meaningless). Exhibit 3.1 (Fidgety Girl) illustrates the case of a person who has mastered the art of being unpleasant in order to do exactly what she wanted.

Using an Interpreter

Sometimes an impression needs to be gathered through an interpreter. In New York City, an interpreter is appointed for people who face legal proceedings but who do not speak English. Evaluations through an interpreter for a defendant who speaks Arabic, Chinese, Greek, Hindi, Korean, Spanish or Vietnamese are not uncommon and — needless to say — should never be taken to suggest that people who came from communities who speak those languages are more prone to have confrontations with the law. It is a reflection of the

simple fact that these languages are well represented in New York City. I am
a bilingual (Spanish and English) individual, and I do not need an interpreter
to make evaluations in Spanish. However, my experience as a bilingual person
gives me an insight into the difficulties and the information that is sometimes
lost while performing evaluations through an interpreter. Chapter 19 — Other
Handicapping Conditions — discusses additional issues regarding this point.

Examinees with Speech or Language Problems

Sometimes, an impression needs to be gathered from individuals suffering
from communication problems. I have conducted evaluations of individuals
who are deaf mutes and who face legal proceedings; sometimes, they are people
who speak the sign language of other languages. Exhibit 19.1 (A Taste of Sex)
illustrates the case of a deaf-mute defendant whose primary language was
Spanish and who, as a result, required two sign-language interpreters during
the forensic evaluation.

Sensibility and Acumen of the Examiner

It is true that evaluations through an interpreter are as good as the quality
of the interpretation and the sensibility of the interpreter. Sometimes the simple
knowledge that the individual is unable to speak English after having lived ten
years in the United States tells a lot about the individual's capacity — or
willingness — to "tune in" to mainstream culture, revealing sometimes antisocial personalities, or serious forms of mental disorder.

In the main, everything that has been discussed about skin marks, tattoos,
dresses, and personal possessions applies equally to the foreign-born or to the
one who has lived in the country for many years. As a rule, although knowledge
of countries and cultures is helpful, the job of the forensic neuropsychologist
is not that of an anthropologist. If the law has been broken in Manhattan, the
defendant is confronted by the law in New York State (or the Federal Law, if
committing federal crimes). In cases of an individual who has battered his wife,
one needs to be judicious about the extent to which one is willing to justify his
behavior because in the individual's original country women are battered as a
matter of routine.

☐ **EXHIBIT 3.1**

Fidgety Girl

Ms Hunter was an 18-year-old Black female with 10th grade education. At the time
of the interview she had been released into the community and was awaiting her
sentence. The neuropsychological evaluation was requested with the cryptic note "as an
aid in sentencing."

She was found to be suffering from crack addiction. It was felt that despite the fact that the defendant stated that she had not used crack for the past "months," her addiction was considered to be current because there was no verified information that she had control over the addiction (e.g., she was not attending a drug rehabilitation program). Drug abuse was pinpointed as contributing to her current behavioral problems, as the main reason for her current problems with the law, and to be the focus of treatment interventions recommended.

The defendant met the diagnostic criterion for Attention-Deficit Hyperactivity Disorder. According to the diagnostic criteria of the DSM (*Diagnostic and Statistical Manual* of the American Psychiatric Association) system, this is a disturbance in which the following are present: Fidgeting with hands and feet and squirming while sitting; difficulties in remaining seated when required to do so; easily distracted by extraneous stimuli; difficulties in waiting turns in group situations; blurting out answers to questions before they have been completed; difficulties in following instructions, these difficulties not being due to oppositional behavior or failure of comprehension; difficulties in sustaining attention; verbiage; interruption or intrusion of others; often did not seem to listen to what was being said to her; and often engaged in physically dangerous activities without considering possible consequences. This disturbance was severe as signs and symptoms were in excess of those required to make such a diagnosis; in addition, there was a significant and pervasive impairment in functioning at home and with peers. Attention-Deficit Hyperactivity Disorder was considered to be the primary diagnosis — above and beyond the diagnosis of crack abuse described above. The defendant had suffered from severe conduct disorder as a child, a disorder that — as an adult — had turned into an antisocial personality disorder.

Ms Hunter was also diagnosed as suffering from Fetal Drug Syndrome. The defendant was born from a mother who was addicted to heroin when pregnant with her, and opiates were found in the defendant's blood at birth; thus, her Attention-Deficit Hyperactivity Disorder was likely to have had a neurological basis. This was thought to be most likely a "subcortical" dysfunction characterized by dyskinesia, that is, involuntary movements that were quasi-purposive (or after an involuntary movement had been executed she tried to mask it as if it were purposive). The defendant could not stay still even if she tried. The defendant had a sister — described as being mentally retarded — born from the same mother.

One of the defendant's psychosocial stressors, in the past, was thought to be her mother, a drug abuser. The defendant lived in many different foster homes as a child; at the time of her interview, she was under the care of her grandmother. As a crack user and drug dealer, the defendant created her own stressors, such as her current confrontations with the law.

The defendant showed serious symptoms and serious impairment in social and occupational functioning. She did not seem to have a buffer zone between the time she wanted to do something and actually doing it. Her level of mental functioning suggested a mild form of mental retardation. She stereotypically classified people who came into contact with her into "good" people — those who went along with her wishes — and "bad, evil" people — those who were unwilling to put up with her.

Stating the prognosis of diagnosed illness, it was felt that the dual diagnosis of Attention-Deficit Hyperactivity Disorder, with antisocial trait features and crack abuse had a very poor prognosis. The prospect of her social rehabilitation was thought to be poor. Ms Hunter had not reflected on the events that led to her charges and in general had poor insight; had a long history of conduct problems; had an inadequate level of functioning, i.e., her IQ suggested a mild form of mental retardation; had many signs and symptoms of an attention and impulse-control disorder that affected her social, family, and occupational spheres; was very manipulative; had no job and was not seriously looking for one; and the events leading to the charges — criminal sale of drugs — had occurred as a result of the need to support her drug addiction to crack cocaine.

The quality of information was thought to be poor as the defendant was not cooperative during the interview and psychological testing. The defendant had to be told to stop cursing (as she was saying expressions as "I do not give a shit about this fucking place") and in general was very disrespectful toward the interviewer. The Probation Officer in charge of the case was called during the middle of the interview because of difficulties with her behavior. She composed herself for a few minutes after talking to the Probation Officer; however, she soon resumed verbally abusive behavior. At times, during the psychological testing, as she was working on a test, she would hum a nursery rhyme with the words "I want to go home; I want to go home," speaking in a high-pitched voice pretending to be a little girl. Toward the end of the evaluative session, the defendant indicated that she wanted to go to the bathroom. A correction officer sat in the evaluation room until the end of the session because there was no female correction officer available to frisk her after she returned from the bathroom as the rules required.

The defendant was duly advised before the evaluative session started that nothing she said during the interview was expected to be confidential between the defendant and the interviewer.

Ms Hunter's oldest memory was when she was four, she stuck "a thorn in her butt;" she indicated that her mind began to "flip" when she was eight years old, when she was first described as being hyperactive and unruly. She began receiving counseling while in the second grade. She jumped out of windows on two occasions: Once, in Washington, while staying with a group of girls, she took PCP and thought she could fly, and the second time, while resisting the sexual advances of a boy friend. The defendant lived in numerous group homes and diagnostic centers until age 16. When she was 17, she felt depressed and attempted suicide by swallowing as many as 20 aspirins (she denied that her depression was drug-related).

Her grandmother filed a PINS (Person in Need of Supervision) petition against her (two PINS petitions were filed, one in 1986 and the other in 1987). At the time, her grandmother complained that she was a truant, stealing from home, being verbally and physically abusive and threatening. According to the background documentation, the present situation represented the defendant's second adult arrest and her first conviction.

At the time of her evaluative interview and testing, Ms Hunter lived again with her grandmother (aged 66) and grandfather (aged 76). As indicated above, she had a sister (age 21) who was mentally retarded and is said also to be a drug abuser. The defendant said that she "saw her mother everywhere;" the defendant did not wish to clarify what she meant, but the background documentation indicated that her mother was still a drug abuser and sexually promiscuous. In the background documentation, she admitted that she was following in her mother's footsteps. The defendant appeared to have a relationships with a man (age 26) whom she expects to marry sometime.

Ms Hunter indicated that she was "studying" for her GED (General Equivalency Diploma); she said that she went to a "tutor whenever the tutor said that she should go" amounting to two hours, two times a week (which, as indicated below, was not supplemented by home studying). Ms Hunter indicated that she was not working now; she said that she worked at Burger King last summer.

Ms Hunter slept late and did not appear to have many or any responsibilities around the house. She said that she spent the time either sleeping or "doing nothing." Although she claimed that she was "working to obtain her GED," during a description of a typical day, no time for studying was indicated.

Ms Hunter was addicted to heroin at birth; she began to use drugs on her own at 13. She used first marijuana and then, at 14, she began snorting cocaine. She began using crack on a regular basis when she was 16, spending — before her latest incarceration — as much as $400 a day. The defendant also tried LSD and PCP. She began using alcohol at 14, and she appears to have drunk anything available, including beer, wine, vodka, and whiskey. The defendant was placed in a residential rehabilitation center in upstate New York, but she was expelled two months after her admission after she was found having sex with a man residing in the same center. The defendant claimed that she has not been using crack or alcohol "for several months," but she indicated that she never was asked to submit to urine analysis or to attend a drug rehabilitation center.

Ms Hunter was an obese young woman (5'6", 190 pounds) who appeared much older than her stated age. As indicated above, the defendant was restless, and interrupted the evaluative session several times threatening to "go home." At times, she behaved like a little girl, and needed to be told not to sleep on the desk; she constantly yawned loudly. The structure and content of her speech was characterized by poor grammatical construction and a rather limited vocabulary, mixed with expletives and obscenities. Her eye contact was poor.

A screening battery of probes that included examination of posture, gait, whole-body balance, muscle strength, tremor at rest, intentional tremor, motor coordination, general appearance of the eyes, eye movements and reaction of the eyes to light was performed and the following was noted: The defendant could not stand still, even if she tried to do so; abnormal body movements were suggestive of "cortical dysinhibition" with gross incoordination of gross movements; presence of abnormal eye movements (the defendant could not follow the evaluator's fingers without moving her head; and inappropriate laughter.

From an extensive checklist of signs and/or symptoms possibly indicative of neurological or mental disorders, Ms Hunter was asked whether she had ever experienced them, and if so, to give examples. The following was volunteered: Tiredness; overeating; lack of concentration; got lost on the streets without being "high" on drugs; forgetfulness; irritability; depression, sometimes with suicidal ideation (she denied that she was currently suicidal); constant temper outbursts; sometimes she broke things, "a TV, a table, a chair, anything"; and she often fought with men, most of the time when completely sober. Paranoid ideation, delusions, and hallucinations were volunteered but they did not appear to be genuine. The defendant stated that she had constant nightmares in which she dreamt she was falling into the dark and dying.

Ms Hunter thought of herself as a very beautiful person, who knew she had problems with other girls because of her beauty. She also said that she was the devil, and tried to tell a poorly credible history of how she could be a "good devil" and sometimes "a bad devil." These two statements were thought to be figures of speech rather than delusional ideation. Once told that if she was found to be mentally ill, she would have to be referred to a psychiatric hospital, she took back all these statements saying that she is "tired of being considered crazy." She indicated that she was not close to anybody, and that she preferred to be by herself.

The Wechsler Adult Intelligence Scale — Revised (WAIS-R) was administered. Ms Hunter's verbal IQ was found to be 68 and her performance IQ was 70; the overall test

IQ was 68. These IQ levels represent a level of intellectual functioning suggestive of mild mental retardation.

As indicated above, Ms Hunter was thought to be suffering from a combination of neurological, pharmacological, and psychological problems that needed to be treated in a specialized residential setting for neuropsychological disorders, probably with the aid of psychotropic medication. A major consideration was to understand that her superficially "volitional" behavior was often the result of a severe form of impulse control disorder having an organic basis. Unfortunately, many years had gone by, during which the label of "emotional disorder" (without further specification) had been given to her, in what was clearly an incomplete diagnosis.

Another important consideration was that she had apparently mastered the art of being unpleasant, an art that she used well to obtain exactly what she wanted, namely, no thorough evaluation of her neuropsychological conditions, no referrals, and no treatment. It was concluded that if the nature of her disorder was not recognized and treated soon, the defendant was likely to spend the rest of her life in prison, as laws and social rules that govern other people's social behavior were either not perceived as such by her or were not strong enough for her.

□ QUESTIONS FOR REVIEW AND DISCUSSION

 Δ Explain the following: (1) Criminal possession of a controlled substance; (2) criminal possession of a controlled substance with intent to sell; (3) criminal sale of a controlled substance 1° and 2°; (4) loitering; (5) steering; and (6) acting in concert. Ms Hunter is 18 and has been charged with selling drugs as an adult. How would her legal situation be different if she were 16?

 Δ Describe your own impression of Ms Hunter. How would you judge your own capacity of fairly evaluating a person who is obnoxious during a two-hour interview and psychological testing?

 Δ How would you judge Ms Hunter's capacity to work with her own attorney?

 Δ You are asked to recommend the most adequate drug rehabilitation facility for Ms Hunter. (1) What would you recommend?; (2) If you think that she needs a residential treatment, what is her legal situation if she fails to seek and continue to participate in such a treatment after being sentenced?; (3) How is incarceration different from a residential drug rehabilitation treatment?

4: INTERTWINED HISTORIES

AT THE COURT CLINIC, THE CLINICAL NEUROPSYCHOLOGICAL EXAMINATION IS typically carried out by a single professional and includes the recording of the individual's family and social history, the occupational history, including the individual's latest job or professional independent practice, a history of residence and travel — all of which often provide background documentation. To this, the clinician adds the medical and neuropsychiatric history, sexual development (which is required in a defendant charged with rape or sexual abuse), and a history of use of illegal drugs and/or alcohol use. However, a history — or more appropriately, the vignette which is the result of probing such a history — can appear in many unexpected places, when the defendant tells the events leading to his or her charges, or when one sums up many pieces of information in order to assess and evaluate the information. All this information and the physical examination, the evaluation of mental status and a review of neurological signs and symptoms (to be reviewed in later chapters) complete the clinical examination.

If one thinks of these histories as paintings, then defendants — most on their own, sometimes on the advice of their lawyers — bring a number of them for our scrutiny. There are sometimes empty canvases; other times the defendant shows us large, complex creations reminiscent of Titian or Delacroix. Some paintings are well-balanced but most often distorted and/or incoherent creations resulting from a biased recollection of an individual who is facing five years in jail, whose main characters and details have either been highlighted or selectively edited for "our benefit." Most importantly, the defendant has the right to make a choice of showing or not showing these paintings.

Probing the History

As indicated earlier, probing a history is not the same as writing about it. Textbooks where the systematic clinical evaluation is explained might give the impression that most professionals record these histories methodically and in an orderly sequence; the fact is that most do not. The implication is that one must adopt the posture of an objective scientist in this important phase of data-collection. This is far from the truth, as we saw in the previous chapter on the unreliability of impressions. A mental health worker or a probation officer who cannot be open-minded and even sympathetic probably has no business working for the courts. Textbooks rarely tell that one also has to be a good writer to be able to describe the person that has been in front of you and who has "touched" you.

Information leading to a history can appear from anywhere, and not necessarily as a result of systematic probing.

- ☐ Some striking features of the clinical evaluation may appear at the end of the session, when the defendant is relaxed, answering questions that have been perceived as non-threatening, as in Exhibit 19.1 (A Taste of Sex).

- ☐ The opposite is also true; the defendant who is alert and cooperative at the beginning of the evaluation, now may turn restless and threatening, making the continuation of the evaluative session close to impossible.

☐ The individual may reveal nothing of his or her history. A court officer was unable to get a social history from a 71-year-old man found guilty of murder because he thought that the officer was "sarcastic and making jokes about him." The defendant was afflicted by an alcohol-related paranoid personality disorder.

☐ He or she may be suffering from mental retardation; thus the information one reviews is provided by the defendant's parent to the probation officer in charge of a case (a person whose professional credentials range from lacking experience to being a critical observer).

These histories — sometimes written in the form of vignettes by a large variety of individuals — are, in this chapter, thought to be "intertwined" because although they furnished important information about the individual each by themselves, the most useful information sometimes is revealed when they are compared to each other.

☐ For example, comparing the chronology of the education history with that of the history of drug abuse, one sometimes finds that the defendant was expelled from school about the moment he or she began heavy involvement with drugs.

☐ An occupational history revealing a long string of menial jobs in a person who appears to have an "average" IQ — and who has some college training — sometimes is the only indication of the individual's rather serious mental disorder.

☐ The lack of formal education in a person who is in the middle 20s, was born abroad, and who — after 10 years of residence in the United States — is still unable to carry out a simple conversation in English may indicate mental retardation or overt mental illness.

Family History

The family history is, literally, a probe about the family: Who is the defendant's father and mother, whether the defendant has brothers and sisters, and whether he or she has a spouse and children of his or her own. The background documentation often contains a social history sometimes indicating whether any member of the defendant's immediate family has or has not had problems with the law, or is alcoholic or a drug abuser, or both parents had been absent during the defendant's early childhood for reasons of death, divorce, or desertion.

Young teenagers who are sometimes charged as adults are also probed as to whether they lacked parental control as children and whether this lack of control was due to ignorance, indifference, or illness (or a combination of these), or lack of congeniality in the home as shown by dominance, favoritism, oversolicitude, severity, neglect, jealousy, crowded housing conditions or interfering relatives, religious or other culturally determined factors (particularly, clashes over these issues), economic difficulties such as unemployment, poverty, or poor control of financial family affairs. The family history is also aimed at determining the defendant's marital status, whether the defendant is single, living with a common-law spouse or friend, whether the defendant is living with a group of friends, or whether he or she was homeless prior to incarceration.

Among successful young drug dealers it is not uncommon to find that the defendant has three girlfriends and children with each of them. Is the defendant contributing to the welfare of his friends and children? Sometimes yes, most likely with drug money. Interesting is the fact that everyone in the harem knows everyone else; the defendant indicates that he was forced to turn to drug sales as a result of his overwhelming "family" responsibilities.

Sometimes, one can read between the lines and detect a history of loneliness and past miseries. Mr Zurbaran said that he has a wife (aged 39) and two sons (aged 20 and 18) and that he feels "very close to his family." His sons — who love him very much — have "attempted to visit him at Rikers Island several times" since his incarceration seven months ago, but after the long journey to the island, and after many hours of waiting, the correction officers always call the wrong name and, as a result, he cannot see them. He cannot call them at home because his sons have no telephone. His two "boys" who have been always "very good kids" have maliciously been persecuted by teachers and principals alike until these professionals managed to expel his boys from school, depriving them of an opportunity for education.

Educational History

The educational history clarifies important questions such as whether the defendant was said to be "slow" in school, whether an evaluation by an educational psychologist or counselor was needed to determine whether special education was deemed necessary at some point. The educational history often contains indications that the defendant had "behavioral problems" — perhaps the earliest manifestations of a conduct disorder — or had "learning disabilities" or was "hyperactive." One needs to ascertain whether he or she was finally expelled from school or he or she left on his own. From individuals migrating from other countries, one sometimes sees no apparent effort to complete one's education. The educational history sometimes reveals a catastrophic decline in mental functions often associated with the onset of a major mental disorder, or the initiation of a pattern of drug abuse; the background documentation tells you that the defendant was once a bright college student, an individual who now is homeless and penniless.

Occupational History

The occupational history is a chronological account of all the jobs a defendant has had since he or she entered the work force. Whenever an occupational link of neuropsychological signs and symptoms is suspected, it includes exposure to neurotoxic agents — such as lead, pesticides, solvents, etc., use of protective equipment and hygiene practices. One defendant — who was a former welder — gave an occupational history revealing exposure to the neurotoxic agents lead and manganese, exposures that may have caused mild neurological problems; but chonic alcohol abuse was most likely to be causally related to the events leading to the defendant's charges.

Today, workers change occupations many times in their lifetimes. As a result, the relationship between job and health is a complex one and these suspected links need to be established by careful probes into the past work history as well as the present occupation. Very frequently individuals who are mentally ill or have had a rather successful "employment" as drug leaders, are found to have no job history in their late 20s.

The job that the defendant has or the profession he or she independently practices, the income he or she receives, are all important pieces of information in specific forensic cases. It is too well recognized that crime and poverty are related; if you are poor, you have a greater probability of being apprehended; if wealthy, all the knowledge and the wisdom of the judicial system is available to you, because you can afford the best lawyers.

Changes in Residence

The history of residence and travel reveals a great deal about our character. If you have ever requested a loan, it is almost certain that you have been asked where you live, for how long, where you lived before you moved to your current address, whether or not you have a telephone in the place you live, and how much you pay for rent. The answers one gives to these questions sometimes tell the difference between someone who has never moved from the street block where he or she was born, a drifter who has lived in various states during the course of a single year, and a person who enjoys a financially sound situation.

◻ A history of travel reveals the fact that a person was born and lived for 18 years in New York, never leaving the city. Life is centered on one street, one block, or — at the most — six to eight squared blocks. People are born, live, and die in New York City and for all practical purposes the lives they have lived could have been lived anywhere because they are so limited. A history of travel sometimes reveals a history of crushed dreams, but sometimes it reveals the continuation of antisocial behavior. Occasionally we need to evaluate a defendant who has been picked up in an airport, with nothing known of his or her prior residence.

❏ Exhibit 4.1 (Love for Fireworks) illustrates the travel history of a former drifter who suffered from a bipolar mood disorder and who has been charged with arson and reckless endangerment.

Medical History

The medical history seeks information on medical conditions thought to have a direct bearing on the evaluation of the defendant's mind and behavior. It includes data on hospitalization(s) and reason(s) for hospitalization, present or past: cardiovascular, gastrointestinal, genito-urinary, skin, blood, ear-nose-and-throat conditions, nervous system, musculo-skeletal, metabolic diseases, cancer, etc. A history of accidents is also usually recorded. The medical history also includes past and present use of medication, alcohol intake, tobacco and illegal drug use; in special cases, alcohol and use of illegal drugs are gathered in a separate history to be described below. Finally, it also includes family history to assess hereditary, degenerative, nutritional deficiencies, and possible metabolic diseases.

The medical history provides information that is essential to make the diagnosis of illness; however, in the court some individually significant items are not volunteered, the time sequence of events is sometimes distorted, and relatives who are called to illuminate a point manipulate facts and try to create a picture-perfect history of the defendant; sometimes the presence of mental illness is perceived as advantageous for the defendant's case — in which case an extraordinary art for recounting catastrophic events may be revealed. It often happens that the defendant brings medical reports (sometimes from prominent specialists in the field) that one is required to read critically.

❏ One defendant brought a detailed medical report on chronic fatigue syndrome and newspaper clippings describing the illness (Exhibit 7.1, Chronic Fatigue Syndrome). A physician may be asked to write these reports for one specific purpose (to claim health insurance) and the defendant brings the report intended to shed light in the court case. Thus, a physician who writes such a report, attempting to be helpful, is manipulated.

❏ Sometimes the background medical information indicates — or the defendant himself is able to relate — a history of his or her mother's pregnancy, when his mother was a heavy drug abuser (Exhibit 3.1, Fidgety Girl); or information about a premature birth is volunteered; others recall having been told by their families about difficult parturitions where "he almost did not make it."

❏ Some others are motivated to perpetuate "tragic" events that they hope or believe will explain their shortcomings as adults: "Falling from the crib as a baby," or a "car accident," or "falling from a swing," or "lead poisoning." The occurrence of head injury is frequently described as "severe"; however, unless the "injury" resulted in unconsciousness and/or required hospitalization, that characterization is often dubious.

☐ Asthma can sometimes be associated with a chronic dependence on the individual's mother, as she is a sure source of support during a sometimes life-threatening attack.

In the previous chapter, I have explained how revealing the close examination of the defendant's skin can be; scars resulting from "accidents" or admitted as having resulted from fights often reveal frequent episodes of violence. It is not uncommon for the defendant to reveal a severely deforming scar resulting from a gunshot said to have never been medically treated; the defendant admits to having avoided too many questions as these wounds are reportable.

Neuropsychiatric History

The neuropsychiatric history focuses attention on whether the defendant was born as a result of a difficult pregnancy, ages at which he or she began to walk, talk, and control his or her sphincters, history of hospitalizations, whether sometimes these hospitalizations have occurred after the crime, and whether the hospitalization(s) are in any way related to the offense. When there are charges such as rape, sexual abuse, endangerment of the welfare of a child, the individual's sexual development needs to be probed. The defendant is asked whether he remembers the age at which he could tell the "difference between boys and girls," when he first masturbated, had his first sexual contact with an individual of the opposite — or the same — sex. Depending on the individual's cooperation — which as a rule is minimal — recurrent sexual fantasies are discussed.

Exhibit 4.2 (Trapped in the Body of a Woman) illustrates the case of Ms Prieto, who meets the diagnostic criteria for female transsexualism, charged with writing harassing letters to women.

History of Drug and Alcohol Use and Abuse

In taking the history of drug and/or alcohol use, it is necessary to determine the age at which the defendant began to use any drugs, however "experimental." Then it is asked whether he or she smoked marijuana, snorted cocaine or heroin, injected cocaine either alone or in combination with heroin, whether he or she smoked crack cocaine, or took LSD, sometimes known by the street name of "acid," amphetamines ("uppers"), Valium and/or other "downers," powerful hallucinogens such as PCP ("Angel dust"), peyote or mushrooms. Less frequently, painkillers such as Darvon are abused; one mentally retarded individual told me that every Friday he drank two bottles of a cough suppressant because it made him "happy."

The language that the defendant uses to describe drug use is often a clue to the insight that the defendant has about the harmful effects of drugs. Once a defendant told me that his five brothers "played" with drugs; and that his ex-girl friend "only" sniffed cocaine. As many drug-abusers do, he established a sharp distinction between the "good" habit of snorting or smoking drugs contrasted with the "bad" habit of injecting drugs or drinking alcohol.

A history of drug abuse calls for assessment of the "magnitude" and the "frequency" of drug abuse, with the former assessed by the money the defendant would have to spend on the streets if he had to buy the drugs for himself. Stories of individuals spending $50 to $100 a day are common; that of adolescents spending as much as $1000 a day during a long "trip" are sometimes reported. Exhibit 16.1 illustrates the case of a man who had been "brought to his knees" by the use of crack. Taking a history of alcohol abuse usually begins by asking the individual the age at which he or she drank the first drink, continuing by asking when the defendant first drank beer, wine, vodka, whiskey, etc. Taking a drink "first thing in the morning" or "drinking a beer to clear his or her head," or to drink alcohol, stop withdrawal symptoms such as "shakes" (or anxiety and restlessness) are all habits that reveal advanced stages of alcoholism. Frequently, defendants mix drugs and alcohol.

The Issue of Older Defendants

Documenting the social history and life style of an elderly defendant is always a challenging task. An alert defendant, say in his 70s often — though not necessarily "always" — has more to tell than a person who is in the early 20s. Elderly inmates that sometimes spend months in detention centers awaiting their sentences sometimes feel very lonely and welcome an opportunity to talk about themselves. A defendant may "open up" to a mental health worker only a few days before his sentence — sometimes for many years — after persistently refusing to talk to a court officer. Sometimes, an elderly person is motivated to commit a crime by authentic, or delusional, religious beliefs (see Exhibit 13.1, The Priest).

☐ **EXHIBIT 4.1**

Love for Fireworks

Mr Joseph — who was referred for evaluation during a pre-pleading investigation — was a 24-year-old Black male with two years of college education. Mr Joseph gave a history suggestive of Bipolar Disorder (Manic Depressive Disorder). The defendant also showed pyromania. These included: Deliberate and purposeful setting of fireworks and explosive devices on more than one occasion; tension or affective arousal before the act or around times when society condones such activities (e.g., the two incidents leading to serious damage occurred around the 4th of July); life-long fascination with, interest in, curiosity about, or attraction to fireworks and explosives and their situational context and/or associated characteristics (e.g., paraphernalia, uses, consequences, exposure to fireworks and explosives, travel around the country to learn more about how fireworks are constructed and displayed); the setting of fireworks and explosive devices was not done for monetary gain, as an expression of sociopolitical ideology, to conceal criminal activity, to express anger or vengeance, or to improve his living circumstances; and it did not appear that these activities were in response to delusions or hallucinations.

An explosion of a homemade metal pipe-bomb in his house blew up his hand, and literally opened up his abdominal cavity. The defendant still had numerous pieces of metal lodged in his body; he needed a special eye operation to remove pieces of metal in that area.

The defendant's father — who died a few years ago — was described as an authoritarian individual who imposed strict rules around the house, rules that he expected to be followed. Since childhood, there were constant family arguments about the defendant's behavior; these arguments intensified after the house explosion. The family was in family therapy even before the incident happened. His father was described as a person who, until his death a few years back, could not cope with his son's not having a hand. The defendant had had numerous problems in finding a job because people would just tell him that they cannot hire a "crippled man." Finding a job had become even more difficult when people found out about his prior confrontations with the law.

Mr Joseph appeared as a very anxious and frustrated individual who — now approaching his mid 20s — felt humiliated to require his mother's help once again; the control of his impulses appeared to be marginal. Hypomanic traits of personality were seen during long monologues of rapid speech and when he talked about the wide range of his professional interests. However, the defendant exhibited a normal range of intellectual functioning.

It was pinpointed that the combination of a bipolar disorder associated with pyromania carried a guarded prognosis. The prospect of his social rehabilitation was felt to be guarded as Mr Joseph tended to rationalize the seriousness of the events leading to his charges. The defendant had a long history of fascination with fireworks and — although he says he had stopped manufacturing fireworks — the extraordinary interest for fireworks and explosive devices was unlikely to be readily diminished. He was yielding to the pressures of the legal circumstances of his case but was likely to feel continuing interest and pressure to be involved with explosives.

The quality of information was mixed, as the defendant was highly motivated to show that he did not suffer from mental illness and mental disorder, and was very concerned about the prospect of having a criminal record as a result of the events leading to his latest charges. Absence of a criminal record and/or mental disorder was essential in maintaining a certification — the defendant claims to possess — to keep and sell rifles and ammunition. The defendant tended to trivialize two major events — blowing up a pipe bomb that almost killed him and a fire that destroyed his apartment where dangerous chemicals, firearms, and ammunition were stored — as "accidents."

The following were the data surrounding the events leading to the charges. The defendant explained the events as follows. He was inside his mother's apartment and at some point he heard a "pop" — similar to the sound produced by a photographic flash lamp. Smoke began to fill the house and fire soon ensued. The whole apartment caught fire and boxes of ammunition in his apartment began to explode. The defendant said that he lost an important collection of firearms in the fire. He said they were both modern, operable firearms as well as antiques, and stated that his possession of them was legal.

The defendant described a life-long interest in pyrotechnics and explosives. He often prepared his own mixtures and did "experiments," going alone to deserted areas in Manhattan to set off fireworks he had just manufactured. He acknowledged the fact that some of the explosives he used were unstable and likely to explode as a result of "spontaneous" combustion.

In 1981, he was preparing "fireworks" for the 4th of July celebration of that year. He built a pipe bomb himself because he said he "could not depend on unreliable fireworks" bought in Chinatown. The explosive device exploded in his home as he was setting it up, destroyed his left hand, and created major damage, including injury and burns on his chest and abdominal area. On a sketch of the human body, he drew the picture of a scar extending from the lower portion of his chest to his genitals. He said that pieces of metal are still lodged under the skin and still "popped out" spontaneously from time to time. At times, the defendant experienced pain at the places where these pieces of metal were lodged. The defendant underwent eye surgery as a result of eye damage suffered during the same incident.

The defendant first denied a psychiatric history (as indicated above, a positive history of mental disorder would have made it difficult to obtain a permit to keep firearms); however, on a subsequent interview he said that he did not feel comfortable talking about his past psychiatric history because he had not seen his lawyer before the first interview and that his lawyer now advised him to fully cooperate with this evaluation.

The following was volunteered: He said that he went to counseling at his high school because of his poor grades; continued counseling at a New York City hospital and at several major medical centers. The need for counseling arose from increasing depression, fights with his father, the death of his grandmother, and the traumatic experience caused by the explosion that almost killed him. He spent five weeks at an institute for physical rehabilitation after his injuries. He was subsequently admitted to a New York City hospital with the probable diagnosis of Manic Depression and lithium was prescribed for two years thereafter. He suspended the medication on his own because the drug made him drowsy and he generally lacked the "energy and vitality" he once had. The same year he received the near-fatal injuries, he was hit by a model airplane and suffered a concussion requiring hospitalization.

Mr Joseph was an only child. His father — a chemical laboratory technician — died from a heart attack. His mother had a senior management position at a large factory. Before his death, the defendant claims that the father had difficulties in coping with the defendant's missing hand, and that his parents had frequent arguments over this matter. The defendant was single and had no children of his own.

Mr Joseph claimed that he had an academic diploma from a high school in New Jersey; He also claimed that he attended a Community College in Manhattan where he majored in Chemistry. Mr Joseph said he had numerous jobs, most of them lasting less than a year. The background documentation did not indicate whether any of these jobs were independently verified and the reason for the job discontinuation ascertained. Some of these jobs were held in many states throughout the continental United States. Before the events leading to his latest charges, he was trying to make a living repairing firearms and occasionally selling ammunition at fireranges, some of which were located outside New York City.

As indicated above, the defendant stated that he travelled extensively through the states to find out how people in other states prepared "fireworks." These travels sometimes were associated with an obsessive preoccupation with the technical details of construction of fireworks and fireworks display shows. For example, whenever he saw a sign "Fireworks," he would stop and would make sure he would meet people and ask for details about firework construction and display. He was interested in how fireworks achieved the twirling and whistling effect as they went up in the air. At other times, he would ask how professionals managed to create such an array of colors during fireworks displays. On many occasions, he would attempt to be hired by companies that manufactured fireworks in order to know more about details of firework construction.

The defendant appeared to have tried to learn about fireworks and explosives from almost any source he could, including books, professors, etc. He said: "If anyone tried to do what I did, I told them to do exactly what I did, experiment, study, and read." There was a grandiose quality in the way he described his preoccupation with the "physics" of explosives; at the same time, the preoccupation appeared to have been carried out largely as a private, secretive activity with little connection to the practical, social world.

The defendant said he used LSD ("acid"), mushrooms, and quaaludes around 1986. The defendant claimed to be an occasional beer drinker.

Mr Joseph was a well-developed (5'6", 191 pounds) man who during the evaluative interview and testing appeared alert and very articulate. He attempted to have an explanation for every topic he discussed. The structure and content of his speech was that of an educated person. At times — and particularly during the second interview — he spoke with a high degree of pressure and circumstantiality giving little opportunity to his interlocutors to cut in. His eye contact was adequate, that is, he did not avoid eye contact or inappropriately stare at the interviewer.

A screening battery of probes that included examination of posture, gait, whole-body balance, muscle strength, tremor at rest, intentional tremor, motor coordination, general appearance of the eyes, eye movements, and reaction of the eyes to light was performed and the results were all within normal limits.

From an extensive checklist of signs and/or symptoms possibly indicative of neurological or mental disorders, Mr Joseph was asked whether he had ever experienced them, and if so, to give examples. He denied ever having experienced these signs or symptoms. Paranoid ideation, delusions, and hallucinations were denied.

The Wechsler Adult Intelligence Scale — Revised (WAIS-R) was administered. Mr Joseph's verbal IQ was found to be 104 and his performance IQ was 106; the overall test IQ was 105. These IQ levels represent a normal average level of intellectual functioning. His performance in the Picture Arrangement Test is noteworthy. The test consists of a series of pictures which, when placed in the right sequence, tells a story, like a cartoon. Because the stories involved humans in various situations, this test is used to assess the so-called "social intelligence." The test requires the individual to evaluate the social relevance of pictured situations, to anticipate the consequences of the characters' actions, and to distinguish essential from irrelevant details. This subtest is sometimes considered a measure of planning ability. The defendant did poorly in this test — his worst performance in the battery — often placing the individual illustration in a wrong sequence, forcing an unlikely story into the sequence or placing the stories in the right order but missing the "punch" line of the story. If the results of this test would be averaged out with the others, his performance IQ would have been considerably reduced.

Mr Joseph was shown outlines of common figures — such as a house, a knife, a fork, eyeglasses, etc. — superimposed on other outlines. People who suffer from subtle to severe forms of brain damage often fail to identify figures presented in such a fashion. There are four such plates, with ten figures on each plate amounting to 40 outlines. Mr Joseph correctly identified 34 out of the 40 outlines. In addition, there were no anomias

— the inability of coming up with the name of a figure one sees. There were no confabulations — an important sign of neurological or psychiatric disorder consisting of making up figures rarely seen by other people.

In the Thematic Apperception Test (commonly known as TAT), Mr Joseph was shown pictures of people in different situations and was then asked to tell a story about each plate, to indicate the characters of the story, the events that led to the present situation and the possible outcome. The following was verbalized: A man clinging to a rope was seen as "art picture," similar to the ones the defendant saw in a museum; he said that it was hard to ascertain whether the man was climbing or going down; then he thought he was going down; a picture of a man who is clutched from behind by three hands, was turned upside down first and then described as a "bad photographic print"; then he thought that perhaps there was a person behind the man holding a paper man; the man in the picture looked intelligent; a picture of a woman squeezing the throat of another woman was seen as a scene of English theatre often seen on PBS; these were said to be middle class women, perhaps mother and daughter. For the most part, the "stories" were mere descriptions of the illustrations; in each case, the defendant judged either the artistic or the photographic quality of the picture. This tendency is often seen in individuals afflicted by serious mental disorders.

☐ **QUESTIONS FOR REVIEW AND DISCUSSION**

△ This case illustrates a defendant who is highly motivated to show that he is mentally healthy because otherwise he may not be allowed to keep firearms. Can you think of other circumstances in which defendants — appearing at the criminal or other courts — are highly motivated to show that they are mentally healthy?

△ The defendant may not tell you that he or she has been diagnosed as suffering from a bipolar mood disorder (in fact, he may not know that); however, he remembers the medications that he was given as an outpatient. What psychotropic medications are used to treat mood disorders?

△ Discuss pyromania; name key elements to make the differential diagnosis between pyromania and the setting of fires that result from other mental and/or circumstantial conditions (e.g., setting fire for profit).

△ Mr Joseph did not suffer brain damage as a result of the numerous accidents while "experimenting" with firearms and explosives; assume that the next time in court Mr Joseph is reported to have suffered extensive brain injuries as a result of an explosion. Discuss the consequences of: (1) knowing Mr Joseph's prior psychiatric history; (2) not knowing such a history (namely, you have to reconstruct from what he says at the time of the interview).

☐ **EXHIBIT 4.2**

Trapped in the Body of a Woman

Ms Prieto — who was evaluated when she was free in the community awaiting sentence — was a 34-year-old Hispanic female with a fifth grade education. Ms Prieto met the diagnostic criteria for Transsexualism as the following were present: A persistent discomfort and sense of inappropriateness about her gender; preoccupation with getting rid of her primary and secondary sex characteristics and acquiring the sex characteristics of the male sex; a wish to live as a man; feelings of being uncomfortable wearing woman's clothing, and dressing as a man. To varying degrees, the defendant's behavior, dress, and mannerisms were those of a man. The defendant experienced much anxiety and at times she appeared to be delusional. However, a more focused diagnosis could not be made due to the sparcity of information surrounding important details of relationships between the defendant and the victims to be explained below.

Ms Prieto discovered by herself that she had a masculine orientation when she was about eight when she often wore her father's clothing and shoes. At the time, her parents punished her severely for engaging in sexual plays with girls of her age. Her parents were said to go to considerable length to "cure" her of her masculine orientation, spending money equally on physicians and priests, the latter hired to get rid of her "evil spirits." She said that she did gain considerable independence when she moved to New York to live by herself. She lived with a heterosexual man and from this union three children were born.

Ms Prieto's background was a mixture of Caribbean Black and American (Caribbean) Indian. The diagnosis of transsexualism was not apparently associated with any obvious physical intersexuality or genetic abnormality although the defendant claimed that gender identification was prevalent in her wider family (cousins).

There were severe stressors during her childhood as her neighbors mortified her by calling names and making public denunciations of her male orientation. During the 1970s and until the mid-1980s, once she moved to the United States the defendant was much into drugs, taking marijuana, cocaine, and opium (she identifies herself with people of the "Woodstock generation"). She felt "terribly paranoid" during those times and thought that everybody was after her. For the past two years, she had remained relatively isolated and she was barely aware of current events. Her current stressors, if any, were unknown.

Ms Prieto's general level of intellectual functioning appeared to be borderline; periodically the defendant felt delusionally threatened to be "robbed of her masculinity," under which circumstances she would cut her hair as close to the scalp as possible and behave exaggeratedly as a man. At times she appeared to suffer from manic episodes under which she would write numerous passionate letters to the women she loved. The events leading to her charges — harassment — appeared to have originated from these episodes. She described herself as having a loving relationship with her own children.

It was felt that transsexualism was well-embedded into the defendant's personality and behavior. She was not expected to change much during the coming years. The failure to fully accept herself as the person she was, was likely to be helped with psychotherapy. The probability of a continuation of the delusional components of her personality that led to confrontations with the law was difficult to estimate.

It was felt that the prospect of her social rehabilitation was guarded. Ms Prieto denied the charges against her, asserting that she has had numerous affectionate and even sexual contacts with the women victims of her harassment. She stated that she was willing to take the latest victim to court. The defendant had had only one prior arrest that, importantly, occurred under similar circumstances leading to similar charges. Once the delusional system was triggered, the defendant had inadequate control of her impulses.

Ms Prieto stated that she suffered a caesaerian surgical intervention when she bore her first child. Her current health was described as being "good." Until this year — after being ordered by the court — Ms Prieto stated that she never sought or received help from a psychiatrist, psychologist, or mental health worker.

Ms Prieto attended school abroad until the 5th grade; when she moved to the United States (at 14), she was placed in 8th grade but she dropped out of school after a few months of attendance. Ms Prieto had been on public assistance for the last 11 years. She said that she used to enjoy attending both "straight" and "lesbian" parties but, for the past two years, she remained at home.

Ms Prieto began using drugs soon after she moved to New York City. She smoked marijuana, snorted cocaine, and used LSD, PCP, and opium. At 25 she stopped briefly following "medical treatment." She resumed again and stopped once more on her own at the age of 33.

Because of the nature of her charges, Ms Prieto's sexual development was probed. She said that she discovered her male orientation on her own. When she was eight, she would stuff stockings with newspapers and tied them around her waist, pretending she had a penis. Sometimes she would engage in sexual play with girls of her age pretending she was the man. She indicated that she entered into a heterosexual relationship with an older man only because he provided much-needed shelter. After the separation, she continued to have homosexual relationships with various women. The evaluation of the charges against her was sometimes difficult because situations involving women — with whom the defendant said to have had consenting homosexual relationships — appeared to be delusional. Even more difficult to evaluate were numerous "love triangles" in which lesbian relationships and the ladies' husbands were involved.

Ms Prieto was a heavy, although well-developed, individual (5'6", 190 pounds) who often behaved in a manner that resembled a woman trying to imitate the behavior of a man. She wore a man's white shirt, a man's type of pants, and masculine-looking shoes; her crew-cut hair was covered by a man's cap. Her arms looked very much like a man's as a result of her vigorous exercise (the defendant performed frequent push-ups) and were covered by numerous tattoos. Her facial expression — combining American Indian and Black features — was remarkable in that when she was in an introspective mood, she appeared to be a young adolescent boy. The defendant appeared to have a good insight into the nature of her problems. Her eye contact at times revealed a slight paranoid stare. Her communication skills in Spanish were excellent.

A screening battery of probes that included examination of posture, gait, whole-body balance, muscle strength, tremor at rest, intentional tremor, motor coordination, general appearance of the eyes, eye movements, and reaction of the eyes to light was performed. The following was noted: When asked to follow this evaluator's finger with her eyes, the defendant followed the finger with her entire head. People who suffer mental disorder often exhibit this pattern of behavior.

She said that she no longer compares herself with other people; she had learned not to consider herself "neither less nor more than other people." She has suffered daily humiliations with her obvious transsexual ways of life only because people were shocked. In New York — where people have been always more tolerant — she was sometimes puzzled about the fact that people would not say anything about her; she almost expected others to point fingers and call her ugly names.

Ms Prieto appeared to suffer somatic delusions in which she often — particularly during dreams — was frightened by the thought that "somebody" tried to rob her of her masculinity. These dreams involved seeing her muscles disappearing and her breasts developing excessively; at other times, she felt as if people were undressing her so that she was totally naked. During these episodes, she scratched herself and tried to cut her hair as short as possible.

The defendant said that she still had flashbacks of the times her father would pay the church to sing psalms for the salvation of her soul and for her return to feminine ways of behavior. Once, church people made a collection and purchased a girl's dress, and a girl's shoes. She made everybody mad when she flatly threw away the gifts. Her parents even resorted to witchcraft to "cure" her. Her father is said to have spent so much money in such effort that at some point he had to sell the house to pay all the expenses.

Individual items of the Wechsler Adult Intelligence Scale — Revised (WAIS-R) were administered. Her level of intellectual functioning was estimated to be borderline.

☐ QUESTIONS FOR REVIEW AND DISCUSSION

△ Make the differential diagnosis between homosexuality and transsexualism.

△ Let's assume that Ms Prieto tells you that she is unjustly accused of harassment, that she in fact did have a love affair with the wife of a person who is the owner of a major retail company in New York City, and that the victim of harassment is lying. As a psychologist, do you need to handle the matter of the burden of proof? Recall that Ms Prieto said that she pled guilty on the advice of her lawyer and particularly because she did not want to embarrass a well-known citizen by forcing her to appear in court.

△ A teacher voices concern about Ms Prieto's ability to function as a homosexual parent — primarily because she is now living with a new female lover. As a psychologist in a family court, how do you prepare yourself (what do you do) in order to address this issue as an expert witness in court?

△ An endocrinologist who writes on behalf of the victim of harassment suggests that Ms Prieto may benefit from hormonal treatment for her "sexual disorder." Discuss the following: (1) Homosexuality, legally and psychiatrically defined; (2) state-of-the-art and issues surrounding the "treatment" of homosexuality; and (3) the effectiveness of psychotherapy and biological intervention in both male and female homosexuals.

△ Ms Prieto argues the point that — as a lesbian who has sexual contacts with nobody else but females — she has no risk factors for AIDS. Is she correct? How would you go about probing for possible risk factors for AIDS in a homosexual female?

5: THE PHYSICAL EXAMINATION

IN THE PREVIOUS TWO CHAPTERS, WE HAVE SEEN THAT APPEARANCES ARE sometimes deceiving and that the stories we are told are often biased, inaccurate, and twisted. Will the information derived from the defendant's physical examination provide more accurate data giving new insights into the "criminal intent" during the events leading to the defendant's charges or point to "mitigating circumstances" or "diminished capacities"?

As defined by *Black's Law Dictionary* (Campbell-Black, 1983), *mitigating circumstances* do not constitute a justification or excuse for the offense in question, but in fairness and mercy may be considered as extenuating or reducing the degree of moral culpability. In the commission of the killing in a sudden heat of passion caused by adequate legal provocation, mitigating circumstances will reduce, for example, the degree of seriousness of the offense from homicide — a more serious crime — to manslaughter — a less serious crime.

In previous chapters, we have referred to cases in which an objective syndrome — cerebral palsy, communication disorders, epilepsy, mental retardation, drug and alcohol abuse, chronic fatigue syndrome, depression, etc. — is sometimes seen as a mitigating circumstance for the execution of a criminal act. As resident expert witnesses, we are called upon to write a professional opinion as to whether these conditions are real; sometimes we are asked to evaluate the comparative likelihood — relative to other factors also present — that these physical conditions are "proximate causes" during the commission of the crime.

If one conceives the nervous system as a computer, the physical examination amounts to checking the inner workings of the hardware of such a computer. The "physical examination" is a part of the neuropsychological evaluation in which such a screening is made. The clinician performs three types of evaluations:

☐ The symptomatic examination, in which he or she observes symptoms and signs of a — primarily, but not exclusively neurological — disease.

☐ The anatomical examination, in which the probable portions of the nervous system affected are ascertained.

☐ The diagnosis, i.e., a statement of the type and possible causes of neurological illness. The cause of a disease is called its etiology. A neurologist — and sometimes, a neuropathologist — is often called in to make a judgment of the possible etiology of abnormal signs and symptoms.

Probing the Nervous System

The physical examination consists of a series of probes performed in a systematic manner. A probe is different from a psychological test or other specific laboratory diagnostic procedure. A probe is the examination of the functioning of the nervous system of an individual with the naked eye or by using very simple equipment. In the clinic, a simple chart containing paragraphs with letters of decreasing sizes is used for a person complaining about visual difficulties; an ophthalmologist who needs to write a new prescription for his client's glasses needs to have access to more elaborate optical equipment. As a rule, a test is a probe that has been standardized on the basis of a statistically representative number of healthy people satisfying various criteria of test development.

It is close to impossible not to have had an encounter with the workings of the nervous system even if one is a perfectly normal individual. A muscle cramp, an arm that goes to sleep when one rests in an awkward posture, the momentary blindness that occurs when one enters a dark room after spending most of the day sunbathing, the embarrassing situation of not remembering the boss' wife who was introduced to us only a few minutes before, the inability to understand a proverb as pertaining to a description of an individual's character are all examples of the normal function of the brain or — more correctly — of the nervous system.

Many of us have developed an intuitive understanding of how the nervous system controls movement by assuming that — from the physical point of view — we are made up of bones and flesh, that we maintain posture and walk through the magnificent combination of pulleys and muscles, and that nerves send electrical signals instructing those muscles to contract or relax.

We may have learned that these electrical signals are generated within the nervous system and that our brain can be conceived of as an extraordinary computer. We might be equally aware of the fact that biochemical processes control the brain; that biological drives — such as hunger, thirst, control of the body temperature, sex, etc. — are regulated by the brain; that our brain can be programmed by education and experience; that scientists have still to learn what unique combination of the brain and the environment produces an Einstein, a Mother Teresa, or a serial rapist. The physical examination is one of the three exams that allows us to collection basic information — basic facts — about the individual.

In law, facts are sharply distinguished from opinions. Black's Law Dictionary defines a fact as ". . . an event or circumstance; an actual occurrence; an actual happening in time, space or an event mental or physical." When facts are presented as evidence they refer to ". . . a circumstance, event or occurrence as it actually takes or took place; a physical object or appearance, as it usually exists or existed." For the most part, rules of evidence do not allow a witness to testify about opinions and/or conclusions. Only an "expert witness" can.

Black's Law Dictionary defines an expert witness as "one who by reason of education or specialized experience possesses superior knowledge respecting a subject about which persons having no particular training are incapable of forming an accurate opinion or deducting correct conclusions." This source also defines "opinion evidence or testimony" as "the evidence of what the witness thinks, believes, or infers in regard to facts in dispute, as distinguished from his personal knowledge of the facts themselves.

As a rule, neurologists, psychiatrists, or psychologists would not report their findings as "facts" but as "signs," "symptoms," or "syndromes." A *sign* is an objective manifestation of a pathological condition. Signs are observed by the examiner rather than reported by the individual. A *symptom* is a manifestation of a pathological condition, and some professionals limit its use to denote subjective complaints. A *syndrome* is a group of symptoms that occur together and that constitute a recognizable condition. "Syndrome" is less specific than "disorder" or "disease." The term *disease* generally implies a specific etiology or pathophysiologic process. (In Chapters 7 and 8, dealing with mental disorders and the use of the DSM, this topic is discussed at some length.)

Contributions from Many Experts

There are several expert witnesses who can potentially contribute to the process of gathering information about basic facts on a defendant's biological and mental processes; sometimes these professionals appear in court to present expert testimony about whether the offense is likely to be linked to such processes. As a rule, neurologists are expected to contribute information about the clinical examination dealing with the "physical examination" and with signs and symptoms of nervous sytems dysfunction, the subject matter of this chapter. Psychiatrists have traditionally been concerned with the "examination of the mental status" and with the signs and symptoms of mental disorder. Some professionals take boards (examinations) in both neurology and psychiatry and call themselves "neuropsychiatrists." Psychologists have long been recognized as expert witnesses in court and have often testified in court in various branches of the law including civil and criminal law; in addition, these professionals are trained in the administration and interpretation of tests which allow forming an opinion regarding matters such as competence to stand trial and rehabilitation potential.

As seen in Chapter 1, some psychologists have dual training in the neuroscienes and clinical psychology and are called "neuropsychologists." Nurses and social workers working with inmates at detention centers and prisons provide information about the physical and mental condition of a detainee because of their daily contact with inmates. In this book, neurologists, psychiatrists, psychologists, psychiatric nurses, social workers, rehabilitation workers, and many other professionals who provide information linked to the court and criminal will, for brevity's sake, be called mental health workers. There are many professionals who are both physicians and lawyers (or psychologists and lawyers). Some of these professionals are called to court to establish "causation" between the offense and the state of mind; a jury establishes that the defendant is "guilty" or "not guilty."

Essential Probes

The following probes are essential in the course of a routine physical examination:

☐ Gait and posture

□ Cranial nerves

□ Motor examination

□ Tendon reflexes

□ Coordination

□ Sensory evaluation

□ Examination of the autonomic system

In the maintenance of the upright posture and walking, a substantial portion of the nervous system is brought into action. The examination of the posture and gait provides important clues as to the status of the nervous and musculo-skeletal system, general health and, sometimes, mental status. The gait examination includes the observation of presence of arm swing, the ability to perform rapid turning without losing balance, and the ability to walk on toes and heels. The defendant may be asked to walk in tandem — that is, he or she is asked to walk heel-to- toe down a line on the floor — a very sensitive probe for general motor coordination. In normal walking, weight distribution over both legs and feet provides a firmer basis for balance than in tandem-walking, while in tandem-walking balance necessarily shifts from one leg and foot to the other. Thus, tandem-walking demands greater ability to compensate for changes in posture and weight distribution. It is a widely-used test for assessing overt signs of alcoholic intoxication, for example.

As stated earlier, sometimes gait and posture reveal the individual's mental status. An elderly individual suffering an impairment in space orientation who has just climbed a steep flight of stairs while exiting a subway station may not be aware that when he stops at the entrance to take a breath, to see where he is, and where he needs to be heading, or may not realize that he is blocking a flow of angered people trying to leave the subway as well.

Often, the presence of psychiatric signs are detected while using these simple probes.

□ Mr Simpson — for example — was able to maintain his balance during a normal erect position with feet together while his eyes were either open or closed. However, when he was asked to repeat the probe while having one foot in front of the other in tandem, he lost his balance. Catatonic behavior was noted. When told the probe was over, the defendant persisted in maintaining the position of feet in tandem in spite of having great difficulty in maitaining his balance. At the time of the probe, the clinical impression gained was that the defendant was not faking his catatonic behavior.

Signs of Catatonia

Catatonic behavior is almost invariably an expression of a serious mental disorder such as schizophrenia, and it is often detected during the physical examination. Sometimes, the individual shows catatonic posturing, that is, voluntary assumptiom of an inappropriate or bizarre posture, usually held for long periods of time. A patient may stand with arms outstretched as if he were Jesus at the cross. At other times, the defendant shows catatonic rigidity, that is, maintenance of a rigid posture against all efforts to be moved. Catatonic stupor is a marked decrease in reactivity to the environment and a reduction in spontaneous movements and activity, sometimes to the point of appearing to be unaware of one's surroundings. Catatonic or "waxy" flexibility is sometimes observed — that is, the person's limbs can be "molded" into any position, which is then maintained. When the limb is being moved, it feels to the examiner as if it were made of pliable wax.

Examination of Cranial Nerves

The examination of the cranial nerves includes the examination of the sensory organs, muscles, and functions that depend on the functional integrity of the cranial nerves, those which arise from the base of the brain. Traditionally, cranial nerves are designated by Roman numerals. The examination is performed seriatim from the first to the twelfth nerve.

The examination of the olfactory nerve — the first cranial nerve — is performed by using aromatic substances, such as vanilla bean, coffee, tobacco, peppermint, etc. Loss of olfactory sensation can occur as a result of traumatic conditions, such as a car accident. The olfactory nerves are two tiny bands of fibers linking the nose to the brain. When one is standing or driving slowly and is suddenly hit by a car from the rear, the body is suddenly accelerated and — as the result of inertia — the body mass of the brain tends to remain in the same position. The olfactory nerves can snap under such stress beyond repair and with total loss of the sensation of smell. However, in the forensic clinic, olfactory dysfunction is more often linked to long term snorting of illegal drugs, such as cocaine or heroin. Some individuals afflicted by serious mental disorders suffer from olfactory hallucinations.

Four probes are used to evaluate the second cranial nerve, the optic nerve: Fundoscopy, visual acuity, visual fields, and color perception. Fundoscopy is the examination of the fundus of the eye where the surface of the retina can be visualized. The fundoscopical evaluation is made by means of an optical instrument called the ophthalmoscope. Although with the aid of the ophthalmoscope, the clinician explores many inner physical aspects of the eye — such as opacities of the cornea or the lens; a neurologist looks at the appearance of the optic papilla. The optic papilla is where neural fibers originating in the retina gather to become the optic nerve. The optic papilla is an oval area crossed by small blood vessels devoid of visual receptors. Change in the appearance and coloration of blood vessels are in some cases indicative of a variety of medical problems such as atherosclerosis. Edema or swelling of the papilla is associated with an increase in intracranial pressure, sometimes indicative of tumors.

Visual Acuity

Visual acuity is the ability to detect, resolve, and perceive the fine details of a visual display. People who face legal proceedings are often poor and — although they are badly in need of glasses — they have rarely had their eyes examined. Defendants who are in jail waiting their sentencing sometimes have their glasses stolen or broken during fights; aging inmates often lose them. The evaluation of visual acuity is essential for the interpretation of the findings of tests requiring normal vision. Most of the psychometric tests described in the Appendix are relatively insensitive to changes in visual acuity.

Nonetheless, when in doubt, the examiner uses simple probes — such as requesting the examinee to read written material of different sizes — to make a quick evaluation of this important confounder. Many factors account for a reduction in visual acuity. Some are changes in the transparency of the optical media of the eye, such as corneal lacerations or cataracts, an opacity of the lens located inside the eye. Some others are due to damage to the neural pathways involved in visual perception. Visual acuity is also important to test in individuals who are suspected of malingering or trying to avoid detection of the impairments to be observed. For example, the inability to read sometimes is hidden as an inability to see.

Our visual field is everything we can see around us with both eyes without moving the head. Changes in the visual field make it possible to localize the site of neural lesions in the visual pathway. A simple test of the visual field is performed in the clinic with one's fingers and sometimes with the aid of colored pencils.

But the characterization and extent of scotomas — loss of vision in specific regions of the visual field — are detected by means of a more comprehensive procedure called visual field testing. In the latter, movable visual targets are used to map the contours of the visual field and to locate where vision is absent. Needless to say, visual testing is essential in cases where partial or total visual loss is claimed. Some people afflicted by hysterical neurosis — now called conversion disorder — experience a very credible blindness.

Color Perception

Assessment of color perception is possible by the use of simple tests. Some of them are plates with letters and numbers shaped by arranging circles of different colors; others involve color sorting. However, as indicated above, the ability to perceive brightness is important in perception of color. The determination of anomalies in color perception is sometimes crucial in forensic investigations, such as in toxic torts involving a worker that makes a mistake in sorting merchandise due to his or her congenital color blindness, or drivers involved in fatal car accidents who suffer from advanced stages of cataract.

Examining the third cranial nerve usually means observing pupil size, reaction to light, and the action of some extraocular muscles allowing the elevation of the eyelids. The pupil dilates as the iris — the colored portion of the eye — contracts; conversely, the pupil has a pin-point appearance as the sphincter muscle of the iris relaxes. These muscles are under the control of the autonomic nervous system and drugs affecting autonomic functions are likely to cause alterations in pupil diameter.

Although pupillary changes can be associated with numerous medical conditions, in the forensic clinic the most common cases are related to drug abuse. The presence of dilated pupils is a common cause of photophobia, an exaggerated sensitivity to light. It is common practice to examine the kind of glasses the individual carries even if he or she does not use them during the course of examination. Heavily tinted glasses are sometimes an indication of photophobia. However, teenagers sometimes use heavily tinted glasses to imitate entertainment idols; some others use dark glasses to avoid being recognized; still others use dark glasses to be able to scan the environment without scanning eye movements being noticed.

Failure to open the eye (dropped lid or ptosis) may be due to lesions of the third cranial nerve. To evaluate the extraocular muscles — controlled by the third, fourth, and sixth nerves — the examiner asks the individual to move the eyes about in a horizontal and vertical plane. Limitations of eye movement and double vision can thus be noted.

Nystagmus — repetitive movement of the eyes — has a fast and slow phase. By convention, the direction of the nystagmus is designated by the direction of the fast phase. Nystagmus may be elicited normally by stimulation of the vestibular organs, such as when the ears are irrigated with cold or warm water (caloric nystagmus). Alterations of eye movements are often observed among people who suffer from chronic alcoholism and/or abuse of illegal drugs.

Signs of Paranoia

During the course of a physical examination, abnormalities in behavior are often observed. Individuals who suffer from paranoia — for reasons that sometimes are known and sometimes unknown — feel suspicious. Sometimes a defendant is instructed to follow the evaluator's finger asking the defendant to keep his head steady. Some defendants appear to have difficulties in following the evaluator's finger as they keep looking at the evaluator. This behavior does not appear to be the expression of a neurological defect but rather a strong urge to be "on guard" or to be "in control;" by following the finger, the defendant feels that this puts him in a submissive or out-of-control position.

The Trigeminal Nerve

Pin pricks and touch over the face are used to assess the functional integrity of two overlapping sensory systems carried by the fifth nerve, the trigeminal nerve. The corneal reflex is tested by touching each cornea with a wisp of cotton. The corneal reflex disappears in advanced stages of coma and presages imminent death. Police officers are often trained to perform these procedures after finding severely wounded invididuals while patrolling the streets or responding to a call.

The examination of the symmetry of facial movements is performed to evaluate the seventh nerve controlling facial muscles. These nerves are tested by observing and touching the muscles of the face as the individual closes the jaw tightly and moves the mandible — or lower jaw — from side to side. The anterior two-thirds of the tongue is innervated by the sensory branch of the seventh nerve carrying taste sensations.

The Sense of Hearing

Hearing can be severely affected by toxic drugs — such as in the use of the antibiotic streptomycin. Deafness often occurs after the early massive use of an antibiotic to treat tuberculosis. Noise-induced hearing damage, quite prevalent in many worksites, may be a more likely explanation of hearing impairment. Many defendants exhibit hearing damage as a result of exposure to "hard metal" music or to the excessive volume of their personal tape players. In the clinic, the noise produced by rubbing the index finger against the thumb can be used as an effective stimulus. Some individuals need audiometric testing to determine the sensitivity of a wide range of frequencies — generally from 125 to 30,000 Hertz (cycles per second).

The Production of Speech

The functions of the 9th through 11th cranial nerves are assessed by carefully observing speech — particularly slurred speech — the presence of gag reflex, and the ability to swallow.

The 11th cranial nerve innervates the muscles that control the symmetry of shoulder muscles and rotation of the head whereas the 12th cranial nerve controls the movement of the tongue. The examiner assesses the functional integrity of this nerve by observing midline presence of atrophy or abnormal tongue movements.

Motor Coordination

The motor examination is directed at the evaluation of muscle tone, motor strength, and motor coordination. Some neurological conditions are characterized by neuromuscular disorders such as the presence of atrophy (muscle degeneration), fasciculation (involuntary twitches of the muscles), tone-resistance to passive movement, and tremor. Evaluation of atrophy and fasciculation sometimes calls for testing of individual muscles. Often, electrophysiological procedures — particularly electromyography and nerve conduction velocity determinations, described in Appendix B — aid the diagnosis.

Evaluation of muscle tone and resistance to passive movement may lead to the diagnosis of either spasticity or rigidity. Spasticity is characterized by a "clasp-knife" resistance: The resistance increases as the clinician continues to apply force. Rigidity is a sort of "lead-pipe" resistance characterized by uniformly increased resistance throughout the range of motion.

Tremor is the involuntary periodic oscillation of a body member. Three categories of tremor are recognized: Resting tremor, intention tremor, and postural tremor.

  □ *Resting tremor,* as its name indicates, is present at rest. It is exaggerated when limbs are relaxed and lessens during the execution of a voluntary movement. Resting tremor needs to be differentiated from physiological tremor, a normal oscillation of body parts between 8 to 13 Hertz.

  □ *Intentional tremor* is manifested while attempting to perform a movement at will (volitional movement). It is often a sign of cerebellar disease. A maneuver to elicit intentional tremor is to ask the patient to touch his or her nose with the index finger of one hand.

  □ *Postural tremor* is observed with the part of the body maintaining a posture, such as holding the hands outstretched. It diminishes when the limbs are relaxed, reappearing as soon as movement begins.

Motor coordination results from the integration of sensory input and motor outputs. One important set of clues is brought by muscle sense or kinesthesia. There are many neurological probes to evaluate proprioception, the ability to recognize the position of limbs in space. The individual may be asked to place his arms in front of him with his eyes closed. Or he is asked to elevate one arm — for example, the left — and then position the right arm at the same height. In other instances, the individual is asked to touch his nose alternatively with the index finger of the right and left hand with eyes closed.

Motor coordination is a learned sequence of motor acts, such as those involved in buttoning one's shirts or tying one's shoes. The cerebellum is the main neural structure involved in the scheduling and appropriate sequencing of motor acts including motor learning. The timing of these learned sensory and motor clues are easily disrupted as a result of a large variety of neurotoxic chemical agents. That is why motor coordination probes have long been used in the quick assessment of intoxicated persons, such as the assessment performed by police officers who need to ascertain possible alcohol intoxication in a person driving a car.

Intellectual Functioning

The physical examination can sometimes reveal features of the defendant's intellectual performance that would require further evaluation with the aid of psychological tests. For example, individuals who suffer from mental retardation or severe forms of psychotic disorder cannot, at times, tell the difference between the probes they are expected to perform and the evaluator's normal range of movement during these probes. One defendant, for instance, would imitate the evaluator's to the smallest detail, such as grabbing his belt while waiting for his response. Some others would imitate not only the movements but the verbalizations of intructions, e.g., "now you move your hand this way and touch your nose."

Examination of Reflexive Behaviors

The so-called "reflex examination" consists of the examination of deep tendon and superficial cutaneous reflexes. Deep tendon reflexes are elicited by tapping the tendon of major muscles with a soft rubber percussion hammer. The reflex activity of the biceps, triceps, quadriceps and gastrocnemius are thus examined.

The clinical interpretation of findings resulting from the "reflex examination" is always challenging. The absence of these reflexes may be associated with alterations at many different levels of the functional organization of the nervous system including the integrity of receptors within muscles. Exaggeration of reflexes is often part of spasticity, a syndrome caused by alterations in upper motor neurons, neurons located at higher levels of the spinal cord.

The *Babinsky response* – a cutaneous reflex — is an abnormal neurological sign seen by the extension of the great toe and fanning of the other toes as a result of striking the most lateral portion of the sole with a sharp object, such as a key or safety pin. Normally, there is no flexion of all toes as a result of this type of sensory stimulation. The Babinsky sign is normal in babies; its disappearance is a measure of the myelinization of the nervous system. (Myelinization is the progressive covering of nerves with myelin, a fatty sheath substance that — among many other properties — plays a role in the transport of nerve impulses.) In the adult, the Babinsky response is found when there are lesions in the bundle of fibers called the cortico-spinal tract.

The sensations of pain, cold and warm sensations, on the one hand, and of touch and mechanical vibration on the other are mediated by the somatosensory system. Sensation of pain and temperature are conducted by thin fibers devoid of myelin whereas touch and vibration are mediated by thick, myelinated fibers. Thus, in lesions affecting the dorsal (or rear) column of the spinal cord, sensations of touch and vibration disappear — or are greatly diminished — while pain and temperature sensations remain unchanged.

Autonomic Nervous System Functions

The evaluation of autonomic nervous function is part of a thorough neurological examination. This includes questions and probes regarding frequency of urination, changes in regularity and frequency of heart beat, amount of urinary output, presence of diarrhea or constipation, impotence, sudden reduction in blood pressure leading to fainting, lacrimation, changes in pupil diameter, dryness of mouth and skin, among others. When necessary, a physician may require the performance of specific tests of autonomic system function — e.g., sweating tests, special electrocardiographic tests, etc. People who are drug abusers — or are temporarily held in jail after long use of drugs — show numerous autonomic symptoms such as fast heart beat, constipation (or diarrhea), dryness of the mouth, etc. The "heat of passion" and some autonomic nervous symptoms that drug users experience are not easily distinguishable from each other.

Widely prescribed tranquilizers, antidepressants, anti-hypertensive medications — particularly the so-called beta blockers — and medications prescribed to regulate cardiac rhythm such as per-xylene also cause autonomic signs and symptoms. Some poor people who do not have access to expensive drugs become addicted to gasoline, nail polish, and glues that cause a variety of autonomic, central, and peripheral nervous system signs and symptoms. Neurotoxins of plant and animal origin often produce marked autonomic effects, sometimes fatal. Well known are the autonomic effects of the bite of the black widow spider, the cobra snake, the sting of the scorpion, and toxins released by bacteria — such as those that cause botulism and tetanus as well as mushroom poisoning (e.g., Amanita muscaria). Intentional poisoning with such agents can occur.

Physical examinations — as described in this chapter — are often absent in psychiatric reports or dismissed in a few lines in a section where the appearance and the physical impression of the individual is discussed. There is a sense of disappointment in the fact that the physical examination is not likely to contribute to understanding an individual's "state of mind;" this is because this type of examination is about the individual's "nuts and bolts" or the functional integrity of the individual's "hardware."

A report of the physical examination of a person charged with murder may read as follows: "A screening battery of probes that included examination of posture, gait, whole-body balance, muscle strength, tremor at rest, intentional tremor, motor coordination, general appearance of the eyes, eye movements and reaction of the eyes to light was performed and the results were all found to be within normal limits." However, when the matter of diminished capacity is at stake, a forensic evaluation without the physical examination may be incomplete.

□ **EXHIBIT 5.1**

New York Child Learns to Walk by Himself

This defendant was evaluated while in custody, before sentence. Mr Barrios was a 28-year-old Hispanic-Black male with 12th grade level of education. Mr Barrios suffered from cerebral palsy which most probably resulted from temporary lack of oxygen to the brain at the moment of his birth.

The defendant now exhibited motor and articulatory speech problems but both his understanding of language and his general level of cognition were virtually intact. His level of functioning could not be adequally assessed because of the defendant's handicap; however, his contact with reality appeared to be intact. The degree of control of his impulses were thought to be adequate and the defendant was not thought to be posing a threat to himself or to others.

Mr Barrios had the appearance of a neurologically-impaired person. Through probing — and in the absence of medical records to support this clinical impression — it was felt that it was likely that this condition came about at birth as a result of brain anoxia, that is, oxygen deprivation to the brain prior to parturition. The following was noted: Numerous scars on his arms acquired at a time in which he used to smash his hands into things including glass; these impulsive behaviors were said to have occurred between the ages of nine and nineteen.

A screening battery of probes that included examination of posture, gait, whole-body balance, muscle strength, tremor at rest, intentional tremor, motor coordination, general appearance of the eyes, eye movements and reaction of the eyes to light was performed and the following observations were made: His whole-body balance was poor and his gait was unsteady; he had poor muscle strength on his upper limbs (he could offer resistance to my moderate pushing down of his upper limbs); the articulation of his wrist was abnormal (vis-à-vis his lower upper limbs, his hands formed some sort of a goose neck with both his wrists abnormally protruding; he showed considerable hand tremor (shakes) while extending his hands; he also showed ataxia (he pointed past his nose when attempting to touch with his fingers with eyes open or eyes closed); he showed moderate jerky eye movements on finger following, a sign of impaired brain control of eye movements; and he was deaf in his right ear (the defendant was told that he had speech problems because he was deaf in one ear which is medically unplausible as his left ear seems to be intact).

A significant finding that needed to be highlighted in his medical history was the fact that the defendant learned to walk and to talk by himself at the age of ten; he had never received adequate treatment for the diagnosed conditions described above as during his childhood and early adolescence his family thought he was "crazy" and attempted to place him in various hospitals which he left on his own.

Mr Barrios was read an extensive list of signs and/or symptoms possibly indicative of neurological or mental disorders. The following was either observed or volunteered as currently present:

He had a speech articulation problem; and at examination, he had trouble sleeping (it took several hours until he could go to sleep every night). An important element of his developmental history is that Mr Barrios was homosexually raped by two teenagers when he was a young boy; the defendant describes himself as a homosexual.

This reporter interprets Mr Barrios' past explosive behavior and seemingly self-mutilating behavior as an expression of rage resulting from the physical limitations caused by his organic condition. The defendant did not seem to harbor hatred for his past misfortunes and did not blame anybody for the lack of adequate treatment.

The defendant seemed to be quite philosophical about his handicap and seemed to regret not having achieved a greater level of skills. During the evaluative interview with this reporter, the defendant seemed to be genuinely remorseful about having to "sell that shit" by which he meant selling drugs that led to his charge.

The Wechsler Adult Intelligence Scale — Revised (WAIS-R) was administered. As prorated — that is, calculated on the basis of 9 of 11 tests, Mr Barrios' verbal IQ was found to be 63 and his performance IQ was 70; the overall test IQ was 65.

These IQ levels represent a level of functioning of a person affected by mild mental retardation; however, it was felt that these IQ levels should not be intepreted literally. The defendant was affected by a neurological condition that made it difficult for him to perform tasks involving both motor behavior and the motor aspects of language, that means the correct pronunciation of words (the defendant had no difficulties in interpreting the meaning of words).

The defendant was given the Embedded-Figures Test. He was shown outlines of common figures — such as house, a knife, a fork, eyeglasses, and the like — superimposed on other outlines. People who suffer from subtle to severe forms of brain damage often fail to identify figures presented in such a fashion. There are four such plates, with ten figures on each plate amounting to 40 outlines. Mr Barrios correctly identified 28 out of the 40 outlines.

The defendant seemed to be perplexed by the task at first but he managed to gain confidence. This performance was poor; qualitative features of his performance — such as the defendant's exaggerated changes in posture and grimaces while inspecting the plates — were consistent with the presence of brain damage.

Mr Barrios was given the following to read: "Once there lived a king and a queen in a large palace. But the king and queen were not happy. There were no little children in the house or garden. One day they found a poor little boy and girl at the door. They took them into the beautiful palace and made them their own. The king and queen were then happy."

The defendant read the paragraph with only moderate difficulty.

☐ **QUESTIONS FOR REVIEW AND DISCUSSION**

△ Discuss the relative contribution of the neuropsychological evaluation and the observation of the defendant in his or her natural setting in the forensic evaluation of a
handicapped individual who is charged with a serious crime such as manslaughter.

△ Mr Barrios has been waiting for his sentence for about a year; the defendant's girlfriend
is now pregnant with his child; Mr Barrios' lawyer argues the point that the defendant's
incarceration will further disrupt his family life and would be an unusual and cruel
punishment. How do you incorporate this new information in your overall evaluation
of the defendant?

△ While Mr Barrios was incarcerated, the temporary facility at the detention center lacked
accommodations for handicapped individuals; the defendant said that he fell while
using the showers and broke his jaw. However, a note signed by a correction officer
indicates that Mr Barrios broke his jaw during a fight for a radio with another inmate.
Discuss the following: The halo effect created by a defendant having a severe physical
handicap; and the issue of the rights of the handicapped while incarcerated.

△ Discuss Mr Barrios' prognosis for social rehabilitation; in your discussion, incorporate
the issue that many agencies created to help the physically handicapped reject anyone
who exhibits antisocial behavior.

6: EVALUATION OF MENTAL STATUS

IN THE PREVIOUS CHAPTERS, WE CONCLUDED THAT IN THE COURSE OF THE
forensic neuropsychological evaluation we had to be cautious about first impressions, that sometimes a family and medical history could be manipulated, and
that the neurological examination — intended for assessing the function of the
nervous system — might not be useful in elucidating matters of the individual's
criminal intent or competency.

In this chapter, we make the first attempt to enter the inner workings of the
mind by discussing the evaluation of the defendant's mental status. The
evaluation of mental status is routinely performed during the course of any of
the various stages of the criminal proceedings such as competence to stand trial,
pre-pleading, and pre-sentence investigations, or as a result of a violation of
probation or parole.

But the evaluation of mental status achieves prominence when the individual's competence is questioned or the matter of criminal intent is raised. There
are several kinds of competency: Capacity to stand trial, to make a will or to
manage one's affairs (guardianship). This chapter refers to the evaluation of
the mental status of the individual at present; later, I will refer to the difficulties

of evaluating the mental status of an individual at the time the events leading to the charges occurred. Unless otherwise indicated, this chapter deals with issues of the evaluation of the mental status in criminal law.

Competence to Stand Trial

As defined by Black's Dictionary of Law competency is "the presence of those characteristics, or the absence of those disabilities, which render a witness legally fit and qualified to give testimony in a court of justice." Until well into the latter part of the 19th century, mental health experts and lawyers used to shared a common language. The word "insane," in particular, carried a meaning that was well understood by both. Suffice it to say here, competence is a legal term and mental disorder is a clinical term; it is now generally accepted that an individual suffering from, say, psychosis, organic brain disorder, or mental retardation can still be competent to stand trial.

The evaluation of the defendant's mental status consists of observations of the subject's behavior and simple probes to evaluate nervous system function. A mental health worker is sometimes called on to perform this evaluation very quickly and under unusual circumstances. An example is the teenager who — while incarcerated — has attempted suicide by hanging himself. However, for the most part, in the forensic evaluation the clinical neuropsychological examination of the mental status is a methodical set of steps aimed at the evaluation of the following:

- □ Level of consciousness
- □ Orientation to person, space and time
- □ Attention and concentration
- □ Prevailing mood
- □ Memory
- □ Language
- □ Constructional abilities
- □ Cognitive functions
- □ Judgment
- □ Insight

The clinical evaluation of these basic dimensions aim to the ascertainment of whether they are within normal limits or the expression of brain disease — that is, whether underlying structural or toxic-metabolic changes in the nervous system can be demonstrated. The limits that supposedly separate normalcy from neurological disorders resulting from organic factors or psychiatric diseases — often called "functional diseases" — are not as distinct as once thought.

Level of Consciousness

The evaluation of level of consciousness is designed to determine how a defendant is placed in a continuum ranging from a reasonable state of alertness to deep coma. Specific terms used for key stages within this range are: Alertness, lethargy, stupor, and coma. In the prison clinic, one can sometimes observe acute episodes of poisoning, such as from inmates that have hoarded psychotropic medications and then one day they take them all at once for suicide purposes. Exhibit 6.1 — A Most Convenient Medicine — illustrates a case of a defendant who suffered from a mental disorder and who took an overdose of his prescribed psychotropic medication prior to the forensic evaluative interview and testing to create the impression of being afflicted by a mental disorder. The adequate evaluation of almost all other dimensions of mental functioning depends on whether the mental health worker can talk to an alert, cooperative individual, or whether the evaluator has to rely on the information given by a relative or friend of a comatose patient in an emergency room. The level of alertness can also be evaluated by simple tests that can be applied at the bedside. In one, the patient is requested to count numbers from one to ten and then from ten backwards. It is possible to make the test more difficult by asking him or her to serially substract sevens from 100 (e.g., 100, 93, 86, 79, and so on).

Orientation

Orientation refers to one's awareness in relation to person, place, and time. The person is revealed in the recognition of one's name and sometimes the recognition of the interviewer who is performing the probing. Place means — in a restricted sense — where the individual presently is: Home, the emergency room, jail, court's building, etc; in a wider sense place is also the city, the county, the state in which the individual resides. Time is also probed for its restricted and wider meaning, ranging from the time it is now, today's date, the day of the week, the current month, and the season of the year.

Attention and Concentration

Probes of attention are aimed at ascertaining the subject's ability to focus his or her mind on specific external or internal stimuli at will or on command. At bedside, the mental health worker is interested in whether the defendant is "tuned" to the environment, reacting to what is probably personally meaningful. But many factors — such as age and education — affect a person's interest in his or her surroundings.

Concentration is related to attention. Concentration is the ability to maintain the focus of personally meaningful stimuli for an appropriate period of time. Inability to concentrate, exemplified in the remark "my mind wanders," may be a common symptom of clinical significance. Distractibility refers to the ease with which stimuli may disrupt the focusing of one's attention.

Affect

Affect is the pattern of observable behaviors that is the expression of a subjective experience of an emotional state. Common examples of affect are euphoria, anger, sadness, or depression. Affect is variable over time, in response to changing emotional states, whereas mood refers to a pervasive and sustained emotion. A range of affect may be described as "broad" (normal), "restricted" (constricted), "blunted," or "flat."

Ms Gilbert — a defendant — appeared to be an emotionally exhausted person whose moods shifted from second to second. She often bent over the desk as if she wanted to go to sleep and she often yawned. She wore thick 180° dark glasses that, when they were removed at my request, revealing sickly-looking eyes, and she appeared to have difficulty in keeping them open. She appeared to be photophobic (an extreme sensitivity to light, possibly drug-related). At one time or another she appeared childish, playful, romantic, beaten down, depressive, hopeful, and careless. During the first 10 to 15 minutes she was seductive and manipulative but after several attempts of trying to force me to smile at her silly remarks she stopped that attitude and adopted some composure.

Depression is a common mood disorder often encountered in the clinic. Depression may be associated with a cloudiness of consciousness which might be the reason why a subject does not perform well during the administration of psychometric tests. Apathy, sudden or slow changes in mood, or elation states not resulting from any particular personal event, feelings of being "high," and inappropriate laughter all are examples of moods with clinical significance that need to be taken into account in evaluating an individual.

Learning, Memory, Recall

In the so-called mini-mental status evaluation, learning, memory, and recall are evaluated by asking an individual to repeat three common names such as "car, shoe, and tree" and then asked to recall them, often a mentally challenging task that acts as interference (such as counting backwards). However, since learning is so dependent on consciousness, motivation, and moods, the information provided by the patient's relative may be more appropriate in evaluating alterations in learning and memory.

Memory disturbances are often found in many clinical descriptions of the effects of neurotoxic agents at the workplace. Office filing technology and computer jargon permeate the description of this important mental process. Memory is described as a process involving "registering," "storing," and "recalling" information and motor acts.

A mental health worker often is called upon to evaluate the "recall" capacity for visual, auditory, and motor skills in three arbitrary time spans: Immediate, recent, and remote. "Immediate" recall — sometimes called short-term memory — refers to the ability of recalling a meaningful event that has occurred in the past few minutes. Aging individuals may leave a pot boiling on the stove for hours or, place water into the pot but not remember moments afterwards what they meant to do. In extreme cases — such as those suffering from Alzheimer's disease or AIDS-related dementia — relatives are forced to remove the knobs of the stove of people living alone to avoid such dangerous actions. Exhibit 14.1 (The Man Who Lost All His Friends) illustrates the case of a defendant who exhibited a behavior consistent with an early phase of AIDS-related dementia. "Numbers recall" during clinical examination may or may not capture these extreme examples of disturbances of "immediate" or "recent" memory. Examiners cannot always put together whether significant failure in a test of immediate recall is in fact due to alterations in concentration, mood, or to lack of interest, rather than to "recall" capacity.

Alterations in memory can be very profound, even leading to total memory loss, called amnesia. But most often memory defects are subtle: The inability to remember where one's favorite tools have been placed or missing highway exits while driving in familiar environments are examples. Forensic professionals are very aware of the presence of "amnesia" among malingerers. Exhibit 20.1 (One for the Road) is a case of a defendant who has been charged with vehicular manslaughter; the defendant — who most likely was under the influence of alcohol — claims not to remember the events leading to his charges.

Language

Language is an acquired skill in the uses of body-generated signs for communication purposes. It encompasses both the signs and the set of usage rules which the individual learns in a given culture. Speech refers specifically to the communication process carried out by sounds generated by the phonatory (speech-producing) system registered by auditory, muscle, and skin receptors. The written language is a valuable source for the evaluation of communication, personality, and even motor disorders (e.g., those revealing hand tremor).

The clinical evaluation of language and speech is difficult because of the diversity of theories of the nature and neural control of speech. The clinician is familiar with classical speech syndromes in making a differential diagnosis (e.g., is it a neurotoxic-induced language defect or aphasia?). Aphasia is the inability to communicate. An extensive vocabulary exists to describe the large variety of aphasic syndromes. An important controversy currently exists regarding the classification and labelling of many speech disorders, particularly their localizing value — i.e., where the neural lesion is located.

Forensic neuropsychologists pay close attention to a large variety of motor and sensory mechanisms and demographic factors such as native language, age, education, and ethnic background in the interpretation of language disorders. Slurred speech, for example, caused by acute ingestion of alcoholic beverages or some drugs — or when the effect of certain drugs is wearing off — is a common observable phenomenon in the clinic.

Readily available labels such as alexia (loss of reading ability), dyslexia (difficulties in learning to read), agraphia (difficulties in writing), and disprosody (alterations in speech intonation) can be misleading and may inhibit further observations of unique patterns of speech disorders. It is universally recommended that restraint be exerted in the use of these terms in favor of explicit descriptions of the language deficit whenever health professionals need to use them.

☐ The following is an example of concrete thinking and clanging, a type of speech in which the external characteristics of objects and word sounds — rather than meaningful, conceptual relationships — govern the choice of words of a defendant. Question: "What is winter?"; Answer: "Winter is window" (probably in reference to the fact that in winter one must close windows tightly, or one looks outside during a winter day through a window); Q: "What's a penny?"; A: "Penny is yellow"; (that is, the color of the coin) ; Q: "What's breakfast?"; A: "Breakfast is eggs"; (what one eats) Q: "What's the shape of a ball?"; A: "White" (the color of the ball).

☐ Another example of how possible malingering can be detected in the analysis of language, is that of the defendant Mr Simpson, a well-developed male (5 feet, 6 inches, 140 pounds). During the evaluative session, the defendant often engaged in delaying tactics, such as giving vague answers to specific questions, repeating the questions he was just asked and delaying the answer to some questions. After giving answers of low-informational content, he would carefully study the reporter's minute reactions and then selectively add additional comments also of very low-information content. He often avoided eye contact.

Constructional Abilities

Subtle qualitative features of mental status are seen when subjects are asked to do things, such as to reproduce pictures or to assemble simple puzzles. These are referred to as constructional abilities. Individuals challenged with such tasks have to plan a solution in their minds and then execute the steps toward the solution of the problem. Defects may be present in the perception of the task, in the planning of the task or in its execution. That is why tests to assess constructional abilities are sometimes called "visuomotor" tests. There are numerous psychometric tests specifically developed to assess constructional abilities. The Block Design test (see Appendix A), in which the subject duplicates geometrical patterns with cubes, is such an instrument used for forensic purposes.

Despite a concerted research effort to understand the nature of intelligence, this highest order of cognitive function remains elusive. There is a vast array of primary mental functions considered essential. For example, a mental health worker will ask a 14-year-old boy to perform simple arithmetic calculations, and ask him information about his name, the name of his dog, and to recite a sentence or repeat numbers or assemble a puzzle, such as the figure of a person. (One sometimes is asked to evaluate children who will be charged with adult rather than juvenile offenses as a result of the seriousness of the offense, especially in cases of homicide or sexual assault.) In evaluating children, the amount of detail in the drawing of a person and how the parts of the body are linked is a good measure of cognitive functioning. However, a mental health worker will often need the help of a trained child neuropsychologist in the evaluation of difficult cases where neuropsychiatric signs are observed.

Insight

Insight is the awareness of our own mental life, attitudes, and behavior. It relates to the capacity of introspection (that is, to look inside ourselves) but more closely to the understanding of the outcome of such a search inside ourselves relative to community standards. A crack addict with a $200-a-day habit often claims that he is not truly addicted and that he can really stop using drugs whenever he wishes. Such a person is said to suffer from "denial of illness" or lack of insight into the nature of his or her own problems. A mentally-retarded person, on the other hand, may have a remarkable insight into what he can or cannot do. Some questions of insight are indeed questions of prevailing standards of care. Exhibit 9.2 (The Young Man Who Got no Respect) is an example of an individual who is mentally retarded but who has good insight into the nature of his problems.

Judgment

Judgment — as a psychological aptitude — is the ability to appreciate court proceedings and its consequences. Black defines judgment as "a sense of knowledge sufficient to comprehend the nature of a transaction." During the psychological evaluation, professionals often evaluate judgment during a test of comprehension ("Why do foods need to be cooked?"), or in the form of intepretations of proverbs ("What does one mean when one says that people who live in crystal houses should not throw stones?").

For highly educated individuals who need to be challenged with more difficult tasks, I often combine two proverbs: "In what way do the sayings 'Still waters run deep' and 'Shallow brooks are noisy' contrast?" When the defendant is evaluated for his or her competence to stand legal proceedings, judgment means specifically knowledge of the roles of different individuals in the court, whether the defendant knows the name and the functions of the defense lawyer, the role of the district attorney, the role of the judge, and the consequences of being found guilty.

It has been indicated above, that this refers to the evaluation of mental status of the individual at present. However, at times, mental health workers have to develop an opinion about the mental status of an individual at the time the events leading to the charges occurred. This task is particularly challenging because the events sometimes occurred a long time ago. A common problem is the temptation to conclude that the signs and symptoms that the defendant suffers from today — perhaps after one year of incarceration and after daily antipsychotic medication — are the same ones as those occurring during the events leading to the charges. A similar problem is that of trying to understand the "instant offense" on the basis of the defendant's childhood. Mothers of some defendants sometimes say that, early in childhood, their sons were "perfectly normal kids;" however, some tell different stories and acknowledge to have requested petition of individuals in need of supervision (PINS), a desperate move.

To conclude this chapter, it is important to highlight the fact that few mental health workers in good professional standing rarely write an opinion about an individual without having a personal, face-to-face, interview with such an individual. In many occasions, videotapes need to be evaluated, but these evaluations are always compared with the impression created by an individual whom one actually has seen.

Past psychological literature — including the works of Freud — refers to the "reconstruction of the minds" of prominent and sometimes historical individuals never actually seen by the writer. This is not now considered a legitimate professional endeavor.

☐ **EXHIBIT 6.1**

A Most Convenient Medicine

Mr Carreras — in custody, before his sentence — was a 19-year-old Hispanic male with 8th grade education in the Dominican Republic. The defendant was known to this clinic: Mr Carreras was examined earlier the same year to determine his competence to continue with the legal proceedings. In addition, the defendant was scheduled to be examined a week before as an aid in sentencing; however, the defendant was "produced" — a term that indicates that a defendant is brought to court — at the clinic in a state of acute delirium and was re-scheduled for further evaluation.

Mr Carreras met the criteria for Schizophrenia, disorganized type. He was incoherent, showing some loosening of associations; sometimes showed disorganized behavior; and exhibited flat or inappropriate affect. In addition, the defendant showed disturbances in content and form of thought, impaired interpersonal functioning and psychomotor behavior. His mental illness was thought to be chronic, as it had been present since childhood. Although it was adequately controlled by means of antipsychotic medication, on at least two occasions the defendant had ingested an overdose of his current antipsychotic medication with the intention of malingering (feigning a mental disorder). Mr Carreras still suffered from delusions but he would not discuss the content of these delusions (the defendant felt that if he revealed them, he would be killed). He also showed a decrease in reactivity to the environment, with reduction of spontaneous movements and activity. Schizophrenia was thought to be the primary diagnosis. The defendant had also abused illegal drugs in the past, particularly marijuana, snorted cocaine and crack. He was suspected of being an alcohol abuser as well.

Mr Carreras was once told that he was born by Caesarean section. He held a mythical interpretation of his mental disorder: He was told that he began suffering a mental disorder after a fall from his crib when he was eight months old. His early difficulties with formal schooling in the Dominican Republic at the age of 12 or 13 and later when he moved to the United States suggested a chronic nature of his mental disorder.

The defendant suffered a variety of motor signs that appeared to be side effects of his antipsychotic medication: He showed overall rigidity, walked without normal arm swing, and his face was expressionless.

He showed serious symptoms and serious impairment in social and occupational functioning but he understood the charges against him and the consequences of his behavior. He admitted malingering when he took an overdose of his antipsychotic medication at least on two occasions, the first time, when he was expected to see his probation officer. His IQ could not be adequately assessed because he was, first, in an acute state of drug intoxication and still recovering the second time. It was estimated however, that — at best — the level of his intellectual performance was borderline, close to a mild form of mental retardation.

The prognosis of this form of schizophrenia was thought to be very poor; the defendant was likely to need antipsychotic medication in the future. Even when effectively controlled by medication, the residual effects of many signs and symptoms of his mental disorder were felt to be likely to continue to affect his social, family, and occupational spheres. Most likely — it was felt — he would be unable to hold a job and, for many years to come, he would be unable to take care of his basic needs for himself.

His moods at times were erratic and the defendant had been described as suicidal in the past. It was not clear whether his moods were related to his delusions or to the bona fide information that the defendant may have, as he (delusionally or not) was afraid of being killed if he revealed such information. Finally, the defendant seemed to have an inadequate control of his impulses and under the right set of circumstances might become assaultive. Most importantly, the defendant had no social supports and he did not have anyone who really cared whether he was well or not.

The defendant was asked whether he understood the idea of being found mentally incompetent to stand trial. He said that he understood that he would then be placed in a hospital for mentally ill people, hospitals similar to ones to which he has been admitted since childhood. The defendant indicated that he did not want to be placed in a mental hospital and that he would like to face the proceedings as he had faith in the judicial system.

Mr Carreras stated he was admitted to a psychiatric hospital on several occasions. Significantly, the defendant indicated that at least on one occasion he took an overdose of his own antipsychotic medication. He was interviewed on at least four different occasions by several psychiatrists. On the first of these examinations, the defendant was found by one of the psychiatrists to be "agitated, suicidal and preoccupied with auditory hallucinations." He was given Haldol and Cogentin, and the symptomatology improved. In the three subsequent interviews that defendant was self-described as "feeling well," denied being depressed and denied auditory hallucinations. The second psychiatrist found him alert and oriented; his speech was generally relevant and did not reveal loosening of associations.

At one of these evaluative interviews the defendant was found to be in a state of acute delirium, with long latency times in response to questions and catatonic posturing. He would stare at the ceiling and either he would not respond or would respond to questions in a manner barely comprehensible. It was suspected that the defendant had either overmedicated himself or took illegal drugs prior to referral to this clinic. Later, he himself confirmed the fact that he had taken an overdose of his antipsychotic medication.

Mr Carreras was charged with murder and violation of his probation. The defendant denied the charges of murder and described the victim as a person who was run over by an automobile and then suffered a heart attack. Mr Carreras' life style at the time of the events leading to his first arrest were difficult to characterize on account of the defendant's marked communication problems. During the events in which a man was killed, he described himself as playing the slot machines in a bodega.

The defendant had apparently discovered that he can create a much worse picture of himself by overdosing with his antipsychotic medications at crucial times in which his level of intellectual functioning, moods, and personality characteristics need to be professionally assessed. It was thought that if the defendant was incarcerated, he would have to be placed in a facility where his current illness could be closely monitored and treated. As indicated above, it was not clear whether the defendant was also a drug and alcohol abuser. However, because of the chaotic state of the defendant's personal affairs, it was very unlikely that he would benefit from a chemical abuse rehabilitation program at this time. Psychiatric supervision was also advised because the defendant suffered rapid mood swings and was suicidal from time to time. It was also felt that it was unlikely that the defendant could work, and vocational rehabilitation was not recommended at the time. Finally, Mr Carreras was very unlikely to function in the community without a reliable system of close supervision of his psychiatric problems as he appeared to be an individual with poor control and therefore potentially dangerous.

QUESTIONS FOR REVIEW AND DISCUSSION

Δ   Discuss the relative contribution of the clinical interview and psychological testing in cases similar to that discussed above (suspected excessive use of antipsychotic medication to fake mental disorder).

Δ   Discuss the issues of the defendant's right to refuse antipsychotropic medication.

Δ   The defendant is scheduled to appear in court and the psychiatrist in charge of the inmate at the detention center gives his usual dose of Haldol; discuss the pros and cons of giving antipsychotic medication to the defendant during his or her court appearance in a case in which the insanity defense has been invoked.

Δ   The defendant is charged with rape 1° and the defendant's lawyer argues the case that he has been under a severe emotional stress for which he is under care of his private psychiatrist. Discuss the following: (1) The issue of the confidentiality of information (argue the case in which the therapist knew that the defendant has raped his nephew); (2) the defendant has sought psychiatric help after he has been charged (argue the case of a prior psychiatric history and the case of no prior psychiatric history).

7: SIGNS, SYMPTOMS, AND SYNDROMES

WE HAVE INDICATED EARLIER (CHAPTER 5) THAT NEUROLOGISTS, PSYCHIATRISTS or psychologists report their findings as either "signs," "symptoms," or "syndromes."

A sign is an objective manifestation of a pathological condition; signs are observed by the examiner rather than reported by the individual. A symptom is a manifestation of a pathological condition which some professionals use in a limited way to denote subjective complaints. Finally, a syndrome is a group of signs and symptoms that occur together and that constitute a recognizable condition or disease. The diagnosis of a neuropsychological disorder — or disease — is made as the result of integration of information derived from the appearance of the individual, medical history, physical examination, review of signs and symptoms, and results of psychological and electrophysiological testing, imaging procedures and sometimes special laboratory procedures, such as the presence of neurotoxic drugs in blood or urine or other biological markers. In the adversary situation — that is, in court — not even the presence of a readily observed sign is an unquestionable fact; the presence of a syndrome definitively requires an expert opinion.

A number of "checklists" have been developed for rough screening purposes that purport to quickly identify the "signs" of neuropsychological deficit and are available through commercial publishers. The utility of such instruments in forensic situations is limited, principally because signs and symptoms need to be interpreted within a context of comphrensive syndromes and etiologies. A universal list of neurological symptoms and signs that could be used by, say, court professionals (e.g., probation officers) to evaluate people suspected of suffering from mental or brain disorders would be difficult to construct, and probably prove misleading.

☐ First, certain behaviors that are severely punished by the law may not be associated with any overt manifestation of neurological and/or mental disorder. As indicated earlier in this book, popular stereotypes suggest that the appearance of an individual may give a clue about his or her offenses. However, a person who has been charged, say, with sexual abuse of a child may appear as a clean-looking, normally-behaving, God-fearing man wearing a three-piece suit.

☐ Second, there is the overriding problem of malingering. The defendant may not be telling us the truth or may have a reason or motive not to share health information with us. Someone who is not ill may volunteer credible signs and symptoms of a severe mental disorder; a person who is very ill may hide important clues of a serious mental disorder.

☐ Third, there is the matter of how these signs and symptoms are interrelated. Signs and symptoms taken in an individual evaluation and out of context can be misleading. Signs and symptoms need to be viewed in the context of known syndromes; a careful evaluation of the medical history and the result of laboratory tests are needed to establish a more precise diagnosis.

Acute and Chronic Dysfunctions

Signs, symptoms, and syndromes develop over time. Clinical neuropsychologists are trained to reconstruct the evolution of signs and symptoms over time — also known as the time course or the natural history of the disease. Some syndromes develop in a matter of minutes or less — e.g., loss of consciousness due to an attempted suicide with carbon monoxide; others may take a few days — e.g., the polyneuropathy that follows certain degenerative disorders such as multiple sclerosis.

Short-lived mental disorders are called acute. Illicit drugs — such as cocaine, heroin, PCP, and others — produce acute effects. In the vast majority of cases, acute neurotoxic effects caused by street drugs are reversible after neurotoxic exposure ceases. Minutes, hours or days after cessation of the neurotoxic exposure, individuals may return to their baseline of neuropsychological functioning. However, as a pattern of alcohol and/or drug use is firmly established, craving for these neurotoxins becomes the "baseline."

Symptoms, signs, and syndromes that develop or persist over longer periods of time are called chronic. Chronic sometimes, but not always, implies "irreversible," meaning that a permanent damage to the nervous system has occurred. However, this is an oversimplified statement because the limit of the nervous system's recovery power is largely unknown. An example of a chronic syndrome is the severe neuropathy produced in AIDS-dementia.

Level of Severity

There are other important terms. Subclinical refers to the neural effects experienced by the affected individual but leading to no major condition requiring medical attention. Subclinical refers to subtle forms of brain damage, and neurotoxic effects that cannot be observed during the course of the clinical examination either by the naked eye or by means of simple probes; thus, subclinical is a matter of "degree."

Another term, preclinical, refers to neural effects that may lead to metabolic changes, behavioral effects, subjective symptoms or neurological or psychiatric signs or symptoms creating the impression that if the cause of brain disorder or absorption of neurotoxin were to continue, these conditions might eventually lead to a full blown neurologic or psychiatric disorder; thus "preclinical" is a matter of "time."

Functional and Organic Disorders

A still important source of disagreement in terminology is the designation of a disease or illness as *functional* or *organic*. A *functional disorder* is considered by some to be the expression of changes in nervous system function — i.e., inability of neurotransmitters to act on target brain cells. The term "functional" means that no structural damage to the nervous system can be demonstrated, either in experimental laboratory animals or at post-mortem examination. The term organic disorder implies an objective change in some anatomical portion of the nervous system structure caused by trauma, the burst of a major blood vessel (stroke) or by a neurotoxic agent, sometimes observable by means of imaging procedures or specially-designed clinical laboratory procedure.

The appendices describe the variety of procedures and the specialized language that is sometimes used to describe "findings" derived from such technology, ranging from paper-and-pencil psychological testing to computer-based brain imaging procedures. Thus, what the clinician describes as "psychomotor retardation" is later interpreted as an overall reduction in "reaction time" as measured by a reaction timer; "alterations in visual spatial organization" is — after careful examination of eye movemens — found to result from alterations in eye scanning; lack of speech "understanding" is sometimes the result of loss of upper auditory frequencies that occurs as a result of chronic exposure to noise; "tiredness" or "feeling weak" — both subjective symptoms

— are found to be correlated by a reduction in nerve conduction velocity of limbs; "memory problems" are observed in the confabulations of details of a story whose details are not remembered; "drug abuse" — that is denied — can be verified by analytical-chemical techniques.

☐ **EXHIBIT 7.1**

Chronic Fatigue Syndrome

Mrs Miller — who was in the community awaiting sentence — was a 40-year-old Caucasian female with High School education. The defendant was concluded to suffer a Personality Disorder Not Otherwise Specified. The background papers indicated that the defendant stole close to a million dollars from her employer over the period of three years and that she failed to report the stolen funds as income in New York State. The defendant showed some narcissistic traits, experienced difficulties in "reading" the motives of other people and felt a sense of entitlement. She acknowledged that once she was successful in stealing money without her boss noticing, she could not stop stealing. It was pinpointed that this may indicate a compulsive personality trait and a "high" similar to those experienced by kleptomaniacs and compulsive gamblers. In addition, various informants had also indicated that she has been depressed in the past, and that she sometimes shows self-defeating personality traits. Her husband had speculated that at times, she may have felt a "father-and-daughter" dependent relationship with the victim of grand larceny. However, there appeared to be only a tenuous correlation between these personality characteristics and the charges against her.

The defendant presented documentation showing that she has suffered from viral and fungal diseases; these physical conditions were said to be known to produce marked fatigue. However, these physical disorders did not appear to play a major role in determining the defendant's state of mind during the three years in which the events leading to the charges against her occurred.

The defendant was experiencing financial difficulties at the time the events took place, and the family appeared to be in chronic debt. The background documentation indicated that there were family pressures to "keep up with the Joneses."

Mrs Miller had a superior intelligence (her IQ was estimated to be more than 135). During the evaluative interview and testing, she was anxious, and experienced embarrasment for the events for which she was charged. These symptoms and conditions that were present in the defendant were transient, understandable and expectable reactions to psychosocial stressors (awaiting her sentence).

Although the defendant was cooperative during the interview and psychological testing and furnished information that was potentially verifiable, the defendant presented an overabundance of information as if trying to argue the point that her physical and "mental" illnesses during the years the events leading to her charges occurred, were contributing factors or mitigating circumstances. At least one of these documents appears to reveal manipulative personaliy traits; the defendant told this evaluator that her present employer did not know the charges against her or that she is facing court proceedings. However, she managed to obtain from him a signed letter in which he attests her "strong character and judgment" (she said that she did not tell him that she was going to submit such a letter to court).

Mrs Miller presented medical documentation indicating that she had suffered from spastic colon, candida albicans (a fungal disease), allergic headache, and Epstein-Barr virus/mononucleosis. Other sources indicated that she has been treated for benign cystic mastitis. The defendant indicated that she sought psychiatric counseling in 1970-71 for depression and again in 1979 around the time she was divorcing. She saw a psychiatrist two to four times per month since 1989.

Mrs Miller denied alcohol and/or illegal drug use. She said that she did not gamble and that she was not involved with gambling debts at the times the events leading to her charges took place. She said that during the events leading to her charges nobody was blackmailing her and she did not have pressure from anyone to steal the money. Said the defendant: "Once I told myself, you should stop doing this." Question: "Did you ever think you could be caught one day?"; Answer: "Yes, but I just could not stop."

Mrs Miller said that she was born into a very conservative family and that she clung to "old-fashioned" values. She said that she had wanted to go to college but there had been much pressure from her family to marry and to have a family; she explained that decisions about her future were taken before the "women's movement." She described herself as shy person, who feels uncomfortable among crowds.

Her medical conditions — e.g., her chronic sense of fatigue at the time the events leading to her charges occurred — were felt to be less plausible contributing factors. The major flaw of the defendant's character was the dissociation between her superior intelligence, her lack of judgment, and her chronic pursuit of self esteem through materialistic values. It was not clear at the time of the evaluation whether major pressures to "keep up with the Joneses" and the chronic tendency to live a standard of living beyond the means of her family — that were said to be contributory factors leading to the charges — have changed.

☐ QUESTIONS FOR REVIEW AND DISCUSSION

Δ Discuss the following concepts: (1) mitigating circumstances; (2) proximal cause; and (3) remote cause.

Δ Many legal concepts are borrowed from both classic and modern logic; some of these concepts are helpful to clarify faulty errors in judgments or wrong deduction from statements; discuss the concepts of inductive logic; deductive logic; *a priori; a posteriori; a fortiori; sine qua non;* conditional contrafactics (hypothetical situations or "hypotheticals"), and the conceptual differences between overlapping conditions and causation.

Δ Exhibit 7.1 illustrates the attempt to invoke a relatively rare and poorly known medical condition to explain *mens rea;* discuss other medical conditions that may be argued to shed light on the defendant's state of mind during the events leading to his or her charges.

Δ Assume that Mrs Miller has been charged with endangering the welfare of a child (child neglect); how persuasive does the argument between a medical condition (chronic fatigue syndrome) and the events leading to the defendant's charges then become?

Δ A branch of criminology concerns "questioned" documents. Why is it important to try to identify the circumstances and the purpose of reports on medical information that the defendant brings to court to support his or her case?

Δ Discuss kleptomania as an impulse control disorder; make the differential diagnosis with antisocial personality disorder.

8: MENTAL DISORDERS AND THEIR CLASSIFICATION

IN CHAPTER 2, WE HAVE DEFINED THE CLINICAL NEUROPSYCHOLOGICAL EVALU-ation as the systematic study of signs and symptoms associated with the normal or abnormal function of the nervous system and behavior through observation and probes. In Chapter 7, we discussed signs, symptoms, and syndromes. The diagnosis of mental disorder — discussed here — is the ascertainment of the possible causes of the syndromes, that is, the etiology of mental disorders.

Not all mental disorders are caused by brain disorders, although many are suspected of having originated from such beginnings. A number of personality disorders are generally recognized as unlikely to have such an organic basis, including sex disorders and paraphilias that may or may not lead to confrontations with the law, and a large variety of maladaptive personality traits such as lying, conning, or compulsions such as stealing and gambling. *Antisocial personality disorder* (previously known as sociopathy), is a leading diagnosable disorder at court clinics.

This chapter deals with all mental disorders focusing primarily on Antisocial Personality Disorder and Malingering; the next chapter covers the subject of mental disorders that have an organic basis and conditions that are physically handicapping both of which are likely to be the focus of a forensic neuropsychological investigation.

THE ICD-10 AND DSM-IV CLASSIFICATION SYSTEMS

The *International Statistical Classification of Diseases and Related Health Problems, Tenth Edition* (ICD-10), published in 1992, is a system of classification of all medical disorders and conditions published by the World Health Organization. The ICD-10 represents a considerable improvement over the ICD-9 published in 1978. Inclusions that call the attention of the forensic neuropsychologists are found in the following chapters:

- ☐ IV. Endocrine, nutritional, and metabolic disesases
- ☐ V. Mental and behavioral disorders
- ☐ VI. Diseases of the nervous system
- ☐ VII. Diseases of the eye and adnexa
- ☐ VIII. Diseases of the ear and the mastoid process

☐ XVI. Certain conditions originating in the perinatal period

☐ XVII. Congenital malformations, deformations, and chromosomal abnormalities

☐ XIX. Injury, poisoning, and certain other consequences of external causes

Chapter V of ICD-10 (on Mental and Behavioral Disorders, also issued independently of other chapters) lists organic (including symptomatic) mental disorders; mental and behavioral disorders due to psychoactive substance use; schizophrenia, schizotypal, and delusional disorders; mood (affective) disorders; behavioral syndromes associated with physiological disturbances and physical factors; disorders or adult personality and behavior; mental retardation; disorders of psychological development; behavioral and emotional disorders with onset usually occurring in childhood and adolescence; and unspecified mental disorder.

The *Diagnostic and Statistical Manual of Mental Disorders (DSM)* is published by the American Psychiatric Association and has been traditionally considered as an expansion of mental and behavioral disorders found in the *International Classification of Diseases*. The first edition of the DSM was published in 1980. The third revised edition is known as the DSM-III-R and was published in 1987. DSM-IV was published in mid-1994.

In the DSM-IV, as well as in the DSM-III-R, " . . . a mental disorder is conceptualized as a clinically significant behavioral or psychological syndrome or pattern that occurs in an individual and that is associated with present distress (a painful symptom) or disability (impairment in one or more important areas of functioning) or with a significant increased risk of suffering death, pain, disability, or an important loss in freedom."

Greeks and Romans called what we now call psychosis *insania* or *furia*. Galen (130-200 AD) offered a physiological explanation for various forms of mental status, attributing them to an imbalance of body phlegms. The theory of the existence of four basic human temperaments (sanguine, phlegmatic, choleric, and melancholic) was developed by Galen, and these and other notions survived unchallenged throughout Europe in the Medieval Age.

A new classification of mental disorder would not be attempted until late in the eighteenth century. At the time, dogma was refused as the only mode of teaching, leading to the advent of the Enlightenment movement — with an emphasis on the observation that resulted from experimentation. This marked the beginning of a more humanistic attitude toward the mentally ill. In 1798 the French physician Phillippe Pinel (1745-1826), often regarded as the father of modern psychiatry, wrote the highly influencial *A Treatise on Insanity*. Pinel divided mental disorders into four groups: Mania, melancholia, dementia, and idiocy. The German psychiatrist Emil Kraepelin (1856-1926) after studying thousands of cases of people afflicted with mental disorders, proposed a comprehensive classification system of mental disorders, much of which is still in use today. He distinguished between endogenous disorders — caused by inherent constitutional factors — and exogenous disorders, caused by external conditions. The pattern of a mental disorder, he noted, depends on the time course of the disorder. In 1896 he made the distinction between dementia praecox (an endogenous mental disorder showing progressive deterioration), and manic-depressive psychosis, the course of which tends to be cyclical, with periods of normal behavior alternating between the attacks. In 1911, the Swiss psychiatrist Eugen Bleuler (1857-1939) gave the name schizophrenia to dementia praecox. Manic-depressive disorders fell into a new category of affective psychosis or mood disorders.

Late in the nineteenth century, as new groups of mental disorders began to be identified, a group of mental disorders characterized by pathology of sexual behavior — sometimes associated with perversion, episodes of severe obsessive-compulsive behavior, phobias, episodes of anxiety and panic, memory disorders, alterations in sensation and motor functions began to be identified as psychoneuroses. By the mid-1950s, the term psychoneurosis was "shortened" to neuroses.

Between 1950 and 1980, three different types of criteria were used to make the diagnosis of mental disorders; these criteria were sometimes separated and sometimes combined, but rarely with clarity. Mental illnesses were ranked on a scale of seriousness and based on the concept of presence or absence of insight. Mental illnesses were classified on the basis of the presence or absence of specific signs and symptoms. The DSM classification system is based on the third type. Unfortunately, the system suffers from all of the advantages and all of the disadvantages of any system created by "committees" whose members are often subjected to numerous pressures (e.g., for "political correctness") and in which many compromises — sometimes without scientific justification — need to be made.

A radical position — primarily that of Thomas Szasz, the author of *The Myth of Mental Illness* and *Insanity: The Idea and Its Consequences* — is that mental disorders do not exist. Szasz is the author of that memorable metaphor in which an individual afflicted with a severe mental disorder is compared to a musician who insists on playing in a 100-piece orchestra in spite of the fact that he has been told again and again that he plays out of tune.

A system to classify mental disorders is not a system for classifying individuals. In contemporary forensic reports written by mental health professionals one is unlikely to find terms like "the schizophrenic" or "the alcoholic" to refer to the men and women under scrutiny, but rather as "an individual who suffers from schizophrenia" or "an individual who is afflicted with alcoholism." It is interesting to note that in the legal system, a similar effort has been made when a longer — but fairer — wording is used to differentiate the individual from his or her charges; witness the evolution of such descriptions as "murderer" changed to "individual who has been charged with murder."

DSM-IV retains the "multiaxial" diagnostic-classification pattern established with the publication of DSM-III in 1980 and continued in DSM-III-R in 1987. The five axes are:

- ☐ Axis I (the "manifest" pathological conditions): Clinical Syndromes and V Codes, representing other conditions that are not strictly speaking mental disorders but may become a focus of clinical attention (e.g., "simple bereavement")
- ☐ Axis II (often called the "underlying" pathologies): Personality Disorders
- ☐ Axis III: General medical conditions
- ☐ Axis IV: Psychosocial and environmental problems (or "stressors" which exacerbates either Axis I or Axis II conditions, or both)
- ☐ Axis V: Global assessment of functioning

DSM-IV contains 18 major classifications for mental and emotional disorders:

- ☐ *Disorders usually first diagnosed in infancy,* childhood, or adolescence, including mental retardation, learning disorders (academic skill disorders), motor skill disorders, pervasive developmental disorders, disruptive behavior and attention-deficit disorders, feeding and eating disorders of infancy or early childhood, tic disorders, communication disorders, elimination disorders, and other disorders of infancy, childhood, or adolescence
- ☐ *Delirium, dementia, amnestic, and other cognitive disorders*, including deliria, organic dementias, dementias due to other general medical conditions, and amnestic disorders
- ☐ *Mental disorders due to a general medical condition* not elsewhere classified
- ☐ *Substance-related disorders*, including alcohol use disorders, amphetamine (or related substance) use disorders, caffeine use disorders, cannabis use disorders, cocaine use disorders, hallucinogen use disorders, inhalant use disorders, nicotine use disorders, opiod use disorders, phencyclidine (or related substance) use disorders, sedative, hynoptic, or anxiolytic substance use disorders, polysubstance use disorders, and other (or unknown) substance use disorders
- ☐ *Schizophrenia* and other *psychotic disorders*
- ☐ *Mood disorders,* including *depressive disorders* and *bipolar disorders*
- ☐ *Anxiety disorders*
- ☐ *Somatoform disorder*
- ☐ *Factitious disorder*
- ☐ *Dissociative disorders*

☐ *Sexual and gender identity disorders,* including sexual dysfunctions, paraphilias, and gender identity disorders

☐ *Eating disorders*

☐ *Sleep disorders,* including primary sleep disorders, sleep disorders related to another mental disorder, and other sleep disorders

☐ *Impulse control disorders* not elsewhere classified

☐ *Adjustment disorders*

☐ *Personality disorders*

☐ *Other conditions that may become the focus of a clinical attention,* including medication-induced movement disorders, relational problems, problems related to abuse or neglect, and additional conditions that may become the focus of clinical attention

☐ *Additional codes,* a category that, in DSM-IV, is reserved largely for "conditions warranting further study" before inclusion in the official lexicon of mental disorders (such as "late luteal phase dysphoric disorder," commonly known as premenstrual syndrome, and "sadistic personality disorder")

Any specific disorder may etiologically be classified (with appropriate medical documentation) as having arisen "secondary to" a physical illness or accident, including neurological anomaly or trauma.

This system is useful in the forensic clinic because it allows one to understand quickly not only the primary and secondary conditions that afflict a single individual (if any) but also physical disorders, past and current stressors, and present level of functioning.

The widely used DSM system for the classification of psychiatric disorders covers most (but not all) the cases normally referred to at a forensic clinic, detention centers, or jails. Frequently, reports that are written by court personnel or on behalf of the defendant by various mental health workers refer to this classification system. The system also involves a procedure for assigning code-number identifiers for each specific disorder, which is sometimes used for statistical purposes.

To cite an example, the following are the diagnostic criteria used for *major depressive episode* as contained in DSM-IV. To make the diagnosis of depression, at least five of the following symptoms must have been present during the same two-week period and represent a change from previous functioning:

☐ Depressed mood — or an irritable mood in children and adolescents — most of the day, nearly every day, as indicated by either subjective accounts or observations by others;

☐ markedly diminished interest or pleasure in all, or almost all, activities most of the day, nearly every day;

☐ significant weight loss or weight gain when not dieting, or decrease or increase in appetite nearly every day;

☐ insomnia or hypersomnia nearly every day;

☐ psychomotor agitation or retardation nearly every day;

☐ fatigue or loss of energy nearly every day;

☐ feelings of worthlessness or excessive or inappropriate guilt nearly every day;

☐ diminished ability to think or concentrate, or indecisiveness, nearly every day; and/or

☐ recurrent thoughts of death, recurrent suicidal ideation without a specific plan, or an actual suicide attempt or specific plan for committing suicide.

These are the criteria for the presence of only one episode; a depressive mood disorder is diagnosed only after the presence of several such episodes. The matter of whether the depression is "reactive" or "endogenous" is sometimes settled only after a careful evaluation of whether there was or was not a clearly identifiable environmental stressor that precipitated the depressive episode. However, a crack abuser with a severe case of depression — the "crash" that follows many consecutive days of crack abuse — will often deny his or her habit and even when admitted to an emergency room will claim a purely "psychiatric" disorder or that the depression was caused by the separation from his wife.

The current DSM multiaxial system is a widely accepted system of classification of mental disorders; most importantly, the DSM system adheres to no single theory on the etiology (the causes) of mental disorders. With such a classification system, one is encouraged to correctly observe and identify the condition of suffering, say, Attention Deficit, Hyperactivity Disorder.

In the forensic clinic, this process of pigeonholing is quite adequate because of the following:

☐ Members of a forensic clinic attached to a court examine individuals who suffer from a variety of neurological, mental and communication disorders, drug and alcohol abuse, mental retardation, individuals that suffer "nothing but" antisocial personality disorder, disorders representing every chapter of Clinical Neurology, Clinical Psychiatry and Clinical Psychology. If one is able to pinpoint "what is wrong" with the individual whose folder we have examined for the first time only a few minutes ago, our task would be quite satisfactory.

☐ Most of the time, with the information that is made available to us, one does not really know what causes the condition because — as we have seen in previous chapters — the information is unreliable and in most cases we do not have the resources to perform additional ancillary laboratory procedures. As we have seen earlier, in Exhibit 7.1 (Chronic Fatigue Syndrome), defendants who can afford the professional opinion of experts come for evaluation already prepared with "theories" and ample documentary "evidence" about what "caused" the syndrome — that is, the mitigating circumstances surrounding their criminal offense.

☐ According to DSM-IV, a neurotic disorder is a mental condition in which the predominant disturbance is a symptom that is distressing to the individual and is recognized by him or her as unacceptable and alien; but contact with reality (or reality testing) is fairly intact. The disturbance may be enduring or recurrent, but there is no demonstrable organic etiology or factor. Examples of neurotic disorders are psychosexual disorders, and adjustment and personality disorders.

☐ Psychosis is a term indicating a gross impairment in reality testing, i.e., the individual incorrectly evaluates the accuracy of his or her perceptions and thoughts and makes incorrect inferences about external reality, even in the face of contrary evidence. As a rule, reality testing in psychosis shows gross impairment.

MULTIPLE DIAGNOSES

In the forensic clinic as well as in most detention centers and prisons, it is not uncommon to have to evaluate an individual who suffers two, three, and — less frequently — four overlapping mental disorders and organic disorders (the topic of the next chapter). The following are only a few of the possible combinations: Mental retardation and drug addiction; schizophrenia and drug addiction, in a person who is monolingual (non-English speaking), thus creating serious communication problems; and organic mental disorder (such as AIDS-related dementia), drug abuse and antisocial personality disorder. However, Antisocial Personality Disorder and Malingering are, by far, the most frequent Conditions Not Attributable to a Mental Disorder that need to be taken into consideration to make the differential diagnosis of Organic Mental Disorders and Conditions.

DSM-IV lists these as conditions not attributable to a mental disorder but which may nonetheless become a focus of professional attention: (1) Marital Problems; (2) Occupational Problems; (3) Noncompliance with Medical Treatment; (4) Parent-Child Problems; (5) Other Interpersonal Problems; (6) Other Specified Family Circumstances; (7) Phase of Life Problem or Other Life Circumstance Problem; (8) Academic Problem; (9) Borderline Intellectual Functioning; (10) Malingering; (11) Adult Antisocial Behavior; (12) Child or Adolescent Antisocial Behavior; and (13) Uncomplicated Bereavement. *Synopsis of Psychiatry: Behavioral Sciences and Clinical Psychiatry* (6th edition) by Harold I Kaplan and Benjamin J Sadock (1991) contains a lucid discussion of each of these topics.

ANTISOCIAL PERSONALITY DISORDER

According to DSM-IV, the diagnostic criteria for Antisocial Personality Disorder requires

☐ A. Current age of at least 18

☐ B. Evidence of Conduct Disorder with onset before age 15, as indicated by a history of at least three or more of the following:
  ☐ Was often truant
  ☐ Ran away from home overnight at least twice while living in parental or parental surrogate home (or once without returning)
  ☐ Often initiated physical fights
  ☐ Used a weapon in more than one fight
  ☐ Forced a person into sexual activity with him or her
  ☐ Was physically cruel to animals
  ☐ Was physically cruel to other people
  ☐ Deliberately destroyed other people's property (other than fire setting)
  ☐ Deliberately engaged in fire-setting
  ☐ Often lied (other than to avoid physical or sexual abuse)
  ☐ Has stolen without confrontation of a victim on more than one occasion (including forgery)
  ☐ Has stolen with confrontation of a victim (e.g., mugging, purse-snatching, extortion, armed robbery)

☐ C. A pattern of irresponsible and antisocial behavior since the age or 15, as indicated by at last four of the following
  ☐ Is unable to sustain consistent work behavior, as indicated by any of the following (including similar behavior in academic settings if the person is a student)
  ☐ Significant unemployment for six months or more within five years
  ☐ Repeated absences from work, unexplained by illness in self or family
  ☐ Abandonment of several jobs without realistic plans for others
  ☐ Fails to conform to social norms with respect to lawful behavior, as indicated by repeatedly performing antisocial acts that are grounds for arrest (whether arrested or not), e.g., destroying property, harassing others, stealing, pursuing an illegal occupation
  ☐ Is irritable and aggressive, as indicated by repeated physical fights or assaults (not required by one's job or to defend a person or oneself), including spouse- or child-beating
  ☐ Repeatedly fails to honor financial obligations, as indicated by defaulting on debts or failing to provide child support or support for other dependents on a regular basis
  ☐ Fails to plan ahead, or is impulsive, as indicated by one or both of the following:
    ☐ Travelling from place to place without a prearranged job or clear goal for the period of travel or clear idea about when the travel will terminate
    ☐ Lack of fixed address for a month or more
  ☐ Has no regard for the truth, as indicated by repeated lying, use of aliases, or "conning" others for personal profit or pleasure
  ☐ Is reckless regarding his or her own or others' personal safety, as indicated by driving while intoxicated, or recurrent speeding
  ☐ If a parent or guardian, lack of ability to function as a responsible parent, as indicated by one or more of the following:
    ☐ Malnutrition of the child;
    ☐ Child's illness resulting from lack of minimal hygiene;
    ☐ Failure to obtain medical care for a seriously ill child;

☐ Child's dependence on neighbors or nonresident relatives for food or shelter;
☐ Failure to arrange for a caretaker for young child when parents are away from home;
☐ Repeated squandering on personal items or money required for household necessities
☐ Has never sustained a totally monogamous relationship for more than a year
☐ Lacks remorse (feels justified in having hurt, mistreated, or stolen from another)

Many mental disorders — particularly organic mental disorders and conditions that are the subject of the next chapter — may contain behaviors that mimic Antisocial Personality Disorder. Individuals afflicted either by Antisocial Personality Disorder or Organic Mental Disorder are often charged with offenses such as these: Abandonment of a child, aggravated harassment, arson, assault, bail jumping, burglary, criminal possession of a controlled substance, criminal possession of stolen property, criminal mischief, criminal possession of a weapon, criminal trespass, disorderly conduct, endangering the welfare of a child, incest, kidnapping, loitering, manslaughter, menacing, murder, public intoxication, public lewdness, rape, reckless endangerment, resisting arrest, robbery, sexual abuse, sodomy, unlawful creation of hazards, unlawful use of a vehicle, vehicular manslaughter and many other offenses listed in the Penal Codes of most US states. The operational definition of Antisocial Personality Disorder is virtually by exclusion.

The coexistence of Antisocial Personality Disorder with many other disorders and conditions, primarily alcoholism and drug abuse — disorders and conditions that have various degrees of volitional control over the events leading to a criminal offense — makes the issue of criminal responsibility difficult. A neuropsychologist who is asked to provide a written opinion on the issue of whether a person, during the events leading to the charges, (e.g., murder) knew and appreciated the nature and consequences of his or her behavior and that the behavior was wrong would be ill-prepared without a first-hand and extensive acquaintance with individuals afflicted with Antisocial Personality Disorder.

MALINGERING

Possibly, there is no other branch of professional activity where one needs to be more aware of malingering than in the practice of forensic neuropsychology in the courts. DSM-IV defines malingering as the "intentional production of false or grossly exaggerated physical or psychological symptoms, motivated by external incentives such as . . . avoiding work, obtaining financial compensation, evading criminal prosecution, obtaining drugs, or securing better living conditions." There are no clear rules for detecting and/or preventing malingering or minimizing its occurrence.

There are two conditions of which one needs to be aware:

☐ Malingering of signs and symptoms (the topic of this entry)

☐ Faulty logic regarding the association between organic mental disorders and/or conditions and the offense.

Malingering needs to be differentiated from many other conditions (such as hysteria) which can produce an impression that signs and symptoms are under the subject's control. Elsewhere, this author (Valciukas, 1991) has discussed "Mass Psychogenic Illness."

Malingering is hard to detect even for the most experienced professionals. Malingering should be strongly suspected if any combination of the following is noted:

☐ Signs and symptoms of disorders are presented in a medicolegal context, e.g., the afflicted person is being referred by his or her attorney.

☐ There is a marked discrepancy between the person's claimed distress and disability and the result of objective methods (e.g., psychometric, electrophysiological testing, imaging procedures).

☐ There appears to be lack of cooperation during the diagnostic evaluation and lack of complying with prescribed treatments if any.

☐ Antisocial Personality Disorder (a diagnostic category in DSM-IV).

Many professionals who work in forensic disciplines allied to the occupational and environmental health sciences — forensic psychiatry, forensic psychology — have proposed their own methods for detecting malingering. The following is an adaptation of one developed by Resnick (1984) in the context of forensic psychiatry in which the defendant has something to gain if found "mentally incompetent." A brief critique of such attempts follows.

☐ The individual who is malingering often shows an over-reaction to being "mentally sick." By subtle — or sometimes not so subtle means, often very early in the evaluation — the defendant tries to make sure that it is understood that he or she is a "very sick person."

☐ The individual suspected of malingering often shows eagerness to call attention to his or her illness. If one happens to try to follow a questionnaire in which questions are scheduled to be asked in one particular order, one often finds that the individual soon manages to tell a lot of what he or she wants to relate but is unable to follow the planned order of questions.

☐ He or she often shows inconsistencies in responses and behavior. There are personality tests — such as the MMPI-2 — that contain specially-designed scales to tap when the subject's pattern of responding is inconsistent. Some of these inconsistencies are best detected by several different people in different contexts. An individual may volunteer cocaine/crack abuse at the time of the environmental incidents to a "sympathetic" interviewer, and later vehemently denies its use to a person who appears threatening. The inconsistencies are detected when all the information from several individuals collecting the data — independently of one another — is put together.

☐ He or she may be able to imitate the content but not the form of a mental disorder. Trained professionals pay attention not only to the things defendants say but the manner in which the ideas are communicated. An alert clinician may be able to detect that a 15-year-old has suffered a stroke even if he or she has never suspected that he or she has suffered a cerebro-vascular accident.

☐ Symptoms often do not fit a known diagnostic entity — or fit too well. Occasionally, people who are examined in a forensic clinic bring clippings — and even studies published in the scientific literature — describing signs or symptoms that are "exactly" those affecting the defendant (see Exhibit 7.1, Chronic Fatigue Syndrome). The individual brings the information sometimes with the totally honest belief that the examining professional may not be aware of the symptoms of the disease and in order to show that he or she fits perfectly what is described in the literature.

☐ Sudden onset of illness is a common complaint among people who malinger when experts know that the complaints are known to take several weeks, months, or even years to develop.

☐ Inconsistency between mental symptoms (what the individual says he or she feels) and behavior (what he or she does).

☐ People who malinger may tell far-fetched stories to fit their needs. In addition, he or she may show contradictions in accounts of his or her stories; this is the reason why the evaluative session of individuals suspected of being malingerers needs to be especially long, "exhaustive" and "exhausting," to allow the interviewer to recognize these contradictions.

☐ The net result is that the malingerer is blameless within the framework of the feigned illness; often "others" are responsible for "symptoms" of disease; alternative — and sometimes very plausible ones — are selectively ignored.

☐ Malingerers often engage in delaying tactics to buy time and often to think of the "right answer" to the question. Sometimes, people who malinger give vague answers to specific questions, repeat the questions they were just asked, and/or delay the answer to some questions.

☐ At times, individuals appear to attempt either to "please" the interviewer or to create a favorable impression of himself or herself. At other times, the defendant will try to express curiosity about the scientific professional background of the interviewer.

☐ Malingering should be suspected in a defendant's pleading of mental disorder if a partner — or a large group of individuals — is involved in the litigation.

Signs and symptoms that individuals who malinger do not show should also be suspected:

☐ It is rare for malingerers to show signs of perseveration, a sign one often encounters in mental and neuropsychological impairment.

- ☐ Malingerers are unlikely to show "negative symptoms" of a serious mental illness, such as blunted affect or total indifference to his or her surroundings. On the contrary, signs and symptoms of anxiety are prevalent among malingerers.

- ☐ It is rare for malingerers to complain of hallucinations, possibly on grounds that if one experiences them one is "crazy" to start with. Hallucinations — when they occur — are often seen by relatives and friends based on the defendant's odd behavior. However, when convenient, malingerers who have suffered hallucinations in the past may malinger hallucinations.

- ☐ Malingerers often have studied, or have close relatives or friends who have studied psychology, psychiatry or mental health. They are often the children, spouses, companions, or close friends of psychologists, psychiatrists or journalists.

Subjective neurological symptoms do not fare well in court because of the ever-present possibility of malingering; signs — and less often neurological syndromes and even neurological diseases — can also be malingered. Findings and the results of studies by means of techniques described in the Appendix are often essential to be brought to court because they are relatively more objective measures over which the defendant has little control.

THE DSM SYSTEM AS THE TARGET OF A COURT DEBATE

Although there are many mental health workers who are not familiar with, ignore or avoid DSM, the classification system is used increasingly in the mental health sciences and for legal purposes. As indicated above, most court-appointed psychologists use the DSM multiaxial system as a vehicle of intra-agency and inter-agency communication; many local, state, and federal agencies use the DSM-IV numerical code for statistical purposes. Neuropsychologists, on the other hand, have not generally adopted this classification system. Sbordone's (1991) *Neuropsychology for the Attorney* does not mention the current DSM multiaxial system at all. Dywan, Kaplan, and Pirozzollo (1991), in *Neuropsychology and the Law,* make only a cursory reference to the DSM-IV in the context of developing legislative concepts of disability.

The neuropsychologist who needs to testify in court needs to be aware of the following issues:

- ☐ If he or she chooses to ignore the current DSM multiaxial system, he or she may be asked to explain why. A neuropsychologist can make a poor showing if he or she is unwilling or unable to define terms properly, to state criteria for the diagnoses of various mental disorders and organic conditions, or to spell out the differential diagnosis. Statements such as "my clinical experience" or "my clinical judgment" which may be widely accepted in clinic and training centers, are questioned in court. This is the very reason why many excellent clinicians refuse to appear in court.

☐ If the neuropsychologist chooses to use the current DSM multiaxial system as the basis for the diagnostic criteria for a possible mental disorder or condition, mental health professionals working for the opposing party may use the same source to argue against such a diagnosis.

The DSM system was never meant to be used in such confrontational situations; its diagnostic criteria were not constructed to stand such beatings. Neither DSM-III-R or DSM-IV, for example, spell out the criteria one must follow to determine when behavior is isolated or a part of a pattern. What makes an antisocial pattern of behavior? How many times does a behavior need to occur to establish a pattern? Finally, Antisocial Personality Behavior does not illuminate individual differences between a person who has a long history of petty offenses, and a person who faces the first and only charge of murder-for-hire.

Prevailing community rules, and legal definitions and practices also must be taken into consideration.

☐ Consider the issue of *age*: There are 11-year-old "boys" who father children; there are 12-year-old "girls" who have babies (neither contribute to the welfare of the children). At the discretion of the judge in charge of the case, a 16-year-old adolescent may be charged as an adult because of the seriousness of the offense (e.g., manslaughter).

☐ Sometimes we have to evaluate illegal aliens who are described by their counsels as facing the "first confrontation with the law" in the United States (Defendants' legal counsel argue against the inclusion of such information in the forensic evaluations if they do not pertain to the current offense). Is not a violation of US Immigration laws another instance of crime?

☐ **EXHIBIT 8.1**

The Vietnam War Veteran

Mr Wald was a 46-year-old Black male with a High School degree. The evaluation was directed to the issues raised by the probation officer in charge of the case, namely: "The defendant's responses to questions at times seemed inappropriate and confused. Please evaluate because of the nature of the offense."

As a result, the following was explored: Whether there are signs and/or symptoms of possible neurological disease or psychiatric disorders; to what extent Mr Wald's behavior is determined by organic conditions — that is, conditions arising from neurological or other physical defects; Mr Wald's intelligence; his personality; his reality testing — whether he is thought to be psychotic — and the ability to control his own impulses (e.g., whether he is viewed as a potential threat to himself or others).

Mr Wald met the diagnostic criteria for *schizophrenia, disorganized, chronic*; the following were present: Flat and/or inappropriate affect (range of feelings); sudden and often unpredictable changes in affect involving inexplicable outbursts of anger; a disorder of form of thought, expressed in rambling speech; a disturbance in the sense of identity, e.g., he had no insight into the nature of his mental problems; did not suspect that he suffered from a serious mental disorder; showed a decrease in reactivity to the environment with reduction of spontaneous movements and activity; experienced social withdrawal and emotional detachment; and exhibited difficulties in self-initiated, goal-directed activity, which grossly curtails work activities and his ability to earn a living.

The defendant was a poor historian, and the time course of his mental disorder could not be easily characterized; from various sources, it was likely that he had a long psychiatric history starting as early as 1970.

He was severely injured with a metal fragment, said to have occurred in Vietnam; the possibility that this disfiguring neck injury in fact had a different origin could not be discounted since it was not confirmed that he ever was in Vietnam. Mr Wald said that he served in the Vietnam War and that he was in active combat duty. Most recently, he had been jobless and homeless.

The defendant showed some impairment in reality testing and communication, along with major impairment in several areas, including work, family relations, judgment, thinking, and mood. Although denied, the defendant was likely to suffer delusional (paranoid) ideation. The events leading to his charges appeared to indicate that the defendant could become assaultive even when unprovoked. His level of intellectual functioning was borderline; he suffered severe visual organization problems which are not totally explained by his antipsychotic medication, as he claimed.

The prospect of his social rehabilitation was poor as Mr Wald thought that the events leading to the charges — assault on an individual on the street that resulted in the victim's losing vision in one eye — constituted merely an accident; he had not reflected on the events that led to his charges; he had a long history of violent behavior although some did not lead to confrontations with the law; he had an inadequate level of functioning, e.g., his IQ was borderline; he had many signs and symptoms of mental disorder that affected his social, family, and occupational spheres; he seemed to have an inadequate control of his impulses; and he had few marketable skills, had no job and was unlikely to be able to hold one due to his severe mental disorder.

Mr Wald's psychiatric history prior to his latest arrest was known only in bits and pieces through notes written by mental health professionals in the past. In a previous psychiatric evaluation, he was found to be unfit to proceed with his legal proceedings. One psychiatrist described the defendant as "a malodorous male of average build who was unkempt. . . His thinking processes were disconnected and irrelevant so that he was unable to focus his thoughts on the charges against him." Another psychiatrist found that ". . . his thinking process was fragmented and disorganized." In-patient treatment was recommended to restore competency.

He was admitted to a hospital for chronic mental diseases and in another psychiatric evaluation he was found fit to proceed with the legal proceedings against him. The defendant was evaluated for the third time as a pre-sentence case; he showed no awareness that he suffers from a mental disorder; he faced mandatory incarceration.

☐ QUESTIONS FOR REVIEW AND DISCUSSION

    △ Discuss the issues surrounding the insanity defense.

    △ Discuss the significance of insight in the characterization of mens rea.

    △ There is growing concern that the mental health workers — psychiatrists, psychologists, mental health workers — have too much influence in the determination of criminal intent. Contrast this assertion with the fact that the defendant has the right to present his or her case under the most favorable light.

PART III

ORGANIC MENTAL CONDITIONS AND THEIR FORENSIC RELEVANCE

PSYCHOLOGISTS, ALONG WITH SUCH OTHER MENTAL HEALTH PROFESSIONALS AS psychiatrists, neurologists, and psychiatric nurses, should be able to recognize and sometimes diagnose those mental disorders catalogued in the DSM-IV classification system described in Chapter 8. A neuropsychologist is specifically trained in the recognition of "organic conditions" that affect mind and behavior, the focus of this chapter. In the concluding chapters, we will see how forensic neuropsychologists use their clinical and legal expertise to render an opinion, not only of medical conditions affecting mind and behavior, but also how they argued for or against claimed (or suspected) links between neuropsychological and numerous physical conditions and criminal offenses.

In psychopathology (the discipline that studies the causes of mental disorders) the term organic is used to describe the notion that a mental disturbance is caused by hereditary, genetic, or in-utero factors or acquired through physical damage or disease — e.g., mongolism, fetal alcohol syndrome, or toxic psychosis caused by PCP (Phencyclidine). Traditionally, the term *organic* has been contrasted to *functional*, to express the view that certain disorders or conditions may not have a physical basis (e.g., neurosis, paraphilias, antisocial personality disorder). As Kandel, Schwartz, and Jessell have indicated in a paper titled "Cellular Mechanisms of Learning and the Biological Basis of Individuality" (1991),

> this distinction dates back to the nineteenth century, when neuropathologists examined the brain of patients coming to autopsy and found gross and readily demonstrable disturbances in the architecture of the brain in some psychiatric diseases but not in others. Diseases that produced anatomical evidence of brain lesions were called organic; those lacking these features were called functional . . . (However) everyday events — sensory stimulation, deprivation, and learning — can cause an effective disruption of synaptic connections under some circumstances and a reactivation of connections under others. It is therefore incorrect to imply that certain diseases (organic diseases) affect mentation by producing biological changes in the brain whereas other diseases (functional diseases) do not. The basis of contemporary neural sciences is that all mental processes are biological and any alteration in those processes is organic (p 1028).

DSM-IV states that the expression *organic mental syndrome* refers to a group of psychological and/or behavioral signs and symptoms that makes no reference to its cause, although an organic cause is suspected. The expression *organic mental disorder* is used when the cause of the organic mental syndrome can be ascertained or is highly suspected either by history or by imaging, laboratory, psychometric, or electrophysiological procedures.

An organic mental disorder is the result of a variety of biological and environmental conditions; these are genetic, degenerative, traumatic, vascular, metabolic, toxic, viral, iatrogenic (caused by physicians who treat the disorder), or, in many cases, unknown causes or combinations. The cause or causes of the organic mental disorder is/are to be listed on Axis III of the DSM-IV system (now termed "Mental Disorders due to a General Medical Condition").

Historically, the understanding of fundamental mechanisms underlying "organic" mental disorders has progressed from a gross morphological approach to the (current) molecular biochemical approach. First, the characterization of gross morphological changes that occur in the nervous system during a mental illness, then the study of cellular mechanisms of mental disorders, and finally, the search for the molecular basis of mental disorders. These three approaches can coexist; all three can contribute essential information for the understanding of fundamental mechanisms of mental disorders.

The most powerful asset of molecular neuroscience is the attempt to explain and manipulate nervous system function and, ultimately, behavior by means of physicochemical and pharmacological processes. From a practical point of view, molecular neuroscience has contributed to the development of large numbers of therapeutic drugs. Antipsychotic drugs, for example, have changed our view of the nature of psychiatric diseases and the way we manage them. Benzodiazepine (a mood modifier generally known under the trade name Valium) is one of a family of widely used and known drugs today, and has been widely available since the 1960s.

It is almost certain that in the near future the molecular approach will force us to make sharper observations than those which were typical of the gross morphological and even the cellular era of scientific research. For example, the distinction between "organic" and "functional" diseases (a distinction that for many generations divided disciplines such as neurology on the one hand, and psychiatry and psychology on the other) has been progressively abandoned because the distinction is so general that it adds little insight into the nature of a neuropsychological disorder.

In most cases, the diagnostic criteria of organic mental syndromes and conditions listed below are those formulated in the DSM-IV. However, the DSM lacks guidelines for brain disorders that are called to the attention of the neuropsychologist performing a forensic evaluation; neither DSM-III-R nor DSM-IV says much about acute manifestations and chronic neuropsychological disorders caused by environmental and occupational neurotoxic agents, for example.

A point that will be elaborated more fully later is that the presence of an organic mental syndrome or physical condition may or may not be causally related to the offense of the person being brought to court; the offense and the organic mental disorder or the physical handicap may just coexist in the same individual, with no causal link. It is the task of the forensic neuropsychologist (1) to obtain a good understanding of the circumstances under which the offense occurred in order to make the best clinical judgement of organic mental disorders or handicapping condition, and (2) to argue for or against such a link. The core of the argument, however, is rarely that simple. There are no "decision trees" that allow one to make the best judgments under all circumstances. The task of the forensic neuropsychologist is to deal with a larger perspective of causation.

The chapters in this section discuss eleven of the most frequent organic mental disorders and physically handicapping conditions that are the focus of a forensic neuropsychological evaluation:

- Mental retardation
- Organic mental syndromes
- Brain trauma
- Brain disorders other than brain trauma
- Dementia
- AIDS-related neuropsychological disorder and AIDS-related dementia
- Organic mental disorders caused by specific neurotropic chemical substances
- Organic mental disorders caused by alcohol and illegal drugs
- Organic mental disorders caused by environmental and occupational exposure to neurotoxic agents
- Specific perceptual dysfunctions that are the focus of the forensic neuropsychological evaluation
- Other handicapping conditions

With an intuitive understanding that criminal offenses and mental and physical conditions sometimes overlap and may or may not be causally related, one needs to be forewarned that any offense listed on the criminal codes of a given state can be studied in relation to all neurological disorders, all mental disorders, and all physical conditions.

But this compilation is probably not very useful. Even if one makes a selection of organic mental disorders and physically handicapping conditions that are frequently associated with such offenses, one cannot conclude that such a causal link exists. There are ten large groups of disorders and conditions that are often put to the neuropsychologist for evaluation. One can argue the point that this selection occurs as a result of culture, tradition, currently prevailing community standards, and how lay people (i.e., prospective jurors) perceive associations between criminal offenses and mental disorders and handicapping conditions; cynics may argue the point that defendants manipulate the court system to get a personal advantage over their individual cases.

However, one needs to be alerted to the fact that, in a large number of cases, an individual with poor or no insight (such as cases of severe schizophrenia), may tell you that there is nothing wrong with him or her; they do not see the relationship between the offense and their mental disorders; in some cases the very occurrence of the offense is denied. But then again, an individual who suffers from Antisocial Personality Disorder may say, "They say that they found vials of drugs on me, but they could not prove anything."

9: MENTAL RETARDATION

MENTAL RETARDATION IS FREQUENTLY THE FOCUS OF A FORENSIC NEUROPSY-chological investigation. In most manuals of mental health and allied disciplines, mental retardation is a chapter on pediatrics or child psychology covering key life periods, such as preschool age (0 to 5), school age (6 to 20) and adult (21 and over). The forensic psychologist who works in family courts or tort law is likely to handle cases of mental retardation falling in one or another of these developmental periods. In the forensic clinic where criminal cases are sent for referrals, individuals who suffer from mental retardation are highly self-selected.

- ☐ There are adult cases or cases in which (because of the seriousness of the crime) adolescents as young as fourteen years of age are charged as adults.
- ☐ It is rare to see individuals afflicted by profound or severe mental retardation; most fall in the category of mild and moderate as defined below.

Characterization of Mental Retardation

The American Association on Mental Deficiency has defined mental retardation as "a significantly subaverage general intellectual functioning existing concurrently with deficits in adaptive behavior, and manifested during the developmental period." The upper limit of the developmental period is arbitrarily set at 18 years in this definition. By adaptive behavior is meant the individual's ability to meet standards of personal independence and social responsibility expected of his or her age and cultural group. Intellectual functions include sensory and self-help skills, the beginning of speech and socialization during the early years, reasoning and judgment, use of academic skills, communication and social interactions. Mental Retardation (MR) and Developmental Disorders (DDs) — such as Language and Speech Disorders and Motor Coordination Disorders — are considered by the DSM-IV separate diagnostic categories. In the forensic clinic, one frequently sees individuals in which these two diagnostic categories coexist (See Exhibit 9.1, Mother Wants Him to Strive in Academia).

The Causes of Mental Retardation

Experts have identified no less than 200 specific causes of mental retardation, but the precise etiology is impossible to determine in about 75 to 85 percent of the cases. These specific causes are generally grouped into three broad categories, namely genetic and congenital factors, organic disorders and conditions, and environmental factors (e.g., poverty, lack of education).

☐ That mental retardation can be an inherited condition has been known since the mid-1800s; there have been numerous studies in which mental retardation has been shown to be a characteristic passed on to the offspring by the genes of the parents. Since the mid-1950s, the study of chromosomal abnormalities has revealed a more precise genetic determination (e.g., chromosomal abnormalities associated with Down's syndrome, fragile X chromosome).

☐ An area that continues to be of growing interest is the ability to predict the chances of parents having children who will suffer from some form of mental retardation, based on the genetic makeup of the parents. Since the 1960s there have been many effective procedures to analyse the chromosomal composition of the fetus during early pregnancy, and (if personal ethics allows) elect abortion when an abnormal fetus exists. Cretinism (a condition created by a severe thyroid deficiency in fetal life) and phenylketonuria, or PKU (a congenital metabolic disorder characterized by the increased concentration of phenylalanine and the presence of metabolic byproducts such as phenypyruvate in the urine) are both examples of congenital inherited conditions. There are many other congenital disorders associated with mental retardation but these are rarely seen in the forensic clinic.

☐ It is generally recognized that organic factors account for the vast majority of cases of mental retardation. These include pathological conditions in the mother during pregnancy such as toxemias (excess of poisons and wastes in the mother's blood), rubella (German measles) during the first three months of pregnancy, numerous viral disorders such as hepatitis, parasitic conditions, metabolic and kidney disorders, congenital syphilis, excessive radiation, Rh incompatibility, malnutrition, neurotoxic agents in the enviroment and the workplace such as lead and industrial solvents, the mother's use of alcohol (Fetal Alcohol Syndrome or FAS) or drugs during pregnancy (Exhibit 3.1., Fidgety Girl), the presence of brain hemorrhage during delivery, or lack of oxygen to the brain (Exhibit 9.2, The Young Man Who Got No Respect).

☐ A new devastating problem is that of babies born with AIDS, but the author is unaware of children born with AIDS who are as yet old enough to have had confrontations with the law. In the forensic clinic, many conditions resulting from perinatal and early infancy conditions are often observed in defendants who have been battered as babies. There are also numerous complications of childhood diseases such as measles, whooping cough, encephalitis, meningitis, and tuberculosis which can result in mental retardation. Many defendants evaluated in a forensic clinic are born abroad; knowledge of prevailing health conditions in the countries a defendant comes from and the local health conditions prevailing during his or her early infancy is of paramount importance in understanding the possible origin of diseases that might have affected the brain.

☐ Poverty and socio-cultural deprivation are associated with many other environmental conditions such as malnutrition, unsanitary conditions, poor housing, exposure to environmental neurotoxic agents (such as lead in old housings, or pesticides in rural environments), lack of adult role models and early exposure to crime, lack of intellectual challenge, and emotional deprivation (Exhibit 5.1, New York Child Learns to Walk by Himself). The link between poverty and crime has been well established by now; in New York City one often sees teenagers who live in poor neighborhoods with a high incidence of crime who, because of their so many injuries, appear to come out of a war.

Evaluation of Mental Retardation

Psychologists working in forensic clinics in the courts administer "intelligence tests" in the form of comprehensive batteries. Among the most widely used is the revised form of the Wechsler Adult Intelligence Scale (WAIS-R), but many other professionals use other tests appropriate to their local conditions. For example, very often in both verbal and written communication, the psychologist and court personnel involved in the legal proceedings are likely to be asked about the defendant's or probationer's IQ (Intelligence Quotient). IQ is used to characterize levels of mental retardation, namely

☐ *Mild* (IQ 50-55 to approximately 70)

☐ *Moderate* (IQ 35-40 to 50-55)

☐ *Severe* (IQ 20-25 to 35-40)

☐ *Profound* (IQ below 20 or 25)

Mild levels of mental retardation are present in a great many of the cases examined in a forensic clinic; moderate levels are rare; and although individuals suffering severe and profound forms of mentally retardation are known, in those charged with crimes, they rarely are seen for evaluation at a forensic clinic.

Legal Issues

Mental retardation is associated with numerous legal issues. Only a few of these can be discussed in this chapter which reviews organic mental disorders that are sometimes the focus of the forensic neuropsychological evaluation.

Psychological testing for possible mental retardation is often requested in the context of examinations to determine the competence to stand trial. Is the individual charged with a crime able to undertand the charges against him or her? Or what are the roles of different key individuals during court proceedings? Is the notion of pleading guilty or not guilty understood by the defendant? What are the consequences of being found guilty? Psychologists may or may not get involved in the answers to these questions, but they play a key role in ascertaining whether the individual is malingering, a situation found less frequently in a regular clinic or school setting.

Until a generation ago, individuals who suffered mental retardation used to be lumped into a single classification scheme, thus overlooking the rich variety of personality differences that may coexist with mental retardation. It therefore is impossible to mention the variety of cases in which a mentally retarded individual can be involved in a crime.

☐ An individual suffering from mental retardations may sometimes be charged with serious crimes such as rape in which (as a result of a competence examination) a psychologist may ascertain that if a concrete mode of language is used to communicate with the individual, he does undertand the nature of his behavior and that what he was doing was wrong.

☐ Sometimes, a mentally retarded individual is charged with sexual abuse but a psychological evaluation reveals that (in the mind of the 28-year-old retarded individual) the defendant regarded himself as a young boy playing with the penis of another 7-year old boy (the victim).

☐ Sometimes, the court needs to know whether a mentally-retarded adult is competent to consent to a sexual act, information that may be vital in charges of rape.

☐ Mentally retarded individuals are often "hooked" by drug dealers and they quickly become addicts (there are cases in which a mentally retarded became addicted to cocaine at a very early age, as early as nine).

☐ One of the saddest cases are those in which a drug dealer uses a mentally retarded person as a "mule:" When the couple "mule/drug dealer" is discovered by law enforcing agents, drug dealers quickly escape leaving the mentally retarded individual loaded with large amounts of drugs to face criminal charges.

Mentally retarded individuals also often have antisocial personality traits and can also be involved in crimes of assault, robbery, and murder; in the latter, a mental health worker may play a crucial role in the determination of the degree of criminal intent in the commission of the crime.

Although having objective information about levels of intellectual functioning is always important in forensic neuropsychological evaluations, these levels need to be corroborated using many other sources of information:

☐ Significant delays in achieving landmark developmental stages (such as the defendant telling that he was once told that he learned to walk and talk at age four)

☐ Poor schooling (which in individuals also suffering from Antisocial Personality Disorder is often rationalized as "lack of interest," or "I was more interested in girls than school at the time")

☐ Being placed in special education programs

☐ In individuals who are born abroad and speak languages other than English, inability to learn English after, say, two to three years of US residence (depending on age and local conditions)

☐ Inability to work in other than menial jobs

One needs to be reminded that defendants examined at the court (and particularly those who are inmates in detention centers) are often the only source of information; as a consequence, essential details about the medical history of the defendant's parents, or about his or her own medical history, are often lacking.

Almost without exception teachers avoid using the diagnostic category of mental retardation because of the known harmful effect that the label "mentally retarded" can have in the self-esteem of an impressionable, still-growing individual. One should be aware of the potential damage of other labels used by teachers in the interpretation of multiple "diagnoses;" these include being told that they were "slow," had a "learning disorder," they were "hyperactive," suffered from an "attention disorder," or were an "underachiever."

☐ **EXHIBIT 9.1**

Mother Wants Him to Strive in Academia

Mr Davis was a 33-year-old Black male with two years of grammar school education in Jamaica. The evaluation was directed to the issues raised by the Probation Officer in charge of the case, namely: "Mr Davis has been diagnosed as having a Developmental Reading Disorder and an Intermittent Explosive Disorder." At the time of the forensic neuropsychological evaluation, the defendant was in the community awaiting his sentence.

Mr Davis met the diagnostic criteria for Pervasive Developmental Disorder Not Otherwise Specified. This is a quantitative and qualitative impairment in the development of social interaction and of verbal and non-verbal communication skills (his IQ was 63), and markedly restricted repertoire of activities and interests.

This evaluator was in agreement with the defendant's prior diagnosis of Intermittent Explosive Disorder. This disorder is characterized by several discrete episodes of loss of control of aggressive impulses resulting in serious assaultive acts or destruction of property. The degree of aggressiveness expressed during the episodes were grossly out of proportion to any precipitating psychosocial stressors (e.g., sibling quarrels about the use of each other's clothing). There were no signs of generalized impulsiveness or aggressiveness between the episodes (in fact, the defendant projected the image of a calm, controlled individual). Episodes or loss of control were not the expression of a psychotic disorder, although organic (congenital) factors could not be ruled out.

The defendant exhibited facial features of an individual suffering from a physical developmental disorder (e.g., very narrow forehead) sometimes associated with congenital maldevelopment of the brain's frontal lobes.

There were no acute events or enduring circumstances that may be related to the diagnosed personality disorder or the events leading to the defendant's charges (robbery). There was no family history of mental illness or chemical dependency; in fact, and because of his unruliness, the defendant himself appeared to be a frequent source of family conflicts.

Mr Davis showed a mild form of mental retardation afflicting areas of social and family interactions and his ability to seek and maintain employment. His explosive behavior sometimes was triggered by trivial events (he had violent fights with his ex-wife; they eventually separated because of loud arguments about his wife breaking the television's antenna in his bedroom). He also showed antisocial personality traits (e.g., "I 'took' the camera from the store because it was Christmas time and I needed the money"). Intelligence testing revealed a concrete form of thinking (e.g., Question: "Which direction does the sun rise in the morning;" Answer: "Over there;" Q: "In which ways are a coat and a suit alike?"; A: "Nothing, a coat is a coat and a suit is a suit."

At 33, Mr Davis had achieved the highest intellectual potential he probably would ever have. Statistically speaking, many individuals who suffer from serious developmental disorders (such as the defendant's) sometimes show an early decline of intellectual functioning, even an early dementia. His inability to work had arrested the possibility of independent living and (at times) responsible behavior.

As indicated below, this report was written after consulting with several people. According to the Probation Officer in charge of the case, Mr Davis' mother strongly believed that the defendant would be able to read and write as a result of his attendance at a local university-sponsored special adult education program. This expectation appeared to be unwarranted, since (as indicated above) the defendant was likely to show early signs of decline rather than showing further intellectual growth. His father appeared to have a more realistic approach when he indicates that "one is not sure what is going to happen to him when we (Mr Davis' father and mother) are gone." Over the years, his siblings had grown tired of putting up with him and mostly had learned to ignore him.

The Probation Officer in charge of the case had indicated that the defendant faced mandatory incarceration. It was felt that if sent to prison, Mr Davis' episodes of intermittent explosive behavior were likely to be interpreted as willful acts stemming from an antisocial personality disorder, and as a result be severely punished. Other inmates may react to his explosive behavior by reacting toward him with violence. Sexual abuse from other inmates was also possible.

It was recommended that attendance at school be discontinued as it tended to perpetuate the hope of achieving a level of performance that in all possibility was unrealistic. This continuation of school attendance, in fact, was likely to accentuate his antisocial behavior.

Participation in a community program where he could learn to accept and maintain personal responsibility was a strong recommendation.

The Wechsler Adult Intelligence Scale, Revised (WAIS-R) was administered. The Verbal Tests included Information, Digit Span, Vocabulary, Arithmetic, Comprehension and Similarities; the Performance Tests included Picture Completion, Block Design, and Digit Symbol. The IQ has been prorated (that is, calculated on the basis of 8 of 11 tests). His best performance was on the Digit Span, a test used to assess concentration and recent memory; his worst was on the vocabulary test. Mr Davis' verbal IQ was found to be 64 and his performance IQ was 65; the overall test IQ was 63. These IQ values represent a mild form of mental retardation.

Mr Davis was given to read the following:

A boy had a dog.

The dog ran into the woods.

The boy ran after the dog.

The defendant was unable to read the paragraph representing first grade reading (the individual reads individual letters, "A," "b," "o," "y" and so on).

Mr Davis was asked to write a sentence of his choice. He did not understand the concept of "sentence." It was explained again, and then he wrote the word "TOPS." The defendant was asked to write from dictation: "Today is a nice day" (he wrote "TO" and he could not continue).

□ **EXHIBIT 9.2**

The Young Man Who Got No Respect

Mr Guthrie was sent for evaluation while incarcerated and waiting for his sentence. He was an 18-year-old Black male with 10th grade special education. He suffered from crack addiction. Drug abuse was considered to be the primary diagnosis; drug abuse was the focus of his current behavioral problems, the main reason for his current problems with the law, and the focus of treatment intervention recommended.

He was diagnosed as suffering from Pervasive Developmental Disorder Not Otherwise Specified. The defendant showed quantitative and qualitative impairment in the development of social interactions and verbal and nonverbal communication. In addition, he exhibited a restricted repertoire of activities and interests.

He showed the physical features of Alcohol Fetal Syndrome. This chronic condition was associated with physical maldevelopment (particularly in the head and limbs) and a low level of mental functioning. This condition markedly affected the image the defendant had of himself, as friends often told him that he was "ugly" and humiliated him. The defendant was born from alcoholic parents; his mother drank when she was pregnant with him. His father was neglectful and abusive; his family changed homes frequently when the defendant was a child. Later, he himself lived in different foster homes.

The defendant showed serious symptoms and serious impairment in social, occupational, and school functioning. He knew that he projected an image of a passive and vulnerable individual. However, it appeared that when by himself the defendant had poor control of his impulses and could physically harm people.

The prognosis for his social rehabilitation was thought to be poor. Mr Guthrie had not reflected on the events that led to his charges and had not come to terms with the consequences of his behavior. He harbored a great deal of anger and often engaged in violent behavior, had an inadequate level of functioning, e.g., his IQ suggested mild mental retardation; had many signs and symptoms affecting his social, family and occupational spheres; seemed to have an inadequate control of his impulses; had no job and chances were that it will be difficult for him to get one; and the events leading to the charges occurred under the influence of a toxicant (crack). The quality of information was marginal to poor on account of Mr Guthrie's mild mental retardation.

Mr Guthrie has been psychologically evaluated on numerous occasions. The common theme of these evaluations, which covered a period until he was approximately 16 years of age, was that the defendant was striving to overcome his difficulties. Mr Guthrie completed 10th grade in a special-education school program. It appeared that the defendant became a drug abuser and a drug dealer about a year ago, and such information did not appear in previous evaluations.

Mr Guthrie had taken crack and marijuana since the age of 15. However, he began using drugs on a regular basis for the past year. The defendant stated that nobody noticed when he returned to his community home when he is "high" on drugs because they took him for granted (e.g., "people do not respect me," he said). He also said that if the adults at the home where he was staying knew he was on drugs, they could not have done anything about it. He often spent about $50 dollars a day on drugs; he took drug about four times weekly. He said that he was often high on drugs when stealing. He also volunteered that he also dealt drugs. A few months back, he had a serious fight with another youngster over non-payment of drug money and the defendant beat the youngster so badly his friend was admitted to a hospital where he stayed for "weeks or even months." The defendant did not know what happened to the youngster involved in the incident. The defendant said that he would like to stop using crack because he tends to "get in trouble" when he takes it (an apparent reference to loss of control and aggressive behavior). The defendant also drank alcohol since he was 15; when he drinks beer, he often drinks a quart.

Mr Guthrie was a poorly developed male (5'4," 120 lbs). He had a small cranium, poorly developed ears, flat, sunken nose, small-rounded eyes with unusual skin foldings that were also noted in his hands and large lower lips. The structure and content of his speech was that of a poorly educated person. His communications skills were very poor. His eye contact was adequate. A screening battery of probes the following was noted: Poor whole-body balance; poor quality in motor coordination; and his eyes showed jerky features on finger following.

From an extensive checklist of signs and/or symptoms possibly indicative of neurological or mental disorders, Mr Guthrie was asked whether he had ever experienced them, and if so, to give examples. He denied ever having experienced these signs or symptoms. Paranoid ideation, delusions and hallucinations were denied.

The Wechsler Adult Intelligence Scale, Revised (WAIS-R) was administered. Mr Guthrie's verbal IQ was found to be 67 and his performance IQ was 66; the overall test IQ was 65. These IQ levels represent mild mental retardation.

Recommendations included that, because of his limited intellectual capacity, an effort should be made for the defendant to receive a clear message concerning sentencing. It was thought that the defendant should receive a face-to-face, clear, strong and unequivocal signal from a person of clear authority, that robbery and the use and criminal sales of drugs on the street is something that the law does not condone.

It was further emphasized that Mr Guthrie was a Mentally-Ill Chemically Addicted (MICA) individual and should be referred to a facility appropriate for such individuals. In spite of the diagnosis of mental retardation, drug abuse was still the principal problem to be addressed. Unfortunately, at that time, most public-funded rehabilitation centers in or around New York City turned down such individuals because of overcrowding conditions and, sometimes, for "safety" reasons. In addition, sometimes such centers imposed a rule that the afflicted individual should call every day to ascertain whether a bed is available that day, a condition that Mr Guthrie would have had difficulty fulfilling.

⬜ QUESTIONS FOR REVIEW AND DISCUSSION

△ Discuss the similarities and differences between mental retardation and developmental disorders.

△ One persistent argument is that mothers addicted to drugs should be incarcerated because (as a result of their continuing abuse of drugs) they are harming their fetus (putting them at risk of developmental disorders and mental retardation). What are the merits and the flaws of this argument?

△ Discuss the concepts of intelligence and insight.

△ A mental health worker argues the point that a defendant who has an IQ lower than 55 should not be criminally accountable. What are the flaws in this statement? Argue the point of the instruments that are used to determine IQ as well as the correlation — or absence thereof — between IQ and criminal intent.

△ In evaluating mentally retarded individuals who were raised in low socio-economic conditions, one often needs to use a vocabulary that is appropriate to the defendant's own vocabulary. Is a mental health worker allowed to use "dirty language" during the forensic neuropsychological evaluation (e.g., in rape, incest)? Do you think that the court should tolerate such language in written legal documents filed in court? Discuss the consequences of ascertaining competence to stand legal proceedings in a mentally retarded individual as a result of using a language inappropriate for such an individual.

△ Argue on the facts and statistics linking criminal behavior to mental retardation.

△ The lawyer of a male defendant suffering from a moderate level of mental retardation argues the point that incarceration of her client would represent unusual punishment as he will certainly be at risk of homosexual rape while in jail. Review the facts and statistics regarding this concern.

△ Discuss the physiological and ethical issues surrounding chemical castration in mentally retarded defendants convicted of rape.

10: ORGANIC MENTAL DISORDERS

THE FOLLOWING CONDITIONS ARE DIAGNOSED AS EITHER AN ORGANIC MENTAL syndrome, when the organic cause is unknown, or as an organic mental disorder, when the cause is known. Only those most likely to be the focus of a forensic neuropsychological investigation are listed here. They include:

- ☐ Organic Delirium Syndrome
- ☐ Organic Amnestic Syndrome
- ☐ Organic Anxiety Syndrome
- ☐ Organic Mood Syndrome
- ☐ Organic Personality Syndrome
- ☐ Organic Delusional Syndrome

Organic Delirium Syndrome

This syndrome is characterized by a reduced ability to maintain attention to external stimuli (e.g., questions must be repeated because of wandering attention) and to appropriately shift attention to new external stimuli (e.g., perseveration of answers to a previous question). It involves disorganized thinking, as indicated by rambling, irrelevant, or incoherent speech.

The diagnosis of delirium is made when at least two of the following are present:

- ☐ Reduced level of consciousness, e.g., difficulty keeping awake during examination
- ☐ Perceptual disturbances: Misinterpretations, illusions, or hallucinations
- ☐ Disturbance of the sleep-wake cycle with insomnia or daytime sleepiness
- ☐ Increased or decreased psychomotor activity
- ☐ Disorientation in time, place, or person
- ☐ Memory impairment, e.g., inability to learn new material, such as the names or several unrelated objects after five minutes, or to remember past events, such as the history of the current episode of illness.

The clinical features develop over a short period of time (usually hours to days) and tend to fluctuate over the course of the day. There is evidence from history, physical examination, or laboratory tests of a specific organic factor (or factors) judged to be etiologically related to the disturbance; or in the absence of such evidence, an etiologic organic factor can be presumed if the disturbance cannot be accounted for by any nonorganic mental disorder, e.g., manic episode accounting for agitation and sleep disturbance.

The acute phase of the delirium (e.g., associated with susbtance abuse disorders, such as drug overdose) is often present during emergency admissions to hospitals. When they are the sole source of information, defendants often distort or rationalize the meaning of such emergencies calling them "mental breakdowns." The time course of delirium is characteristically brief and reversible.

Delirium is diagnosed clinically or by means of simple clinical probes; there is no formal testing for delirium except the Mini-Mental Status Evaluation usually performed at the bedside.

Organic Amnestic Syndrome

Here, there is a demonstrable evidence of impairment in both short- and long-term memory, usually a result of neuropsychological testing. With regard to long-term memory, remote events are remembered more clearly than more recent events. Impairment in short-term memory (inability to learn new information) may be indicated by the inability to remember three objects after five minutes. Long-term memory impairment (inability to remember information that was known in the past) may be indicated by inability to remember past personal information (e.g., what happened yesterday, birthplace, occupation) or facts of common knowledge (e.g., past US Presidents, well-known dates). The diagnosis is made when the disturbance is not occurring exclusively during the course of delirium, and does not meet the criteria for dementia (i.e., there is no impairment in abstract thinking or judgment or other disturbance of so-called higher cortical function and no personality change); there is evidence from the history, physical examination, or laboratory tests of a specific organic factor (e.g., gunshot wounds) judged to be etiologically related to the disturbance.

Organic amnestic syndrome and disorder are conditions often referred to the neuropsychologist for forensic evaluation. The focus of the referral is to determine whether evidence (perhaps, poor performance in memory tests) or impairment in both short- and long-term memory, which require testing, can be demonstrated. Although memory tests are available (such as the Wechsler Memory Scale, Benton Visual Retention test), some are difficult to administer in the forensic clinic for a variety of reasons. One may be the defendants' demographic profile, including poor education and monolingualism (in languages other than English). However, the neuropsychologist's most challenging task is the evaluation of a malingered memory impairment when the defendant has an obvious motivation not to remember the events leading to his or her charges or other information that is crucial in the determination of criminal responsibility. There are no general rules regarding the detection of malingering in a claim of memory impairment; if the experienced neuropsychologist creates a list of such rules, these are surely to be challenged in court. An erratic performance sometimes provides a hint (not remembering the name of the President of the United States but remembering that Goethe is the author of Faust).

A good source of information for tests employed in civil law is Sbordone (1991). Exhibit 10.1 (The Car Tinkerer) is an example of an individual who claims to be unable to recall the events leading to his charges.

Organic Anxiety Syndrome

The diagnostic criteria for this disturbance are the presence of prominent, recurrent panic attacks or Panic Disorder. At some time during the disturbance, one or more panic attacks (discrete periods of intense fear or discomfort) have occurred that were unexpected (i.e., that did not occur immediately before or on exposure to a situation that usually caused anxiety, and were not triggered by situations in which the person was the focus of another's attention).

At least four of the following symptoms developed during at least one of the attacks: Shortness of breath (dyspnea) or smothering sensations, dizziness, unsteady feelings, faintness, palpitations or accelerated heart rate (tachycardia), trembling or shaking, sweating, choking, nausea, abdominal distress, depersonalization or derealization, numbness or tingling sensations (paresthesias), flushes (hot flashes) or chills, chest pain or discomfort, fear of dying, or fear of going mad or of doing something uncontrolled.

Individuals who are addicted to Valium often develop Organic Anxiety Disorder. Sometimes, the individual may not be aware of the connection between his recurrent attacks of anxiety and the abuse of both Valium and alcohol.

Organic Mood Syndrome

This syndrome is often present in the clinic appearing as a prominent and persistent depressed, elevated, or expansive mood. The "crash" (major depressive episode) that occurs after a period of heavy use of crack cocaine is a good example; many suicide attempts occur under these circumstances. Drug-related mood syndrome often appears in the psychiatric history, frequently masked as a "mental breakdown" or rationalized as being the result of personal and/or family problems. Individuals who use powerful mind-altering drugs — such as PCP (Phencyclidine, also known by the street name "Angel Dust") — often volunteer episodes in which they feel they can fly (some defendants are seriously injured or killed during such mood-expansive episodes). In making the diagnoses of Organic Mood Disorder, one needs to specify whether the mood syndrome or disorder is manic, depressed, or mixed.

In the forensic clinic, one rarely sees the acute manifestations of organic mood syndrome (either depressive or manic). These manifestations are most likely to be observed by professionals who work in detention centers where inmates suffer a sudden withdrawal from long-abused drugs. The syndrome and disorder are evaluated clinically or by means of simple probes. There are many "Depression Scales," such as that developed by Aaron Beck; however, as these scales explore a single dimension, they often "load" the individual into a pattern of responding. The MMPI, the most widely used test of personality, contains a built-in scale for depression (as does the revised MMPI-2) that, because it is mixed with other scales, does not exhibit the shortcoming found in Beck's. Projective techniques such as the TAT (Thematic Apperception Test) may often reveal stories of hopelessness and people who are driven to suicide.

Organic Personality Syndrome

This is a persistent personality disturbance — either lifelong or representing a change or accentuation of a previously characteristic trait — involving:

☐ Affective instability, e.g., marked shifts from a normal mood to depression, irritability, or anxiety

☐ Recurrent outbursts of aggression or rage that are grossly out of proportion to any precipitating psychological stressors

☐ Markedly impaired social judgment, e.g., sexual misconduct

☐ Marked apathy and indifference

☐ Suspiciousness or paranoid ideation.

An organic personality disorder is said to be of an *explosive type* if the outburst of aggression or rage is the predominant feature.

Organic personality syndrome and disorder is frequently the focus of a forensic neuropsychological evalution; these are episodes that often lead to a variety of criminal charges. Individuals afflicted by the explosive type are frequently charged with physical assault, criminal mischief, child (physical) abuse, and homicide. However, less suspected (and often present in individuals who give the impression of self-control) are sexual misconduct, lewdness, and sexual abuse of children. In the forensic clinic, the most frequent causes of organic personality disorder are chronic alcoholism and/or drug abuse (Exhibit 10.2, Christmas Celebration).

A probe of the events leading to the defendant's charges is often enough to reveal one or many of the ingredients which are required to make the diagnosis of organic personality testing. However, some of the events may not be remembered (because he or she was intoxicated) or amnesia for the events may be faked. Sometimes, projective techniques such as the TAT are useful to reveal themes of violence in individuals engaged in a variety of antisocial activities; however, individuals with borderline cognitive levels do not provide more than monosyllabic interpretations of the test. In the clinical histories, defendants sometimes tend to reveal problems of dyscontrol by negating even the slightest irritability. Sometimes individuals deny ever being irritable when in fact they have been charged with criminal behavior several times as a result of their assaults. The MMPI or MMPI-2 can be used with educated individuals who show an adequate level of reading (that is, 4th-grade level).

A good source for additional information on Organic Mental Disorders is *Synopsis of Psychiatry: Behavioral Sciences and Clinical Psychiatry* by Harold I Kaplan and Benjamin J Sadock (1991).

Organic Delusional Syndrome

The organic basis of many delusional disorders can sometimes be recognized. A delusion is a belief (less frequently, a system of beliefs) involving situations that occur in real life, such as being followed, poisoned, infected, loved at a distance, having a disease, or being deceived by one's spouse or lover, with at least one month's duration. Although auditory or visual hallucinations may sometimes be present, these are not prominent. Behavior is not obviously off or bizarre in an individual afflicted by delusional disorders.

In the forensic clinic, almost all types of delusional disorder can be observed. These include:

☐ *Erotomanic Type*, in which the predominant theme of the delusion(s) is that a person, usually of higher status, is in love with the subject. Individuals (both men and women) who suffer from erotomanic delusion often exhibit sexually promiscuous behavior; erotomanic delusions need to be differentiated from prostitution linked to the need for money to obtain illegal drugs; both male and female drug abusers may sometimes be very seductive during the course of a forensic evaluation.

☐ *Grandiose Type*, in which the predominant theme of the delusional disorder is one of inflated worth, power, knowledge, identity, or special relationships to a deity or famous person. One occasionally sees professional boxers who have had confrontations with the law as a result of these delusions.

☐ *Jealous Type*, a delusional disorder in which the predominant theme of the delusion(s) is that one's sexual partner is unfaithful. Many individuals afflicted by chronic alcoholism delusion exhibit jealousy which often leads to assault, physical abuse, and sometimes to homicide.

☐ *Persecutory Type*, a delusional disorder in which the predominant theme of the delusion(s) is that one (or someone to whom one is close) is being malevolently treated in some way. People with this type of delusion may repeatedly take their complaints of being mistreated to legal authorities. They are often charged with assault or criminal possession of weapons carried to "protect themselves."

☐ *Somatic Type*, a delusion in which the predominant theme of the delusion(s) is that the person has some physical defect disorder or disease (e.g., that one leg is thinner than the other, that one's face is grossly asymmetrical).

☐ **EXHIBIT 10.1**

The Car Tinkerer

Mr Morrison is a 21-year-old Caucasian male with 8th grade education. The evaluation was directed as an aid to determine his competence to stand trial.

The events leading to the charges as described by available sources are that the defendant was accused of entering the rear seat of a taxi, grabbing the victim around his neck, holding a gun to the victim's head and asking him for his money. In the background documentation the victim is described as having recovered the gun after the victim hit the defendant with his car as the defendant was running away.

The events leading to the charges as described by the defendant are that he remembers entering a night club where he went to spend some time with his usual friends and the next thing he remembers is being in a hospital bed ten days after.

Mr Morrison stated that he had never suffered a condition for which he was admitted to a hospital except during the events leading to his arrest. He was not currently taking any physician-prescribed and/or over-the-counter medication. However, the attorney did not have the defendant's medical records. The defendant stated that he has returned to one of the city hospitals for follow-up, but reports on this follow-up were not available. Therefore, information that the defendant suffered a fracture of the skull, loss of hearing and a total loss of memory from minutes after entering the night club to close to ten days after being hit by a car came from the defendant's lawyer and the defendant himself.

The defendant indicated that he was found to have had "blood" accumulated within his skull. He has been told that his mother was against opening the defendant's skull to remove the blood and she was told that chances were that the condition would resolve itself (probably meaning that blood would gradually be reabsorbed). The defendant said that he was also told that the "nerve" that carries hearing sensation on the right side was severed and that hearing loss on that side would be permanent. It is unclear how the "nerve" carrying hearing sensation could be selectively affected without affecting balance (the eighth cranial nerve carries both vestibular [balance] and hearing sensations); however, the defendant did not appear to suffer a unilateral balance problem, or if he did, it has been resolved in the past three months. The lawyer who was acting as the defendant's counsel indicated that the defendant suffered from a "retrograde ammesia," that is, a memory loss for the events that supposedly happened before any brain injury. Mr Morrison stated that he never sought or received help from a psychiatrist, psychologist or mental health worker, except for school counseling when (during the 8th grade) he decided to abandon school.

The defendant indicated that he lived with his mother (aged 47) who was a real estate broker in Westchester. The defendant said that he was single, that he had a girlfriend, and that he had no children of his own.

Before his incarceration, Mr Morrison completed 9th grade; he indicated he left school because it was "too slow." He later completed his education at mechanical trade school with a certification as a mechanic.

Before the events leading to his charges, Mr Morrison worked at a station attached to a car dealer where he performed repair work for cars. The work sometimes consisted in disassembling a car's entire motor, making the diagnosis of needs, writing up estimated costs, and performing the needed repair work. The defendant also indicated that he was a certified car inspector for the State of New York. The defendant stated that on the advice of his doctors, he had not returned to his regular job after the events leading to the defendant's charges. However, the defendant was still "tinkering" with his own race car (he said that he sometimes he raced in New Jersey, and he hoped to race in Indianapolis in the future). He said that, uncharacteristic of him, after the event in which he was hit by a car, he made mistakes in the sequence in which, say, the pieces of a carburetor should be placed; he said that he recently made a mistake with the placement of washers in the carburetor of his own car, and the carburetor was damaged. He indicated that if he did that mistake at his own job, that would have created serious problems.

Mr Morrison denied use of illegal drugs and described himself as a "social drinker." He said that he began drinking on his own when he was 17; he said that he liked cocktails such as "7 & 7" . The defendant said that he did not remember drinking at the night club. He said that he did not remember taking illegal drugs and that it would be uncharacteristic of him because he did not use drugs. The lawyer indicated that he did not have a record of the defendant's BAC (Blood Alcohol Concentration) and he did not know whether such evaluation — or any other toxicological evaluation — was performed to determine the presence of illegal drugs in the defendant's urine at the time the defendant was brought to the city hospital.

Mr Morrison is a well-developed, muscular young man (5'10", 180 lbs) who during the evaluative session and testing was amiable and cooperative. The defendant was well oriented in space, time, and person. The structure and the content of his speech were unremarkable; the defendant's communication skills were excellent. His affect was normally-ranged and his mood was neutral.

A screening battery of probes that included examination of posture, gait, whole-body balance, muscle strength, tremor at rest, intentional tremor, motor coordination, general appearance of the eyes, eye movements and reaction of the eyes to light was performed. The defendant showed slight problems with whole-body balance; his body bobbled a little when asked to stand with two feet in tandem (but not so much when asked to stand on two feet together). The presence of severe "disorder" on the the right side of his brain, was likely to cause him to fall toward the side of the "injury." However, the defendant did not show such a tendency (or if he showed that in the past, it has already disappeared at the time of this evaluation).

From an extensive checklist of signs and/or symptoms possibly indicative of neurological or mental disorders, Mr Morrison was asked whether he had ever experienced them, and if so, to give examples. The following were volunteered: Throbbing pain in the head, which was said to be markedly affected by the weather; occasionally, he said he sees flashes of light particularly when he bends to pick up something from the floor; he said he often feels tired and requires about 12 hours of sleep to feel completely rested; he said he has lost weight (about 15 lbs in recent weeks); that he sometimes felt lightheaded and/or dizzy; about a week after his release from a city hospital he said he found himself walking in a area of Long Island he did not recognize and was able to return home with the aid of a friend; and he said that (except for the events leading to his charges) his memory of past and more recent events were intact. Because of the lack of information from the city hospital, a clinical assessment whether the defendant is suffering from a "traumatic amnesia," "anterograde amnesia" (memory loss after the traumatic event) or "retrograde amnesia" could not be made at the time of the evaluation. (This was not to say that the defendant was suspected to be malingering; this was to clarify that a diagnosis of amnestic disorder was made after several clinical pieces of information are integrated). Paranoid ideation, delusions and hallucinations were denied.

The defendant appeared to use arguments a *fortiori,* e.g., he indicated that he has never had a confrontation with the law before and therefore the events leading to his charges could never have happened. However, he appeared to be at a genuine loss to explain how he was found in an area "frequented by prostitutes and pimps," an area where he said he has never been before and it would be uncharacteristic of him to have patronized. The defendant said: "To tell you the truth, I would like to go to trial to find out what really happened that night." Question: "Is it possible sometimes to do something that is uncharacteristic of oneself?"; Answer: "Yes, I think so;" Question: "Would you give me an example in which you would have experience?"; Answer: "I once remember that returning with my girl from some place she was drunk, and she kept saying 'kiss me, kiss me'; the following day when I told about her about the previous night, she told me she did not remember a thing."

The Wechsler Adult Intelligence Scale, Revised (WAIS-R) was administered: The IQ has been prorated (that is, calculated on the basis of 10 of 11 tests).

General Information assessed his fund of general knowledge, whether obtained formally or informally. Individuals who do well on this subtest usually are alert to the environment and have a good long-term memory for facts. This subtest also assesses the individual's memory for facts, or distant events. The defendant did very well in this test.

The Digit Span Test was used to assess multiple mental functions including his attention span and ability to concentrate. The defendant was required to repeat a series of numbers of increased lengths; the defendant was able to repeat the series "5-9-1-7-4-2-8" and "4-1-7-9-3-8-6" without errors, thus revealing a better-than average capacity to concentrate and to remember most recent events.

Vocabulary scores indicated the individual's knowledge of word meaning and the ability to express these meanings verbally. The defendant had no difficulty or hesitation in remembering and explaining the meaning of words.

Arithmetic required the individual to solve numerical problems without the aid of pencil and paper. In the execution of this test the individual needs to use basic arithmetic skills. The defendant did poorly in this test.

Comprehension tapped common-sense reasoning and the ability to exercise social judgment in practical situations as well as the individual's exposure to "mainstream" culture. The defendant's second highest score was obtained in this test.

The Similarities subtest was used to assess Mr Morrison's ability to discriminate between essential and superficial likeness. This test calls for the ability to see relationships between things and ideas, and to categorize them into logical groups. It also measures the capacity to form conceptual units from verbal material and to express these concepts in words. The defendant had no difficulties with this test.

In the Picture Completion Test the defendant was required to discover and name the missing part of an incompletely drawn picture. The defendant did very well in this test.

Picture Arrangement Test consisted of a series of pictures which, when placed in the right sequence, tells a little story, like a cartoon. Because the stories involved humans in various situations, this test is often used to assess the so-called "social intelligence." The test requires the individual to evaluate the social relevance of pictured situations, to anticipate the consequences of actions, and to distinguish essential from irrelevant details. This subtest is sometimes considered a measure of planning ability. The defendant obtained his highest score in this test.

Block Design is a measure of the ability to analyse abstract figures visually and construct them from their component parts. It is essentially a measure of ability to handle spatial relationships. The defendant had no difficulties in this test, nor did he reveal difficulties with visual spatial organization.

Digit Symbol requires looking at geometrical symbols placed under one-digit numbers and then copying the codes associated with the number as quickly as possible. This test requires a quick switch of attention and visual-motor speed. The defendant did very well in this test.

Mr Morrison's verbal IQ was found to be 104 and his performance IQ was 108; the overall test IQ was 113. These IQ levels represent a slightly-better-than average level of intellectual functioning. Importantly, there was no mismatch between verbal and performance IQ, a mismatch that often is observed in individuals afflicted with mental disorders.

In the Embedded-Figures Test, Mr Morrison was shown outlines of common figures (such as a house, a knife, a fork, eyeglasses, etc.) superimposed on other outlines. People who suffer from subtle to severe forms of brain damage often fail to identify figures presented in such a fashion. There are four such plates, with ten figures on each plate amounting to 40 outlines. Mr Morrison correctly identified 40 out of the 40 outlines, a perfect score. In addition, there were no anomias (the inability to name a figure one sees; however, the defendant misnamed objects (e.g., a "nail" for a "bolt"). There were no confabulations — an important sign of neurological or psychiatric disorder consisting in making up figures rarely seen by other people. Finally, there were no perseverations.

Mr Morrison was shown cards printed with geometrical designs of various levels of complexity; he was instructed to copy as well as he could. In drawing the figures, the defendant needed to rely on perceptual and motor abilities that are sometimes disrupted due to brain damage. The defendant made some errors in the reproduction of the figures; however, the number and qualitative features of these errors were not sufficient to conclude that the defendant exhibits signs of organicity (e.g., brain damage).

The defendant was asked to read the following:

> Once there lived a king and a queen in a large palace. But the king and queen were not happy. There were no little children in the house or garden. One day they found a poor little boy and girl at the door. They took them into the beautiful palace and made them their own. The king and queen were then happy.

Five minutes later (and after the defendant completed some other psychological tests) he was asked to recall the story. The defendant was able to recall all the key components of the story. When challenged about the factual content of the story, and told that there was only one character (the king) he indicated that he "thought he read that there was a king and a queen." The defendant appeared to have a good recall and did not confabulate, that is, he did not make up events that were not recalled.

In conclusion, there was no information to suggest that the defendant suffered from a significant mental disorder at this time. Individuals who are afflicted by traumatic head injuries sometimes suffer selective loss of memory for events around the times the traumatic episode happened; this memory sometimes is regained, sometimes not. It would be important to know whether the defendant (during his stay at the city hospital) remembered all, or had at least any partial recollection of, these events. Mr Morrison appeared to be an alert, bright, amiable, and cooperative individual who did not appear to suffer any handicap, condition, or disorder likely to interfere with his ability to communicate. However he indicated that he suffered subjective distress as a result of his inability to recall the events surrounding his charges.

EXHIBIT 10.2

Christmas Celebration

Mr Tasso is a 44-year-old Caucasian man with 8th grade education. The neuropsychological evaluation was ordered by the Court as an aid in sentencing.

Mr Tasso was diagnosed as suffering from Alcohol Dependence (severe, self-reportedly in remission; he also met the criteria for Organic Personality Syndrome). This is a persistent personality disturbance, involving: Affective instability, e.g., marked shifts from normal mood to depression, irritability, or anxiety; recurrent outbursts of aggression or rage that were grossly out of proportion to any precipitating psychological stressors; marked impaired social judgment, e.g., events leading to his latest charges; and marked apathy and indifference when sober. The condition was of explosive type; aggression — as a prominent feature — appeared when intoxicated. The defendant (who suffered from mental retardation) had also experienced delirium tremens in the past during these phases of forced alcohol withdrawl.

Physical disorders and conditions were observed or volunteered: Scoliosis (hunched back); a tumor now removed (which in the documentation is described as a "brain tumor the size of a football" but was likely to be a benign tumor the size of a tangerine) was located outside critical brain structures, but probably affecting his sense organs controlling balance on his right side; he was still recovering from the gunshot wound on his lung that he suffered during the events leading to his charges during Chirstmas the year before; his mental retardation may be related to perinatal medical problems (he was told that he was born afflicted with jaundice, with a twin brother; his twin brother died at birth); some early documentation shown by the defendant indicated that he suffered from a "seizure" disorder (self-reported); however, a neurologist was unable to confirm such a diagnosis either clinically or by means of electroencephalographic (EEG) procedures; and the defendant had sex with a female now suspected to suffer from AIDS. Today, he volunteered information to the effect of suffering bouts of diarrhea, weight loss and night chills with profuse sweating. However, the defendant and his brother both said that an HIV test taken six months ago was found to be negative.

Until a few months prior to his latest charges (shooting with a starter's gun at the Empire State Building), the defendant used to befriend a lady who is described as a drug and alcohol abuser; the defendant's brother said that the woman was a "constant source of problems" as they appear to abuse alcohol together (it would appear that the defendant was in her company the night of the events leading to his charges). The defendant had been living with his brother for the last 18 months.

The events leading to his latest charges appear to be a repetition of events which happened in the past events that also led to confrontation with the law. The defendant was evaluated by professionals who specifically recommended attendance to an alcohol rehabilitation program. The defendant went to these programs only as a result of pressure from the court. As soon as the pressure was perceived as subsiding, the defendant discontinued attendance. It was felt that the defendant may repeat such cycle in the future.

According to the background documentation, the offense involves the defendant "standing in the middle of the Empire State Building holding a gun (later found to be a starter pistol)." The defendant accepted the fact that he was returning from a Christmas party and was under the influence of alcohol. The background documentation also indicates that he was ordered to drop the gun, he ignored the command and was shot by the arresting officer.

Mr Tasso was subjected to an extensive neuropsychological evaluation in 1967 after he was arrested for possession of a gun. A medical report written at the time indicated that he had suffered seizures since he was three days old. He was diagnosed as suffering mental retardation when he was ten. At age 16 he was involved in a riot at school, creating extensive damage to the school cafeteria. He is said to have suffered seizures in 1967 while attending a dance. However, reports from a neurological indicate that he suffers from an "idiopathic form" (i.e., cause unknown) of epilepsy and mental retardation. The neurologist made clear that he was highly suspected to be an alcohol abuser (susceptible individuals who are alcohol abusers sometimes develop seizures). At the time, his full IQ was said to be 65. The documentation also indicates that the defendant has been fired from numerous jobs, that he often had little concern for the consequences of his own behavior, and he tended to blame others for his own faults.

There were additional reports from mental health professionals arising from his second apprehension by the police in 1990 for fighting with someone in a bar while intoxicated with alcohol. The defendant indicated that he was referred to an alcohol rehabilitation treatment center and that he relapsed only four days after he discontinued the program. His brother George said that he had relapsed several months later. Both the defendant and his brother indicated that he had been "alcohol free for more than a year;" however, during the events leading to his most recent charges that happened less than two months ago, the defendant was heavily intoxicated by alcohol (the definition of being "alcohol-free" is the proven abstinence from alcohol for a period of at least six months).

Mr Tasso lived with his mother (said to be in the 70s), his brother (aged 38), his sister--in-law, and children from his brother's family. The defendant never married and said that he has no children of his own.

Mr Tasso said he attended a "vocational training program;" in the past, he was employed in menial jobs.

Mr Tasso had been drinking alcohol since he was a teenager. Until a year ago, the defendant used to drink about 24 cans of beer a day. He used to drink about two cans of beer every day before going to work; the defendant became very anxious and restless if alcohol was not avaible. Forced to stay sober while at the hospital for the tumor operation described above, he developed intense delirium tremens in which he saw snakes on the hospital floor. He had surgery only after he was successfully detoxed from alcohol. He denied the use of illegal drugs.

Mr Tasso was a sickly appearing individual (5'6." 150 lbs) who appeared to be much older than his chronological age. Mr Tasso came to the evaluative interview and testing accompanied by his brother George. During the evaluative interview and testing the defendant was calm and cooperative and slightly apathetic. His affect (the range of his feelings) appeared to be narrow. The structure and content of his speech was that of a poorly educated individual; his eye contact was adequate.

A screening battery of probes (including examination of posture, gait, whole-body balance, muscle strength, tremor at rest, intentional tremor, motor coordination, general appearance of the eyes, eye movements, and reaction of the eyes to light) was performed and the following were noted: The defendant tended to fall to the right on a balance test (this is a consistent with the existence of a tumor affecting his balance sense organs in the past); the coordination of intended movements was poor. The defendant had scars in both hands resulting from punching a glass window while incarcerated in 1967.

From an extensive checklist of signs and/or symptoms possibly indicative of neurological or mental disorders, Mr Tasso was asked whether he had ever experienced them, and if so, to give examples. The following was volunteered: Headaches; tiredness; dizziness; concentration difficulties; forgetfulness (when employed as a kitchen helper, he needed to be reminded constantly about where things were); lack of sense of humor (he often did not understand the jokes from people of his own age and background, a probable indication of concrete mode of thinking); irritability (particularly when intoxicated with alcohol); and insomnia. Visual hallucinations (related to alcohol withdrawal) were present in the past.

The defendant gambled at horse racing in the past; sometimes he would lose up to $200 on bets, a significant amount for an individual who did not work.

Individual items of Wechsler Adult Intelligence Scale Revised (WAIS-R) were administered: Information, Digit Span, Similarities, Picture Completion, Block Design and Digit Symbol. His verbal IQ was estimated to be about 65 (mild form of mental retardation) and his performance IQ about 92 (dull normal). There was a mismatch of close to 30 points between his verbal and performance IQ; this is consistent with a severe handicap in verbal abilities and communication. The defendant showed a significant improvement in performance skills over the past 14 years; IQ tests performed in 1968 revealed a subnormal level of performance as well. This may be related to the stated claim that he has diminished his alcohol intake in the recent past.

As indicated above, Mr Tasso suffered from an organic personality disorder (which is likely to be related to his long history of alcohol abuse) and a congenital form of mental retardation. It was felt that if the defendant was placed on probation, he should attend an alcohol rehabilitation program where he first become alcohol free and then rehabilitated. The defendant had failed previous attempts in his alcohol rehabilitation; although he said that he had not drunk alcohol in the past year, it is clear that the events leading to his latest charges at Chistmas time last year were alcohol related. These failures mean that the defendant was likely to suffer future relapses, hence the need of a carefully supervised program where his alcohol abuse (and medical conditions) could also be adequately evaluated and monitored. The facility that he was currently attending did not require him to undergo urine, blood, or breath analysis.

☐ QUESTIONS FOR REVIEW AND DISCUSSION

△ Name liver, kidney, lung diseases that affect brain functions and — as a result — behavior and neuropsychological functioning.

△ Most of us think of crimes as that of comission (that is, when during the events leading to the defendant's charges, he or she did something that is punishable by the law). Name neuropsychological disoders that often lead to behaviors in which the defendant does *not* do something, which failure to perform leads to confrontation to the law (crimes of omission).

△ Identify psychological tests to assess short-term and long-term memory; discuss the strengths and limitations of these tests to assess memory for forensic purposes.

△ Discuss the pro's and con's of hypnotism as a tool to search an individual's forgotten memories for legal purposes.

△ Discuss the difference between delirium and delusions.

△ You are involved in the court evaluation of a male suffering from an organic delusional disorder caused by chronic alcoholism. The defendant's dominant delusional theme is that his wife is having an affair with another man, and he has assaulted his wife on several occasions. The man has again violated his probation by beating his wife close to death. The parolee has not complied with psychiatric treatment referral. Discuss and justify your recommendations.

11: BRAIN DISORDERS OTHER THAN TRAUMA

THERE ARE MANY OTHER BRAIN DISEASES THAT CAN CAUSE NEUROPSYCHOLOGI-cal dysfunction that are the focus of a forensic neuropsychological evaluation. These include:

- ☐ Metabolic disorders affecting brain and neuropsychological dysfunction
- ☐ Epilepsy
- ☐ Brain tumors
- ☐ Other disorders

Metabolic Disorders Causing Neuropsychological Dysfunction

Clinical neuropsychologists recognize alterations of nervous system function that are caused by conditions, disorders, or diseases affecting organs systems other than the nervous system. Mental health workers who work in hospital emergency rooms and/or detention centers have numerous opportunities to observe the manifestations of these disorders causing acute forms of encephalopathy (a name that applies to any disease of the brain). Forensic neuropsychologists sometimes need to review this information when performing a forensic neuropsychological investigation. Most forensic neuropsychologists who work at court clinics examine defendants during the chronic phase of the brain disorder; this is sometimes days, weeks, months, and even years after the onset of the brain pathological process that causes neuropsychological dysfunction. The following are examples:

- ☐ Myocardial infarction (death of heart tissue because of poor blood irrigation, e.g., artherosclerosis)
- ☐ Cardiac arrest, that can have multiple causes
- ☐ Conditions affecting adequate blood supply to the brain
- ☐ Suffocation or drowining, strangulation, aspiration of vomitus, compression of the trachea or a foreign body in the trachea
- ☐ Diseases that paralyse the muscles involved in respiration
- ☐ Carbon monoxide poisoning

There are numerous other encephalopathies associated with dysfunction of the kidney (e.g., uremic encephalopathy), liver (e.g., chronic hepatic encephalopathy), and others that are caused by electrolyte and endocrine dysfunction. In individuals whose medical history is unknown, some of these conditions may be erroneously diagnosed as clinical manifestations of dementia (e.g., AIDS dementia, to be discussed in Chapter 14).

At the time the individual suffers the acute manifestations of encephalopathy, the clinical evaluation is often very limited. At the bedside, many of the probes to evaluate stages of consciousness may be applied. If the individual is fully conscious, one often needs to ascertain whether he or she is oriented in person, place, and time. Sometimes, during the early phases of recovery, a mini mental state evaluation can be performed. Cooperation in performing more comprehensive neuropsychological testing during the early phase of recovery is often minimal.

It has long been known that the prognosis of the chronic sequelae of these acquired disorders depends primarily on the duration of the acute clinical manifestations of the disorder and the coma that often ensues. In most cases, these conditions are reversible, leaving no apparent signs of brain disorders. Most neuropsychologists attach prognostic significance to coma resulting from encephalopathy that last more than 48 hours. However, there are numerous other factors that are taken into account in evaluating the prognosis of recovery; these include the individual's age, his or her premorbid level of intellectual funtioning, and (most importantly) the motivation to recover. For example, inmates who are chronic drug abusers, who also suffer from terminal stages of AIDS, and who at the same time are held in detention centers often lack such motivation. One needs to be reminded once again that defendants who are examined at the clinic often suffer from numerous coexisting medical, neuro-psychological, personal, and legal problems making the prediction of probable outcome very difficult.

There are numerous legal implications related to the evaluation of chronic manifestations of the encephalopathies resulting from these acute disorders. The vast majority of these evaluations are performed on defendants at various stages of their legal proceedings. However, a neuropsychological evaluation may need to be performed on the the living victim of a violent crime or on a witness to a crime when the conflicting parties need to ascertain his or her reliability.

Sometimes the defendant charged with a crime has been evaluated as having apparently been in a sound state of mind at the time of the events leading to his or her charges. However, myocardial infarction, cardiac arrest, attempted suicides, violent attacks from inmates while the defendant is held in detention centers; diseases contracted while the defendant awaits a court appearance may occur after the events that led to the charges. The counsel for the defense sometimes is highly motivated to show that the neuropsychological conditions that the defendant is suffering today are the same as those during his or her involvement in the events leading to the charges.

The opposite can also be true: A defendant who, during the events leading to his or her charges were experiencing an agitated state associated with acute encephalopathy, may experience total recovery and sometimes it is difficult to perceive that the individual who is described in the basic documentation is the same as the one being interviewed today.

Epilepsy

Epilepsy, or epileptic disorder, refers to a chronic condition characterized by recurrent seizures. A seizure is a transient and paroxismal disturbance of cerebral functions caused by excessive discharge of cortical neurons. It has long been recognized that the clinical manifestations of the seizure depend on the site and the pattern of spread of the electrical discharges in the brain.

Epidemiologic studies have shown that epileptic disorders afflict about one percent of the general population and that as many as 30 to 50 percent of such individuals are afflicted with neuropsychological disorders. Research in which the link between epilepsy and criminal behavior were said to to be established (popular in the 1950s and 1960s) in most cases were performed on single cases or cluster of cases observed in clinical conditions. There has never been a large-scale, scientifically-sound epidemiologic study to support such a link, however.

A classification system of epilepsy that has remained relatively stable over the years makes the distinction between partial seizures (involving localized portions of the brain) and generalized seizures.

A discussion of the clinical manifestation of epilepsy likely to be the focus of a forensic neuropsychological evaluations needs to concentrate on the following:

- ☐ The *ictus* (the convulsion) itself

- ☐ Psychological and behavioral changes that sometimes occur before the convulsion (the *preictal stage*)

- ☐ Psychological and behavioral changes that sometimes occur after the convulsion (the *postictal stage*)

- ☐ To facilitate the review of clinical manifestations of seizure, the preictal, ictal and postictal stages will be collectively called *periictal changes* (that is, clinical changes around the time a seizure disorder occurs)

☐ Psychological and behavioral changes that occur between epileptic seizures (the *interictal* manifestations)

The preictal manifestation of the seizure is called aura. These include:

☐ Autonomic sensations such as fullness in the stomach, blushing, changes in respiration.

☐ Sensation of *dejà vu,* forced thinking or dreamy states

☐ Affective states (fear, panic, depression, elation)

☐ Automatisms (lip smacking, rubbing, chewing).

Family members often recognize the imminency of a seizure by noting the presence of any of these preictal manifestations that are often characteristic in certain individuals.

The clinical manifestations of generalized seizures (the ictus) primarily involve the convulsion. When the differential diagnosis between neurological and psychiatric conditions needs to be made (or when malingering is suspected), the forensic neuropsychologist needs to rely on known features of psychiatric manifestations that may resemble seizure disorders. The clinical features of epileptic seizures usually involve the occurrence of nocturnal seizure, the presence of sterotyped aura (visual, auditory and sometimes olfactory hallucinations that occur before the convulsion), body movements, cyanotic skin changes (the individual looks "blue"), self-injury resulting from a fall or tongue biting, incontinence, and postictal confusion. Individuals who suffer impulse control disorders or other conditions that family members often described as "seizure" may involve none or few of the above. The postictal stage is characterized by a gradual recovery of consciousness and cognitive function within minutes or hours after the epileptic seizure.

A condition called *status epilepticus* is sometimes invoked in defendants charged with violent crimes. This is a clinical condition characterized by the presence of electrical correlates of the seizure although without body movements.

The clinical manifestations of epilepsy, the recommendation for electrophysiological procedures to observed EEG abnormalities supporting the diagnosis of seizure disorder and treatment is the province of the clinical neurologist. The clinical neuropsychologist is primarily concerned with the characterization of cognitive function and personality disorders that occur as part of the interictal manifestation of a seizure disorder. It is not uncommon for experienced neuropsychologists to witness an attack of petit mal (characterized by brief disruption of consciousness without convulsion) during the course of test administration. A defendant may malinger such episodes. The role of the forensic neuropsychologist is not only to have an opinion on such malingered conditions but also to establish or negate links between seizure disorders and offenses. As indicated above, with the increasing sophistication of the lay public in the recognition of mental disorders, the vision of somebody acting as a robot in status epilepticus when killing somebody is not likely to fare well in the court.

Brain Tumors

Brain tumors are often invoked as an explanation of criminal behavior. Some media versions of crimes committed by individuals afflicted by brain tumors are described as if brain tumors acted as an homunculus (a little man) controlling the behavior of a sick individual. It is as if "the brain tumor made that man kill." This contention is supported by high-profile criminal cases in which the connection appears to be accurate and suggests that may be a causal connection. A forensic neuropsychologist may be called upon to express an opinion on the possible links between the presence of tumors and criminal behavior.

It is generally estimated that 1-2% of the general population suffer and die from brain tumors. Although these are called "brain tumors," few originate in the brain tissue itself. For example, glial tumors originate from glial cells, traditionally considered "supportive" tissue, although the glia may have more important functional properties than suspected, rather than from neurons.

Most brain tumors may involve tissues that originate in the membranes covering the brain (meningiomas originating in the meninges) or cerebral metastasis of tumors that originate in some other organ system. In Chapter 14 in which the neuropsychological manifestations of Acquired Immune Deficiency Syndrome (AIDS) are discussed, we will mention neoplasms (tumors) that cause an organic mental disorder linked to this syndrome.

Asssuming that all tumors, regardless of their sites and tissue composition, can cause similar behavioral effects, three stages of clinical, behavioral, and psychological manifestations can be recognized.

☐ The *asymptomatic stage*, in which the tumor does not cause any symptoms. The presence of a brain tumor may be found at autopsy after the individual has died, or is discovered by accident when he or she undergoes a medical examination for reasons other than behavioral or psychological problems. An early symptom is an epileptic seizure; focal seizures (originating in electrical storms in well-defined areas of the brain that cause specific groups of muscles to contract) in individuals with no history of seizure disorders are sometimes present. The afflicted individual may show subtle (subclinical) behavioral and psychological manifestations leading to confrontation with the law. Abrupt assaultive behavior (in individuals with no history of impulse control disorder or antisocial personality traits) has been described in the literature; some of these cases have been successfully argued in court in favor of a mitigating circumstance or diminished criminal responsibility. This phase (unless associated with gross neurological manifestations or seizures) rarely is referred for medical attention; members of the family often rationalize such behavior as temporary "mood changes." Some are interpreted as purely psychological in nature and are referred to a clinical psychologist. Although many textbooks perpetuate the description of cases in which someone who has suffered a brain tumor has been treated by means of psychotherapy, most contemporary clinical psychologists are well prepared to recognize signs and symptoms of "organicity" through clinical interviews or psychological testing. Many neurological signs and symptoms may later be clinically recognized. These include weakness, sensory disturbances (some of which can be of sudden onset), disturbances of visual fields leading to a condition called hemianopsia, paralysis of cranial (motor) nerves, such as the facial nerves, speech loss, motor incoordination, and many others.

☐ The *intermediate stage* is characterized by recurrent and more frequently-paced focal epileptic seizures and neurological signs and symptoms that are caused by the pressure of the tumor(s) on adjacent brain structures. At this stage, classical manifestations of frontal, temporal, occipital, parietal lobe disorders or disorders of the hypothalamic and lymbic structures may be recognized. Well localized headaches are common. The defendant may have already seen a clinical neurologist who is able to make the diagnosis of brain tumor with the aid of state-of-the-art imaging procedures such as the CT (Computerized Tomography) or MRI (Magnetic Resonance Imaging). "Brain tumors" some of which are found to be meningiomas may be removed without perceptible loss of cognitive function or changes in personality or behavior. Defendants seen at forensic clinics, who are poor and uneducated, and sometimes homeless, may be suffering behavioral manifestations that are characteristic of advanced clinical stages of brain dysfunction highly suspected to be caused by brain tumors, without ever having seen a physician (street friends suspect that his or her behavior was caused by drug abuse). At this stage, afflicted individuals may become violent, suffering from numerous confrontations with the law. Individuals who are in detection centers waiting for court procedures, are often transferred from facility to facility as they become unmanageable; some may be treated as suffering from mental disorders and given inappropriate medication. Occasionally, this is a stage when an uneducated defendant tries to theatrically malinger, but this requires good knowledge of neurology, and sustained good acting since defendants are being watched by literally dozens of individuals over the course of many days.

☐ The *final or terminal stage* is characterized by the presence of physical signs and symptoms of raised intracranial pressure: Changes in the appeareance of the retina as examined by means of an ophthalmoscope (e.g., papilledema), excruciating headaches, vomiting, clouding of consciousness, coma, and death. Some violent individuals in detention centers may commit suicide at this stage; some are killed by other inmates.

With the advent of advanced imaging procedures, the role of the clinical neuropsychologist in recognizing the psychological changes caused by tumors has greatly increased: The neuropsychologist is sometimes able to recognize subtle changes in perceptual or cognitive function and can identify personality traits caused by brain tumors complementing the wealth of information obtained from modern, powerful imaging procedures. A clinical neuropsychologist is especially trained to recognize signs and symptoms associated with brain tumors and some tests that can result in a differential diagnosis between psychiatric and organic disoders.

However, forensic experts are called upon to offer opinions linking criminal events or tortious acts and neuropsychological dysfunctions.

- ☐ A neuropsychologist is called upon to express an opinion on the possible links between the presence of tumors and criminal behavior.

- ☐ A forensic occupational physican may be called upon to testify as to whether a brain tumor was likely to be caused by occupational exposure to environmental toxic agents (e.g., hydrocarbons), the plaintiff may undego a comprehensive neuropsychological evaluation in preparation for a court appearance in which compensation is sought.

☐ **EXHIBIT 11.1**

A Man Who Did Not Know Where Babies Came From

This was a pre-pleading investigation. Mr Francois, who met the criteria for Organic Personality Syndrome, was a 31-year-old Black man with an unknown level of education. The defendant exhibited a persistent lifelong personality disturbance involving the following: Affective instability, e.g., marked shifts from normal mood to depression, to apparent sexual excitement; marked impaired social judgment, e.g., sexual misconduct; and suspiciousness.

Epilepsy was suspected to be the cause of such a syndrome. This mental disorder was considered to be of explosive type, and the episodes of sexual abuse might have been the expression of impulsivity (but not of epilepsy per se).

The defendant appeared to suffer from a seizure disorder and stuttering since the age of three. Both his organic personality disorder and severe stuttering appeared to be chronic. The defendant's parents were said to be loving ones. There were no acute events or enduring circumstances that could be related to the diagnosed personality disorder.

The defendant appeared to suffer problems with his social and occupational life. However, he appeared to be at a loss to explain exactly what he did at work, at a branch of the an agency that transferred money abroad owned by his parents. He appeared to have tried to hide his skills, as this revelation may imply that he was not as unable of managing his own affairs as otherwise would be implied. Formal testing revealed an individual who was functioning at a mild level of mental retardation; however, it was not clear that the defendant was not malingering (attempting not to do his best).

The defendant suffered from stuttering that severely impaired his communication abilities. The defendant claimed he could not speak English although he was talking to a woman in English as he waited to be interviewed. The defendant said he could speak Creole and read computer-based messages in French, (the language used during monetary transactions at the office where he worked).

It was felt that the diagnosis of organic personality disorder had a poor prognosis as it implied personality traits that had been shaped by abnormal brain functioning.

Although seizures were for the most part prevented by medication, the defendant had restricted options in occupational and family matters.

It was felt that any prospect of his social rehabilitation was guarded as Mr Francois denied that the charges took place in the manner the background documentation describes (e.g., feeling the breasts of as many as seven women at a subway exit in Manhattan around 14th street). Therefore, it could not be said that the defendant had reflected on the events that led to his charges or that he had come to terms with the consequences of his behavior. For the most part the defendant was highly motivated to project the image that he was mentally incapacitated on account of his illness (the defendant understood the consequences of being found mentally incompetent to face the legal proceedings against him).

An early attempt at evaluation was interrupted when he said that he could not respond to the questions because he did not understand English. Mr Francois was interviewed on two sessions afterwards. The interview and testing were performed in Creole with the aid of an interpreter.

The quality of information was poor. At times, the defendant appeared to be malingering; he was suspicious and paid unusual attention to the notes that I was taking. He dwelled excessively on the instructions given at the beginning of testing, that this was a report written for the Judge in charge of his case. After he finished drawing a geometrical picture from one of the tests (whose quality was particularly poor), the defendant asked "Is that going to be seen by the Judge too?"

When Mr Francois was a child in Haiti, he appears to have had limited contact with other children and normal play as a result of his illness. He said that he had an abcess on his left nipple "four years before today" (an expression that reveals memory or calculation problems), that required daily drainage; scar on his chest was noted.

According to the background documentation, the defendant had suffered from seizures since he was three years old. Mr Francois appeared to have lived a very isolated life, overprotected by his parents. His parents seemed to link his stuttering to the onset of seizures. The defendant was once medicated with Dilantin (an anticonvulsant). He is now taking Tegretol 200 mg a day. (The defendant was asked to write the name of his medication on a the form for the neuropsychological evaluation; the defendant's lawyer called the evaluator's office to ask what kind of paper the defendant was asked to sign; obviously either the defendant himself or his parents misinterpreted this event.) The defendant was then seeing a psychiatrist for his seizures.

The last seizure attack (which happened mostly at night when he was sleeping) occurred about three months ago. When that happened, his parents rushed to his bedroom and often found him with his jaw locked, his mouth foaming and his eyes rolled in. This description suggests generalized convulsions. This is said to be the defendant's first and only arrest.

Mr Francois was born in Haiti and came to the USA with his family a few years back. Asked twice on different days, he did not remember the level of schooling obtained while in Haiti (he did remember that courses were given in French). The defendant received a diploma from a New York City school for handicapped children in 1980. Courses were given in English and emphasized, in his case, speech education.

Mr Francois said that he worked for his father at the money-transfer agency owned by his father. He said that he did "research work" there, receiving phone calls from clients who wish to travel to Haiti and others who want to make money transactions to that country. He said that "he watches the computers (in French) until there was an indication that the transfer of money has been successfully completed." At times, he also stuffed envelopes.

Mr Francois denied alcohol and/or illegal drug use. The defendant denied that he was under the influence of alcohol and/or drugs the day the events leading to his charges took place.

Because of the nature of the charges, Mr Francois' sexual development was explored. The defendant said that he became aware about the "differences between boys and girls" at the age of 17. The defendant said that he never masturbated and that he never had a sexual contact with anybody (either a woman or a man). The defendant said that he sometimes had erections but he did not do anything about them. He said that he has never tried to have sex with a woman because it is "too complicated;" he added "the simpler you keep things, the better." He only recently entered a store where they had "dirty pictures" and looked at one of the magazines. The defendant said that he "did not know where babies come from;" he said his mother never told him and he never had the curiosity to ask. Asked whether he would have a family and perhaps children one day, he said that he would. Question: "How could you get children if you just told me you dont know where babies come from?." Answer: "I will adopt them." The defendant is aware that he has been charged with feeling the breast of a woman; he said that he was walking on the street with his arms crossed over his chest, as he normally did whenever he is on the streets, and he accidentally touched the woman and that he tried to apologize to the woman. However, the background documentation indicated that several women were involved.

☐ **QUESTIONS FOR REVIEW AND FURTHER DISCUSSION**

Δ   This report is read by the defense counsel and by the counsel for the District Attorney. In this report, what statements are consistent with the presence of a mental disorder and/or other handicapping conditions? What statements support the view that Mr Francois is a functional individual?

Δ   Is Mr Francois at age 31 discovering sex?

Δ   Discuss the Klüver-Bucy syndrome as it pertains to this case.

12: TRAUMATIC BRAIN DISORDERS

THERE ARE MANY BRAIN DISORDERS RESULTING FROM TRAUMATIC CONDITIONS causing neuropsychological dysfunction that are the focus of a forensic neuro-psychological investigation. However, the context when and where these traumatic events occur is crucial.

BRAIN TRAUMA IN CIVIL AND CRIMINAL LAW CASES

Although often the focus of a criminal offense, the neuropsychological evaluation of traumatic brain disorder is also often of paramount importance in civil (tort) law in cases of head injuries resulting from preventable vehicular or workplace accidents or medical malpractice. The DSM-IV does not contain specific diagnostic categories for these conditions.

The forensic neuropsychologist who handles civil cases and who is likely to see these brain disorders as disabling conditions resulting from vehicular or workplace (industrial as well as farm) accidents sees brain disorders from a different perspective from that of the neuropsychologist who needs to evaluate criminal cases. In the latter case one sees defendants afflicted by brain disorders where the claim is made the brain disorder negates or reduces criminal responsibility. The causes of some traumatic brain disorders may be quite different in the criminal cases from tort cases (e.g., assaultive acts, being shot during the course of robbery and sometimes the result of force used by law enforcing agents during the suspect's apprehension). There are accidents as well. Neuropsychologists who work in civil (tort) law and those who work in criminal law sometimes need to conduct different lines of reasoning.

☐ A neuropsychologist who needs to evaluate the potentially long-lasting consequences of head injuries for the plaintiff (the victim of the accident) may unintentionally lower the threshold for concluding that head injury indeed was caused by the car accident where the defendant was driving recklessly. The neuropsychologist argues the point that the "minor" head injury (that is, an injury not necessarily associated with loss of consciousness or memory) resulted in subtle personality changes that only close relatives can detect.

☐ The neuropsychologist who works for the defendant (the individual allegedly responsible for the accident) may argue the point that the relatives (his wife, his children) are biased in favor of detecting personality changes and that these "changes" are only subjective impressions of people who have normal family problems. Reports may contain the defendant's wife statements to the effect that "we have been married for 30 years; my husband was a nice person before the accident, and now, after the accident, we cannot get along any more; he is not the person he used to be." However, no data obtained by means of objective procedures (CT scans, electrophysiological procedures, psychometric testing, etc.) support the claim that there is something wrong with the plaintiff.

In civil law, sometimes one of the most important issues is compensation: If the wife's contention turns out to be true, how does one establish guidelines for a fair compensation? In criminal proceedings, however, the possibility of malingering — or just the reflection of the fact that people make untruthful statements because they fear for their lives — cannot be ruled out entirely. What of the hypothetical woman who turns out to be the wife of a mob criminal?

How can these "close relatives" or "close acquaintances" be believed or trusted?

Neuropsychologists on opposite sides of an argument in a criminal case face important dilemmas. A 72-year-old man — a known figure of the mob with a long criminal history who is now charged with yet another murder — claims that he cannot remember the events leading to his charges. A neuropsychologist acting for the defense explains that the defendant suffers from an organic amnestic disorder as a result of a cardiovascular accident two years ago.

A neurologist acting for the prosecution, after reviewing medical records, concludes that the defendant indeed suffered a cardiovascular accident; a neuropsychologist, also acting for the prosecution, reviews old original data from testing performed at the hospital, and after comparing the results with recent testing, fails to find a significant impairment in short-term or long-term memory for an individual of his age, background and education. Malingering is suspected because the defendant has a motive for not remembering (the possibility of being incarcerated for the rest of his life).

The forensic neuropsychologist is likely to play a larger role in charges dealing with civil cases established for the rehabilitation involving centers for the head injured. On March 16, 1992 the *New York Times* published an article in which agencies organized for this purpose promised near-impossible cures, then neglected patients or discharged them once the insurance coverage ran out. Although the article refers to new investigations in the area of brain-damage rehabilitation, it also referred to allegations about for-profit psychiatric hospitals and the filing of false medical claims under workers' compensation programs.

"Accidents" and Antisocial Personality Disorder

In a forensic neuropsychological evaluation, the notion of "accident" in someone suspected to be afflicted by Antisocial Personality Disorder is often different from the notion of "accident" in people not so afflicted. An alert mental health worker always asks the circumstances under which the "accident" happened.

As reported by the defendant, often there are many surprises. For example:

☐ The defendant may tell you that he and a friend were playing with a loaded gun and another boy was killed when the gun "accidentally" fired (note the "gun" killed the boy, not "the defendant" or "the defendant's friend").

☐ The boy suffered a "brain injury" when crossing the street and was "accidentally" hit by a car; the defendant pictures himself as a victim of circumstances — perhaps being run over by a drunken driver; the boy later indicates that he was being chased by somebody with whom he was arguing and he crossed the street at night in the middle of two cars; the reason for the argument is not revealed.

- ☐ A man "accidentally" bumped the lamp during the course of an epileptic seizure (the epileptic seizure was later found to have be triggered by crack; someone died in the house during the incident and the defendant is being charged with manslaughter).
- ☐ Two school girls ride the subway together; the defendant tells you that she was only asking to "hold" her friend's gold ring; the victim refused and she was "accidentally" cut in the struggle.
- ☐ A prison inmate suspect in the killing of a policeman may tell you "I was in the wrong place at the wrong time and a cop was hurt by accident."

Many epidemiologic studies and my own clinical experience in a court clinic support the view that a large percentage of inmates report a history of head trauma and traumatic brain injuries. If these statistics are not analyzed critically they may lead to wrong conclusions.

- ☐ First, it is generally reported that at least 20% and as much as 80% of prison populations involve individuals who also suffer from Antisocial Personality Disorder. It is part of the personality of such individuals thus afflicted to have a need for rationalization of their behavior; a history of head trauma — however minor — appears to fulfill such a basic need. The thought appears to be "I was a good person, then 'things became different' (which means, 'I became a bad person') when I was injured in my head."
- ☐ Second, it is common that people afflicted with congenital mental retardation repeat mythical stories told by their parents: "My child was OK until he fell from the bed as a child." Under these circumstances, the family finds a socially acceptable justification for the child's inadequacies. "My husband and I have 'good blood;' it was the accident that caused our boy to be slow."

TRAUMATIC BRAIN DISORDERS

The most frequent brain traumata, the etiology of which is typically accident or injury, are these:

- ☐ Minor head trauma
- ☐ Cerebral concussion
- ☐ Cerebral contusion
- ☐ Cerebral compression
- ☐ Severe traumatic brain damage
- ☐ Post-traumatic epilepsy

Minor Head Trauma

Traditional criteria for minor head trauma have been developed by neurologists and neurosurgeons. Behavioral and psychological sequelae of minor brain traumata are thus often evaluated by clinical probes and simple commands such as opening of the eyes, asking his or her personal name, or probes aiming to ascertain whether the patient is oriented in space, time and person. A paramedic at the site of a car accident may perform such simple probes. At the bedside, a clinical neurologist may choose to use the Glasgow Coma Scale, or GCS (Teasdale and Jennet, 1974).

The duration of the post-traumatic amnesia (PTA) often gives an indication of the severity of the head trauma for "normal" individuals with no prior history of mental disorders. The neuropsychologist is often called upon to evaluate the long-lasting consequences of such "minor injuries." Sbordone (1991) refers to the useful criteria of comparing self-reporting complaints with those of a family member, relatives, or individuals close to the injured person. Obviously, the latter criteria applies to "normal" individuals who have "functional" families. A homeless individual who reports a head injury, is suspected of being an alcoholic, and who is charged with a crime, typically has nobody to speak on her or his behalf.

The loss of memory may extend to events that may have occurred before the brain trauma; this is called retrograde amnesia. For example, a defendant who was charged with a crime (e.g., manslaughter) may claim that he does remember the events prior to the shooting where he himself sustained a brain injury. For someone with a long history of criminal behavior, who is facing life in prison, the possibility of malingering retrograde amnesia is substantial.

Cerebral Concussion

Neuropsychologists who work in criminal cases describe a concussion as a violent shaking or jarring of the brain, such as one resulting from a blow or shaking or a bullet that hits the skull without penetrating it. Neuropsychologists who work in civil cases (often evaluating victims of car accidents) tend to think of a concussion as a brain injury resulting from a rapid acceleration (such as caused by someone hit from behind the car), or rapid deacceleration (such as caused by a car hitting a tree). The physical forces that cause concussion, contusion, or traumatic brain damage (and sometimes post-traumatic epilepsy) will be assumed to be basically the same and will not be elaborated further. Concussion is a common form of mild brain injury often involving brief loss of conciousness. Hypersensitivity to bright light (photophobia) or to loud sounds is a common symptom in individuals who have recently suffered a brain concussion.

Neuropsychologists often describe a "post-concussive syndrome," characterized by somatic (fatigue, excessive need for sleep), cognitive (lack of concentration, concrete mode of thinking), and personality changes (irritability, low tolerance for frustration, intrusive recollection of the traumatic events that caused brain concussion). Most of these somatic, cognitive and personality changes are observed by clinical interviews requiring simple probes; but standardized tests such as Wechsler Adult Intelligence Scale, revised edition (WAIS-R) are often very appropriate to tap the integrity of these functions. In criminal cases in which one often required the examination of people afflicted by various degrees of mental retardation who later suffer from traumatic brain disorders, these probes may be misleading and there is the danger of linking low level mental functioning to the "brain injury."

Cerebral Contusion

This is a bruise of the surface of the brain with extravasation of blood (from broken blood vessels to brain tissue) but without rupture of the membranes (the pia-arachnoid membranes) that normally protect the brain. Neuropsychologists who routinely evaluate victims of car accidents often see three common conditions:

☐ Frontal lobe damage that results from front car collisions

☐ Occipital lobe damage (sometimes with loss of smell, because of rupture of the olfactory nerve as the brain mass is suddenly pulled backwards) resulting from a rear collision

☐ Damage to other portions of the cerebral cortex such as the temporal and parietal lobes.

Needless to say, for a neuropsychologist who works at detention centers or courts, and who often needs to evaluate victims of violence, the anatomical sites are less predictable. Brain imaging sometimes allows early objective verification of the brain contusion which is coincidental with a myriad of neuropsychological dysfunctions whose severity depends on the location, the extent and the severity of brain trauma. Days, weeks, and even months after brain trauma, the afflicted individual may suffer from lingering clinical neurological signs and symptoms. The unique contribution of clinical neuropsychologists is, in such cases, the demonstration of chronic but subclinic long-lasting post-traumatic neuropsychological changes.

Cerebral Compression

Cerebral compression occurs when the head injury is followed by intracraneal hemorrhage which may may be either epidural (or extradural), subdural, or intracerebral.

Severe Traumatic Brain Damage

As indicated above, the vast majority of head injuries that are the focus of a neuropsychological forensic investigation in civil law result from vehicular and workplace accidents. Hundreds of thousands of individuals are brought to hospitals every year; thousands become the focus of civil law investigations requiring the evalution of a neuropsychologist.

The neuropsychologist working in criminal courts is likely to see traumatic head injuries as a result of violence. Penetrating missile head injuries are not infrequent and many defendants indicate that they still have a bullet lodged in the brain. During a violent act (as a result of the defendant's being assaulted) the brain may be extensively damaged without skull fracture. It is also possible that the skull may be fractured without brain damage. The clinical neuropsychologist is also trained to recognize that some brain injuries may occur as a result of infections that may cause meningitis or intracranial abscess.

The role of the clinical neuropsychologist in the evaluation of the sequelae of severe brain damage is significant. As the defendant recovers from his injuries, the neuropsychologist may be called in to follow the recovery of cognitive function associated with such a recovery. A clinical neuropsychologist may be involved in the cognitive rehabilitation of victims of a serious crime who have suffered extensive brain damage. During the long, personal contact between the defendant and therapist, the defendant may volunteer information about the circumstances of the criminal events that later may be denied in court. The mental health worker who works at detention centers and who has the opportunity of listening to such recollection of events may hear them but may choose not to write them down. (The mental health worker discovers early in the communication with a defendant that inmates do not trust a mental health professional who takes too many notes.)

"Brain death" resulting from severe brain injury is a matter that surfaces many times as an ethical issue. Today, medical technology allows the support almost indefinitely of the life of an individual who suffers from brain death. A defendant may be involved in events in which the victim has suffered brain injury that is the cause of "brain death." While the victim is alive, he or she may be charged with assault; the defendant, therefore, may have a vested interest in having the victim declared "alive," but, if the victim is "dead," the charge can change to manslaugther or even murder.

Post-Traumatic Epilepsy

In the last chapter, epilepsy or epileptic disorder was defined as a chronic condition characterized by recurrent seizures. A seizure is a transient and paroxismal disturbance of cerebral functions caused by excessive discharge of cortical neurons. It has also been noted that the clinical manifestations of the seizure depend on the site and the pattern of spread of the electrical discharges in the brain. In the last chapter, we also referred to idiopathic epilepsy, that is, that caused by inherited mechanisms that causes a propensity to low seizure thresholds.

Partial and generalized epileptic seizures may appear after a traumatic head injury.

☐ A neuropsychologist who handles civil cases may be involved in the extent to which a victim of a car accident may be suffering a disabling condition, perhaps for life; this assessment is crucial in cases where the victim seeks compensation.

☐ The neuropsychologist who works in court sometimes is asked to form an opinion whether epileptic seizures now being suffered by the victim of a violent assault are likely to be linked to the events leading to the defendant's charges.

☐ In certain cases, the defendant may claim that the events leading to his charges were the direct result of a post-traumatic epilepsy resulting from brain injuries received when he was a child.

☐ A post-traumatic epilepsy often needs to be differentiated from other conditions that may cause a lowering of a threshold for a seizure to occur, such as cocaine, amphetamines, and alcohol.

☐ QUESTIONS FOR REVIEW AND FURTHER DISCUSSION

Δ One plaintiff who after a comprehensive neuropsychological evaluation has been found to be severely disabled is shown playing golf in a videotape taken by the detectives hired by the defense. Discuss the merits of clinical and field settings in determination of disability.

Δ The mother of a client being seen at a hospital clinic asks the therapist for "a big favor"; she asks the therapist whether she can have another "letter like this." The letter shown to the therapist reads: "To whom it may concern: This is to indicate that Mr Hernandez suffers from a disabling mental disorder that requires 24-hour attention." The letter is signed by a social worker who is not the patient's primary therapist; the social worker has not visited the client at his home. The client's mother has been successfully avoiding vocational training (and eventual job placement that would remove her from welfare) because of similar letters that she was able to obtain in the past. The primary therapist refuses to write such a letter; however, another social worker writes another letter. These letters are not part of the patient's charts. Discuss the multiple ethical, legal, and social ramifications of this case.

13: DEMENTIAS

WE NEED TO DIFFERENTIATE BETWEEN CHRONOLOGICAL AGE (I.E., THE AGE THE calendar says we are) and functional age (i.e., the age indicated by the appearance and performance of our various physiological systems). Chronological age is not a predictor of functional age; that is, people of the same chronological age may have marked differences in cognition and affect. Recent epidemiologic studies have shattered many preconceptions of how aging individuals feel, think, and behave. True, our swimming abilities reach their peak in the late teens and go downhill after that. However, verbal abilities remain unchanged and (depending on how we collect data) may even improve throughout life.

Decline in neuropsychological functioning with normal aging may be an artifact of epidemiologic study design. Forensic neuropsychologists (particularly those involved in class actions, in which a large number of indivividuals are involved) need to have at least a cursory understanding of such issues. Aging of psychological functioning (the backbone of the definition of senile dementia) is very much in question today. Most of us were led to believe that our mental abilities diminish as we grow older. However, scientific observations do not seem to support this contention. The vast majority of studies of aging individuals have been performed using cross-sectional studies in which people of various ages are studied at a given point in time. Thus, the apparent "decline" in cognitive functions may be due to reasons other than aging, e.g., older individuals will have been less educated than younger ones. Thus, the apparent decline of psychological functions in cross-sectional studies is then a methodological artifact: Cultural and experiential effects confuse the issue of what can be attributed to aging alone.

Longitudinal studies — follow-up studies over time where individuals are tested at regular time intervals for many years — tell a much different story. Follow-up studies have shown that fundamental psychological functions such as "understanding of verbal meaning" actually show an increase with chronological age, while identical functions when tested in cross-sectional studies show a decline. Anastasi (1982) concludes that

> the results of the better-designed studies of adult intelligence strongly suggest that the ability decrement formerly attributed to aging is predominantly due to intergeneration or intercohort differences, probably associated with cultural changes in our society. Genuine ability decrements are not likely to be manifested until well over the age of 60.

Anastasi (1988), an authority in the field of psychological testing, believes that what counts are the changes in individual performance that occur with age. Many people, of course, experience a decline in intellectual abilities and performance with age. But others, in proportions which are still unknown, show no changes. These new facts do not fit our prejudices.

The Causes of Aging

It is impossible to review all the etiological factors that may affect aging; the scientific literature on aging and health issues associated with the elderly is huge. The forensic neuropsychologist who works in either criminal or civil law needs to be alert to these factors because they sometimes surface during the course of the forensic investigation. In this section dealing with elderly individuals facing criminal charges, we will mention primarily Alzheimer's disease and the evaluation of cognitive and affective disorders among the elderly. In the next section, we will focus on dementia as a frequent mental disorder that the neuropsychologist is asked to address while evaluating individuals who suffer from AIDS and who face criminal charges.

Scientists have proposed several conceptual models for Alzheimer's disease, such as genetic, abnormal protein, infectious agents, nutrition, abnormal blood flow, changes in biochemical properties of neurotransmittors in the brain, and toxic agents. A brief review of these models is appropriate before considering the possibility that dementia may be caused by chronic environmental or occupational exposure to neurotoxic agents.

Genetic causation. Certain families have a very high rate of longevity while in others the incidence of Alzheimer's disease is disproportionately high. Yet, there is the possibility that what is labeled "genetic" is in fact the sharing of common environmental factors (e.g., rural living or nutritional habits), and thus the environment cannot be ruled out. Abnormalities in the genetic material of cells of the aged are however also suspected; the inability of DNA to code for normal proteins which in turn may affect neurotransmission between neurons has been reported. Chromosomal aberrations have been proposed as possible cytogenetic markers of aging.

Abnormal protein. When Alzheimer first described the disease in 1907 that now bears his name, he observed that the neural tissue exhibited a characteristic neurofibrillar appearance. He found that a substance (later demonstrated to be a protein) could be observed to be wrapped around cerebral blood vessels replacing degenerating nerve terminals. The hypothesis is that the presence of abnormal proteins lead to the formation of neural plaque which in turn causes severe intellectual impairment. This hypothesis seems to be supported by the common observation that in post-mortem examination of the brains of Alzheimer's cases, the more numerous the neural plaques, the more profound the mental deterioration appears to be while the individual was still alive.

Poor blood circulation. "Bad circulation" and "hardening of arteries" have been popular explanations of why mental capacity declines with age. It has been postulated that people suffering from Alzheimer's disease suffer from a marked reduction in blood flow. Thus, the brain may lose its ability to receive adequate oxygen and glucose from blood, both vital to normal brain functioning. Today, the hypothesis of brain atherosclerosis has few supporters. But it is possible that numerous subclinical strokes may lead to dementia, for example, in those who are occupationally exposed to head trauma, such as boxers.

Lathyrism. Excessive consumption of chick pea or vetch, *Lathyrus sativus,* and related species is associated with a non-progressive, irreversible neurological disease called lathyrism. Paralysis of the lower limbs occurs in both sexes and all ages but it seems more prevalent among young males. It is one of the oldest neurotoxic diseases known to humans, and once it was prevalent in Europe, northern Africa, the Middle East, and parts of the Far East. Now, it is restricted to India, Bangladesh, and Ethiopia. The disease tends to develop in times of flood or drought when the usual crops are ruined or become unavailable; at those times, the hearty plant Lathyrus becomes the major dietary staple. The causative agent is suspected to be beta-(N)-oxalyl-amino-L-alanine (BOAA).

Biochemical hypothesis. Spontaneous or environmentally-induced biochemical disturbances in neural transmission have been thought to be very plausible causative factors in senile dementia. The hippocampus and the cerebral cortex of patients suffering from Alzheimer's disease show markedly reduced levels of the enzyme choline acetyltransferase (CAT). It is speculated that some of the profound memory disturbances and cognitive deficits seen in this disease are the results of biochemical alterations in the acetylcholine-mediated neurotransmitters.

Slow-acting viruses. Viruses are known to be causative agents in many progressively debilitating and fatal diseases such as Creutzfeld-Jacob's and AIDS (acquired immune deficiency syndrome). It has been found that 25% of all AIDS cases develop neurological problems including dementia. Certain degenerative diseases such as Creutzfeld-Jacob's may be caused by prions, infectious agents which lack RNA or DNA — unlike viruses which usually contain either RNA or DNA.

Alterations in the immune system. Some investigators have proposed changes in cells generated by the thymus gland (T-cells) and bone marrow-generated cells (B-cells) are biological markers of aging. In the next chapter we will discuss AIDS-related dementia.

Aging as an abiotrophic process. In the mid-1980s comprehensive hypotheses have been proposed for common mechanisms underlying several neurodegenerative diseases. Calne et al. (1986), for example, have proposed the hypothesis that

> Alzheimer's disease, Parkinson's disease, and motor neuron disease are (all) due to environmental damage to specific regions of the central nervous system . . . The damage remains subclinical for several decades and makes those affected specially prone to the consequences of age-related neuronal attrition.

The authors of this hypothesis argue that several neurodegenerative diseases may be initiated by environmental factors, such as linking the presence of methyl-phenyltetrahydropyrine with Parkinsonism, polio virus infection with post-polyomyelitic syndrome, chick pea ingestion with lathyrism, and still unindentified factors and amyotrophic lateral sclerosis-PD complex of Guam, and trauma with pugilist's encephalopathy. All these neurodegenerative diseases may be the expression of abiotrophy, a selective, premature decay of a functionally-related population of neurons. It is speculated that abiotrophic disorders have not been recognized earlier because few people had reached 50 years of age before the 20th century.

Definition of Dementia

In dementia there is a demonstrable evidence of impairment in short- and long-term memory, and other cognitive functions and affect. Impairment in short-term memory (inability to learn new information) may be indicated by inability to remember three objects after five minutes. Long-term memory impairment (inability to remember information that was known in the past) may be indicated by an inability to remember past personal information (e.g., his or her birthplace, occupation, what happened yesterday) or facts of common knowledge (e.g., past U.S. Presidents, well-known holidays).

The following conditions need to be present to make the diagnosis of dementia:

☐ Impairment in abstract thinking, as indicated by an inability to find similarities and differences between related words, difficulty in defining words and concepts, and other similar tasks

☐ Impaired judgment, as indicated by an inability to make reasonable plans to deal with interpersonal, family, or job-related problems

☐ Other disturbances of the so-called higher cortical functions, such as aphasia (disorder of language), apraxia (inability to carry out motor activities despite intact comprehension and motor function), agnosia (failure to recognize or identify objects despite intact sensory function), and constructional difficulty (e.g., inability to copy three-dimensional figures, assemble blocks, or arrange sticks of specific designs)

☐ Personality change, i.e., alteration or accentuation of premorbid traits

The generally recognized categories for severity of dementia are:

☐ *Mild:* Although work or social activities are significantly impaired, the capacity for independent living remains, with adequate personal hygiene and relative intact judgment

☐ *Moderate*: Independent living is hazardous, and some degree of supervision is necessary

☐ *Severe:* Activities of daily living are so impaired that continual supervision is required, e.g., unable to maintain minimal personal hygiene; largely incoherent or mute. It has been recently recognized that AIDS-dementia is likely to have a different neurological basis as it tends to affect deep brain structures (thus, the name subcortical dementia).

Dementia significantly interferes with work, usual social activities, or relationships with others; it is often the focus of attention for the neuropsychologist who is asked to assess the multiple dysfunction that enters its diagnostic criteria; individuals afflicted by dementia sometimes become assaultive (see Exhibits 13.1, The Priest, and 14.1, The Man Who Lost All His Friends).

The Wechsler Adult Intelligence Scale (Revised) is a must; in cases where AIDS-dementia or pseudodementia needs to be ruled out, assessment of depression (Beck's Depression Scale) needs to be used. Pseudodementia is the presence of diminished memory and cognitive functions resulting from the simultaneous presence of a mood disorder, generally depression.

The Study of Geriatric Felons

An interest in the health problems of the elderly is relatively new. Butler, (1975) in his award-winning *Why Survive? Being Old in America*, reviewed the numerous issues and health concerns of the elderly. As a result of this interest, numerous medical and health subspecialties began to concentrate on the growing needs of this demographic group. Specialties in geriatric psychiatry (also called geropsychiatry) and geriatric neuropsychology have developed professional specializations concerned with the diagnosis, prevention, and treament of physical and psychological disorders of the elderly. Rosner and Schwartz's (1987) *Geriatric Psychiatry and the Law* focuses on the issues concerning geriatric law-offenders. Richard Rosner and his collaborators have also published many research articles concerning specific issues of geriatric offenders.

Approximately two-fifths of geriatric offenders between the ages 62 and 88 years are diagnosed with organic mental disorders, dementia, alcoholism, and/or substance abuse. DSM-IV contains diagnostic categories of organic mental disorders (called Dementias Arising in the Senium and Presenium) that include primary degenerative dementia of the Alzheimer type, multi-infarct dementia, and senile and pre-senile dementia.

As indicated by Rosner and his collaborators, the competence to stand trial and pre-pleading evaluations are the main reason for examining an elderly offender. The role of the neuropsychologist in a forensic clinic is the evaluation of possible organic mental disorders and, most importantly, of the likelihood of their relationship to the offense. Equally important is the evaluation of the offender's cognitive level of functions to determine whether this level may or may not hinder his or her competence to stand trial.

The Evaluation of Aging Individuals Facing Criminal Charges

Most elderly people show a substantial degree of psychomotor retardation, sometimes doubling the time required to administer a basic core of tests. This limits the scope and variety of psychological tests that can be performed during a "typical" session. In most cases, one is limited to a selection of subtests from the Wechsler Scale and other instruments geared to the presence of cognitive deficits associated with the generalized brain dysfunction, such as the Bender Gestal Test or the Embedded Figures Test. Visual and hearing impairment among the elderly are other factors that affect the interpretations of tests; in such cases, higher-order cognitive deficits cannot be interpreted as playing a role. Individuals who claim memory impairment may be administered psychological tests available for the evaluation of such functions. In addition, a large percentage of geriatric offenders are poorly educated (as a rule, the younger the individual, the higher his or her level of education). The possibility of chronic mental retardation among individuals who have lived all their lives in poverty without the intellectual challenges of more affluent groups is an important point to be taken into consideration.

Occupational Exposure to Neurotoxic Agents and Aging

The forensic neuropsychologist working in civil law is aware of new issues regarding behavioral and psychological changes said to be linked to occupational exposure to neurotoxic agents. By the late 1970s, a growing number of reports (particularly from Finland, Sweden and Denmark) had demonstrated that workers occupationally exposed to organic solvents are at risk of developing polyneuropathy. By the middle 1980s, some investigators had proposed that occupational exposure to solvents may also induce senile dementia (WHO, 1985).

Although the hypothesis that occupational neurotoxic agents may cause dementia is hardly new, testing of neurotoxic hypotheses on accelerated aging is difficult. Dr. Alice Hamilton (1943) observed early in this century that lead workers looked twice their age. Dr. Irving J. Selikoff (one of the leaders of occupational medicine in our time, who died in 1992) made a similar observation to describe patients who were occupationally exposed to solvents.

Thus far, the hypothesis that chronic, low level occupational or environmental exposure to neurotoxic agents may accelerate functional aging has not been postulated in a manner that could be adequately tested in epidemiologic studies. However, the idea has been proposed time and time again. There are many methodological questions that make it difficult to design an appropriate study, including inadequate epidemiologic design, lack of availability of cohorts, the quantitative definition of long-term exposure and absorption of neurotoxic agents, and matters of statistical analysis of data.

A forensic neuropsychologist involved in civil cases in which workers claim to have suffered impairment in cognitive function as a result of neurotoxic agents at the workplace needs to be aware of epidemiologic issues. These issues refer to the applicability of epidemiologic (group) data to single cases.

Most reports claiming an association between environmental or occupational exposure and early aging are cross-sectional studies (comparing different individuals at one point in time) with the limitations discussed above. In a prospective study, a cohort of individuals occupationally exposed to neurotoxic agents that can be observed for a number of years needs to be identified and examined.

The identification of people who are exposed to neurotoxic agents (such as solvents) at the workplace are difficult because such exposures are not likely to be known outside the premises in which they occur. In addition, chronic exposure to neurotoxic agents often occurs in small shops with a rapid turnover rate. Affected individuals may drop out of their jobs and the subjects who are available for study might not be the most appropriate to study, since their exposure might not be known to be health threatening.

In order to claim that an occupational neurotoxic agent is the causative factor of dementia, long-term exposure to such an agent needs to be thoroughly documented. For example, quantitative assessment of environmental exposure to solvents in every job where painters are exposed to solvents in paints is a formidable task.

In the United States, the cooperation of management in making such an assessment is the exception rather than the rule. Sometimes, in order to define "personal dose," diaries documenting paint use need to be kept; from these diaries, industrial hygienists need to identify the chemical composition of paints used in every case. Valciukas (1991) discusses other issues regarding occupational exposure to neurotoxic agents as a possible cause of accelerated aging.

☐ EXHIBIT 13.1

The Priest

Mr Fernandez (who was in custody, before sentence) was a 56-year-old Hispanic male with a 10th grade education in the Dominican Republic. The defendant met the criteria for Organic Personality Syndrome as the following were present: A persistent personality disturbance probably representing a change or accentuation of a previously characteristic trait; affective instability, e.g., marked shifts from normal mood to depression, irritability, or anxiety; recurrent outbursts of aggression or rage that were grossly out of proportion to any precipitating psychological stressors; and paranoid ideation. The organic personality disorder was thought to be of explosive type as aggression and rage were predominant features. In recent years, there appeared to be a progressive deterioration of Mr Fernandez' mind.

His psychosocial stressors were felt to be moderate. The defendant lived in a church together with the victim who was a priest in charge of the church; a deep spiritual bond was said to exist between the victim and the defendant. The defendant was said to become progressively disillusioned as a result of the lack of spirituality of the priest's message. The defendant often rebelled against the victim's orders that the defendant considered ruthless and dictatorial. At the moment of the event leading to the charges, the parish had little or no attendance.

The defendant showed moderate symptoms or moderate difficulty in social functioning. He also exhibited a borderline level of intellectual functioning, close to a mild level of mental retardation. Memory signs or organicity (including circumstantiality of speech and forgetfulness) were also noticed. However, his contact with reality was good. The events leading to his charges were not thought to be the expression of a delusion. Although the defendant experienced depression, he did now show suicidal ideation.

Mr Fernandez had known the victim (an 84-year-old priest) for a number of years and had lived in the church while working as a messenger. When he met him for the first time, the defendant said that he had a deep admiration for the victim; the relationship was described as that of "father and son." Over the years the victim allowed the defendant to take responsibilities around the church. The defendant (an uneducated person) felt very proud about these responsibilities that included scheduling church activities, such as afternoon prayers, around the time the events leading to his charge happened. The victim was described by the defendant as a ruthless man who had become progressively concerned about his personal power over the progressively smaller number of members of his parish located in Spanish Harlem. In recent years, some of the scheduled church events had no attendance. The priest was described as often using the defendant and his brother as messengers between the victim and the parishioners. The priest's directives were said to be often unfair and sometimes plainly wrong; in recent years, the defendant and the victim constantly argued over how un-Christian the victim's demands sometimes were. The defendant said that the priest had "the devil" in himself; and he had "put the devil in his brother's soul;" but these remarks appeared to be figures of speech coming from an uneducated person rather than delusions.

The defendant knew many of the priest's "little secrets," including the fact that sometimes the victim made sexual advances to female parishioners and that he once had an affair with a woman in the parish. The defendant appeared to feel guilty on disclosing the deceased man's pecadillos. The defendant indicated that the priest and himself "lived together" for many years, that the arguments often took place in the priest's bedroom at the moment the victim was about to go to sleep. A homosexual relationship was denied although he often described an early "deep spiritual" relationship between the victim and the defendant.

The day the events leading to his charges took place, they had one of their constant arguments and the defendant lost his temper and killed the victim. Importantly, the defendant did not describe his action as an act of liberating the community of his tormentor. The defendant did not say that it was God who ordered him to kill the priest.

The defendant used the language of someone who killed him for a personal reason, as his admiration and love for the priest were betrayed to the point that the defendant lost all respect for the victim.

Mr Fernandez stated that until 1967 he himself was a very promiscuous man, even when he was married and had children. He said that he suffered from venereal diseases including syphilis; it was not clear whether the defendant understood the seriousness of the illness and whether the defendant ever received an adequate treatment for syphilis. (Syphillis, when untreated, sometimes creates a psychosis characterized by excessive and inappropriated mysticism). While discussing possible drug abuse, the defendant stated that he was so "scared of needles" to the point that sometimes "he would not go for treatment even when he knew he needed one."

The background papers indicated that Mr Fernandez received psychiatric attention for his "nerves" on one occasion in the past. The defendant stated that he began drinking on a regular basis at 15 and until an unspecified time he was an alcohol abuser; he drank beer, vodka, and whiskey. Drug abuse was denied.

Mr Fernandez was a sickly appearing person (5'4", 130 lbs) who during the initial phase of the evaluative interview appeared confused and bewildered. As the evaluative session progressed, the defendant became progressively more talkative sometimes revealing circumstantiality. (Circumstantiality is a term that describes a pattern of speech that is indirect and delayed in reaching the point because of unnecessary, tedious details and parenthetical remarks.) The defendant's circumstantial replies or statements were prolonged for many minutes; it was felt that if the speaker was not interrupted and urged to get to the point, he would never get to it.) The defendant appeared remorseful for the events leading to charges, and he was tearful during the recounting of these events. His eye contact was adequate.

A screening battery of probes that included examination of posture, gait, whole-body balance, muscle strength, tremor at rest, intentional tremor, motor coordination, general appearance of the eyes, eye movements, and reaction of the eyes to light was performed and the following was noted: Motor incoordination; the defendant had difficulties in touching his own nose with his fingers; and he could not follow this evaluator's finger with his eye; the defendant could not hold his eyes in position; they would jump side to side in no apparent pattern.

From an extensive checklist of signs and/or symptoms possibly indicative of neurological or mental disorders, Mr Fernandez was asked whether he had ever experienced them, and if so, to give examples. The defendant appeared to be affected by depression and memory problems; he did not appear to experience suicidal ideation. Paranoid ideation, delusions, and hallucinations were denied.

The Wechsler Adult Intelligence Scale, Revised (WAIS-R) was administered. Mr Fernandez' verbal IQ was found to be 76 and his performance IQ was 65; the overall test IQ was 70. His verbal IQ levels represented a borderline level of intellectual functioning and his performance IQ suggested mild mental retardation. The overall IQ is just between borderline and mild mental retardation. There was about 10 point difference between his verbal and performance IQ; people who are depressed or who are suffering from the acute effects of neurotropic medications sometimes shows this mismatch between verbal and performance scores.

☐ QUESTIONS FOR REVIEW AND FURTHER DISCUSSION

Δ Discuss crimes of comission and crimes of omission by individuals suffering from dementia.

Δ   Discuss the importance of naturalistic observations in individuals whose lawyers claim
     unaccountability by reason of dementia.

Δ   Discuss the difficulties usually encountered in the psychological evaluation of aging
     individuals.

Δ   Discuss the issue of competence. Is someone who is incompetent to face legal
     proceedings by necessity also incompetent to take care of his or her financial affairs?

Δ   An insurance company denies insurance to a Mrs LeBlanch because she has been found
     demented; the basis of such decision is a neuropsychological report performed two
     years ago in which the neuropsychologist (who was hired by the patient's husband,
     now separated from Mrs. LeBlanch) argues the point that she is incompetent to care
     for the children. Discuss the case.

14: AIDS-RELATED NEUROPSYCHOLOGICAL DISORDERS, INCLUDING DEMENTIA

MANY VIRUSES CAUSE ORGANIC MENTAL DISORDERS AT SOME CRITICAL POINT
during the course of infection. These include Amyotrophic lateral sclerosis (a
degenerative disease of the nervous system causing progressive weakness and
paralysis), Creutzfeld-Jacob diseases, general paresis, kuru, multiple sclerosis,
and others. However organic mental disorders associated with these illnesses
are unlikely to be the focus of a forensic neuropsychological evaluation. Acquired Immunodeficiency Syndrome (AIDS) — a disease caused also by a virus
— has become one of the most significant health and societal problems of our
time. The forensic neuropsychological investigation involving individuals who
are infected with the AIDS virus or who suffer from the clinical manifestations
of the disease and who face criminal charges needs to rely on a wealth of
epidemiologic, clinical, and legal facts.

THE EPIDEMIOLOGY OF AIDS

Transmission

AIDS was first reported among homosexual men in June of 1981. Between
1981 and 1983 many populations were clustered in mutually exclusive "risk
groups" for epidemiological surveillance and reporting purposes. In 1983 the
human immunodefiency virus (HIV) was identified as the cause of AIDS. HIV
has been found in varying amounts in blood, semen, vaginal secretions, saliva,
breast milk, tears, urine, cerebrospinal fluid, and alveolar fluid. However, only

blood and semen have been directly implicated in the transmission of HIV, since the level of virus in the other fluids is minimal.

Three routes of transmission have been shown to be important:

☐ Inoculation of blood (such as transfusion of blood and blood products, needle sharing among intravenous drug users, needle stick, open wound, injecting with unsterilized needles)

☐ Sexual transmission (homosexual, men to men, and heterosexual, both men to women and women to men)

☐ Perinatal (intrauterine and perinatal)

The risk factors for AIDS have now been well recognized; these include most prominently sexual contact and intravenous use of drugs. Generally recognized as unsafe sex practices are vaginal or anal intercourse without a condom, sex practices in which body fluids (such as semen, urine or feces) are allowed to penetrate the mouth or vagina (as in unprotected fellatio or cunnilingus, blood contact of any kind), and sharing sex instruments with an infected individual during sexual intercourse or other activity. However, intravenous drug use is, by far, the most significant route of tranmission in the individuals who are the focus of a forensic neuropsychological investigation.

It has been estimated that 25% of all the cases of AIDS in the United States have occurred in individuals who are drug abusers, and the number is rising. This percentage is often extrapolated to individuals being held in detention centers in large metropolitan areas such as New York, Los Angeles and San Francisco. However, the percentage of HIV-infected individuals in detention centers is likely to be higher. More that 80% of the cases of AIDS among intravenous drug abusers have occurred in the New York City metropolitan area where at least half of the 400,000 drug abusers nationwide are known to reside. It was recognized early that intravenous drug users represented the bridge to HIV infection of the adult heterosexual population. In the early 1990s, while the homosexual population began to show a measure of success in cutting down the incidence of AIDS as a result of intense education programs, HIV infection among heterosexual individuals and in the drug-abusing population continued to raise.

The court neuropsychologist who often needs to write case recommendations is familiar with the guidelines formulated by the Centers of Disease Control (CDC) for prevention of HIV transmission. These guidelines are periodically modified and at the time of this writing should not be considered the most updated source of information. Prevention of infection is accomplished by:

☐ Informing prospective sex partners of his or her infection with HIV

☐ Protecting a partner via condom during any sexual activity

- Once the person is known to be infected, informing previous sex partners or individuals with whom needles were shared about their potential HIV exposure
- For intravenous drug users, enrolling in drug rehabilitation programs to end the dependence on drugs
- Not sharing personal items that can be easily contaminated with blood (razors, toothbrushes)
- For an individual known to be HIV-positive, abstaining from donating blood, plasma, body organs, other tissue, or semen
- For women infected with HIV, avoiding pregnancy
- Cooperating with physicians, dentists, and other appropriate health professions in curtailing the spread of the disease

HIV Infection among Persons Confronting the Law

Epidemiologic studies of people who are HIV-positive or suffer from AIDS confronting the law are very difficult to perform.

- Some individuals spend only a few hours or a few days in detention centers and they are never tested for HIV.
- Because of serious communication problems with inmates due to mental disorders, mental retardation, AIDS-related dementia to be described below, severe forms of schizophrenia, etc., an adequate medical history often cannot reliably be reconstructed and one simply cannot know whether the inmate is at risk of HIV infection.
- An incarcerated individual who is at risk for AIDS (e.g., shared needles with other drug abusers, was a bisexual or homosexual individual who had unprotected promiscuous sex, had contact with a female who soon after the sexual contact died from AIDS), may hide these risk factors and may not volunteer for HIV testing. Current estimates are that at least 25% of the inmates in the New York City detention center are either HIV-positive or suffer from AIDS.
- Someone who is already incarcerated and knows that he or she is HIV-positive may not disclose this fact to medical staff and refuse HIV testing for fear of being physically attacked by inmates (and sometimes by correction officers), or placed in confinement.
- Someone who had confrontations with the law and has been released on bail may falsely volunteer that he is HIV-positive to gain sympathy or to be removed from the premises as soon as possible.

Epidemiology

At the time of this writing, HIV is a worldwide problem. In 1994, it was estimated that approximately 1.5 millon people in the United States, were infected with HIV, more than one millon in Latin America, half a million in Europe, and as many as 10 millon in Africa. In 1995, there were approximately 500,000 AIDS cases in the United States. The geographic distribution of HIV infection heavily favors large urban centers such as New York, Los Angeles, and San Francisco which collectively represents 50% of the US cases, but HIV-infection and AIDS cases are present in smaller cities and rural areas.

The ethnic composition of individuals infected with HIV, suffering from ARC (AIDS-related complex) or AIDS is likely to vary from community to community. Nationwide, Caucasians still represent more that 60% of all cases, African-Americans about 24%, and Hispanics 14%. However, because of the well-known link between socio-economic status (roughly defined as an index considering an individual's education and income) and the ethnic background of individuals who are held in detention centers facing legal proceedings, the facts are quite different. Hard statistics are difficult to obtain for the reasons named above.

In New York City about 45% of such infected inmates are Afro-Americans, 45% Hispanics and 10% of other ethnic backgrounds. More affluent Caucasians can post their bails, so the ethnic distribution of HIV-positive individuals or those afflicced with ARC or AIDS who are evaluated as bailees are Caucasians. Thus, it is close to impossible to estimate the percentage of HIV-infected individuals who appear in criminal courts. Although the vast majority of individuals who have AIDS and face legal proceedings are males, the proportion of females with AIDS are on the increase reflecting nation-wide trends.

Screening

A neuropsychologist who evaluates individuals from the community of inmates who are HIV-positive, or those who are suffering from ARC or AIDS, must be aware of the basic issues of screening for AIDS. What follows is not a quick substitute for the information and training that needs to be obtained by specific training courses now widely available nation-wide.

The antibodies produced by the immune system after being infected with HIV can be detected by two serum tests: Enzyme linked immunosorbent assay (ELISA) and immunoblotting. Nationwide, ELISA can be performed anonymously and free of charge in many health centers. The ELISA test is normally used first as an initial screening procedure. It is generally recommended that if the ELISA test is found to be positive, it needs to be followed by a second ELISA. If both results are positive, then the final verification of HIV seroconversion (seroconversion is the fact that antibodies are now shown in blood serum) is determined by immunoblot.

After infection, it has been estimated that it takes six to twelve weeks for antibodies to the virus to develop and six to twelve months for seroconversion (to be found HIV-positive) to take place. The percentage of individuals who are infected with HIV who later develop AIDS still cannot be accurately ascertained but it may take years. It has been estimated that the average survival times of those who have been diagnosed with AIDS is about 18 months.

Issues of Counseling

There are issues of counseling that a neuropsychologist performing a forensic evaluation (who may not be primarily involved in this specific professional activity) may encounter while the defendant is still pondering the wisdom of being tested for HIV exposure. These issues include the exploration of known high-risk practices, the discussion of the meaning of a positive or negative screening result, being prepared for referral to agencies capable of handling an individual's fears and concerns, counseling of a type that is adequate to the defendant's needs (e.g., mental retardation, limited knowledge of English), the potential effects of disclosure on family, social status, health and life insurance, the individual's past reaction to stress, and the prevention from catastrophic reactions (primarily, but not exclusively, suicide).

In detention centers, it is not uncommon to examine individuals whose HIV status is has been recently known (e.g., while in jail after apprehension for criminal charges). A forensic evaluation sometimes needs to be conducted under very difficult conditions. Although primarily the province of a physician, a non-physician cannot confess ignorance on these issues or handle an emotionally-charged interview by promising prompt referral. In fact, the psychologist sometimes is the best prepared to discuss facts with individuals who are mentally retarded or are afflicted with a a serious mental disorder.

By now, it has been recognized that a good professional needs to know how to share information about the meaning and correct interpretation of the positive test result, the need for active sources of social support (when available), the recommendation for prevention of HIV transmission, recommendation on the followup of sexual partners and individuals with whom needles were shared in the past, recommendations against donating blood, organ, or tissues and referral to psychological support. A mental health work needs to be aware of the fact that the risk of suicide is real.

Confidentiality

Guidelines on the confidentiality of the defendant's HIV status have been slowing evolving. One needs to appreciate that the mental health professional working at the court is constantly torn about these issues. On the one hand, one would normally feel that a judge needs to be informed about the defendant's HIV status. In addition, one needs to know enough about the screening issues and clinical manifestation of AIDS to alert court personnel when one feels that HIV status or even AIDS is fabricated for manipulation purposes. The two cardinal rules are that no person should be given the HIV test without his or her knowledge and consent, and that defendants should be advised regarding the advisability of unnecessary disclosure of HIV status or affliction with AIDS.

An additional issue that has not been entirely resolved is the fact that an HIV-positive individual continues to place other individuals at risk by practicing unprotected promiscuous sex or sharing needles. The attempt to explain that there is an urgent need to modify his or her own behavior to a mentally-retarded individual, or someone with a long history of drug abuse, or someone afflicted with a severe mental disorder, or someone who cannot effectively communicate in English, or who suffers a speech disorder as a consequence of a stroke is sometimes a formidable task. Discussion of issues dealing with the involuntary hospitalization of such individuals creates heated debates. The attempt to notify all potential individuals who might have been infected by a mentally disordered individual who has been homeless is generally recognized as a close to an impossible task.

CLINICAL MANIFESTATIONS

Knowledge of AIDS and HIV-Related Disorders

In the mid-1990s, knowledge of AIDS is no longer considered an exclusive province of the medical profession but the concern of everyone. The following is just an example of how information about AIDS may be used by the court neuropsychologist. Often, one needs to perform a forensic neuropsychological investigation on homeless individuals who have had a confrontation with the law; in many cases, such individuals afflicted by drug abuse or severe mental disorders cannot provide a medical history. The presence of *Pneumocystis carinii pneumonia* (PCP), for example, is almost pathognomonic (characteristic or indicative of a disorder because it is typical) of AIDS. One needs to be reminded that not all individuals afflicted with AIDS show visible signs of physical deterioration; inmates of detention centers, for example, may show excellent muscular development and feel motivated to keep in good physical condition by performing isometric exercises and push-ups until advanced stages of the disease become debilitating. It is not infrequent that an individual afflicted with a mental disorder, but whose physical appearance is otherwise unremarkable, may recall being told that he or she was once admitted to a hospital with PCP claiming that he has never been told that he suffers from AIDS.

There are several additional reasons why the neuropsychologist needs to be aware of signs and symptoms, and conditions of the disease process that are rarely included in the training of such professionals.

☐ As a member of a medical team at a detention center, the neuropsychologist needs to have an understanding of the various disease processes associated with HIV-infection and target organs including the nervous system. This knowledge enhances the planning for adequate clinical probes and neuropsychological testing, followup, and, whenever appropriate, monitoring of medical treatment. The medical team, for example, is interested to know what level of a given drug, AZT (azidothymidine), causes neuropsychological side effects as the result of the need to administer the drug at almost toxic levels to be effective.

☐ The neuropsychologist who (as a part of the medical team) performs the initial clinical neuropsychological evaluations needs to use adequate protective equipment such as masks, gloves and sometime cover-all suits both to protect himself and the patient who is very susceptible to opportunistic diseases.

The neuropsychologist who works at the court may be at risk of incurring infectious diseases other than AIDS. It is unavoidable, for example, for the defendant who works with the cubes from the Block Design subtest of the Wechsler Adult Scale of Adult Intelligence Scale to hand back the cubes to the psychologist to be returned to their original container. A defendant afflicted with hepatitis, for example, can transmit the disease not only to the evaluator but to other examinees that follow him as well.

Knowledge of AIDS and accompanying disorders and conditions, alone, provides only limited protection. Individuals who are inmates in detention centers sometimes receive adequate medical screening (although this information is not available in the background documentation as a rule). One would hope, for example, that individuals who suffer from acute manifestations of an infectious disorder may not be sent to a court appearance. Defendants who suffer from antisocial personality traits may decide, with the aid of counsel, that it is best not to appear in court to make an impression on the severity of their illness. Others, however, are impatiently waiting for their court appearance and are willing to appear in court at any cost. A neuropsychologist who works at the court is aware of the fact that individuals who might be seriously ill and yet in the community might not be able to appear in court because of serious illness. The neuropsychologist must sometimes exercise his or her own judgment about the seriousness of the defendant's, bailee's, or probationer's medical as well as psychiatric condition. This writer once performed a neuropsychological evaluation on a patient afflicted by leprosy.

ARC, AIDS, and HIV-Related Diseases

AIDS-Related Complex (ARC) is a condition caused by HIV in which patients test positive for the virus, have a specific set of clinical symptoms, but the severity of these symptoms is less than AIDS. Signs and symptoms of ARC include loss of appetite, weight loss, fever, night sweats, skin rashes, diarrhea, tiredness, lack of resistance to common infections, and/or swollen lymph nodes. The Federal Centers for Disease Control (CDC) in Atlanta has provided guidelines for the diagnosis of AIDS and HIV-related diseases; these are available to health professionals at no cost.

Signs, Symptoms, and Non-Neurological Conditions

In the early stages of infection, people who are infected with HIV experience flu-like symptoms that are sometimes accompanied by physical signs such as enlarged lymph nodes (particularly around the neck area), skin rashes, and liver and spleen disorders. However, some of the recently-infected individuals do not experience signs and symptoms at all.

At the earliest stages of HIV infection some individuals may show defects in tests of immunological and hematological function and nonspecific symptoms. Cutaneous anergy (the absence of sensitivity reaction to substances that would be immunogenic or allergenic to most individuals) may be shown. Other hematological changes may include anemia, leukopenia (i.e., the total amount of leukocytes in the circulating blood is less than normal), or decreased T-helper lymphocytes, one type of white blood cell important to the normal function of the immune system. The development of nonspecific symptoms such as malaise, low-grade fevers, and fatigue is also possible. At this early stage an individual may infect other individuals without realizing that he or she was infected with HIV.

Symptomatic individuals develop opportunistic infections by protozoa or virus, including fungal infections, Herpes infections, and antibiotic-resistant tuberculosis. Although, as indicated above, *Pneumocystis carinii* pneumonia (PCP) is generally considered a pathognomonic sign, it occurs in about 60 percent of the cases. This type of pneumonia is characteristic in that it is associated with an unproductive cough, low-grade fever, exertional dyspnea, and generalized chest pain. Other complications such as chronic diarrhea, weight loss, malaise, fatigue, fevers, and night sweats are common.

Neurological Disorders Associated with AIDS

The nervous system can be the target of opportunistic infections or directly infected with HIV. Opportunistic infections — that is, as explained above,

those caused by protozoa and viruses to which the individual is highly susceptible because of his or her immunosuppressed system — may be associated
with numerous neurological disorders and conditions. An aware neuropsychologist may notice some of these signs and symptoms and must alert the
medical team.

☐ Meningeal infections — generally with the bacterium.

☐ *Cryptococcus neoformans* — associated with fevers, headaches, and alterations
of mental status. Examination of the spinal fluid verifies the presence of this
fungus.

☐ The brain may be infected with *Toxoplasma gondii* (a sporozoan species) often
causing seizures because of focal brain lesions.

☐ Brain infection with CMV (*Cytomegalovirus*) may cause meningitis, cerebritis,
and blindness rapidly leading to death.

☐ Other areas of the nervous system such as the brain stem, cerebellum, or spinal
cord may also become infected, giving rise to clinical manifestations characteristic of lesions of these portions of the nervous system, such as effects on
balance, posture, ability to walk, etc.

☐ Several forms of neuropathies and myopathies, such as cranial and peripheral
neuropathies, radiculitis, and myopathies may also be present.

☐ Other neurological disorders caused by AIDS include aseptic meningitis, neoplasms (brain tumors) and peripheral nervous system manifestations.

☐ Aseptic meningitis occurs in five to ten percent of all patients with AIDS and is
characterized by fever, headaches, and cranial nerve involvement.

☐ Neoplasms such as Kaposi's sarcoma (KS) or lymphoma often occur in AIDS
patients. Signs and symptoms include purple spots on the body, altered mental
status, lethargy, confusion, dysarthria (alterations in speech articulation), and
motor incoordination.

☐ The peripheral nervous system may be involved as a result of the involvement
of the spinal cord. These lesions are characterized by progressive paralysis, leg
weakness, gait ataxia, and incontinence. Peripheral neuropathy is often associated with pain, numbness, and paresthesia. Sometimes, peripheral nervous
system involvement is the first clinical manifestation of AIDS, and therefore they
often occur in individuals who do not suspect that they have been infected with
HIV.

Imaging techniques such as MRI (Magnetic Resonance Imaging) and CT
(Computed Tomography) often are helpful in identifying the presence of the
above conditions.

AIDS-Related Dementia

The neurological syndrome associated with AIDS that is often the focus of
the forensic neuropsychological evaluation is AIDS dementia. Although there
are no accurate statistics, it is estimated that AIDS dementia may develop in

about 60 percent of afflicted individuals. The criteria for HIV-associated dementia complex are:

Acquired abnormality in at least two of the following cognitive abilities (present for at least one month): Attention/concentration, speed of processing information, abstraction/reasoning, visuospatial skills, memory/learning, and speech/language. The decline should be verified by a reliable history and mental status examination. When possible, history should be obtained from an informant, and information should be supplemented by neuropsychological testing.

At least two of the following: (1) Acquired abnormality in motor function or performance verified by clinical examination, neuropsychological testing, or both; and (2) Decline in motivation or emotional control or change in social behavior. This may be characterized by changes in personality with apathy, inertia, irritability, emotional lability, or onset of impaired judgment characterized by social inappropriate behavior or disinhibition.

AIDS may be also characterized by a myelopathy (a neurological disease affecting the control of muscle). The diagnostic criteria are:

☐ Acquired abnormality in lower-extremity neurological function disproportionate to upper-extremity abnormalities.

☐ The myelopathy is severe enough to require constant unilateral support for walking.

☐ Although mild cognitive function may be present, the criteria for HIV-associated demential are not fulfilled.

Epidemiologic data of AIDS dementia is hard to come by because of the difficulties of making differential diagnosis with other conditions and disorders. Information that is available from studies (such as those involving homosexual men for example) may not be applicable to inmates held in detention centers because of their confrontations with the law. For example:

An inmate suffering from AIDS may suffer from mental retardation as shown by a history of late development such as walking and talking, poor schooling, and life history of menial jobs. It is important to differentiate mental retardation and dementia.

☐ An individual who has had several confrontations with the law may exhibit a long, complex history of alcohol and drug abuse, including the use of powerful mind-altering drugs such as PCP. Organic mental disorders caused by alcohol and drug abuse need to be differentiated from dementia.

☐ Before contracting AIDS, an individual may have already been suffering from a serious mental disorder such as schizophrenia. Cognitive dysfunction resulting from such severe mental disorders cannot be equated with dementia.

☐ Inmates in detention centers in large urban areas such as New York City include a large population of Hispanics, many of whom are poorly educated and who exhibit limited communication skills in English. Such individuals cannot be easily included in a study of AIDS dementia.

☐ Homosexual men who have confrontations with the law not because of their lifestyle but because of their antisocial behavior including criminal activity and who later develop AIDS may volunteer a history of high standard of living. When formally tested during the course of a neuropsychological evaluation, one finds that such individuals never completed high school and are poorly informed of basis facts of mainstream culture. An imposing physical figure and a flashy lifestyle may be erroneously equated with high intelligence. Appearances and (most importantly) departures from expectations generated from these appearances should not be interpreted as a "decline" of intelligence.

In Chapter 13, we defined dementia as a demonstrable impairment in short- and long-term memory, abstract thinking, judgement, other disturbances of the so-called higher cortical function such as aphasia (disorder of language), apraxia (inability to carry out motor activities despite intact comprehension and motor function), agnosia (failure to recognize or identify objects despite intact sensory function), and "constructional difficulty" (e.g., inability to copy three-dimensional figures, assemble blocks, or arrange objects of specific designs), and personality change, i.e., alteration or accentuation of premorbid traits. Dementia thus defined is characteristic of older individuals. As we saw in the last chapter, sometimes, this is called Alzheimer's type dementia.

AIDS dementia is likely to have a different neurological basis as it tends to affect deep brain structures (thus, the name subcortical dementia). Previously, dementia has generally been recognized as a pathognomonic of cerebral cortical injury. It is now known that lesions of the basal ganglia (causing neurological disorders such as Parkinson's disease) may be accompanied by dementia, abnormal movement, psychomotor retardation, apathy in absence of other "cortical signs" such as aphasia.

Drastic reduction in cognitive functioning and personality changes may be caused by depression (pseudodementia). Inmates who are dying of AIDS in detention centers and who know that, if they get better, they are bound to face many additional years in prison, may suffer profound bouts of depression. Hence, suicidal ideation and actual suicide attempts are not uncommon. There are no clear-cut rules to differentiate dementia from pseudodementia. Probes with standardized psychological tests called depression scales sometimes help to clarify the differential diagnosis.

The Forensic Neuropsychological Investigation

Although numerous neuropsychological studies on individuals afflicted with AIDS have been performed, few have addressed the numerous issues of differential diagnosis among individuals facing legal proceedings discussed above. An additional difficulty is that because of past abuses, research of any kind in detention centers (even organized thinking that may potentially benefit the health of inmates) is often discouraged. Finally, individuals afflicted by antisocial personality disorder may falsely denounce a well-intended mental health professional for engaging in "experiments" trying to obtain an advantage in their legal situations.

Having already recognized the possibility that HIV may infect multiple targets within the central and peripheral nervous system — and that the unique demographic composition of individuals who are infected who face legal procedures — one still faces the issue about what strategies and what batteries of psychological tests are most appropriate when the inmate appears in court for an evaluation. The following are conditions that need to be addressed in a forensic report.

Levels of current cognitive function can best be tested by means of standardized intelligence scales such the WAIS-R (Wechsler Adult Intelligence Scale, Revised). However, is the substandard level in cognitive functioning linked to AIDS-related nervous system disorder, or are these levels likely to be the ones the individual always had?

Memory impairment can be assessed by means of the many available psychological tests such as the Benton Visual Retention Test (BVRT). Is it likely that the poor performance is related to the general apathy currently experienced by the individual because of AIDS?

Inmates often develop adjustment disorders while in prison. Some inmates facing sure death and many years of incarceration, develop deep religious ideation and sudden (and often unrealistic) attachments to long-ignored family members. After several weeks of counseling a 22-year-old inmate suffering from AIDS (a severe drug abuser) once told me that he was "prepared to die an honorable death." He was released soon after. Someone who knew him told me that the day of his release he stole a large sum of money from his mother and disappeared from the city. Are the personality traits of the AIDS-afflicted individual the same ones that he always had, or did they originate from present conditions?

Forensic Issues

Forensic issues as they apply to civil law need to be distinguished from those applied to criminal law. Unless they are wealthy, well-connected, or famous, individuals who are not endowed with these personal attributes and who are found to be HIV-positive are still the target of discrimination. When these cases are brought to civil courts, the neuropsychologist may offer important professional opinions on the intactness of superior skills that such individuals may have.

Some others may involve rare cases in which someone claims to have developed AIDS as a result of faulty workplace practices, such as those existing in hospitals a decade ago when guidelines for safe handling of human fluids did not exist. In such cases, the neuropsychologist may provide evidence of early manifestations of cognitive dysfunction in someone who until several years ago was an outstanding professional.

There is no demonstrable association beween HIV-infection, AIDS, and the nature and extent of criminal offenses. Individuals infected with HIV or afflicted with AIDS may be involved in any criminal offenses and any causal link between infection and crime cannot be easily established. However, AIDS may sometimes be a factor in their criminal behavior.

☐ Male homosexuals who are not drug abusers but suffer from AIDS may have confrontations with the law for petty crimes such as larceny. However, cases in which male homosexuals are charged with serious crimes such as assault or manslaugher of their lovers are sometimes related to the onset of dementia. There are many reported cases in which homosexual lovers both of whom are suffering from AIDS engage in murder-suicide pacts.

☐ Drug abusers who are not homosexuals, either male or female, but suffer from AIDS may be involved in posession or sale of drugs.

☐ Individuals who had been suffering from mental retardation or a serious mental disorder before contracting AIDS may be homeless and are sometimes charged with crimes such as trespassing, criminal mischief and other minor charges that stem from the perceived oddity of their behaviors.

☐ **EXHIBIT 14.1**

The Man Who Lost All his Friends

Mr Seidel — who was free in the community awaiting his sentence — was a 44-year-old Caucasian male with an associate degree in marketing. The defendant said that he had lied about his age so often that he was no longer certain how old he was; however, he was sure he was born in 1946.

The defendant suffered from a mild form of dementia. He showed demonstrable evidence of impairment in short- and long-term memory that he rationalized as voluntary "lying." Impairment in short-term memory was also indicated by his inability of recall the time sequence in which events had occurred in the past. In addition, the defendant showed an impairment in abstract thinking, as indicated by inability to find similarities and differences between related words, difficulty in defining words and concepts, and other tasks; inability to understand the overt behavior of people in everyday situations and the motivations that led to their actions; impaired judgment, as indicated by inability to make reasonable plans to deal with interpersonal, family, and job-related problems and issues; disturbances of higher (brain) function, such as "constructional difficulty" (e.g., inability to copy three-dimensional figures, assemble blocks); and personality change, i.e., alteration or accentuation of premorbid traits. These disturbances significantly interfered with his personal plans (e.g., such as deciding to go to trial in spite of not having reassurances that he could win such a trial). The capacity for independent living remained, with adequate personal hygiene, although his current judgment was impaired.

The defendant had many narcissistic and egocentric traits. He appeared to suffer from denial of illness; although from his history and current observations he appeared to be a very sick person, he said that there was nothing wrong with him.

The defendant said he was a homosexual and that he had been diagnosed as having AIDS. The defendant was running a high fever during the evaluative session; he said that a few days ago he had walked away from a New York City hospital when he was told he needed to be admitted. However, he said that he has never had an HIV test performed.

His stressors were severe: Eighteen of his gay friends had died from AIDS during the past three years; two of these people were his lovers in years past; he had been sexually attacked on the streets, and he attended the Crime Victim program at a city hospital for at least one year.

The defendant showed considerable impairment in reality testing and severe communication problems; he showed impairment in several areas, such as judgment, thinking, and mood. The defendant hid his memory problems with confabulation, that is, the fabrication of facts or events in response to questions about situations or events that were not recalled because of memory impairment. (It differs from lying in that the person is not consciously attempting to deceive.)

The prognosis was poor, since Mr Seidel had not reflected on the events that led to his charges (he did not undertand why these events happened; and, as a consequence of his illness, he had not come to terms with the consequences of his behavior.

Moreover, he had an inadequate level of intellectual functioning (his IQ showed borderline/mental retardation); he had many signs and symptoms of mental disorder that affected his social spheres; and he seemed to have increasing difficulty with control of his impulses.

Mr Seidel stated that he had suffered from gonorrhea, syphilis, and hepatitis. During the last weeks he had been sick with high fever; the defendant rationalized his illness as being a "cold." He has a pattern of checking in hospitals during the acute episodes of illness and walking out of the hospital before any effective treatment could begin. Once in North Carolina, his father took him to a hospital when he was very sick and then he walked away; while driving in the car and passing in front of another hospital, he told his father to stop to check into that hospital as well.

Mr Seidel stated that he went to a city hospital and attended a program for crime victims for a year three years ago after being sexually attacked at knifepoint on the streets. The defendant claims that he has never been arrested before.

Mr Seidel was adopted as a child. His father (aged 76) and his mother (aged 75) are still alive and live in Virginia where the defendant was raised. The defendant was married for a number of years and then divorced. He had no children.

Mr Seidel spent most of his time working; his social life had been markedly changed in the past three years as a result of the death from AIDS of most of his friends.

Mr Seidel said that he used to "experiment" with drugs (including LSD and hallucination-producing mushrooms) in the 70s but he stopped using drugs. The last time he took any drugs was last Christmas, when he snorted cocaine. The defendant described himself as someone who enjoyed wine but who did not abuse alcohol. Under doctor's recommendations, he sometimes took sleeping pills; the doctor would not give sleeping pills in quantities because he feared the defendant might be suicidal.

Mr Seidel (6'1", 155 lbs) had a sickly appearance and he coughed with abundant production of phlegm; at times, he appeared to be choking on his own phlegm. The defendant appeared as someone who tried to maintain dignity and a bygone elegance. His clothes were of apparently good quality but they looked as if they had not been at the cleaners for a significant time. His mood changed significantly during the interview; at times, he cried when recalling the events leading to his attendance at the Crime Victim program. During the initial phase of the interview, he appeared to have a boyish face and a relatively youthful expression; after the episodes of coughing and crying, the defendant looked aged and defeated. He showed psychomotor retardation; the typical "tempo" of his reactions was very slow, sometimes requiring several seconds to come up with the answers he was clearly motivated to give. He suffered from anomia, the inability to come up with words he obviously used to know. At times, his expression was that of bewilderment. His eye contact was adequate. However, his verbal communication was very poor. The defendant appeared to begin to articulate his thoughts and then expected this evaluator to reconstruct the defendant's words and line of thinking.

A screening battery of probes that included examination of posture, gait, whole-body balance, muscle strength, tremor at rest, intentional tremor, motor coordination, general appearance of the eyes, eye movements, and reaction of the eyes to light was performed and the following was noted: The defendant was unable to follow this evaluator's finger with his eyes; his eyes continued to look fixed, straight ahead. He also had problems with holding his eyes in a cross-eyed position. This was interpreted as a significant neurological sign. The defendant (a two to three pack cigarette smoker a day) had what appears to be a growth on the left side of his lower lip; he has never seen a doctor for this condition.

During the evaluative interview and psychological testing the following was noted. The defendant was asked to remove his jacket to perform a series of motor coordination tests. When he put his jacket back on, he continued his dressing and added his scarf and his overcoat. Then he realized that the evaluation was to continue and he removed his scarf and his overcoat. This behavior suggests the possibility of perseveration, also a sign of neurological disorder.

From an extensive checklist of signs and/or symptoms possibly indicative of neurological or mental disorders, Mr Seidel was asked whether he had ever experienced them, and if so, to give examples. He denied ever having experienced these signs or symptoms. However, the defendant appeared to suffer from denial of illness. He said that he suffered from insomnia and occasionally he has to take sleeping pills to be able to sleep. Paranoid ideation, delusions, and hallucinations were denied.

The defendant said that he has little sense of humor, revealing a concrete mode of thinking. He often brooded on things. Although he appeared to be worried about his health, he has not recently taken a medical examination. He began to carry a knife after the homosexual attack. He said that he denied that he had a knife, thinking that nobody was going to notice it; however, the matter of the knife surfaced during his trial, and he lost his trial and now was facing mandatory incarceration.

The defendant could not really explain why he decided to go to trial and the reason of his confidence in winning the trial after having been caught during the commission of the crime.

The Wechsler Adult Intelligence Scale, Revised (WAIS-R) was administered. Mr Seidel's verbal IQ was found to be 90 and his performance IQ was 74; the overall test IQ was 82. There was a mismatch between verbal and performance scores; this may be indicative of a serious neurological disorder. The defendant was not under medication but he was extremely slow in his reactions. Psychomotor retardation accounted for his poor performance scores. The defendant appeared not to realize that, in the recent past, he indicated that the speed of his reactions had been slowed down. These IQ levels represented a low normal to borderline level of intellectual functioning.

During the administration of this test, the following was noted. In one of the stories of the Picture Arrangement test, the defendant was unable to see the face of one of the characters in the story. This was suggestive of agnosia, a significant neurological sign.

His deteriorating mental status may have first played a part in the commission of the crime, and may have handicapped him in the decision to go to trial. Only on the day in which the evaluation was performed did the defendant have the full realization that he would be incarcerated. At times, there appeared to be an element of self-destruction as the defendant either did not seek legal options that had been open to him in the past or did not attempt to take advantage of any chances of putting his case in a favorable light. The defendant had made no personal arrangements about his life in case he has to spend time in prison. In addition, Mr Seidel was not consulting or even talking to his lawyer.

Because of the early stages of dementia that may be interfering with the defendant's judgment, it was felt that the court might consider ordering an evaluation to determine competence to continue to face legal proceedings before he was scheduled to be sentenced.

☐ QUESTIONS FOR REVIEW AND DISCUSSION

△ Discuss pseudodementia and subcortical dementia.

△ During the course of counseling, a homosexual man who has recently found out he was exposed to HIV tells you that he plans to "get even" and infect as many people he can. Discuss the legal similarities and differences with the Tarasoff ruling (duty to inform the potential victim).

△ Discuss incarceration facilites for inmates afflicted with AIDS.

△ Review matters of your own health protection and protection of inmates suspected to be afflicted with AIDS but who are still awaiting the results of important medical laboratory tests.

15: NEUROTROPIC AGENTS AND DRUGS

A CHEMICAL SUBSTANCE IS TERMED NEUROTROPIC WHEN IT DISPLAYS AN affinity for the nervous system. A neurotropic agent can be a beneficial drug (such as an antipsychotic medication) or a harmful substance (such as a neurotoxic poison).

In the forensic sciences, it is the intended use of a chemical substance that distinguish a beneficial substance from a poison. Arsenic, for example, is commonly found in many foodstuffs, but at such a low dose that it causes no harmful effects; it is also an effective raticide, and one can be harmed by accidental ingestion; or someone can intentionally use arsenic to kill a person. Thus, toxicologically, it is the *dose* that determines whether or not it is a poison; from the forensic point of view, it is the *intended use* that determines criminal intent.

This chapter is an introduction to some basic notions of forensic neurotoxicology. Chapter 16 reviews some fundamental concepts of illegal drugs, their use and effects, and the instances when illegal drugs are the focus of a forensic neuropsychological investigation. Chapter 17 is an overview of environmental and occupational neurotoxic agents, and issues that are important to the forensic neuropsychologist in evaluating either individuals or groups of persons.

A chemical substance is neurotoxic when it can cause a harmful change in an individual's nervous system. The neurotoxic environment is the sum of all the chemical compounds present in the human habitat that have a potential of creating a health hazard for humans. Neurotoxic agents found in the environment and the workplace will be distinguished from drugs, the topic of this chapter. Neuropsychologists are increasingly called upon to offer an opinion in cases of individuals exposed to neurotoxic agents in the environment or the workplace. Per force, this chapter is only a superficial treatment of the subject; readers interested in more detail may consult Klaassen, Amdur, and Doull (1986) or Valciukas (1991). First, some definitions are necessary.

Definitions

- *Poison* is any agent that is capable of causing a deleterious response in a biological system or is capable of destroying life or seriously injuring a vital function. At a high dose, for example, cyanide becomes a poison.

- *Toxic* is a synonym for "poisonous," but the latter term is now rarely used. A substance that is toxic has the property of causing a harmful or lethal effect. Asbestos is a toxic substance; but asbestos is not known to be neurotoxic, affecting the lungs rather than the nervous system.

- A *neurotoxic substance* is capable of causing a deleterious effect on the nervous system at the structural (macroscopic or molecular) or functional (behavioral or psychological) level. Methylmercury, for example, is a powerful neurotoxic substance.

- The *neurotoxicity* of a given chemical compound relates (among other factors) to its amount and concentration. Zinc, for example, is often listed (appropriately) as a neurotoxic metal. Yet, zinc is also a vital nutrient when present in the diet in only very small quantities.

☐ The level of organization at which neurotoxicity can be demonstrated is important. *Neurotoxic effects* can occur at the gross morphological, cellular, or molecular level of organization. Often, compendia of toxic chemicals list "neurotoxic agents" irrespective of the level of organization where it has been demonstrated. For example: Sometimes a powerful neurotoxic agent capable of causing human death may be described alongside another which has been found to produce minor pharmacological alterations only in cells of the spinal cord of chicken embryos in vitro.

☐ The *neurotoxic properties* of many compounds may be overlooked in lists where the primary target of toxicity is cited. For example, some drugs whose primary target is the cardiovascular system are also neurotoxic. Digitalis, for example, increases the force of contraction of the myocardium (heart muscle) but at toxic levels it can also cause blurred vision, loss of visual acuity, and disturbances in color perception. Most toxic agents have multiple targets of toxicity.

☐ The intrinsic association between a group of chemical compounds and neurotoxic properties should never be suggested or implied without clinical, experimental, or epidemiologic evidence. For example, many industrial solvents are neurotoxic. But one does not actually imply that all solvents are neurotoxic. Thus, water is generally regarded as the "universal solvent;" yet, only under exceptional circumstances is water toxic. (Water is toxic when — as a result of ingestion of large amounts, often by mentally disturbed individuals — an imbalance in electrolytes vital for neural transmission occurs).

☐ A *neurotoxin* is any toxic substance that occurs naturally in the environment or is produced by living organisms such as plants or animals but is capable of causing a biological effect on the human nervous system. In many cases, neurotoxins are part of a plant or animal's defensive or offensive mechanism. Nicotine and caffeine, for example, occur naturally in plants as protection against predators. Neurotoxins can also kill. The sting of some spiders (such as the Black Widow) can cause human death.

Some neurotoxic agents (such as anthrax and botulism) while naturally occurring, are part of the arsenal of human chemical warfare. A neurotoxin is generally an organic, naturally-occurring compound — i.e., the venom contained in the sting of the marine animal Portuguese man-of-war. But toxins can also be produced synthetically or by means of genetic engineering in the laboratory. The term neurotoxin should not be construed to mean the nervous system as the only target. For example, snake venoms are often classified separately as neurotoxins, cardiotoxins, hemotoxins, cytotoxins, myotoxins, and the like. Snake venoms appear to affect many membranes and perhaps most tissues of the body. These naturally-occurring toxins are sometimes used for criminal purposes.

□ A *neurotoxicant* is any neurotoxin, neurotoxic agent, or neurotoxic drug. Although the term is useful for its broad connotations, it is not widely used in the environmental and occupational toxicology literature.

□ A *neurotoxic drug* is:

   □ A naturally-occurring substance or (more frequently today) a manufactured chemical compound developed for therapeutic purposes to alleviate medical conditions, such as the use of salicylic acid (aspirin) to relieve pain.

   □ A chemical compound used to arrest the progress of a neurological disease. L-dopa, for example, is used to halt the devastating degenerative effects of Parkinson's disease.

   □ A chemical substance that can control behavioral changes, such as the use of lithium to alleviate severe swings in mood.

□ A *xenobiotic agent* is any chemical compound developed by humans; the Greek word "xenos" means "foreign," indicating that the compound is not part of our natural habitat. But not all xenobiotic agents are harmful. In fact, the vast majority of chemical compounds and drugs created by humans have beneficial effects on humans at appropriate doses or have directly or indirectly improved the quality of our lives.

□ *Neurotoxic agents* are chemical compounds capable of causing a temporary or permanent change in nervous system function. The term refers to a large family of chemical compounds developed for useful purposes in industry, agriculture, or the household, but are inadvertently harmful to humans. There may be several interrelated factors explaining why they may be harmful.

□ The dangerous neurotoxic properties of a given chemical compound may be unknown. For example, until its accidental release to the environment, PBBs (polybrominated biphenyls) were not known to be toxic.

□ The presence of a neurotoxic chemical compound in the human habitat may be unsuspected. For example, children have died after consuming insecticides thinking it was sugar.

□ A chemical compound may be a neurotoxic agent when used for purposes other than intended or when inadequately handled. For example, mercury was used as a fungicide to protect wheat seed intended for planting. It caused devastating health effects in Iraq when, during a period of famine, seeds were used to make bread.

ABSORPTION AND DISTRIBUTION

The mere presence of a neurotoxicant in the environment is not necessarily a cause for neurotoxic illness: The chemical compound must enter the human body and reach a target somewhere in the nervous system. In the previous chapter chemical compounds that are neurotoxic were discussed; in this chapter we will understand why they are neurotoxic by considering their absorption, distribution, metabolism, and excretion. In Environmental and Occupation Health Sciences, this information is essential for designing effective strategies for biological monitoring and for accurate reconstruction of the workers' occupational history (a topic discussed in Chapter 17).

Neurotoxic agents can enter the body via various routes. Some of these routes may not be suspected; thus it is important to identify them so that inadvertent exposure does not occur; some of these unsuspected routes are utilized for criminal purposes. For example, a weekend gardener working in his shorts may absorb a significant amount of pesticides via testicular absorption which is as effective and toxic in causing illness as oral absorption of certain pesticides. Cigarette smoking at a lead smelting facility, for example, is a practice that may result in increasing levels of lead absorption. Lead particles may be inhaled along with the cigarette smoke. Lead deposited on the cigarette paper as a result of handling the cigarette with contaminated hands may be both inhaled and ingested.

The locus of action needs to be recognized. A local effect is the direct effect of a toxic agent at the site of the contact between the toxicant and the biological tissue. A chemical compound may thus be caustic to the stomach; some others are lung irritants. The nerves of the peripheral nervous system can be affected locally as a result of *percutaneous* (skin) *absorption*. A systemic effect is that requiring absorption and distribution of the toxicant from its entry point to a distant site at which deleterious effects might occur. For example, the alcohol ingested by a partygoer or solvents inhaled by a professional painter produce their neurotoxic effects when the toxicants reach the brain. Figure 15.1 is a simplified view of the absorption, transport, and fate of neurotoxicants.

Inhalation

Many neurotoxic agents are absorbed through the lungs. Volatile and gaseous toxic agents, such as industrial and commercial solvents, may be inhaled via the nose and mouth and enter the circulatory system through the mucous membranes of the respiratory tract. In the lungs, the area of absorption is very large and access to blood circulation is rapid.

Physically, toxic agents may be present as either dusts or droplets in air (aerosols). Workers in auto body shops who remove excessive lead applied to gaps by sanding, painters exposed to organic solvents in paints, and chemical workers who manufacture psychoactive drugs (mind modifiers) may be occupationally exposed through this mechanism. The snorting of cocaine, occurring at the olfactory epithelium, is an example of local absorption of soluble dusts.

Ingestion

Oral absorption is an important route of neurotoxic absorption in children. Lead intoxication, for example, can occur as a result of mouthing contaminated soil. It is also a possible route of entry for workers exposed to neurotoxic dusts such as miners and smelter workers where ingestion may take place without the individual realizing it as, for example, when workers eat at a contaminated workplace.

There are numerous factors that regulate gastrointestinal absorption:

☐ The concentration of the neurotoxic agent or drug at the site of absorption; this is fundamental.

☐ The physicochemical properties of the neurotoxic agents or drugs, especially lipid solubility. The greater the ability of an agent or drug to be dissolved in fat, the greater its chances of being absorbed, since all living cells of the body have fat in their membranes.

☐ The physiological factors involved at the particular site of the gastrointestinal tract. For example, many drugs and neurotoxicants are absorbed more readily in the small intestine than in the stomach because of favorable pH, enzymatic activity, and intestinal motility.

☐ The amount of surface area exposed to the neurotoxic agent; the greater the surface area, the greater the absorption. Factors that affect surface area are the intestinal flora present and whether the individual has eaten food that could inhibit absorption.

☐ The maturational state of the individual, the child having a much greater rate of gastrointestinal absorption than the adult, and the fact that body size is related to effective dose. For the same dose, a child's body is more vulnerable than a larger adult.

Dermal Absorption

Some neurotoxic agents readily penetrate the skin. These include a large number of solvents and pesticides. Workers who continually use degreasers for personal cleansing, e.g., acetone, may absorb these agents dermally and later show neurotoxic illness. Improper design of protective gloves and shoes may actually maximize dermal absorption by trapping toxic substances between the inner surface of the glove or shoe and the skin. In hot environments, rolling up the sleeves or pant legs of clothing meant to protect the skin can also increase dermal absorption.

The skin is not a homogeneous organ; different areas of the body have a different potential for dermal absorption. Factors such as skin thickness and local blood circulation play important roles; the thicker the skin, the less the absorption. The skin of the back, for instance, is thick, while that of the lips is very thin. The skin on the genital organs of men and women is an example of thin, highly vascularized tissue, favoring dermal absorption.

Sublingual Absorption

This route of entry is encountered in drug administration for therapeutic purposes. Though the surface area on the tongue is relatively small, the tongue cannot be overlooked as a possible route of toxic exposures. For example, nitroglycerin is taken sublingually to treat heart conditions. Despite the tongue's small surface area, this drug is effective because it is potent and has a high lipid solubility, i.e., only few molecules are needed to produce the desired therapeutic effect.

Local Absorption

Local absorption is also called "area" or "topical" (from the Greek *topos,* meaning place) absorption.

Some toxic exposures occur as the result of the direct contact of neurotoxic agents on peripheral nerves. Dental assistants, for example, may expose peripheral nerves in their hands to methyl methacrylate when manually preparing amalgam, an alloy used for filling cavities.

Topical application on mucous membranes of the nose is another example of local absorption. This route of entry is common in illegal drug administration, such as in cocaine snorting, or in solvent addiction, such as toluene.

Other Routes of Entry

In medicine (as well as in drug addiction or during the criminal use of chemical substances) other routes of entry include injection either subcutaneously, intramuscularly, or intravenously.

Intraperitoneal administration, meaning injecting the drug or neurotoxic agent directly into the abdominal cavity, is often used in laboratory animals.

Rectal administration, for instance, occurs in therapeutic uses of drugs when oral administration is impossible because of vomiting or when the patient is unconscious. This route is also preferred when the drug is destroyed by digestive enzymes if given orally.

To circumvent the blood brain barrier that normally protects the brain, some drugs are administered into the cerebrospinal fluid, as in the case of spinal anesthesia during difficult childbirths.

Effects of Age, Sex, Race, and Body Size

Age. Neurotoxic agents and drugs have a differential effect on children, adults, and the elderly. This is primarily due to the differences in the rate of absorption in the gastrointestinal tract and the liver's capacity to metabolize chemical substances. For a large number of neurotoxic agents and psychoactive drugs, children and the elderly are more susceptible to the toxic effects of such drugs than adults. Experimental work with laboratory animals such as the rat have shown that, in the case of lead, the neonate's gastrointestinal tract surface is more permeable than the adult's. The likelihood and danger that some neurotoxic agents, such as alcohol, can be released from the mother through breast feeding and absorbed by the neonate is also an important issue.

Sex. In epidemiologic studies of neurotoxic illness, biological factors associated with ingestion, distribution, and metabolism are sometime difficult to disentangle from and psychological and cultural factors (such as eating habits). Neurotoxic agents can accumulate in fat and bones. Fat deposition, for example, is genetically different in males and females. During pregnancy, massive toxic doses of lead may be released from storage in fat and bone deposits into the bloodstream. But eating habits are primarily determined by culture. Male North American Indians, for example, eat muskrats which may be contaminated with methylmercury; females rarely eat them. (The source of methylmercury is the fish that muskrats eat).

Race. In the past, racial variations in toxic absorption were thought to be due to genetic predisposition. A classic example involved the occupational absorption of asbestos among insulators. Until a generation ago, asbestosis was thought to be a disease of Caucasians. It was argued that Blacks were genetically "less susceptible" than Caucasians to the toxic effects of asbestos, when in fact, it was eventually realized that because of long-standing discriminating job practices, Blacks were less likely to be hired as insulators. Thus, the lower prevalence of asbestosis in Blacks had no genetic basis. It has been well established, however, that certain racial groups do exhibit greater absorption of particular toxins. For instance, people of Chinese ancestry lack the enzyme aldehyde hydrogenase necessary for ethanol metabolism. Minimal ingestion of alcoholic beverages may result in illness and the development of sudden rashes in these people.

Volume of distribution, body size, and body mass. Some quantitative aspects of the absorption and distribution of toxic chemicals depend on physical properties of the body considered as a single compartment. The volume of distribution within such a compartment is assumed to be relatively uniform (or of not practical consequence if not uniform). A given amount of chemical compound will be in relatively higher concentrations in someone with a small body than in someone with a larger body. This is why "toxic dose" is specified as a unit of volume per unit weight. In addition to body weight, in epidemiological studies it is necessary to know body mass. For certain toxic agents, such as DDT, the greater the body mass, the greater is the statistical likelihood of increased accumulation of toxin in fat. There are several anthropometric measures of body mass, one of which is the Quetelet index, relating height and weight. The presence of fat can be ascertained by means of anthropometric techniques, as for example the use of calipers to measure natural skin foldings.

Effects of physiological conditions. The physiologic activity of an individual at the moment of examination is important in the estimation of the pharmacological properties of neurotoxic agents. Feeding, physical exercise, and emotional state are examples of physiological conditions that have been extensively investigated.

☐ Feeding is a factor. People who drink milk before alcoholic beverages, for example, retard the process of ethanol ingestion by coating the digestive tract and reducing the available surface of gastrointestinal absorption.

☐ In general, physical exercise increases the rate of absorption of neurotoxic agents. Numerous animal and human studies support the role of physical exercise on neurotoxic absorption.

☐ Emotional states are factors that affect drug and toxicant absorption; emotions are difficult to measure and interpret. Emotional states have an effect on a neurotoxic agent's rate of absorption in essentially three ways. First, an emotional state may be associated with agitation and increased respiratory rate, leading to a more effective inhalation of gaseous agents. Second, an emotional state such as depression may lead to apathy and failure to take precautions on possible sources of contamination. Third, emotional states are complex neurobehavioral phenomena controlled by the hypothalamic-autonomic system; the possibility that emotional states physiologically modulate absorption has long been postulated but not yet adequately studied or documented.

EXCRETION AND BIOTRANSFORMATION

Drugs and neurotoxic agents are secreted from the body either unchanged or as metabolites. The knowledge of whether a neurotoxic agent is excreted unchanged or is biotransformed (metabolized) is important. This physiological fact supports the concept of biological monitoring (BM), to be reviewed in the following chapter dealing with the toxicological basis of Environmental & Occupational Health Sciences. Biological monitoring is essential for the control of toxic agents in the environment and the workplace. Most of the excretion of a toxic substance from the body is by the kidney or by biotransformation by the liver.

Renal Excretion

The kidneys excrete the end products of body metabolism (urea) as well as any excess of vital substances such as sodium, potassium, and chloride. The kidneys also maintain a balance of water and sodium, an essential process under the control of hormones generated by the hypothalamus, a brain structure. The

FIGURE 15.1

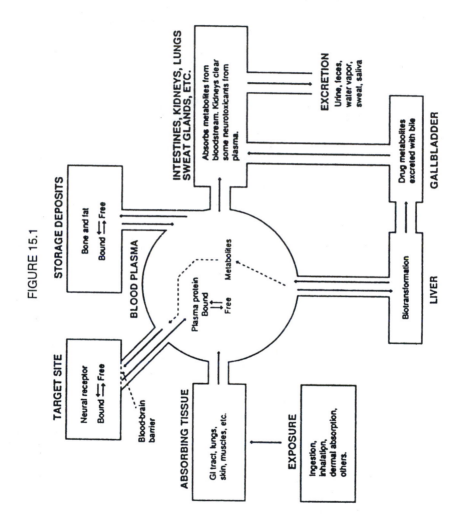

kidneys perform these functions in three major ways: Glomerular filtration, reabsorption, and tubular excretion.

The functional unit of the kidney is the nephron, a long, unbranched tubule extending from a capsule-like structure (the Bowman's capsule) encircling a network of capillaries, the glomerulus. There are one to three million nephrons per kidney totalling about 35 miles of tubules. The internal/external fluid exchange is facilitated by close contact between blood vessels and tubules. The glomerulus has pores of 70 to 80 Ångstrons in diameter, and, under normal positive hydrostatic conditions in the glomerulus, all molecules smaller than molecular weight 20,000 are filtered. Thus, large proteins or protein-bound drugs, and neurotoxic agents remain in the plasma and are not excreted.

The glomerular filtrate contains many essential body constituents such as water and glucose. These (along with lipid soluble drugs or neurotoxic agents) are reabsorbed back or reclaimed into the blood plasma before they leave the body via the urine. There are many factors influencing this process, the pH of the filtrate being one of them.

Elimination of liquid waste as urine occurs via the collecting ducts that converge into the ureters. Tubular excretion of foreign compounds may be accomplished by direct active secretion into the renal tubules by anion and cation carrier processes. Urine analysis is important for the detection of the presence of illegal drugs and neurotoxic agents or their metabolites.

Liver Metabolism

Although biotransformation can occur in the kidney, spleen, intestine, blood, lung, brain, and skin, the liver is the most important organ in this process. The end product of liver activity is the production of single inactive metabolites, and active metabolites. Active metabolites (or breakdown products of toxic subtances) are important since drugs or neurotoxic agents may not, by themselves, produce a neurotoxic effect but their metabolites may.

Drugs and neurotoxic agents are biotransformed by enzymes. The ability of an enzyme to alter a drug or neurotoxic agent is dependent on the liver's ability to form an enzyme-agent interaction. The principles underlying these chemical and pharmacokinetic processes are very similar to those governing the formation of receptor-agent bonds.

The molecules of drugs or neurotoxic agent can be modified by two processes: Synthetic and non-synthetic reactions. A synthetic reaction is the chemical bond of a drug or neurotoxic agent, or its metabolite(s), with naturally-occurring molecules provided by the body. The result of this process is the formation of a pharmacologically inert, generally a water-soluble product which is readily excreted from the kidney. In pharmacology, this process is also known as conjugation.

Four major chemical groups make synthetic reactions possible; these include carbonyl (COOH), hydroxyl (OH), amino (NH), and sulphydryl (SH). For conjugation to occur, one of these chemical groups must be present. A drug or neurotoxic agent may undergo a nonsynthetic reaction before conjugation if there is not a site for the pharmacological bond to occur (that is, if none of these four chemical compounds are present).

Non-synthetic reactions involve oxidation, reduction, or hydrolysis. Oxidation is a chemical reaction where a carbon atom increases its covalent bonds to either oxygen or nitrogen. In a reduction, a carbon atom reduces the number of its bonds to oxygen or nitrogen. In hydrolysis, water molecules take an active part in the biotransformation of the drug or neurotoxic agent. The end result of a non-synthetic reaction may be the formation of an active metabolite more potent (more toxic) than the original drug or neurotoxic agent.

Drugs and neurotoxic agents are metabolized by liver enzymes located in the cells of the smooth endoplasmic reticulum. The enzymes perform primarily non-synthetic reactions of oxidation, reduction, and hydrolysis. Among their functions is the conjugation with glucuronic acid. Repeated exposure to certain drugs (such as mood modifiers) change the enzymatic activity of the liver. Tolerance to drugs (see below) is explained by this mechanism.

Other Routes of Excretion

Neurotoxic agents may be secreted by feces, expired air, sweat, saliva, semen, vomitus, tears, milk, nails, and hair. Forensic investigators who need to know the causes of neuropsychological dysfunction often need to know the fate of chemicals or their metabolites by analyzing these secretions.

☐ The chemical analysis of expired air is important in metabolic studies designed to monitor the effects of industrial solvents in humans. These evaluations are usually performed under laboratory conditions where a known amount of the solvent first inhaled and then the exhaled air is collected in plastic bags for further analysis.

☐ Milk excretion is an important route. Drugs and neurotoxic agents may be secreted via the mother's milk causing health problems in infants whose livers lack fully developed metabolizing enzymes to biotransform them.

☐ Analysis of hair samples receives considerable attention in forensic toxicology, a field with which forensic neuropsychology is very much related. Hair samples of ancient mummies have been studied for their lead content. The levels of arsenic and other metals can be examined in people who have died hundreds of years ago.

◻ Secretion and storage of neurotoxic agents can occur in animal fur. Knowledge of this avenue of excretion is essential in veterinary toxicology during the course of certain types of criminal investigations.

TOLERANCE

Definition of Tolerance

Tolerance is the reduction of potency of a drug or the toxicity of an agent following repeated administration of that drug or repeated exposure to the agent. Tolerance is a function or ability of the organism, not the chemical compound. As a result, increasing levels of the drug or toxic agent are needed to produce the same effect. Sometimes, there can be a dissociation in the development of different tolerance effects. With repeated oral ingestion of Librium, for example, tolerance develops to its sedative properties while its antianxiety properties remain unchanged. Repeated ingestion of barbiturates may reduce its sedative properties (or even produce insomnia) while the properties of dangerously inhibiting the respiratory centers do not show tolerance or adaptation.

Types of Tolerance

Several forms of tolerance are recognized.

◻ *Cross tolerance* is the development of tolerance to a drug or neurotoxic agent by repeated exposure to a second drug or neurotoxic agent. Cross tolerance to alcohol has been extensively studied, for example. Phenobarbital (an anticonvulsant drug) is more potent in individuals who have developed tolerance to alcohol than patients who have not. Cross tolerance exists among many hallucinogenic drugs, such as LSD, psilocybin, and mescaline.

◻ *Drug disposition tolerance* is the induction of tolerance to a drug or neurotoxic agent due to the increased presence of more metabolizing enzymes in the liver. This is also called metabolic tolerance. It is presumed that the drug creates a reduction of effect at its receptor by decreasing the effective concentration of the agonists or by reducing the reactivity of the receptor.

◻ *Cellular tolerance* is an adaptation to the effects of a drug or toxic agent even when the plasma levels of the drug are high. It is also called pharmacodynamic tolerance. It is thought that the tolerance is a property of receptor substances on cell surfaces, a diminished number of receptors or a lower affinity of the receptor for the chemical compound results in lowered effectiveness of the drug or toxic agent. The most common form of pharmacological tolerance, for example, is that to opiates such as morphine and heroin.

◻ *Behavioral tolerance* is a behavioral adaptation to a drug's effects following repeated administration. A person who suffers from severe alcoholism, for example, learns to compensate for the acute effects of alcohol.

THE LANGUAGE OF TOXICOLOGY

Terms

Every chemical substance can be classified as to its potency or *toxicity*. Traditionally, six basic classes of potency are recognized: Extremely toxic, highly toxic, moderately toxic, slightly toxic, relatively non-toxic, and relatively harmless. *Poison* is a chemical term referring to extremely or highly toxic.

What renders an agent neurotoxic is its ability to reach, react, and pharmacologically affect some branch of the nervous system (the brain, brain stem, spinal cord, and nerves). We have already indicated that neurotoxic agents can affect the nervous system locally (as when anesthetics are injected by dentists into the gums without affecting other portions of the mouth) and systemic (as when the toxic agent needs to travel some distance to the brain to produce its toxic effects).

Some of the effects can be direct and others indirect. Halothane (an anesthesic) has a direct effect on the nervous system producing narcosis. Narcosis is a profound loss of consciousness caused by a drug. Some others produce indirect effects on the nervous system through their primary action on the kidney, liver, blood-forming mechanisms, or pulmonary action. Sometimes a toxic agent can cause permanent biochemical changes and traumatic alterations in the nervous system — i.e., chronic toxic psychosis caused by PCP (Phencyclidine, also known by its street name, "Angel Dust").

The effects of a neurotoxic agent can also be *acute* or *chronic*. *Acute* is a term used to indicate both a short period of time — minutes, hours, days, and even weeks. The term is also often used to indicate that the toxic effect is reversible. The period of time for the production of an acute effect cannot always be precisely defined. Thus, the acute effects of certain neurotoxic agents are measured either in a few seconds, or in minutes, hours, days and even weeks, such as the time a human takes to recuperate from poisoning by certain snakes.

A *chronic* effect is one where there is permanent damage to the nervous system and is used to denote a phenomenon that lasts over a long period of time (months or years) and is largely irreversible. Exposure to methylmercury *in utero*, for example, causes chronic damage to the child's nervous system (Minamata disease) associated with profound mental retardation.

Most forensic investigators agree that long-term, low level exposure to a neurotoxic agent needs an additional term. The term subchronic has been proposed to describe such a pattern of toxic exposure. But the reader needs to ascertain how a particular author uses this term in the literature. The expression "long-term low-level exposure" is used by some authors.

In Chapter 7, two terms used in neurology were introduced: *Subclinical* and *preclinical. Subclinical* (literally, not yet seen as causing a disease) indicates a pharmacological, neurophysiological (or even a behavioral or psychological) change that is not detected during the course of the clinical examination of the subject at a given point in time. Certain electrophysiological and psychometric procedures are useful to detect changes that are not observed by examining physicians and, sometimes, by the subjects themselves.

The term *preclinical* is used to designate signs, symptoms or syndromes that occur before the appearance of the overt manifestation of neurotoxic illness. Thus, in the term preclinical, "pre" indicates time. Preclinical is a useful term in preventive medicine to indicate the fact that, if conditions are left by themselves and without control, a clinical manifestation of neurotoxic disease is likely to appear later.

Neurotoxic effects may be observed, on the one hand, immediately after the inhalation, ingestion, injection, and topical application of the agent or, on the other, after several days. The latter is called *delayed neurotoxicity*. Certain pesticides, such as triorthocresyl phosphate (TOCP), leptophos, and mipafox are capable of causing delayed toxic neuropathies, that is, delayed effects on the peripheral nervous system causing paralysis and sensory alterations first in lower limbs and then in upper limbs.

There are numerous terms used to describe the manner in which chemicals interact with themselves. The following is a partial list; some others may be found in Klaassen, Amdur, and Doull (1986).

- An *additive* effect is one in which the combined effect of two chemicals is approximately the sum of the effect of each individual agent. The simultaneous presence of several organophosphorus pesticides may be additive and this effect is explained in terms of the additive effects of the rate of inhibition of cholinesterase (an enzyme) by each pesticide.

- A *synergistic* effect is one in which the effects of two chemical compounds is much greater than the simple sum of their single effects. Ethanol (alcohol) produces a synergistic effect when present along with many drugs and industrial solvents.

- *Potentiation* describes an effect in which a chemical compound itself may not be able to produce a toxic effect but when added to another the latter is much more toxic.

- *Antagonism* describes the inhibitory effects that the two chemicals have when they are simultaneously present.

- *Antidote* (with its original meaning of being capable of arresting or negating the effects of a poison) is now rarely used in the scientific literature.

Mortality and Morbidity Toxicology

Forensic experts are sometimes dependent on information gathered by other professionals such as human toxicologists and epidemiologists. The latter two perform essentially two types of studies: Mortality and morbidity. In mortality studies, one of the basic measurements is the ascertainment of the lethal dose. The concept of lethal dose is well rooted in statistical thinking. When a single dose (that is, the concentration per unit weight of a given toxic agent) is administered to a group of cells, bacteria, or experimental animals, the percentage of individuals who will die is proportional to the dose. At a lower concentration, for example, 30% of the individuals may die; at a higher dose, 75%. Thus, lethal dose is a relative term.

During the initial stages of a toxicological study, several different percentages of lethal dose are plotted. Theoretically (and depending on financial and human resources, and increasing ethical considerations regulating animal research), one could ascertain the percentage of dead experimental animals for increasing amounts of dose of the chemical agent in very fine graduated steps. But this is both inpractical and unnecessary. Few well-chosen steps (usually in logarithmic incremental units) can give a good idea of the overall statistical trends for the group. The LD_{50} (that is, the dose capable of killing 50% of the laboratory animals during experimental trials) is a common reference point and is ascertained by mathematical extrapolation of empirical data. The forensic neuropsychologist needs to know this terminology because it often appears in forensic reports and is discussed in court appearances.

The concept of lethal dose is basic in classical toxicology and epidemiology studies dealing with mortality, for example on toxicological studies of cancer. In neurotoxicology, the terms used in "morbidity toxicology" are important. During the process of a criminal investigation, it is also important to know the concept of lethal dose and how lethal dose is related to effective dose (ED) and toxic dose (TD). What follows is a brief introduction to the terminology of "morbidity toxicology."

Threshold levels to neurotoxic substances need to be known in forensic investigations involving occupational or environmental exposures to chemical substances. "Threshold" as a scientific concept has existed since the middle of the last century. Ernst Heinrich Weber (1795-1878), a physiologist, performed the classic experiment to determine the magnitude of the physical stimuli just sufficient to produce a specific sensation (e.g., pain). Gustav Theodor Fechner (1801-1887) concluded that the magnitude of the sensation and the physical stimuli required to produce the effect were related by a logarithmic law, called the Weber-Fechner law. The branch of experimental psychology dealing with the study of stimulus-response relationships in the sensory systems is called psychophysics.

When and why psychophysicists and toxicologists parted and went their own ways is difficult to ascertain. Psychophysics and toxicology had a common ancestor and a common language in the German science of the last century. Physics was taught alongside chemistry, the physiological sciences, and psychology (then a new discipline, but well rooted in physiology). In addition, most scientists of the period had a particular inclination for philosophy; some of them (such as Fechner) considered themselves "experimental philosophers" and performed their experiments to test or prove philosophical ideas.

A threshold is the minimal amount of energy, either physical or chemical, just sufficient to produce an observable effect. Physicochemists, pharmacologists, and neurophysiologists determine at what concentration (or dose) a given chemical substance appears to produce a physical, chemical, physiological, or behavioral change.

Both the stimulus and the effects are intertwined. For example, the slowing of the electrical conduction velocity of a nerve (the effect) is related to the stimulus, the oral administration of methylmercury (the cause). The effect is defined in terms of the levels of the stimulus (the cause) that is, at what level of ingested levels of methylmercury a statistically significant reduction in nerve conduction velocity is observed.

"Threshold limit values" is almost a tautology, as is the expression "the hazardous effects of dangerous substances." Threshold *is* a limit. However, "limit" has the connotation of "ceiling," the maximum allowable levels of a substance recommended in the environment or the workplace. Threshold limit values (TLV$^{®}$) for a large number of substances have been calculated. The best source for current information is *TLV® - Threshold Limit Values and Biological Exposure Indices,* published by the American Conference of Governmental and Industrial Hygienists.

TLVs are necessary but inadequate. The most serious problem with TLVs is that certain toxic agents (most notably, asbestos and neurotoxic substances such as lead) do not seem to have a threshold. That is, there is no low level of exposure that is "safe." Moreover, TLVs need to be complemented by other concepts. The concept of *no-effect level* (NEL) is obviously inadequate because by "effect" one may mean changes in the physical appearance of nerve cells *in vitro*, changes in the selective permeability of membranes, slowing of conduction of peripheral nerves, or reduction in reaction time. The possibility of delayed neurotoxicity (described above) may need to be taken into account as well. Finally, the concept of no-effect level is subjective and depends very much on who does the observing.

Thus, the concept of no-effect level has been upgraded to include the use of techniques which could be available for public scrutiny giving rise to the concept of *non-observable-effect level* (NOEL). But, how important would the knowledge of and physiological properties of a toxic substance be if no adverse health effects for humans or animals could be demonstrated? The concept of *non-observable-adverse effect level* (NOAEL) originated in response to this criticism.

Dose-Response Relationships

The concept of a dose-response relationship is fundamental in experimental pharmacology, human forensic toxicology, and forensic applications of environmental and occupational health sciences, and it is of increasing concern to neuropsychologists. Toxicologists view the dose and response as causally related, whereas epidemiologists tend to be more cautious when speaking of statistical associations between exposure levels and neurological signs and symptoms or the results of electrophysiological and psychometric tests. This distinction has enormous legal consequences that are the object of current debates.

THE LANGUAGE OF ENVIRONMENTAL HEALTH

The fields of environmental and occupational (E & O) health are rapidly expanding. One of the major objectives of these disciplines is the prevention of environmentally- or occupationally-induced toxic illnesses. As stated earlier, there are many individual attempts to link the principles of environmental and occupational health to firmly-rooted pharmacological and toxicological principles. However, a literal translation is practically impossible and does not always satisfy the large number of professionals who have different backgrounds and who need to apply these concepts in different contexts.

Some of the most basic concepts are *drug* and *toxic agent*. Drugs and toxic agents follow the same pharmacokinetic and pharmacodynamic laws. But the conditions of "administration" are radically different.

- ☐ Drugs are *administered* under clinical conditions for their therapeutic value and the individual who takes the drug (or his or her relatives) agrees to the drug administration.

- ☐ People are unwittingly *exposed* to toxic agents in the environment or the workplace; in many cases, people who are affected by environmental or occupational toxic exposure do not even know about the existence of such exposures.

There is current discussion (with an yet unresolved outcome) about a common terminology that applies to both fields.

There are at least three essential concepts that have originated in the environmental and occupational health sciences. Zielhuis and Henderson, in an editorial published in 1986, urged the proper use of these terms. Quotations are taken from that source.

Terms

Environmental monitoring (EM) is the "measurement and assessment of agents at the workplace and evaluates ambient exposure and health risk compared to an appropriate reference."

Biological monitoring (BM) is the "measurement and assessment of work-place agents or their metabolites either in tissues, secreta, excreta, expired air, of any combinations of these to evaluate exposures and health risk compared to an appropriate measure."

Health surveillance (health effects monitoring, or HEM) is the "periodic medico-physiological examination of exposed workers with the objective of protecting health and preventing occupationally related disease."

Both the external and the internal (our own body) environment are monitored. Industrial hygienists, while measuring ambient levels of a chemical compounds in the workplace, make an evaluation of the external environment while biological monitoring measures humans' internal indications of absorption (blood lead levels) or internal indicators of effects (e.g., ZPP, ALA-D, ALAU). These are sometimes called *biological markers* of absorption (or effects). Some of these indicators are agent-specific: Zinc protoporphyrin for lead; cholinesterase for exposure to cholinesterase-inhibiting chemical compounds. Some others are non-agent specific, since many chemical compounds may produce the same biological response, for example, anemia.

The American Conference of Government and Industrial Hygienists (ACGIH) published in 1984 a list of biological exposure indices (BEI) with the similar meaning to biological monitors. A committee of the Deutsche Forschungs Gemeinschaft proposed the concept of biologically acceptable limits of occupational exposure (BAT).

THE OCCUPATIONAL HISTORY

Occupational history is a chronological account of all the jobs a person has had since he or she entered the work force. It includes exposures, use of protective equipment and hygiene practices. The occupational history is taken by many:

- ☐ A professional during the clinical examination
- ☐ A health scientist during an epidemiologic survey

☐ A scientist who is performing experimental studies with human subjects under laboratory conditions

☐ A forensic professional who evaluates the defendant's objective findings, signs and symptoms, in cases in which the defendant claims occupational-induced neurotoxic illness

This brief section is devoted to the explanation of how an occupational history is obtained.

Quantitative Estimates of Toxic Exposures

An assessment of human dose is made essentially by two types of data: Measurements of environmental levels of chemical compounds and exposure estimates abstracted from the occupational history. (A discussion of techniques of sampling and continuous monitoring of environmental chemicals in air, water and soil, techniques for continuous personal monitoring, and chemical analytical techniques for analysis of these samples are beyond the scope of this book.) Measurement of environmental levels of toxic substances is not always possible, e.g., management does not allow these measurements to be made on the premises; the product that is suspected to cause a health problem is no longer in use; responsible individuals have removed all evidence on the suspected chemical; there is no accepted technology for such assessments, etc. Therefore, sometimes the occupational history is the only source on information of the possible causes of health problems.

An occupational history that is taken by an experienced interviewer, abstracted by a professional person well trained in both job practices and data-reduction procedures can produce the following information:

☐ The classification of an entire workforce by job categories and further by process division or task duties — e.g., custodians, pipe fitters, painters, mechanics, office workers, etc.

☐ Information obtained from environmental measures, a ranking of jobs by exposure — e.g., lead smelters (heaviest exposure to lead), packers and workers in the unloading deck carrying batteries to the smelter (intermediate exposure), and workers in the shipping department (minimal exposure).

☐ Quantitative estimates of length of service in the industry — i.e., duration of toxic exposure. This information can lead to estimates of turnover rates (how quickly workers quit their jobs and why) and whether these turnover rates are related to changes in environmental conditions.

☐ When the information derived from the occupational history is related to measures of biological markers of exposures, quantitative dose estimates are sometimes possible, e.g., levels of lead in blood; levels of metabolites known to be associated with toxic agents such as mandelic acid as a result of exposure to styrene.

Information Contained in the Occupational History

The importance of the occupational history in the evaluation of human neurotoxic effects cannot be overestimated. It was Bernardino Ramazzini (1633-1714) who first recommended that his students add to the anamnesis (the medical history) the important question "In which trade are you in?" or "What is your occupation?" Today workers change occupations many times in their lifetimes. As a result, the relationship between job and health is often complicated, and these suspected links need to be established on careful probes into the past work history as well as the present occupation.

The actual probing is an art. All the professional and personal skills of an interviewer (i.e., ability to establish a professional but frank communication with the worker, patient, victim of an environmental disaster, the defendant in court, etc.) are required for this task. In the clinic, the physician or the neuro-psychologist obtains this information during the initial visit. Current guidelines for occupational history taking include:

☐ Past occupational history: Dates, occupations, places of employment, job tasks, exposures, use of personal protective equipment, and personal hygiene practices.

☐ Present occupation: Place of employment, month, year when current job began, job tasks, exposures, use of personal protective equipment and personal hygiene practices.

☐ The spouse's occupation is often overlooked. The interviewee can suffer bystander toxic exposure leading to illness or even death, e.g., bystander exposure to pesticides, lead, asbestos, etc.

☐ Sometimes the occupation of the interviewee's parents is important, e.g., the possibility of bystander exposure at home with lead brought in a parent's clothing. The child sometimes helps his or her parents in farming, hobbies, small shops, and these activities may be overlooked during the course of a pediatric examination.

One needs to be familiar with work practices and have a knowledge of the toxicity of numerous chemical compounds in order to obtain additional information on exposure data. For example, if a plaintiff claiming neurotoxic exposure arising from work in a chemical plant also acknowledges that he/she engaged in cabinet making as a hobby, questions about the use of glues, varnishes, and solvents become necessary. However, intelligent decisions must be made when probing the depth of a particular activity. A bulkier occupational history of several pages collected by an inexperienced interviewer is not necessarily more useful than a terse one obtained by an experienced industrial hygienist.

Neurotoxic Drugs

A drug is any substance used as a medicine for the alleviation or treatment of diseases and conditions. A neurotoxic drug is a chemical compound that has the nervous system as a primary target of its effect. A forensic neuropsychologist is aware of the neuropsychological of numerous compounds used by examinees.

Medical uses of these drugs include:

- ☐ Analgesics, such as aminopyrine, antipyrine, oxyphenbutazone, and phenylbutazone, which in large doses can stimulate the nervous system

- ☐ Local anesthetics, such as cocaine, procaine and others

- ☐ General anesthetics, including such volatile and gaseous agents as ether, chloroform, divinyl ether, ethyl chloride, halothane, methoxyflorane, and tifluoroethylvinyl ether; ethylene, cyclopropane and nitrous oxide

- ☐ Depressants, including sedatives, hypnotics and anticonvulsants

- ☐ Narcotic analgesics, codeine, heroin, methadone, morphine, opium, antihistamines, phenothiazine drugs, including chloropromazine, bromide

- ☐ Drugs affecting the autonomic nervous system (such as atropine, belladonna, scopolamine and synthetic substitutes), and sympathomimetic agents such as epinephrine, amphetamine, and related drugs such as ergot and derivatives

- ☐ Cardiovascular drugs, including digitalis, and beta blockers to control hypertension

- ☐ Stimulants, depressants and psychomimetic agents, such as anxiolytics and antipsychotic drugs

There are numerous drugs used in research for the purpose of gaining knowledge of the fundamental chemical and physiological processes of the nervous system. They are named for the neurotransmitter with which they interact — cholinergic, adrenergic, and serotonergic drugs. A recent area of intensive research are the new neurotransmitters, notably amino acids and peptides.

☐ QUESTIONS FOR REVIEW AND DISCUSSION

- Δ Review the moral dilemma involving the use of psychotropic agents as "chemical straight jackets."

- Δ Discuss Exhibit 6.1 (A Most Convenient Medicine) and other uses of medication for malingering.

- Δ Explain the concept "the dose makes the poison." Is it true? Discuss other factors involved.

- Δ The use of psychotropic medication is sometimes an important clue that the defendant is suffering from a mental disorder. Name the following: (1) an antidepressant; (2) an anxiolytic; (3) a sedative; (4) an anticonvulsive; (5) antipsychotic; and (6) an hypnotic.

16: ORGANIC MENTAL DISORDERS CAUSED BY ALCOHOL AND ILLEGAL DRUGS

ALCOHOLISM AND SUBSTANCE ABUSE ARE FREQUENTLY THE FOCUS OF A forensic neuropsychological investigation. In civil (tort) law neuropsychological evaluations, alcoholism and drug abuse may be confounding (that is, confusing or complicating) factors in the assessment of head injuries caused by workplace and vehicular accidents. In cases of workplace accidents, for example, alcoholism (and more recently, drug abuse) may be blamed for workers injuries. In criminal investigations, many individuals who are facing criminal charges may claim amnesia for the events leading to the charges.

ALCOHOLISM

History

The exact time when humans began using alcohol is lost in history, but it is certain that the inebriating properties of the products of fermentation (the earliest means of producing beverage alcohol) have been known for a long, long time. In the literature of antiquity, there are many references to the link between alcohol and misconduct and even criminal behavior.

Some historians have speculated that the invention of beer was one of the many reasons why some ancient nomadic tribes in Europe and Asia became settled. The most powerful alcoholic beverage the Greeks and Romans could manufacture was wine from grains; American Indians fermented grains to create alcoholic beverages (e.g., chicha among South American Indians). Inmates sometimes manufacture wine from almost anything that can be fermented, such as fruits (plums, apples, pears) brought by relatives to detention centers.

The process of producing beverage alcohol through distillation was not developed until the 17th century. But the ability to consume grain alcohol on a large scale was not possible until later; with the availability of gin, rum, and whiskey, one could consume larger amounts (i.e., higher concentrations) of alcohol that had been possible with beer or wine. However (as in the 20th century with the availability of certain once "fashionable" drugs, such as cocaine), the consumption of beverages having high alcohol concentrations was a privilege of the upper classes.

In the early 1800s, physicians such as Benjamin Rush (1745-1813) first began to call alcoholism a disease, resulting from the excessive and chronic consumption of alcohol (Keller, 1979).

The U.S. medical, legal, and popular literature of the nineteenth century contain numerous references to the link between alcohol consumption and crime. Alcoholism was also considered a sin. In the United States, a large scale social experiment occurred during the time of Prohibition (1919-1933), when it was found that Prohibition not only did not "cure" the problem, but it intensified criminal activity associated with the distribution and consumption of alcohol and corruption of public officials. But even after Prohibition was repealed, the devastating effects of alcohol were still recognized.

Bill Wilson and Dr Bob Smith, two men who suffered from chronic alcoholism, founded Alcoholics Anonymous (AA) in 1935; AA was to become one of the most successful organizations engaged in the rehabilitation of individuals suffering from alcohol-related problems. The principles of the 12-steps proposed by AA were later adopted by other agencies handling abuse of other psychoactive drugs and other self-help groups such as Narcotics Anonymous (NA), Al-Anon Family Groups (targeted to families of alcoholics), Nar-Anon (for families addicted to narcotics), Alateen (for teenaged children of alcoholics), Women for Sobriety, Pills Anonymous or even other maladaptive behaviors such as Gambling Anonymous (GA) although some of these groups have made compromises to the religious overtones contained in the original AA self-help philosophy.

Acute Alcoholic Intoxication and Chronic Alcoholism

In an individual who is not a chronic alcoholic, the acute phase of ethyl alcohol (or ethanol) intoxication is characterized by disinhibition, slurred speech, dizziness, nausea, unsteady gait, coma, and sometimes death through respiratory depression, the latter particularly among adolescents who are experimenting with alcohol for the first time. "Experienced drinkers" — that is, individuals who have developed a tolerance for alcohol — rarely experience "hangovers." In additional, individuals who suffer from chronic alcoholism learn to manipulate food intake and pace drinks to avoid any unpleasant toxic side effects.

Psychologists who perform neuropsychological evaluations in court clinics often encounter individuals in various phases of acute alcohol intoxication or the "morning-after" syndrome. The fact that some individuals are unable to abstain from drinking alcohol before their appearance in court is itself suggestive of a drinking problem. Sometimes it is possible to smell the aroma of beer, wine, whiskey, gin, brandy, or other aromatic liquors on the breath of an

individual. But experienced drinkers may drink vodka, thought to be comparatively (but not totally) odorless. Individuals who try to mask the aroma of
alcoholic beverages often chew mints; but the alcohol exhaled from the lungs
mixed with mint may make the mint aroma surrounding the defendant suspi-
ciously overpowering.

Neuropsychologists are aware that alcohol ingestion can be used for manipulative purposes. Someone who is examined in the context of a litigation
against his or her employer may purposely drink large quantities of alcohol for
several days before testing in order to alter the result of psychological tests.
There are no rules as to what test results may be more susceptible to this type
of malingering. However, the results of most neuropsychological tests can be
significantly altered in this manner. Certain electrophysiological tests (such as
the determination of nerve conduction velocity of peripheral nerves) are
unlikely to be influenced by a single instance of excessive alcohol intake. Other
electrophysiological procedures such as nystagmography are extremely sensitive to even minute amounts of alcohol intake. Examination of the eye movements of people suspected to be intoxicated by alcohol (the "gaze test") is
commonly used by law enforcement agents in many states.

The neuropsychological picture of chronic alcoholism is important to bear
in mind. Chronic alcoholism has a profound effect on mood, cognitive functioning, impulse control, personality, and social behavior; in advanced stages
of alcoholism, neurological signs (such as peripheral neuropathies and cerebellar disorders) may be present.

Chronic alcohol abuse may cause mood lability, that is, quick shifts from
exhilaration to depression. Inappropriate sentimentality is sometimes apparent
in people suffering from chronic alcoholism. Often, the afflicted person may
cry while listening to music, hearing a story having a particular sentimental
bent, or recalling sad (or even happy) episodes of his or her childhood. Alcohol
is described as anxiolitic (i.e., having the capacity to "melt" anxiety) and its
intake in moderate amounts can indeed have beneficial health effects. Aggressive behavior, too, may be unleashed during episodes of alcohol consumption.
Criminal acts such as wife and child abuse, rape, and murder are often
committed under the influence of alcohol.

People who suffer from chronic alcoholism cannot drink in moderation. A
revaluation of the hypothesis that chronic alcoholics can control their drinking
(the alternative to a total abstinence from alcohol) has failed to support early
contentions such as that of Pendery and collaborators formulated in 1982. A
history of alcohol consumption can have devastating effects. Some experts
refuse to use the expression ex-alcoholic in the classification of people who
have ceased to drink, pointing to the lifelong vigilance on drinking behavior

such individuals must exert. Recidivism or relapse into drinking again is common.

Symptoms of alcohol withdrawal include tremulousness, irritability, gastro-intestinal, and autonomic symptoms. Hallucinations and seizures may also occur. These signs and symptoms may be alleviated by the intake of alcohol. Delirium tremens (DT) is the most severe manifestation of alcohol withdrawal. It includes extreme agitation, confusion, tremors of the face, tongue and extremities, and sometimes visual hallucinations.

Malnutrition often accompanies excessive alcohol consumption. Korsa-koff's psychosis is a disease characterized by confusion and severe memory deficits and alterations of peripheral nervous system function, including pares-thesia and sometimes paralysis. Korsakoff's psychosis is now understood to be caused by nutritional factors, not the alcohol per se. Malnutrition may be voluntary such as in the cases of those who drink to avoid eating to stay thin — the "three martini diet."

Persons at High Risk of Alcoholism

A conservative estimate is that about 10% of the population who drink develop the psychological and physiological dependence on alcohol that char-acterizes alcoholism. On the basis of epidemiological and sociological data, the National Council on Alcoholism has pinpointed the following factors for the development of alcoholism, but there is no complete agreement on the extent of the risk for each factor:

- ☐ A familial history of alcoholism, including parents, siblings, grandparents, uncles and aunts.
- ☐ A history of teetotalism in the family, particularly where strong moral overtones were present and, most particularly, where the social environment of the patient has changed to associations in which drinking is encouraged or required.
- ☐ A history of alcoholism or teetotalism in the spouse or the family of the spouse.
- ☐ Coming from a broken home or one with much parental discord, particularly where the father was absent or rejecting but not punitive.
- ☐ Being the last child in a large family.
- ☐ Heavy drinking often associated with heavy smoking, although the opposite need not be true.
- ☐ Certain cultural groups are recognized where drinking is often common (e.g., Russian, Polish, Scandinavian, Irish, etc., versus Chinese). However, alcohol-ism can be encountered in any culture.

Diagnostic Criteria for Alcoholism

DSM-IV suggests the following diagnostic criteria:

❑ Pattern of pathological use of alcoholic beverages. Need for daily use of alcohol for adequate functioning; inability to cut down or stop drinking; repeated efforts to control or reduce excess drinking by "going on the wagon" (periods of temporary abstinence) or restricting drinking to certain times of the day; binges (remaining intoxicated throughout the day for at least two days); occasional consumption of a fifth of spirits (or its equivalent in wine or beer); amnesic periods for events occurring while intoxicated (blackouts); continuation of drinking despite a serious physical disorder that the individual knows is exacerbated by alcohol use; drinking of non-beverage alcohol.

❑ Impairment in social or occupational functioning due to alcohol use. Violence while intoxicated, absence from work, loss of job, legal and financial difficulties (e.g., arrest for intoxicated behavior, traffic accidents while intoxicated), arguments or difficulties with family or friends because of excessive alcohol use.

❑ Duration of disturbance of at least a month. Signs and symptoms need not be present continuously during this period.

DSM-IV establishes the distinction between *alcohol abuse* and *alcohol dependence*. Alcohol dependence is characterized by all the symptoms of alcohol use plus the pathological characteristic of the daily need for alcohol ingestion for adequate functioning; tolerance or withdrawal must be present. Alcohol tolerance is defined as the need for marked increases in amounts of alcohol to achieve the desired effects or marked diminished effects with regular use of alcohol. "Morning shakes" and malaise relieved by drinking are characteristic of alcohol withdrawal.

Difficulty of Obtaining Reliable Data on Alcohol Consumption

Reliable data on individual patterns of alcohol consumption are difficult to obtain. The toxicologic approach of data gathering is to estimate the amount and frequency of drinks, equating a can of beer to a glass of wine, to a shot of hard liquor, either by itself or in highballs. The toxicological approach has been followed by some forensic investigators of work-related neurotoxic illness. The behavioral approach followed by expert groups such as the National Council on Alcoholism or the DSM-IV is to ascertain the degree to which an individual's behavior is patterned around alcohol intake. The behavioral approach is preferred by most professionals who help alcoholics enrolled in alcohol rehabilitation programs.

The toxicological approach has major flaws:

❑ People have a poor recall of their alcoholic intake; most underestimate their alcoholic consumption.

❑ Some drinkers follow a consistent pattern of alcohol intake but most do not. Some people drink wine with their meals every day while others engage in alcoholic binges lasting several days .

☐ In certain areas of the country where there are marked seasonal changes, drinking intake varies markedly in summer and in winter, being more common in winter.

☐ Behavioral aspects of drinking (the need to drink just when one rises in the morning to "clear one's head") is typical of chronic alcoholics; this information is lost in toxicological-oriented questionnaires.

Signs and Symptoms of Alcoholism

A questionnaire on symptoms of alcoholism has been developed by the National Council on Alcoholism (NCA). The questionnaire is self-adminis-tered and takes only a few minutes to complete. The following is a sample of the questions:

☐ "Do you occasionally drink heavily after a disappointment, or when your boss gives you a hard time?"

☐ "When drinking with other people, do you try to have a few extra drinks when others will not know it?"

☐ "Are you secretly irritated when your family or friends discuss your drinking?"

☐ "Do you usually have a reason for the occasions when you drink heavily?"

☐ "Have you ever tried to control your drinking by making a change in jobs, or moving to a new location?"

☐ "Do you have the 'shakes' in the morning and find that it helps to have a little drink?"

☐ "Sometimes after periods of drinking, do you see or hear things that aren't there?"

The higher the number of signs or symptoms, the more likely someone is to have a problem with alcohol. However, the severity of the symptoms are important. Visual images of a frightening nature occur only in advanced stages of alcohol dependence. A common problem among people who suffer from alcoholism is denial. The individual may deny that she needs to drink in order to be socially attractive in spite of the fact that most people have already told her that when she drinks she makes a fool of herself. People may simply not remember their pattern of intake or their behavior.

Other psychometric methods for assessing the presence and severity of alcohol use or abuse problems include the MacAndrews Alcoholism Scale on the MMPI (Graham, 1987) and the Marlatt-Miller (1984) Comprehensive Drinker Profile.

Epidemiology

The National Institute on Drug Abuse conducts national surveys on drug abuse and publishes its data annually. Data tend to contrast sharply between national and local trends, with some surveys indicating increases and others decreases in patterns of alcohol consumption and, importantly, with the age of onset of alcohol use.

Alcohol and the Child

The neuropsychologist who performs forensic evaluations of children encounters three major problem areas:

- ☐ The Fetal Alcohol Syndrome (FAS), e.g., neuropsychological deficits in the child caused by the mother's excessive drinking during pregnancy.

- ☐ People who drink usually have a positive history of family alcohol abuse, e.g., the study of parents' alcoholism from the child's point of view.

- ☐ Alcoholism has become a major health concern; some defendants who appear in court claim to have been drinking alcohol since the age of five.

Clinical Probes

There are simple clinical probes to determine whether an individual is likely to be afflicted by acute alcohol intoxication. These probes are used by law enforcement officials to apprehend individuals suspected of driving under the influence of alcohol. These include the presence of slurred speech, inability to walk balanced on a straight line, nystagmus (repetitive eye movements, particularly when attempting to follow the examiner's finger), inability to squat and/or rise from a squatting position, inability to track the examiner's moving finger with one's own finger, and many others. Some cities have initiated programs of videotaping the individuals during the performance of these tests to contest a defendant's future claims.

One needs to be cautious about either under- or overestimating the presence of alcohol-related problems in the evaluation of individuals, work groups, or health status of a given community. One needs to understand the circumstances under which personal information about alcohol intake is volunteered; rationalization and denial are almost a pathognomic signs of alcoholism.

- ☐ A mother who wants to regain visitation rights to her children may vehemently claim that she has stopped drinking and that she does not drink as much as she used to in the past.

- ☐ A driver who is charged with vehicular manslaughter would tend to maximize his alcohol intake during the events leading to his arrest.

- ☐ A husband may claim that he drinks because he has been abandoned by his wife; in fact, his wife left him because of his drinking.

- ☐ Someone who has had a confrontation with the law and awaits a court proceeding may claim that she began drinking after the events leading to her charges when in fact she suffers from chronic alcoholism.

Alcohol and Organic Mental Disorders

Alcoholism may be linked to numerous mental disorders. A court neuro-psychologist sometimes has to evaluate recommendations that other experts have made about individuals who are facing legal proceedings. The combination of alcoholism with these disorders may increase the risk of a confrontation with the law.

☐ People who suffer mental retardation sometimes develop alcoholism; these individuals are notoriously difficult to rehabilitate particularly when they lack adequate social support.

☐ Chronic alcohol abusers (particularly those afflicted with nutritional problems) may develop alcohol-related dementia; dementia may be secondary to traumatic brain injury often suffered by people who chronically abuse alcohol.

☐ Many organic mental syndromes (such as organic delirium, delusional, amnestic, mood, and personality disorders) are often caused by chronic alcoholism.

☐ Brain disorders (such as seizure disorders) can occur among people who suffer from chronic alcoholism.

☐ Cerebral tramautic injuries (particularly those suffered in car accidents) are often found in individuals who suffer from alcoholism.

☐ Exposure to risk factors for AIDS (promiscuous sex, failure to use a condom during sex with strangers, risky sexual practices) often occur in individuals intoxicated with alcohol.

☐ Occupational traumatic events that are labeled "accidents" are sometimes linked to workers who drink alcohol while they work.

ABUSE OF SUBSTANCES OTHER THAN ALCOHOL

History

Although we may regard the epidemic of drug abuse as a relatively "new" problem, scholars such as Ray (1974) remind us that drug abuse, like abuse of alcohol, has a long history. For example, the opium capsule was worshiped by many cults in ancient Greece, and, in South American legend, the Incas believed that Manco Capac (the divine child of the sun) gave them coca as a gift to cure human suffering and unhappiness. History also records the link between drugs and crime. Marco Polo wrote of famed assassins of Arabia who enlisted recruits by allowing them brief visits to paradise with the help of hashish.

Blanken, Adams, and Durell (1987) of the National Institute of Drug Abuse have indicated that drug abuse became a problem in the United States in the middle of the last century as a result of the following events:

☐ The perfection of the hypodermic syringe by Dr Alexander Wood in 1853.

- ☐ The Civil War and the attitude of pity toward veterans who were medically addicted but otherwise respectable individuals; opium addiction was called "the soldier's disease."
- ☐ The importation of Chinese laborers between 1852 and 1870, who brought the opium habit with them.
- ☐ The widespread availability of opium and cocaine-containing products from physicians, drug stores and grocery stores, availability that continued into the late 19th and early 20th century. Coca-Cola indeed contained cocaine in the original mixtures early in the 20th century. The Pure Food and Drug Act of 1906 required, for the first time, that manufacturers list ingredients on their labels.

Various pieces of legislation were passed by Congress to limit the distribution of narcotic drugs. In 1914, the Harrison Narcotic Act required anyone producing or distributing opiates or cocaine to register with the Federal Government and to keep records of all transactions. In 1922, an amendment of the Narcotic Act prohibited the importation of cocaine and coca leaves. By 1924, the importation of heroin was also prohibited. Between 1930 and 1960 the Marijuana Tax Act was enacted in 1937, amphetamines were developed, and the death penalty was imposed for sales to minors.

The mid-1960s saw the explosion of the "counter-culture." First the assassination of President Kennedy, the growing Civil Rights movement, the unpopular Vietnam War, and the general rejection of mainstream culture rocked the fabric of our society and social disruptions were associated with an explosion of drug use. Although the use of marijuana was illegal, it became the norm. The use of hallucinogenics such as LSD was also fashionable.

The period between 1967 and the early 1980s witnessed a major departure in patterns of drug use as more and more people became involved. In the mid-1960s, an epidemic of heroin use occurred. In the early 1970s, cocaine use was considered fashionable but epidemiologically inconsequential; but between 1974 to 1983 the number of cocaine users jumped from 5.4 to 22.2 million. The mid 1980s saw an epidemic of the more powerful crack-cocaine. Other more powerful mind-altering drugs such as PCP were developed but their use was restricted to underprivileged populations largely in urban areas.

In 1981 the first case of AIDS was reported among male homosexuals. Still uncontrolled in the early 1990s, the epidemic continued to spread to drug abusers and from drug abusers to heterosexual populations. Also in the early 1990s, the vast majority of AIDS patients in detention centers and among individuals who appear in court because of criminal charges are intravenous drug abusers.

Until recently, substance abuse was considered to be primarily an "urban problem." However, drug abuse has now rapidly extended to suburban and even rural communities. However, drug abusers make use of community standards (e.g., life in New York City) to rationalize their criminal behavior. One needs to be reminded that during a criminal investigation the focus is not on the drug use by itself, but rather on whether drug use is a contributory factor in the events leading to the charges.

Diagnostic Criteria for Psychoactive Substance Dependence

The World Health Organization defines drug dependence as:

A state, psychic and sometimes also physical, resulting from the interaction between a living organism and a drug, characterized by behavioral and after responses that always include a compulsion to take the drug on a continuous or periodic basis in order to experience its psychic effects, and sometimes to avoid the discomfort of its absence. Tolerance may or may not be present. A person may be dependent on more than one drug.

Dependence on psychoactive sustances is established when at least three of the following are present:

☐ Substance often taken in larger amounts or over longer periods than the user intended.

☐ Persistent desire, or one or more unsuccessful efforts to cut down or control substance abuse.

☐ A great deal of time spent in activities necessary to obtain the substance (e.g., seeking an opportunity to purchase), taking the substance (e.g., chain smoking), or recovering from its effects.

☐ Frequent intoxication or withdrawl symptoms when expected to fulfill major role obligations at work, school, or home (e.g., does not go to work because of hangovers, goes to school or work "high," intoxicated while taking care of his or her children), or when substance use is physically hazardous (e.g., driving while intoxicated.)

☐ Important social, occupational, or recreational activities are given up or reduced because of substance use.

☐ Contined substance use despite knowledge of having a persistent or recurrent social, psychological, or physical problem that is caused or exacerbated by the use of the substance (e.g., keeps using heroin despite family arguments about it, cocaine-induced depression, or having an ulcer made worse by drinking).

☐ Marked tolerance: Need for markedly increased amounts of the substance (e.g., at least 50 percent increase) in order to achieve intoxication or desired effect, or markedly diminished effect with continued use of the same amount).

The following may not apply to certain substances, such as marijuana, LSD, or PCP:

☐ Characteristic withdrawal symptoms, e.g., such as the depression that often occurs after crack ingestion.

☐ Substances often taken to relieve or avoid withdrawal symptoms (e.g., Valium is taken to decrease anxiety caused by alcohol withdrawal).

DSM-IV also contains criteria for assessing the severity of the dependence to psychoactive substances.

- Mild: Few, if any, symptoms are present in excess to those required to make a diagnosis; the symptoms result in no more than mild impairment in occupational functioning.
- Moderate: Symptoms of functional impairment between "mild" and "severe."
- Severe: Many symptoms in excess of those required to make the diagnosis of psychoactive substance dependence.

The following classes of substance abuse (other than alcohol described above) are frequently the focus of the forensic neuropsychological investigation.

- Marijuana
- Heroin
- Cocaine or similarly acting sympathetics
- Barbiturates or similarly acting sedatives or hypnotics
- Other mixed or difficult-to-classify substances such as amyl nitrite, mushrooms, peyote, steroids, etc.

Many individuals who are incarcerated or awaiting their court appearances or who come to court for a forensic neuropsychological investigation suffer mixed addictions. For example, intravenous use of cocaine and heroin is frequent among chronic drug abusers.

An important difference between drug abuse and alcohol abuse is the relative risk of addiction. While it takes the consumption of large quantities of alcohol over long periods of time to become an alcoholic, the risk of addiction to illegal drugs is considerably higher. Some experts claim that the addiction to crack-cocaine is almost immediate for some individuals.

Epidemiology

In the last chapter, we mentioned the practical and legal difficulties of carrying out epidemiologic investigations among individuals who face legal proceedings. Statistics collected annually by the National Institute of Drug Abuse show the following trends for the 1990s in the US household population aged 12 and older:

- About 10% of the US household population had used an illicit drug of some sort in the past month, and about 36% in their lifetime.
- About 5% smoked marijuana/hashish whereas about 33% did so in their lifetime.
- About 11% used cocaine in their lifetime.
- About 12% used medically-prescribed drugs such as stimulants, sedatives, tranquilizers, and analgesics for non-medical purposes.

☐ Although the percentage of individuals who used highly addictive crack, and other illicit drugs (such as inhalants, hallucinogens [LSD, PCP], and heroin) is small, the per capita consumption of this group of individuals sometimes reaches staggering proportions amounting to several thousand dollars per week.

☐ Typically, at the time of the survey each year, about 52% of the respondents reported that they had used alcohol in the past month, about 65% in the past year, and about 82% in their lifetime.

Assessing Substance Abuse through Questionnaires

There are several checklists available for the assessment of substance abuse. These typically cover such areas as these:

☐ The age of onset of marijuana use, since the vast majority of individuals who have had confrontations with the law exhibit an early use of marijuana sometimes as young children.

☐ The use of heroin, and whether the drug was injected or snorted, an important distinction in assessing risk for AIDS.

☐ The use of cocaine, and whether it was injected or snorted.

☐ The use of crack, which needs to be asked about independently, since the addictive properties of crack cannot be compared with other illicit drugs.

☐ The use of hallucinogens (LSD, PCP), since PCP is so powerful a mind-modifier that sometimes even "occasional" use may cause irreversible brain damage.

Defendants often describe drugs as "uppers" (such as amphetamines) or "downers" (such as Valium). "Uppers" and "downers" are often used to counteract the withdrawal effects of other drugs

Certain individuals abuse designer drugs, mushrooms, peyote, and/or pain-killers often in combination with other illicit drugs. In order to characterize the behavioral pattern of drug dependence, it is important to ascertain whether the drug is used "occasionally" (most defendants tend to minimize their drug dependence), or "frequently" (many defendants use drugs for several hours at a time; and few, such as those addicted to crack, for several days). Some individuals use alcohol and other drugs to counteract the effects of illicit drugs. Some individuals seek psychiatric help for "mental breakdowns" which are clearly after-effects of long periods of use of illicit drugs. The author is aware of cases in which psychiatric patients were given antipsychotropic medications while continuing to engage in heavy drug and/or alcohol abuse.

Because of the sensitive nature of the questions and the illegality of drug use, taking a history of drug use is confined to clinical settings only. But, even during the course of the clinical examination, one cannot be sure one is obtaining a reliable history of drug abuse. Although some intravenous drug users are easily identified by the needle track marks, some intravenous users inject drugs intravenously in places that are not suspected or are not seen when normally dressed (e.g., eyelids, penis, legs).

Marijuana

Few neurotoxic drugs have received more attention than marijuana and other cannabis products. When smoked or ingested, these substances produce changes in perception, performance, cognitive functioning, moods, etc. Detrimental effect is to be anticipated among motor vehicle operators, pilots, air traffic controllers, law enforcement or emergency aid personnel, military personnel, and industrial workers.

If one reviews the relevant empirical studies of the relationship between cannobioid concentration and effects, it is difficult to escape the conclusion that the extant data base is inadequate. Such a conclusion is primarily based on retrograde temporal extrapolation — or "back calculations" on concentrations of any cannobioid in any human physiological fluid or tissues. Interpretations of effects based on back-calculated concentrations are not scientifically defensible.

Heroin and Other Opiates

In its natural form, heroin is a derivative of opium. Except for alcohol, opium is one of the psychoactive drugs with the longest use in the Western hemisphere. Opium was used in Sumerian and Middle East civilizations some 4000 years ago. The medical and "recreational" effects of morphine were known to the Greeks and are mentioned in Homer's *The Odyssey* as nepenthe, a substance that elicited warmth and well-being followed by sommolence and sleep. Opium has been an important component of the armamentarium of medicine since the Greek physician Galen (130-201 AD) administered opium to relieve the pain of the wounds suffered by Roman gladiators, as well as headaches, gall bladder malaise, colic, kidney stones, asthma, and congestive heart failure. Thomas Sydenham (1624-1689), one the greatest physicians of the seventeenth century and sometimes called "the English Hippocrates," once said about opium,

> I cannot forebear mentioning with gratitude to the goodness of the Supreme Being, who has supplied afflicted mankind with opiates for their relief; no other remedy being equally powerful to overcome a great number of diseases, or to eradicate them effectually (cited in Snyder and D'Amato, 1986, page 29).

Opium was the subject of romantic writers of the early nineteenth century. *Confessions of an English Opium-Eater,* a book that made its author famous throughout Europe, was written in 1822 by Thomas DeQuincy . Morphine was extracted from the poppy plant in its pure form in 1805 by the German chemist

Friedrich Sertürner, who named morphine after Morpheus, the Greek god of sleep and dreams. Heroin was obtained from morphine by a simple alteration of morphine's chemical structure. Only two years after its successful marketing of aspirin, the Bayer pharmaceutical house introduced heroin for use in cough medicines. Public health authorities recognized the severe addictive potential of heroin only 25 years after its synthesis in 1875. About 20 opioid alkaloids are derived from opium; these include morphine, heroin, codeine, and hydromorphone (Dilaudid). Morphine (an opiate) and its derivatives are now available in synthetic forms included in drugs such as oxymorphone (Numorphan), oxycodone (in Percodan) and hydrocodone (in Hycodan). In 1976, MPTP (1-methyl-4-phenyl-1,2,5,6-tetrahydropyridine) was synthesized. Langston, Tetrud, and Irwin (1983) reported the development of marked Parkinsonism-like symptoms after injection of MPTP sold as "synthetic heroin."

In the United States the last major epidemic of heroin use occurred in the mid-1960s. In the 1970s and 1980s, the drug never lost popularity among addicts, and there were early indications of another wave in the early 1990s. It is generally estimated that half of the heroin addicts live in New York City. The vast majority of heroin addicts support their drug habit (sometimes amounting to $200 a day or more) through criminal activity. A significant percentage of inmates awaiting legal proceedings are addicted to heroin or a mixture of heroin and cocaine. In 1991, Switzerland ended a liberal program for the free availability of drugs in Geneva. The "program" could no longer be controlled and was a haven for drug trafficking and drug use throughout Europe.

Heroin (as well as morphine) causes a physical dependence on the drug. After ingestion of heroin, a feeling of euphoria, somnolence, and relief of pain soon ensues. When a chronic heroin abuser suddenly halts the use of heroin, withdrawal symptoms soon follow, including overexcitement, depression, and hypersensitivity to painful stimuli. In the late 1960s it was discovered that opiates are naturally produced in the brain. In DSM-IV, the clinical effects of heroin are used as a model for all opioids.

Small amounts of heroin are associated with analgesia, drowsiness, mood changes, and mental clouding. The psychoactive properties of heroin vary considerably whether it is snorted or injected intravenously. Injected intravenously, its effects can last four to six hours. Larger doses of heroin can cause changes in blood pressure, heart rate, and cerebral circulation. Death can occur as a result of the direct effects of heroin on respiratory centers.

Heroin can cause idiosyncratic effects on people who are already suffering from mental disorders such as mental retardation, traumatic brain damage, mood disorders, and severe psychosis, such as schizophrenia. As indicated above, in the clinic, one rarely sees an individual who is addicted to heroin alone but instead to a combination of other psychoactive drugs and alcohol.

Cocaine

Cocaine is indigenous to South America. The Spaniards discovered, for the rest of the civilized world, that cocaine induced good spirits and endurance. Until early in the twentieth century, Bolivian and Peruvian Indians worked in the mines for meager salaries and a daily ration of cocaine leaves that they kept tucked inside their cheeks. Cocaine reached Europe in the early 1800s and soon was an ingredient of many popular beverages, such as the Mariani Coca Wine that made its inventor, the French chemist Angelo Mariani, rich and famous. As indicated earlier, cocaine was once part of many popular American potions and beverages until the Pure Food and Drug Act became a law in 1906. Cocaine was the drug of choice of affluent individuals, who could afford the habit. When it reached underprivileged masses, it become almost instantly associated with crime; cocaine abusers would go to any lengths and would do almost anything to obtain money for the drugs. Cocaine use is still epidemic. Epidemiological data indicate a steady increase in the use of cocaine among various age groups between 1970-90 on a nationwide basis, although data resulting from surveys on the east coast had detected an opposite trend.

Cocaine is a stimulant and is self-administered by many routes, including inhalation, intravenous use, and (as South American Indians still do) intrabuccal absorption. A case has been reported in which an individual placed cocaine inside his penis to obtain priapism (excessive erection). The priapism lasted three days; soon afterwards he developed blood clots in his genitals, arms, back, and chest; gangrene developed and the individual lost his legs, nine fingers, and his penis. This writer once evaluated a college-educated engineer from South America who swallowed over 50 condoms of pure cocaine and brought them to New York aboard a plane; upon his arrival one of the condoms burst inside his stomach, and the man almost died of cocaine poisoning. Once in the blood stream, the drug is short-acting and needs to be constantly snorted or intravenously injected in order to sustain its stimulating effects. In a court clinic, it is not rare to see individuals who spend the street equivalent of several thousand dollars snorting cocaine nonstop for several days.

Cocaine causes a euphoric, exhilarating effect. People who snort cocaine in the form of crack describe many illusions and hallucinations. A frequent illusion is the thought that the user can see at distances of several miles. Others include odd body image distortions, in which limbs are felt to have the capacity to streatch, so that, for example, one can open a door without rising from a chair.

As a rule, the feeling is of superior strength, power, and overconfidence. It is no surprise that when one talks of rehabilitation to a long-time crack user who has had numerous confrontations with the law, one is talking to a brick wall.

DSM-IV contains diagnostic criteria for cocaine intoxication. The euphoric effects of cocaine are short-lasting and cause a myriad of effects depending on the individual. Moderate doses create a generalized picture of behavioral arousal and excitation, with significant elevation of blood pressure. Many users compare its effect to "something better than orgasm" (and indeed many abusers lose all interest in sex). This writer has seen at least five teenagers who had suffered strokes after inhalation of cocaine; these strokes are often hidden or rationalized, and a few of these individuals did not seek medical attention after these life-threatending medical conditions. Individuals who are afflicted by severe mental disorders (such as schizophrenia) exhibit a marked exacerbation of psychotic signs and symptoms.

Cocaine per se causes paranoid delusions. Cocaine also lowers the threshold for epileptic seizures. The excitatory effects are followed by physiological and psychological depression; many develop suicidal ideation and may actually commit suicide during the "crash" that follows prolonged cocaine use; these depressive episodes are often rationalized as "mental breakdowns" or somewhat explained as "psychological" in nature. Toxic doses of cocaine produce convulsions, coma, and death. "Police brutality" leading to heart attack is very often experienced by individuals who suffer from the acute effects of cocaine intoxication. Some law enforcement officers describe individuals suffering from cocaine-induced convulsions as "fish taken out of the tank."

Withdrawal from cocaine is associated with a persistent craving for the drug; some ex-cocaine abusers claim that the craving persists for life. Because of the euphoric effects — and the general feeling that cocaine is something "good" for them — the rehabilitation of someone addicted to cocaine is very difficult, especially in someone who has little motivation to get rid of the habit (e.g., an individual who has no financial difficulties to support his or her habit).

Inhalants

Although psychoactive chemical substances such as cocaine and heroin can be absorbed through the nasal mucosa (snorting), there are numerous chemical substances in liquid form whose vapors can be inhaled causing euphoric effects.

The first case of trichloroethylene addiction was reported about 60 years ago. At first, most addicts stumble on its narcotic action by accident and subsequently become addicts. Since the 1970s, inhalant use has been primarily a problem confined to young adults with a history of psychological disturbance, exacerbated even further by the addiction. The National Institute of Drug Abuse periodically issues material for the laypublic on inhalants, their general effects, the extent of the problem, and the danger. The following descriptions are abstracted from National Institute publications.

Inhalants are a diverse group of chemical compounds that produce profound psychological effects, particularly alterations in mood. Many addicts describe the action of some inhalants "as a suffusion of pleasant warmth, a feeling of disengagement and relaxation and slowly approaching peaceful sleep." Sometimes they are not recognized as drugs because they were never meant to be used that way. Thus the presence of dried paint or spray on clothes and body, empty spray cans, tubes of glue in a teenager's room are not suspected as a source of problems by a parent. There are products used as cleaners, beauty agents (e.g., acetone used as a nail-polish remover), glues (e.g., used in model airplane making), or as fuel for commercial vehicles (e.g., there are reports of addiction to gasoline).

Inhalants fall into three major categories: aerosol sprays, solvents, (e.g., toluene, n-hexane, trichlorothylene), and anesthesics. Although it is possible to get intoxicated by alcohol via inhalation, most people who ingest alcohol do not take it through this route.

All inhalants produce effects similar to anesthetics. At low doses, users may feel slight stimulation; with higher amounts, they may feel less inhibited; at high doses, loss of consciousness and death can occur. The effects of inhalants are immediate and can last from 15 to 45 minutes. Drowsiness usually follows, and headache and nausea can also occur. Sniffing inhalants for even brief periods of time can produce alteration in vision, cognition, and can reduce muscle and reflex control.

The National Institute of Drug Abuse estimates that about seven million Americans have experimented with inhalants; most are under 20 years old, many as young as seven or eight. They usually start sniffing when they see friends, brothers and sisters, or other neighborhood people doing it. Sometimes the child will experiment with some household products and discover their psychoactive properties by accident. Repeated sniffing over a period of a number of years can produce permanent, sometimes irreversible damage to the nervous system. Sniffing high concentrations of aerosols can produce heart failure and death. Others produce death by acting on the respiratory centers of the brain stem. Deliberate inhaling from plastic bags carries the added risk of death by suffocation.

Since the early 1960s, there have been numerous case reports describing the devastating neurological effects of glue sniffing. In some of them, occupational exposure to these solvents may have been the trigger for the addiction.

Shirabe et al. (1989), for example, reported two patients with poly-neuropathy following glue-sniffing. They were painters, aged 19 and 20 respectively, who worked in the same workshop and who each developed a subacute, predominantly motor polyneuropathy after sniffing vapor for 2.5 to 3 years respectively. The polyneuropathy progressed for three months even after the exposure ceased. As a result of chromatographic analysis, the glue was proven to contain both n-hexane and toluene as volatile substances.

While n-hexane seems likely to have been the major cause, toluene may have been a contributing factor in the onset of the polyneuropathy. As a result of light and electron microscopy, it was concluded that both solvents (primarily n-hexane, however) acted on the peripheral nerves resulting in axonal degen-eration, thus causing a predominantly motor polyneuropathy with marked neurogenic muscular atrophy. Sometimes the source of inhalants can be un-usual. Sahenk and collaborators (1978) reported a generalized toxic poly-neuropathy in a 23-year-old woman after excessive intentional inhalation of compressed nitrous oxide delivered from cartridges through a whipped cream dispenser. Chromatographic analysis of the cartridges revealed an exposure to nitrous oxide and 26 other compounds including trichloroethylene, toluene, and phenol, all known neurotoxic agents.

DRUG ABUSE AND ALCOHOLISM TREATMENT CENTERS

Court neuropsychologists are often asked for referrals appropriate for de-fendants and probationers who abuse drugs or alcohol. The following is a brief description of types of agencies handling alcohol rehabilitation; in some locations, similar programs have also been established specifically to deal with problems of drug abuse.

Crisis Centers

These community-based programs used to be called "Sobering-Up Sta-tions." They provide a medically supervised environment for people who are intoxicated and need to "dry out." At a crisis center, the afflicted person receives bed rest and proper nutrition while professional staff monitor his or her condition. Some people stay for one day, but many remain about five days while staff help make referrals for additional treatment. If the afflicted individ-ual is waiting for a residential program, he or she can usually stay for a maximum of two weeks.

Hospital Detoxification

These programs provide 24-hour care for patients who need to be hospitalized for alcohol intoxication and/or withdrawal. Under a physician's care, patients are guided through withdrawal from alcohol. Professional staff are available to help the patient obtain continuing services after he or she is discharged. Almost all patients go on to some additional alcohol treament. On average, patients stay from five to seven days in a hospital detox program. If additional problems such as other drug withdrawal, medical conditions and/or psychiatric conditions occur, a longer stay is possible.

Inpatient Rehabilitation Programs

These programs provide a medically supported setting for patients who are already safely drug and alcohol free. Patients may stay from three to eight weeks. While there, he or she is involved in a program of alcohol education and individual and group therapy. All program activities are aimed at recovery from alcoholism and specifically address the physical, emotional, and spiritual aspects of this disease. Alcohol education and counseling services are also available for the patient's family and friends. After completing the program, he or she is referred to a halfway house and/or an outpatient clinic to maintain recovery and obtain additional services if required.

Outpatient Clinics

In outpatient clinics, people afflicted with alcoholism and their families and friends obtain a full range or treatment services from evaluation to full-day or evening programs. Most clinics are open from 9:00 AM to 9:00 PM and on weekends. The type of services patients receive — how often they need to visit the clinic, how long each visit lasts, and the total time in treatment — varies based on the patient's needs. Patients receive individual, group and family therapy, and participate in educational sessions covering topics related to recovery. Outpatients clinic services are available to adults, children and adolescents.

Halfway Houses

Halfway houses serve men and women in a safe, secure home-like setting that is alcohol-free. While at the halfway house the patient receives peer and professional staff support combined with frequent visits to an outpatient clinic. Planned social and recreation opportunities help patients to adjust to their new sober lifestyle. Generally, people stay in these community-based programs from three to nine months, depending on their needs and progress of recovery.

Some halfway houses are for women only, some are co-ed, and some are for men only.

Residential Chemical Dependency for Youth

These programs provide treatment services for young people from twelve to eighteen years old in a home-like setting and are jointly certified with the Division of Substance Abuse Services. Both short-term and long-term programs are available. The short-term programs last from six to eight weeks. Here people benefit from a highly structured and intensive treatment program followed by ongoing outpatient services. The long-term program is designed for young people who need six to 15 months of residential care before returning to the community. Family services are an important part of both programs.

☐ **EXHIBIT 16.1**

The Man Who Was Brought to His Knees

Mr Keaton, who was evaluated when he was in the community awaiting his sentence, was a 30-year-old Caucasian male with some years of trade education. The evaluation was directed to the issues raised by the Probation Officer in charge of the case, namely that, during the probation interview, the defendant stated he tried to kill himself last year by jumping off the roof of a building. The Probation Officer in charge of the case also had questions about his statement that at the age of eight he was sexually abused by five older boys in his neigborhood.

The defendant was suffering from crack addiction (thought to be current and severe). Despite the fact that the defendant stated that he had not used crack for the past 88 days, his addiction was considered to be current because there was no verified information that he had control over the addiction. Drug abuse was considered to be the primary diagnosis — above and beyond the diagnosis of borderline personality disorder to be described below. Drug abuse was the focus of his current behavioral problems, the main reason for his current problems with the law, and the focus of treatment intervention recommended.

The defendant met the criteria for Borderline Personality Disorder. This is a pervasive pattern of the following: Unstable and intense interpersonal relationships characterized by alternating between extremes of overidealization and devaluation; impulsiveness in areas that are self-damaging, e.g., spending, sex, substance use, stealing; affective instability, that is, marked shifts from baseline mood to depression; inappropriate, intense anger, or lack of control of anger; suicidal threats; persistent identity disturbance manifested by uncertainty about his sexual orientation and long-term goals; and frantic efforts to avoid real abandonment, primarily by his girlfriend (described as a PCP addict) who had custody of his only son.

The defendant attempted to justify his severe addiction to crack as due to "stressors" that happened 22 years ago (sexual abuse as a child). Most, if not all, of his current "stressors" were drug-related: His "family" problems and his current struggles with his girlfriend were primarily caused by the fact that he suffered from a severe addiction to crack and she to PCP. Some stressors were more tangible but still drug-related: He lost all his life savings (about $50,000) and all his valuable possessions to crack. The defendant showed some mild symptoms and difficulties in social function; his level of intellectual function was borderline to dull normal; his contact with reality was good; he appeared to make a serious effort to stay free from drugs.

It was felt that the diagnosis of crack abuse and borderline personality disorder had a poor prognosis; however, the defendant checked himself into a bona-fide drug rehabilitation program and claimed to have stayed drug free for the past 88 days. A period of six months of cessation of all drug use is needed to make the diagnosis of "drug abuse in remission."

The prospect of his social rehabilitation was considered guarded, since Mr Keaton appeared to be well motivated to stop using drugs and had a very good insight into the nature of his drug-related problems; recently managed to return to his former job of construction worker; had an adequate level of functioning, e.g., his IQ was average; had no signs and symptoms of a major mental disorder; and had adequate social support (e.g., his mother, with whom he was now living).

Mr Keaton stated that he had never suffered a condition for which he was admitted to a hospital or been told by a physician that he has suffered a medical illness or disorder. His current health was described as being "good." Mr Keaton stated that he was "sexually abused" by five older boys; the incident happened when he was eight and the other boys were about 12 or 13. As described by the defendant, one by one, the older boys put their penises in his mouth as a form of "initiation rite" into a group.

Later, as an adult, the defendant was in contact with members of that group and he was told that they also had to perform these "initiation rites" in order to be admitted to the group. Although the defendant appeared to be heterosexual, he admitted to having homosexual passive encounters when he was an adult. Asked whether the memories of his "sexual abuse" as a child had anything to do with the present charges, the defendant indicated "none whatsoever."

Mr Keaton completed 11th grade education and then trained in trade school education. He was currently working as an iron worker. He said that he attended a drug rehabilitation program three times a week until he recently obtained a job; he was now going once a week and attending an AA group every evening seven days a week.

Mr Keaton's father was drug addicted (he injected heroin). The defendant began experimenting with drugs at the age of 12 when he smoked marijuana. At 13 he experimented with LSD; at 14 he used amphetamines; at 15 he used mescaline; and at 16, he used PCP. He began snorting cocaine at 18, used Valium at 19, began smoking crack at 25 and snorted heroin at 26. He denied intravenous use of drugs and consumption of alcohol appeared to have been minimal. Before his incarceration he used primarily crack, a substance that "brought him to his knees;" he spent between $100 and $1,000 a day on crack and (as indicated above) he lost all his savings and personal property to buy drugs and lately had resorted to stealing.

His first suicide attempt occurred after nine days of uninterrupted smoking of crack, a period of time in which he said he did not sleep or eat. The second suicide attempt was related to a likely crack-induced paranoid ideation in which he felt his girlfriend was sleeping "with just everybody."

Most, if not all, signs and symptoms suffered by the defendant in the past were drug-related. After smoking crack, he experienced excruciating headaches which were probably related to the acute hypertension caused by crack; when he was "high" on at least one occasion, he was lost on the streets without being able to return to his home (for a time the defendant slept on the streets). The defendant had episodes of temper-tantrums in which he punched the walls with his bare hands (scars were noted). He suffered from numerous delusions and hallucinations including the feeling that his legs were infested with rats and that his father had contracted someone to kill him. When under the influence of the drug, he often hallucinated seeing his father or his girlfriend, sometimes talking to him, but sometimes dead. At times he felt like Superman and he had unlimited strengh. Very often, he heard persistent whispers. As mentioned earlier, sometimes he became "terribly jealous" and he thought he could hear someone having sex with his wife next door.

During the times in which he used crack, he experienced marked sexual arousal. In his own apartment, he would watch his wife in the bedroom and masturbated without her noticing him. The episodes of passive anal sexual intercourse with men occurred under similar circumstances. The fact that he indicates that he took the trouble to ensure that the partner used condoms points to the consensual nature of these sexual relations. He denied that such episodes occurred beyond the perimeter of his own house. (The defendant never checked his HIV status; he indicated that he was not emotionally ready for it, yet).

Almost all the symptoms mentioned above were said to be in remission but the defendant appeared to have intense flashbacks of these events which are described as "nightmares." He said that when he was alone and walking through the streets where he had used drugs, he still could hear faint whispers. At the time of his evaluation, he was suffering from nightmares in which his dreams were of people trying to hit him with baseball bats.

Mr Keaton was a well-developed, pleasant-looking man (6', 183 lbs). His arms were covered by numerous tattoos (a cross, a scorpion to indicate the month in which his son was born, a skeleton); symbols of gang membership were denied. He was slightly anxious but once the purpose of the evaluative interview and testing was explained to him, he became very cooperative, volunteering very intimate experiences of his life as a drug addict as if he felt relief in doing so. The structure and content of his speech was that of a fairly educated person. His eye contact was adequate.

A screening battery of probes that included examination of posture, gait, whole-body balance, muscle strength, tremor at rest, intentional tremor, motor coordination, general appearance of the eyes, eye movements, and reaction of the eyes to light was performed and the results were all within normal limits.

As indicated above, the defendant experienced numerous drug-related symptoms in the past; he was experiencing a state of mind of spiritual awakening such as the feeling of having been "born again" which is common among many recovering addicts. He also indicated that he was motivated to start to "live over again while I am young and still have energy to work."

Individual tests and items of the Wechsler Adult Intelligence Scale, Revised (WAIS-R) were administered. His level of verbal intellectual functioning appeared to be borderline or dull normal; his performance levels were within normal limits.

17: NEUROTOXIC AGENTS IN THE ENVIRONMENT AND THE WORKPLACE

AS INDICATED IN CHAPTER 15, A CHEMICAL SUBSTANCE IS CALLED NEUROTOXIC when it can cause a harmful change in an individual's nervous system. The neurotoxic environment is the sum of all the chemical compounds present in the human habitat that have a potential of creating a neurotoxic health hazard in humans.

Neurotoxic agents found in the environment and the workplace were distinguished from illegal drugs, the topic of the last chapter. Neuropsychologists are increasingly called upon to offer an opinion in cases of individuals exposed to neurotoxic agents in the environment and the workplace. Per force, this chapter is only a superficial treatment of the subject; readers interested in learning more on this topic may consult Goodman-Gilman, Goodman, and Gilman (1980), Klaassen, Amdur, and Doull (1986), and Valciukas (1991).

NEUROTOXIC AGENTS IN ENVIRONMENT AND WORKPLACE

Neurotoxic agents can be grouped as agents of natural origin, neurotoxic metals, metal salts and metalloids, plagicides, household products, and neurotoxic drugs.

Databases

A forensic neuropsychologist sometimes needs to know whether a given chemical substance is neurotoxic; this information is now available through computer databases. The compilation of comprehensive databases of all toxic agents, their uses in the work environment, and their presence in the living environment of humans is a formidable task. In the United States, one of the most comprehensive databanks is the chemical information system of the National Institutes of Health/Environmental Protection Agency which is continuously updated and includes hundreds of thousands of entries. It has been generally agreed that 25% of all the toxic agents listed are neurotoxic. One needs to read the information from these databases critically. The following are some guiding questions.

Which neurotoxic agents have in fact proven to be so? There may not be a clear answer to this question. At the time of this writing, the most comprehensive list of neurotoxic agents is that of Anger and Johnson published in 1985, which contains approximately 850 entries. However, since no firm neurotoxicity testing protocol has yet been agreed upon, information on the neurotoxic properties of a given chemical compound may not be available simply because no such testing has ever been performed. For example, very little is known about the effects of toxic agents on olfaction because studies of neurotoxic-induced olfactory changes in humans are rarely performed.

What are the most likely uses? "Typical" uses of great numbers of neurotoxic agents are now available. These compilations are essential for the development of health preservation programs. But knowledge of "atypical" uses of a given toxic agent is equally important. An accident, for instance, may constitute an "atypical" use of the toxic compound. For example, in 1973 many chemists knew the use of polybrominated biphenyls (PBBs) as a flame retardant; but for health scientists in Michigan the same year, it took a great deal of research to identify their accidental presence in farm animals' feed.

Irving J Selikoff (1915-1992), one of the most influential leaders in occupational medicine of our times, had warned of the important distinction between product manufacture, product use, and environmental exposure when evaluating people at risk. Until recently, the primary exposure that occurred as a result of product manufacture was the principal, if not the only, object of concern. The case in point is the "lead worker," a category of risk that is gradually disappearing. Instead, far larger groups of product users are at risk. The vast majority of neurotoxic exposures now occur as a result of product use or environmental exposure. The environmental persistence of such neurotoxic agents as lead, DDT, PBBs, dioxins, etc., is of greatest concern.

Under which conditions might people be exposed to neurotoxic agent(s) in the environment? Neurotoxic agents may be present in air, soil, or water. They might be inhaled, ingested, or absorbed through the skin. The design of relational databases allowing the generation of exposure information without the need for compiling all possible permutations is now possible. A relational database is a computer-based filing procedure in which several columns containing information can be linked by following certain rules.

Experts operate on the concept of chemical principles. In an empirical science such as environmental and occupational neurotoxicology, a principle is an educated judgment resulting from familiarity with the field. In an environmental accident where no causative agent is originally known (such as the massive killing of fish, for example) experts may entertain several hypotheses until a causative agent(s) of death is found. The body of universally-accepted scientific laws in environmental health sciences is yet to be compiled.

In which occupations are they likely to be found? This is a variation of Ramazzini's question: "What trade are you of?" In contemporary society "occupations" have lost their old connotation of a fixed activity performed through life. In a typical lifetime, people either engage in multiple occupations or switch jobs several times, or both. In addition, in the very upper and the very lower levels of socio-economic strata, people often do not have "jobs" as we understand them. Thus, matching jobs and neurotoxic agents is often an unrewarding task. The US Department of Health, Education, and Welfare published a valuable guide entitled *Occupational Diseases: A Guide to their Recognition*, last updated in 1977.

This is why fixed, *a priori* preconceptions about which neurotoxic agents are expected to be found in which occupations should be avoided. Databases generated as a result of this effort may produce an oversimplified picture of the prevalence of toxic agents in work environments. Further, fixed databases may inhibit the investigation of novel combinations or patterns of use of neurotoxic agents. Some examples:

- Trichloroethylene is frequently listed (correctly) as an industrial solvent. In fact it can be found almost anywhere, including in drycleaning establishments or in offices as "white out" agents (to cover typographical mistakes).
- DDT was banned a long time ago but it is estimated that in at least 10,000 homes, DDT persists (Lipske, 1986); from time to time the use of DDT is authorized in the United States and abroad to combat pests resistant to other agents.

Catalog of Neurotoxicants

There have been numerous different listings of neurotoxicants. As stated above, the most comprehensive enumeration to date is that of Anger and Johnson's (1985) where names (including trade names) of close to 850 industrial and commercial neurotoxic substances, their mode of action and bibliographic sources are given. In its original source, the list encompassesd 71 pages. For detailed information on these and other sources, see Valciukas (1991).

EFFECTS OF INDUSTRIAL SOLVENTS ON INDIVIDUALS

A large number of chemical compounds are classified as solvents, all having the common ability to dissolve and readily disperse fats, oils, waxes, paints, pigments, varnishes, rubber, and many other materials. We will review some of the issues related to the identification and characterization of solvents in the environment and the workplace and the clinical manifestations of solvent exposure and absorption. This will illustrate the knowledge a forensic neuropsychologist must have when acting as an expert witness on individual cases involving environmental and occupational neurotoxicants.

Chronic occupational exposure to solvents has been known to be associated with toxic polyneuropathy since the last century. In her autobiography written in 1943, Alice Hamilton made reference to the challenge that the study of industrial solvents offered at a time when the safety health effects caused by lead and other metals seemed to be well understood. Several bibliographic sources already available in the middle 1940s had reviewed the neurotoxicity of industrial solvents in a manner indistinguishable from current sources. But it was in the 1950s that a growing literature on the neurotoxicity of solvents began to appear. Experimental studies in the United States and Japan in the 1960s and the bulk of the research published in Italy, Finland, and Sweden in the 1970s constitute the core of our knowledge of the human health hazards posed by industrial solvents in the workplace. In the 1980s, solvents began to emerge as a major human health hazard, a dubious distinction that the metal lead once had. However, a research literature on solvent toxicity in humans with particular relevance to forensic purposes is almost nonexistent.

Measurement of Solvents in the Workplace

One of the fundamental tenets of toxicology is that a chemical compound is the "cause" of a pharmacological, structural, physiological, and psychological process if these show a variation as an effect in proportion to dose. The measure of solvent "dose" in humans is very difficult if not impossible. The most persistent problems in human studies of the neurotoxic effects of solvents are these:

☐ The identification of solvents
☐ Environmental measures of solvents
☐ The quantification solvent dose

Solvents are identified by scientific name, chemical structure, synonyms, code number or name, and commercial name. Ideally, one would like to know which solvents are present and at which concentrations in a specific environment when a worker goes about his or her daily routines. Airborne measures of individual solvents in the working environment may be available in certain epidemiological studies specifically designed to study the correlation between occupational exposures to solvents and nervous system functioning. But for the purposes of making a forensic evaluation this information is often not available.

Single-solvent exposure is rare. Most of the occupational exposure occurs as mixtures of solvents and sometimes the composition of mixtures varies from job to job. An example of this is the occupational exposure to solvents among painters. Even when the characterization of the mixture of solvents is attempted, such information provides only limited help in the characterization of the prevailing levels of solvent exposure because of the extreme variability of solvent concentration in painting operations. Monitoring is possible but rarely done.

There are no universal markers for solvents (i.e., biological indicators of absorption). Solvents have in general a very short half-life; individual solvents are metabolized and eliminated from the body in a matter of hours. Thus, biological monitoring has been attempted but with little success.

A circularity of thought sometimes prevails in the reliance of single biological monitoring. One must know which solvents are present in certain industrial operations (such as painting, spraying, etc.) in order to devise the appropriate biological monitoring. At least in the United States, in most cases knowledge of the chemical agents used during these operations is difficult if not impossible to obtain. Neurotoxic effects of solvents have been studied in relation to three measurements:

☐ Air or personal sampling
☐ Biological indicators of exposure and absorption
☐ Self-assessments

The Hygienic Effect of Solvents

Swedish investigators (e.g., Gregerson et al., 1984; ørbæk et al., 1985) have defined solvent exposure levels in relation to current occupational standards (OS) for each solvent. The hygienic effect (HE) for a mixture of solvents is defined by the formula which follows:

$$HE = C_1 / OS_1 + C_2 / OS_2 + \ldots + C_n / OS_n$$

where

C is the observed atmospheric concentration of solvent 1 and OS is the occupational standard for the same solvent.

The following is an example for the calculation of HE for styrene and acetone derived from figures reported by Gregerson et al (1984).

$$HE = \frac{C_{styrene}}{TLV_{styrene}} + \frac{C_{acetone}}{TLV_{acetone}} = \frac{261}{210} + \frac{176}{1200} = 1.24 + 0.15 = 1.39$$

The "hygienic effect" can also be expressed as a summation:

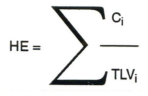

$$HE = \sum \frac{C_i}{TLV_i}$$

where
C_i is the concentration level of any given solvent
TLV_i is the threshold limit value for that particular solvent

An Index of Solvent Inhalation

Fiddler et al. (1987) have provided a comprehensive solvent inhalation index (EI):

$$EI_j = \sum_i \sum_r \sum_m (T_j F_{mrij})(R_{mj} E_m)((1 - P_r) V_i)$$

where:
EI is the exposure index
j is the jth individual
i is outdoor/indoor (1 = indoor; 2 = outdoor)
r is respirator type (1 = none or dust; 2 = cartridge; 3 = airline)
m is the method of paint application (1 = spray; 2 = roll; 3 = brush)
T is the time spent painting (hours)
F is the fraction of time in spraying, rolling, or brushing
R is paint application rate (gallons per hour)
E is the relative vapor emission factor for each method or paint application (2.5., 1.25, and 1 respectively)
P is the protection factor for each type of respirator (none or dust = 0; cartridge = 0.65; and airline = 0.90)
V is the ventilation factor relative to outdoors (1,5, respectively)

Thus, this time-weighted average provides:
Time components (T and F)
An estimation of strength of the emission source (R and E)
An estimation of emission source modifiers (P and V)

Uptake, Distribution, Metabolism and Excretion

Solvents are absorbed through the respiratory tract and the skin. During respiration, solvent vapors are inhaled into the alveoli of the lungs from where they then diffuse into the capillary blood. Equilibrium between alveolar air and capillary blood concentrations is quickly achieved. The amount of solvent taken up depends (among other factors) on the solvent's solubility in water (the blood/air partition coefficient). Solvent uptake can also occur through the skin (percutaneous absorption). Dripping of paint while rolling paint over walls and mists while spraying, capture of solvents inside protective gloves, and the dangerous practice of immersing the arms directly into solvents are examples of ways in which skin can serve as a route of exposure. Protective creams have been developed to avoid this comparatively minor route of solvent entry. However, at the time of this writing, human and experimental work in laboratory animals have shown that such creams do not prevent such absorption.

Solvents tend to concentrate in organs in concentrations proportional to their regional blood flow. The vessel-rich group (VRG) of organs are the heart, spleen, liver, kidney, lung, and brain. Hydrophilic solvents distribute evenly among all tissues, whereas lipophilic solvents concentrate in lipid-rich tissues, such as nervous tissue.

There is little in common in the metabolism of various solvents except that they are generally oxygenated by the cytochrome P-450 system and conjugated by the action of glucuronyl-, sulfo-, and glutathione-transferase. Therefore, the metabolism of solvents needs to be reviewed according to the functional group of these chemicals, a task beyond the scope of this chapter. This is why most experts adhere to the notion that a given solvent (e.g., carbon tetrachloride) does not constitute a "model" for the metabolism of other solvents.

Profound species differences also pose a problem. Neuropharmacological processes induced by acute or chronic solvent exposure observed in laboratory animals may not be applicable to humans because of these species differences. Species differences even exist between closely related species such as the mouse and the rat. Organic solvents are excreted through the kidneys and the lungs.

Mechanisms of Solvent Neurotoxicity

The mechanisms of solvent neurotoxicity can be approached on each of three levels:
- Clinical
- Neuropathological
- Neuropharmacological

Clinical and epidemiological studies support the view that chronic exposure to organic solvents is associated with a neurological picture called toxic polyneuropathy, that is, a multiple-targeted neurological disorder. The peripheral, central, and the autonomic nervous system are jointly, separately, and differentially affected. The peripheral nervous system, in particular, has been the object of intensive analysis. The notion that toxic agents produce neuronopathies (pathologies of the neurons), axonopathies, and myelinopathies is, to a large extent, based on this knowledge.

At the neurochemical level, the acute neurotoxic effects of solvents affecting the nervous system are thought to be caused by the penetration of solvent molecules into the nerve cell, adversly modifying ion transport, or into the lipids of the nerve sheath, affecting nerve conductivity. Some solvents (such as carbon disulphide and 1,1,1-trichloroethane) may exert acute neurotoxic effects by inhibiting energy-dependent processes such as protein synthesis or neurotransmission. Free radical generation, lipid peroxidase, and autoxidative damage, known to result from ingestion of carbon disulphide or carbon tetrachloride, are likely to damage membranes, resulting in impaired conductivity and neurotransmission. Chronic effects are thought to involve the oxidative metabolism of solvents the products of which reactivate intermediates (radicals, epoxides) in the neurons and glial cells which then bind to vital intracellular macromolecules, proteins, RNA, and DNA resulting in prolonged and progressive cellular disfunction and eventual cell death.

Clinical Manifestations of Solvent Neurotoxicity

Much of the current knowledge on the clinical and subclinical manifestation of human solvent neurotoxicity has been gathered in Japan, Italy, Finland, Sweden, and (to a lesser extent) Denmark. Comparatively little research on the human health effects of occupational exposure to solvents has been performed in the United States.

What is described here as "clinical observations" are, in most cases, studies of sick people who have been referred to or sought help in a medical unit. This grouping is contrasted with "epidemiological investigations" where public health workers study people at risk where they work, often during performance medical field surveys or health hazard evaluations. However, in many cases, the justification for two contexts is unwarranted. Epidemiological studies, for example, have been performed by inviting people at risk of solvent exposure but who are not currently sick for a thorough clinical evaluation in hospital units. Some advanced clinical cases are discovered in this manner as a result of an epidemiologic survey.

Solvent Poisoning

The concept of solvent-induced polyneuropathy has been firmly established. These include neurological signs and symptoms such as headaches, lightheadedness, lack of balance and coordination, paresthesia, memory problems, increased perspiration, euphoria, and sometimes tachycardia and hot flashes. The acute effects of solvent exposure are distinguished from their chronic effects. The acute effects are:

☐ Short-lived symptoms such as dizziness, headaches, exhilaration, drowsiness, confusion, and/or disorientation that are time-linked to the presence of solvents in the environment

These symptoms disappear after the worker is removed from the exposure and do not appear during weekends or vacations, when there is no exposure present. The chronic effects are persistent symptoms such as fatigue, sleep disturbances, irritability, lack of concentration, memory problems (recent memory), sleep disturbances, and sometimes changes in libido and potency.

The diagnosis of chronic toxic encephalophathy is made when:

☐ Long-term, high levels of organic solvent exposure can be demonstrated

☐ A clinical neurological picture in one of the following is present:
Paresthesia
Impairment in memory
Impairment in concentration
Changes in mood or emotionality

☐ Abnormal results are obtained in at least one of the following:
Psychometric tests specifically designed for the assessment of chronic toxic encephalopathies (most of currently available batteries are not so designed)
Changes in nerve conduction velocities, particularly of lower limbs

☐ Exclusion of other obvious causes such as chronic alcoholism, head trauma, vascular diseases, degenerative or metabolic conditions, etc.
Note that chemistry (blood or urine) is not recommended for the diagnosis of this chronic condition.

There are large variations in the use of terms to designate this toxic-induced neuropsychological syndrome. In Sweden it is usually named psycho-organic syndrome. Other authors refer to the syndrome as toxic polyneuropathy. The term *painter's syndrome* has been proposed but is not generally accepted. For a good discussion of national variations of terminology (in Europe only), the 1985 WHO publication *Chronic Effects of Organic Solvents on the Central Nervous System* may be consulted. In that source, the neurological effects of solvents on humans are classified into three categories:

☐ In type I, the patient complains of non-specific symptoms such as fatigue, poor memory, difficulties in concentration, and loss of initiative. These symptoms are thought to be reversible if exposure is discontinued.

☐ In type IIa, there is a marked and sustained change in personality as shown by fatigue, emotional lability, and lack of control of motivation and impulse.

☐ In type IIb there are difficulties in concentration, memory impairment, and impairment in the capacity to learn. These symptoms (unlike those in IIa) can be measured using psychometric tests. The complete reversibility of IIb is questionable.

☐ Type III is characterized by dementia with pronounced global impairment in intellect and memory and is often accompanied by neurological signs.

OTHER CHEMICAL COMPOUNDS

Neurotoxic Agents of Natural Origin

These agents can be broadly subdivided into *phytotoxins* (meaning "toxins of plant origin") and neurotoxins of animal origin.

☐ *Toxins* of plant origin do not follow any particular botanical taxonomic pattern. Among the most common are akee, castor and fava beans, hemlock, certain varieties of mushrooms, poison ivy, etc. The seeds of many edible fruits such as apple, cherry, peach, apricot, plum, etc., contain glycosides that release cyanide on digestion.

☐ *Neurotoxins* of animal origin include powerful venoms formed by marine animals, arachnids, insects, and reptiles.

☐ Marine animals include shellfish (i.e., mussels, clams, and oysters that may become poisonous during the warm season) and fish (e.g., sting ray, scorpion fish, etc.). Among the arachnids, the poisonous properties of a powerful neurotoxin secreted by the black widow spider is well known. In desert areas scorpions are found whose lethal sting have been known since antiquity.

☐ Reptiles which secrete venoms include snakes of the crotaloid (e.g., rattlesnake), viperid (e.g., European vipers), and elapid (e.g., cobra) families. The Gila monster, also a reptile, is the only known poisonous lizard. Recently, it has been discovered that certain bright-colored birds are poisonous.

☐ A large number of poisonous organisms secrete neurotoxins. Some of them act individually and are capable of causing serious neurological disorders such as Lyme disease (e.g., ticks). Others need to act in swarms to affect an adult's health — e.g., bees, wasps. Because the toxicity depends on the nature of the neurotoxin, the dose, the body weight of the victims, and the victims' physiological state, the size of the swarm necessary to produce a harmful effect varies from case to case.

A good source of information on prevention, diagnosis, and treatment of naturally-occurring poisonous plants and animals is Dreisbach's *Handbook of Poisoning* (10th edition, 1980), which provides as well a rather comprehensive list of poison centers in the country and around the world.

Neurotoxic Metals, Metalloids and Metals that have Neurotoxic Salts

Published information on neurotoxic metals is available on the following: Aluminum, arsenic, barium, bismuth, cadmium, gold, iron, lead, lithium, manganese, mercury, molybdenum, nickel, palladium, selenium, tellurium, thallium, tin, tungsten, uranium, vanadium, and zinc. In the forensic literature, it is sometimes stated or implied that "heavy" metals are neurotoxic. The use of this term should be discouraged because not all neurotoxic metals are "heavy." Metals, such as tin, are not neurotoxic but their salts are.

Chemical Plagicides

Plagues are groups of plants or animals that are a human health hazard or may cause economic loss. Rachel Carson in *Silent Spring* first called attention to the relative meaning of the term "plague" — that is, the danger of killing a species without consideration of the global ecology. A plagicide is any chemical compound designed to kill such a plant or animal species. Among chemical plagicides are:

- Acaricides — to control mites and ticks (synonym, miticides).
- Baits — to attract pests or to trap in order to destroy them by other means.
- Defoliants, desiccants, foaming agents, foggers, fungicides, growth regulators, herbicides, insecticides, rodenticides, soil fumigants, and sprays.

One tends to associate agricultural neurotoxic agents with pesticides (plagicides). However, pesticides are used in various other circumstances, most commonly in the household. Exposure is high among wood treaters, people who work in the construction industry handling pesticide-treated woods; people engaged in outdoor sports, particularly, golfers who walk over a recently pesticide-spread lawn; fishermen who eat newly-caught fish coming from heavily contaminated water; and compulsive housewives who use exaggerated amounts of insect killers, etc. There is the case of a Seattle woman who used five insecticide bombs to attack fleas; the gas was so concentrated that windows and roofs blew out, ignited by the pilot light of her stove.

Household Neurotoxic Products

Among the most common toxic products in the household are:

- Pest-control chemicals — insecticides, flea and roach powders, weed killers, etc.
- Solvents — paint thinners, turpentine, nail polish remover, furniture stripper.
- Drugs — prescription medications (or even over-the-counter preparations) that can be accidentally ingested by persons other than the ones for whom the medication is prescribed.

18: SENSORY AND PERCEPTUAL DEFICITS

DURING THE COURSE OF A FORENSIC INVESTIGATION INVOLVING EITHER criminal or civil cases, a neuropsychologist may need to have knowledge about, or to evaluate reports involving, numerous specific dysfunctions and handicapping conditions. Among those most frequently encountered in the court clinic are these:

- ☐ Vision and visual perception
- ☐ Hearing and auditory perception
- ☐ Somatosensory system
- ☐ Chemical senses

Handicapping conditions due to limb loss, motor coordination disorders and speech disorders will be reviewed in the next chapter.

VISION AND VISUAL PERCEPTION

Although questions about the functional status of sensory systems such as hearing, taste, and smell can be the subject of forensic neuropsychological investigation, questions involving the visual system are, by far, the most frequently asked. Although usually conceived of as either branches of human engineering or experimental psychology, matters of lighting and illumination are sometimes the focus of a forensic investigation: e.g., "Could she really identify him from such a distance?" Also, many neuropsychological tests used for assessing cognition and memory are based on visual tasks, where questions of visual compentence are important.

Forensic neuropsychologists are or should be conversant with the functional organization of the visual system, photoreceptors and the visual neural pathways, the significance of eye movements for vision, color vision, visual perception, visual masking, and numerous electrophysiological, ophthalmological and psychometric procedures for the examination of basic visual functions and visual perception. Vision is an active phenomenon. Visual perception simply cannot occur without the active participation of body, head, and eye movements. We are curious about something and we walk toward the object of our curiosity; we see after scanning the world around us, locating objects in our environment, locking targets of particular interest, and tracking moving objects with our eyes.

Vision cannot occur without eye movements. At rest, the eyes exhibit physiologic nystagmus, quick and small-amplitude movements of the eye. Retinal images do not fade because of the presence of these almost imperceptible eye movements. The eyes can be moved horizontally from side to side and vertically up and down. The eyeballs can also rotate around an anterior-posterior axis. Eye movements are controlled by three pairs of muscles: The lateral and medial recti, the superior and inferior oblique, and the superior and inferior recti.

Eye movements are controlled by a system that contracts some ocular muscles at the time others are relaxed. The small muscles that move the eyes are controlled by the oculomotor nuclei of the midbrain, nuclei which in turn are controlled by input from the superior colliculus, the cerebellum, the vestibular system, and the cerebral cortex. Double vision — which occurs after moderate or advanced stages of alcohol consumption, for example — results from the disrupting effects of ethanol on the neural pathways that control the mechanisms of eye convergence. (Vergent eye movements are those that allow the focusing of the two eyes on a single object.)

During the course of a forensic neuropsychological investigation, the examination of the functional status of eye movements is sometimes helpful in making a differential diagnosis of neuropsychological disorders and (importantly) for ruling out malingering. It is generally accepted, for example, that cold-water nystagmus can be elicited in individuals who fake seizures; cold-water nystagmus does not occur in persons suffering genuine seizures.

Most of the tests of visual perception and visual spacial organization in forensic investigations by clinical neuropsychologists involve a "challenge" to the normal functioning of one's nervous system. Defects that are not seen during the course of a routine clinical investigation sometimes surface as a result of such a challenge, revealing subclinical manifestations of neurologial disorders.

Visual masking is a testing principle underlying many of the tests in use today. "Masking" means making visual perception more difficult by adding or interfering with other visual stimuli.

In 1921, Edgar Rubin proposed the distinction between figure and ground in perception and since that time there has been a vast literature on the phenomenon of figure-ground relationships. The selection process involved is a basic perceptual mechanism occurring in all sensory channels: Vision, audition, skin senses, etc. Gestalt psychologists (Wertheimer, 1912) used a variety of perceptual tasks in humans and animals to demonstrate the generality of this perceptual mechanism. During the same and later periods, neurologists devised ingenious perceptual tests to challenge the visual system in order to reveal subtle brain dysfunction hitherto hidden during neurological examinations. Many of these tests were designed to evaluate distortions in the perception of figure-ground relationships. One of these, the Gottschaldt test, consists of a test figure presented either alone or within different geometric patterns. The subject's task is to detect the test figure in each of the different background configurations.

There are many other procedures for the examination of visual functions. The forensic expert is likely to need to perform, to have an informed opinion, or to need to examine documentation regarding additional procedures, sometimes performed by other professionals including neurologists, ophthalmologists, and clinical neurophysiologists. They include:

☐ Ophthalmoscopic examinations
☐ Pupillary reaction to light
☐ Visual fields
☐ Visual acuity measurements
☐ Color perception
☐ Electro-retinography (ERG)
☐ Visual evoked responses (VER)

The ophthalmoscopic examination — including pupillary reaction to light — is performed with the aid of an ophthalmoscope. A physician, neurologist, or ophthalmologist can detect important qualitative features of the retina and the nervous system using the ophthalmoscopic examination. This is possible because the retina is the only portion of neural tissue directly observable from outside. The optic disc (the site where the optic nerve originates) may be found to be abnormal, edematous, and hyperemic, with a bloody appearance. The optic disc can show pallor (discoloring) or whitening, indicative of atrophy. The retina sometimes may show changes in pigmentation indicating alterations in the retinal pigmented epithelium.

Color blindness caused by traumatic loss of one eye is not uncommon among individuals evaluated at the forensic clinic. A particularly sad experience is to witness the progressive blindness experienced by individuals afflicted by AIDS (e.g., infection by Cytomegalovirus (CMV) causes this progressive blindness). Although blindness can be arrested, many defendants are poor, often afflicted with severe drug addiction and this robs them of the opportunity or the ability to seek adequate medical attention.

Examination of the eyes (particularly the pupils) is essential because of the large percentage of drug abusers normally seen in the court clinic. It is important to recognize the appearance of a normal pupil and those exhibiting mydriasis and miosis, since pupillary changes are often a sign of drug abuse. Eyelid retraction is common among cocaine abusers.

The visual field is a quantitative estimation of the extent of our vision. It is obtained through a routine examination called the visual field examination. The subject fixates his or her eyes at the center of an apparatus while visual colored targets are moved away and toward the center. The blind spot, the place where the optic nerve leaves the retina and which contains no visual receptors, is readily apparent in the assessment of a person's visual field.

Visual fields are important sources of information to make the clinical diagnosis between intracranial and peripheral lesions. This is possible through the knowledge of the functional organization of the visual system's neural pathways. Students of neuroanatomy learn to relate alterations in the visual field to different lesions of the visual pathway. Gross alterations in the visual field can be detected by means of simple testing methods. One needs to be placed in front of the subject and ask him or her to fixate the eyes on the examiner's nose. With extended arms, the examiner moves a colored pencil vertically and horizontally about the subject's visual field until the subject can no longer see it. Experienced test administrators recognize hemilateral scotoma as a result of left-right differences in the drawing of symmetrical figures. In general, people with hemilateral scotoma tend to ignore the blind area of their immediate environment; they may or may not be conscious of this.

Visual acuity is the ability to detect, resolve, and perceive fine details of a visual display; it can be assessed by simple means — e.g., by presenting samples of reading material of different sizes similar to those used during a routine ophthalmoscopic examination. The importance of assessing visual acuity before any psychometric testing is attempted cannot be overestimated since visual acuity is essential for the performance of most psychometric tests. (The author carries a chart to examine visual acuity both in English and Spanish.)

There are forensic investigations in which the defendant claims that events leading to criminal charges are caused by a deficit in color perception (e.g., vehicular manslaughter, occurring because of professed inability to see traffic light). During a forensic neuropsychological evaluation, there is need to perform some rudimentary examination of color perception. Color perception is achieved by a complex neural system (often described as a "computer") that analyzes the physical parameters of the light reflected by objects. The system is said to perform an "abstraction" of visual information. But "abstraction" has no cognitive connotation here. The human retina is sensitive to light wavelengths in the range of 400 to 700 nm (nanometers). This range covers the perception of the blue, green, yellow, orange, and red portions of the spectrum. Studies performed early in the 19th century suggested the existence of three types of special cells, the cones, that are responsible for color perception.

This hypothesis has been confirmed by the modern demonstration of three different pigments in the cones. (The rods, the other type of cell in the retina, do not detect color.) Alterations or deficits in color perception can be genetic or acquired. Neurotoxic agents and drugs can cause alterations in color perception called acquired achromatopsia. Of interest to the forensic neuropsychologist working in tort law is epidemiologic data suggesting acquired achromatopsy as a result of chronic occupational exposure to industrial solvents.

There are various electrophysiological procedures that may be the focus of attention during a forensic neuropsychological investigation. Since the discovery of the electroencephalogram by Berger in 1929, many investigators have used sensory stimulation to study the resulting changes in the EEG recordings. These electrical changes are known as evoked potentials (EP).

The term "evoked potential" has at least two meanings:

☐ It is the electrical response arising in the cerebral cortex as a result of stimulation of a specific sensory system. Thus, visual, auditory, and somatosensory stimulation will induce a visual evoked potential (VEP), an auditory evoked potential (AEP), or a somatosensory evoked potential (SEP).

☐ Evoked potentials can result from specific cognitive acts — in which case they are called event-related potentials or ERP. Evoked potentials can be recorded before a motor act is initiated (the readiness potential).

To this author's knowledge, event-related potentials and readiness potentials have never been presented to the court during the course of a forensic investigation and thus are not discussed here.

The visual system consists of receptors, neural pathways, relay nuclei, and centers of neural integration. This sensory system is biologically designed to obtain information about the external world and to make appropriate adjustments in the organism's physiology and behavior. Electrophysiologists study the electrical signals as they travel from the receptors (rods and cones of the retina) to their final destination in the cerebral cortex. If the retina is activated by its specific stimulus (i.e., light) receptors give rise to the generator potential. The generator potential is a graded potential which, after achieving a certain level (the firing threshold) is capable of initiating the action potential. Several individual action potentials (derived from single receptors and their associated single fibers) form the compound sensory potential. The message, carried by neurons of the first and second order, continues toward the brain, reaching the third neuron in the thalamus. From specific thalamic nuclei, the electrical signal then reaches the visual cortex where an electrode placed on the scalp can pick up the message. The electronic superposition of 10 to 1000 such signals (commonly called averaging) is necessary to "see" an evoked potential in the midst of EEG background waves.

The forensic utility of EPs is based on their ability (1) to demonstrate abnormal sensory system function when the history and/or neurological examination is equivocal, suspected to be malingered, or in rare cases of hysterical blindness; and (2) to reveal the presence of clinically unsuspected malfunctioning of the visual system. Evoked potentials are used to assess possible blindness in babies when no behavioral techniques can be used for these two purposes because of the infant's age.

Whether accurate visual perception can occur under different conditions of lighting often can be the focus of a forensic investigation. Lighting — as it pertains to the optimal visibility of objects and awareness of space needed for people to perform their daily activities — is an engineering discipline. However, many factors of lighting are also known to experimental psychologists (e.g., human-factor engineers or ergonomists) professional psychologists who sometimes needs to explain the meaning of key facts to the jury. Performance, safety, comfort, and even moods are intimately related to environmental lighting. For example, glare is a lighting problem leading to accidents that sometimes surface during the course of a forensic investigation in civil courts.

HEARING, AUDITORY PERCEPTION, FORENSIC ACOUSTICS

The forensic neuropsychologist is sometimes involved in the evaluation of hearing, auditory perception, and problems involving basic knowledge of acoustics. Many psychological tests (particularly those in which defendants need to react to spoken speech) assume that the examinee has normal hearing in the human voice range. The evaluation of hearing disorders is a subject of forensic investigations involved civil (tort) law cases, such as occupational exposure to unsafe levels of noise. However, forensic acoustical investigations are sometimes essential in high-profile criminal cases.

Some basic notions of the measurable properties of the auditory stimulus are discussed first. The term stimulus has a specific meaning for different scientific disciplines. In sensory physiology, stimulus is defined as a form of energy change that can produce a sensation. Auditory stimuli have two fundamental attributes: Intensity (e.g., the loudness of a sound, etc.) and quality (e.g., the beauty of a melody, the roughness of a sound).

Sound is produced by the periodic compression and expansion of any acoustically-conducting medium including air, water, ground, metals, artificial materials, etc. Although the present discussion is restricted to the propagation of sound in air, the forensic neuropsychologist (especially one who often needs to review facts and documentations on occupationl health problems) knows that physical facts of mechanical vibrations and sound production are often considered a common family of occupational problems. If the successive compression and expansion of air that occurs in the generation of a pure tone is plotted on graph paper, a sinusoidal pattern emerges. However, pure tones are rarely heard in real life. Pure sounds are generated by mechanical devices (such as the tuning fork or a flute) or electronic oscillators (such as the electronic synthesizer). A whistle is also close to a pure tone.

The pitch of a sound is primarily determined by the frequency of its sound waves, measured in Hertz (Hz), and secondarily by its intensity. An increase in the intensity of the sound of 1,000 Hz, for example, is perceived as having an increased pitch, while an increase in the intensity of a sound having less than 1,000 Hz is perceived as having a lower pitch. The loudness of a tone is primarily determined by the intensity of the sound. But the pitch of the sound is also a factor. The detection of sound is primarily accomplished by the auditory sensory system. But sound is also detected by the skin, receptors located in the joints, and the otolithic organs (a component of the vestibular system) and muscle. The present discussion is confined to the acoustical reception that occurs via the auditory system. Chronic exposure to mechanical vibrations causes a variety of illnessess, one of the most frequent is Raynaud's syndrome caused by handling power tools.

Auditory stimuli have properties of intensity which can be measured in terms of our reaction to them. These reactions can be measured by their lower thresholds, upper thresholds — not measurable in all sensory systems — range and resolution.

The lower (absolute) threshold is the minimal energy that can be detected by a specific sensory system. In environmental health, knowledge of the lower threshold for hearing is important in the design of instruments that simulate human hearing. Upper thresholds are more difficult to define than lower thresholds. The upper threshold for hearing is that level of sound that is so loud that the sound is either irritating or painful to a volunteer. However, under normal living conditions, people are exposed to explosive sounds (e.g., rock music) that would be intolerable to a research volunteer. The context in which the sound occurs makes a difference. The context where sound is generated determines the relative annoyance of the sound. It is the annoyance of the sound that is often the focus of the forensic investigation. A few years ago in New York City, a "hissing building" — the building emitted a high-pitched sound during conditions of high winds — was the target of a lawsuit brought by neighbors; the case was dismissed.

The range of sound is the range of sound intensities (or sound frequencies) that can be detected. The range of intensities extends from 0 to 140 dB (decibels); the range of frequencies, 60 to 20 KHz (kilo Hertz = 1000 Hertz).

The upper limit of the ranges varies for every person as we lose approximately 50 Hz per year of life. The decibel (dB) is a unit for expressing the intensity of sound.

There are essentially four methods for (intensity) threshold determinations: Limits, adjustment, constant stimulus, and tracking. Because of their frequent use, only the methods of limits and tracking will be discussed here.

The method of limits, well known to experimental psychologists or even to students who have taken an introductory course in psychology, is used to assess hearing on a single individual. In occupational health, a hearing specialist is sometimes called to evaluate workers en masse to determine the extent of hearing disorders caused by the noisy occupational environment. The method of limits can be used for the determination of both the threshold of intensity and the quality of the stimulus. Here we will discuss the former. The intensity of the stimulus of a given quality (e.g., a tone of 1000 Hz) is either reduced until the subject no longer perceives it (called descending series), or increased until it is perceived, in which case it is termed ascending series.

Most modern audiometers have stimulus-delivery protocols built into the circuitry and the device has a printer that produces a hard copy of the threshold contours. Protocols like these are difficult to follow. They are time-consuming, and subjects are not likely to be cooperative, particularly when the evaluation is performed under field conditions. In the determination of vibratory thresholds, for example, only one or very few selected frequencies are used. It should be emphasized that the method of limits requires minimal use of language on the part of the person being examined. A simple hand gesture or a turn of a switch is enough for the subject to tell the status of the stimulus: Above threshold, just about threshold, or below threshold. The method is easily understood by most subjects.

The method of tracking can be used for a variety of purposes just as the method of limits. The intensity of the stimulus is under the subject's control. The subject is instructed to keep a switch on until the intensity of the stimulus decreases down to an imperceptible level. When the stimulus is below threshold, the subject releases the switch and the intensity of the stimulus increases automatically.

Georg von Békési (1899-1972) designed a method of audiometry that is based on this procedure. In it, the frequency of the sound increases automatically from lower to higher frequencies and the subject hears the slowly increasing sound pitch. The subject controls the increment of the intensity of the stimulus by pressing the switch when he/she can hear the sound and the switch is released when the sound becomes imperceptible. Although developed for hearing studies, it has been adapted for other sensory modalities. As stated earlier, there are many variations of psychophysical procedures for threshold determinations. The reader who is interested in pursuing this topic further should consult some of the many excellent sources available (Marks, 1974). A threshold value is inversely proportional to the sensitivity of a sensory system: The lower the threshold, the greater its sensitivity.

Auditory perception underlies many psychometric tests, which assumes that the defendant has normal hearing. It is essential that the examiner make a quick evaluation when there is any suspicion of hearing loss before the administration of a test. The evaluation of hearing, particularly in elderly offenders, is essential. Simple examinations of the status of the auditory system can be performed, such as the ticking of a mechanical watch. The watch is progressively removed from the subject's ear until its ticking ceases to be perceived. Unilateral traumatic rupture of the tympanic membrane is not unusual among industrial workers; teenagers who use high-powered personal acoustical devices are known to be at risk of early hearing loss. Other simple tests may involve the utilization of the hissing sound produced by rubbing the index finger against the thumb. When in doubt, a thorough evaluation by a professional hearing specialist may be required.

The auditory evoked potential (AEV) is an electrophysiological technique that is sometimes essential in determining whether a young baby has been born deaf (e.g., babies born from drug addicted mothers). It records the electrical response arising in the cerebral cortex as a result of a specific stimulation of a specific sensory system. Thus, when an auditory stimulation induces an evoked potential in the cortex, this is an indication of the intactness of the hearing system.

Auditory perception and cognition are intimately related. Most of us are constantly tuned in to our auditory environment. Quick or unexpected noises elicit the orienting reflex, which is the tendency to turn the head in the direction of the sound. A forensic neuropsychology can make creative use of the orienting reflexes in individuals who are suspected to be malingering apathy. However, a very creative individual (such as a scientist or a musician) may be so deeply involved in their thoughts that they may not normally hear trivial auditory changes in their surroundings. Some severely disturbed individuals (such as autistic children or schizophrenics) show a total apathy even to the loudest noises. Finally, people who are non-English speakers or who do not have a total command of the language may not react to an auditory message as do native English-speakers. These factors are important and must be be taken into account in the psychometric evaluation of the foreign-born.

Some auditory-based perceptual characteristics are affected by age. For example, the cocktail party phenomenon severely affects people of advanced age. The cocktail party phenomenon is our ability to follow the conversation of a friend while in the midst of hearing other voices simultaneously. It is not clear where and how in the auditory system this feat is accomplished. Historically, there have been alternative explanations, some identifying the primary sensory functions of the cochlea as the site of this ability and some invoking cognitive brain mechanisms. The cocktail party phenomena is the auditory counterpart of the phenomenon of figure-ground relationships known to exist in vision, touch, and in the chemical senses, where the background and other stimulus can be separated out, one from the other.

The forensic neuropsychologist involved in cases of occupational exposure to noise at the workplace is familiar with many technical aspects of sound and vibration measurement. The sound level meter is the basic instrument for measuring noise. It contains three weighted networks (electronic circuitry that reproduces several different acoustical characteristics of the human ear) A, B, and C. The A-network is an ideal ear reacting to the characteristics of the sound, very much as the human ear does. To imitate human hearing, the A-network, for example, "hears" high-frequency tones louder than lower-frequency tones of the same decibel level. The A-network is used in monitoring enviromental and occupational health problems because it is sensitive to high-frequency tones which are the most damaging to the ear. The sound-level meter simulates the ear of an ideal observer (someone who is the average of all of us, regardless of important demographic differences such as age) placed in the environment to measure sounds as humans would perceive them. The significance of the level meter can be appreciated, for example, in the case of measuring sounds too intense to be assessed by humans. The sound level meter is used by pretending a human being is there. For example, noise measurements are made at the ear level of the worker, so that the sound level meter registers the same amount of noise that the worker hears.

Environmental noise is measured in octaves. An octave is a concept borrowed from music. In piano playing, the distance between the note A3 to A4 is an octave. A4 has double the frequency of vibration of A3. For example, if A3 vibrates at 440 Hz, A4 vibrates at 880 Hz. Thus, an octave is always double the frequency of a sound taken as a reference. We saw earlier that the sound of a 1,000 Hz is, by convention, a reference sound. Octaves are measured up and down relative to 1,000 Hz. For example, in environmental and occupational health monitoring, the octave scales are sounds of 125, 250, 500, 1,000, 2,000, 4,000 and 8,000 Hz. The sound level meter measures the concentration of acoustic energy in each of these bands of frequencies (e.g., 125-250, 250-500, and so on). For precision measurements, sometimes a third of an octave is measured.

Personal noise dosimeters have been designed that allow the measuring of daily doses of sound [sound dose is defined below]. The dosimeter's microphone is placed on the worker's shoulder or collar. Personal monitors are based on the principle of piezoelectricity in which sound energy is transformed into electrical signals. After the duration of exposure is calculated, the cumulative sound energy for the day is transformed into "sound dose." If on any given day the dosimeter measures, for example, over 100 percent, this indicates that the worker has been exposed to excessive noise that day. The advantage of personal monitoring devices over the sound level meters is that workers' exposures are measured directly as they actually occur under working conditions.

A neuropsychologist who is involved in occupational and environmental health concerns is familiar with basic concepts involved in the noise survey. A noise survey is the characterization of the sounds in a given environment in terms of frequency and intensity in relation to people who live or work in the area where noise is a problem (e.g., the engine room of a ship, the room where metal automobile parts are molded by rivetting, a neighborhood close to an airport, and the like). Thus, the report of a noise survey usually contains a simplified layout of where the noise survey was conducted with recognizable components of such an environment, the registered values in decibels and, most importantly, the probability of incurring hearing damage at the levels of noise that have been measured. The report usually contains a conclusion as to whether measured levels are hazardous to hearing and, if they are, recommendations as to the elimination of the problem.

As a rule of thumb, a sound is damaging in the long term:

☐ If the sound interferes with human speech between two people talking at arm's length so that they are forced to raise their voices in order to be heard. A sound of 50 dB, for example, will interfere with speech; at 60 dB one is forced to speak loudly; at 65 dB, communication is possible only by shouting. (There is also a "frequency factor" that contributes to the interference of voice communication: Low-frequency tones mask high-frequency tones.)

☐ If tinnitus (or ringing of the ear) is present after brief exposure to the source of noise.

☐ If temporary loss of hearing that muffles speech occurs at the completion of a work shift.

Needless to say, acoustical experts are called in when needed in certain high-profile criminal investigations. One is reminded, for example, of the detailed acoustical survey involved in the case of President Kennedy's assassination on November 22, 1963. An important consideration was to determine the likelihood that more than one gun was involved in the shooting by distinguishing primary sources of gun noise from echoes.

In psychoacoustics, speech intelligibility describes the ability to detect spoken words as a result of the acoustical characteristics of the verbal message. For example, one is able to understand a message even if all the frequencies above 3 kHz (a kHz is 1,000 Hertz) are eliminated from a taped, spoken message by means of acoustical filters. However, the intelligibility of the message is impossible if the lower frequencies are eliminated. Often, the difficulty of the aging individual to comprehend test instructions is due to deficits in cognition. But the possibility of severe hearing impairment should be ruled out first.

The acoustical analysis of speech is essential in cases of criminal harassment. A man or a woman frequently calls the same person, sometimes hundreds of time during a single day. The voice is recorded and analysed by acoustical procedures (voice analysis). The acoustical "fingerprint" of the person's voice talking through the telephone is compared with the defendant's, and experts may or may not be able to tell whether they belong to the same person.

Educated defendants with the urge of voicing explicit sexual fantasies as part of a mental disorder (frequently, a delusional disorder involving erotomanic delusions) may sometimes avoid recognition by playing previously recorded commercial tapes. The now widely available possibility of tracking the telephone number of the person making the call is avoided by making the calls from public telephones. An expert sometimes is involved in the task of figuring out the distances of between public telephones and the home of the suspected individual.

SOMATOSENSORY SYSTEM

The somatic sensory (or somatosensory) system is a group of sensory submodalities that conveys and interprets sensory information originating in the skin and muscles. This system is more likely to be relevant to the forensic neuropsychologist who works in civil law (tort cases) than those who handle criminal cases. Evaluation of the health effects of environmental and occupational neurotoxic agents is a case in point.

There are numerous neurotoxic agents and drugs that can affect the somatic sensory system. These include agents such as metals and metallic compounds (e.g., lead, mercury, arsenic), solvents (e.g., trichloroethylene, styrene, methyl n-butyl ketone, carbon disulfide), alcohol, "sniffers" such as toluene, and household products like acetone. How (and whenever possible, why) the somatic sensory system is particularly vulnerable to these neurotoxic agents is reviewed in this chapter. These neurotoxic-induced conditions must be distinguished from hereditary, metabolic, traumatic, viral, or other causes that may produce similar effects on the peripheral nervous system. Four types of somatic sensations are recognized:

- ☐ Pain
- ☐ Temperature
- ☐ Discriminative touch
- ☐ Proprioception

The skin accomplishes many sensory functions — thus the term cutaneous sensation. Touch, temperature, pressure, vibration sensations, and superficial pain are carried out by sensory processes located in the skin.

Nociceptors are the receptors for pain. The stimulus for pain is tissue destruction, chemical irritation, or heat. On the basis of extensive clinical, electrophysiological, and psychophysical research, three types of nociceptors have been identified:

- ☐ Mechanical nociceptors that are activated by strong mechanical stimulation or by sharp objects. During the course of a clinical examination, a pin prick may be sufficient to assess the functional status of pain sensation.
- ☐ Heat nociceptors respond when the skin temperature is raised above 45 degrees centigrade, the pain threshold for heat in humans. Psychophysical experiments for the determination of input-output relationships in heat nociception have been carried out by means of heat generated by infrared sources.
- ☐ Polymodal nociceptors respond equally well to mechanical, heat, or chemical stimulation.

Chemical stimulation is sometimes accomplished by the use of cantharidine, an irritant substance secreted by certain insects. This chemical substance produces blisters which are removed in order to apply chemical substances (the nociceptive stimulus) to the exposed area. Stringent institutional ethical codes have now restricted this type of research in human as well as in animals. The stimulus for temperature is radiant heat. As in the case of pain, simple tests in clinical use can be easily made available, e.g., ice cubes, a mildly warmed iron, etc. However, due to the presence of homeostatic mechanisms (a process by which the organism maintains a state of physiological equilibrium, such as normal levels of temperature, water, salt, etc., in the face of changes in the external environment) the study of temperature sensations under laboratory conditions is difficult. Sweating is one aspect of these homeostatic mechanisms, where heat is removed efficiently through the pores, with a minimum of loss of water from the body. In addition, regional variations in the physical properties of the skin are factors that contribute to the difficulty of studying temperature sensations.

The neuropsychologist involved in a forensic investigation may be required to evaluate pain in criminal cases.

☐ Individuals who suffer from borderline personality disorder frequently burn themselves with cigarettes; inmates held at detention centers sometimes also burn themselves, hoping to seek different housing.

☐ The literature on criminology contains numerous references to the high tolerance to pain found in individuals afflicted by antisocial personality disorder. There are documented reports indicating that such individuals supposedly telling the truth under hypnosis tolerate pinching of the skin with a needle. Such a pinching (and the absence of a reaction to it) is a traditional probe used by professional hypnotists to conclude that the defendant is under the hypnotic state.

☐ Sadistic individuals with a history of causing pain to animals (e.g., a defendant once told this writer that as a child he placed a cat inside a bag, poured gasoline and burned the animal alive).

The neuropsychologist involved in a forensic investigation may be involved in the evaluation of pain in civil law cases.

☐ Neurological cases in which pain is diminished and sometimes lost is the concern of a forensic neuropsychologist performing a forensic investigation in civil law. The neuropsychologist may not be concerned about what causes the pain — but may write on opinion for the courts on the devastating effect that this handicap has on the victim's daily life.

The evaluation of peripheral neuropathies are chiefly of interest to the forensic neuropsychology working on civil cases (e.g., the evaluation of the victim of a car accident seeking compensation). Peripheral neuropathy is a condition involving the peripheral nervous system. There are many conditions (genetic, vascular, traumatic, metabolic, etc.) that affect somatosensory functions. Some are found in certain occupations (e.g., the carpal tunnel syndrome among sign language teachers); in the forensic clinic one often observes peripheral neuropathies associated with chronic alcoholism.

Carpal tunnel syndrome is the most commonly reported nerve entrapment syndrome. It presents itself as tingling sensations and pain in the thumb, index, middle finger, and portion of the ring finger. In chronic conditions, it may result in muscle weakness and wasting. It results from the compression of the median nerve (a mixed nerve containing motor as well as sensory fibers) as it passes through the wrist.

Somatic sensations can be affected by a large variety of medical conditions, physical agents, and chemical intoxications. Those named below serve as illustrations.

☐ Among the medical conditions affecting blue collar workers, the most common are diabetes, carpal tunnel syndrome (i.e., numbness of the hand caused by pinching of hand nerves), and excessive use of alcohol.

☐ The frequent use of vibrating tools may induce a condition similar to Raynaud's syndrome, known as vibration syndrome. Although pneumatic tools producing rapid vibration were in general use as early as 1883, vibration syndrome was reported for the first time in 1911. The vibration syndrome consists of stiffness or numbness of hands, loss of muscle control, inability to hold, grab or manipulate objects, finger swelling, reduced sensibility, paresthesia, i.e., tingling sensations in the hand, cyanosis, and a characteristic blanching of fingers when exposed to cold. Mechanical vibration might be the common etiology of hand-arm somatic sensation alterations and hearing loss among Finnish lumberjacks.

☐ Tight boots might affect somatic sensations in the feet as well.

☐ Excessive cigarette smoking can also affect blood flow of the hand and indirectly can affect somatic sensations.

☐ Mild injury by heat can induce hyperalgesia (painful reaction to the slightest touch).

Valciukas (1991) reviewed the neurotoxins of plant and animal origin, drugs, and other neurotoxic agents that might affect the somatic sensory system. In many (e.g., n-hexane poisoning) changes in somatic sensations are the most prominent symptoms of the neurological picture; in others (e.g., drugs to treat dermatological conditions) disorders in somatic sensation are side effects of the treatment. The clinical and epidemiological conclusion that somatic sensory changes are caused by industrial toxic agents can, therefore, be made, only after these possible causes of peripheral neuropathy have first been ruled out.

CHEMICAL SENSES

Chemical senses are used by living organisms to gather chemical information from the external and internal environment. From the evolutionary point of view, chemical senses (particularly taste and olfaction) are the oldest channels of information, found in lower species of animals and more prominent and important in many animals, compared with humans. In humans, olfaction and taste are both chemical senses.

Chemical senses are responsible for mediating numerous biological processes and species behavior. Ethology has helped to uncover many of these chemical cues. There is much evidence that organisms throughout the phylogenetic spectrum, from simple to complex living things, use chemical signals for species and individual recognition.

Lower organism (e.g., most insects) as well as higher organisms (some say even humans), use chemical signals called pheromones to attract a member of the opposite sex within the same species. Pheromones are hormones secreted by an organism into its external environment where they are sensed by members of the same or opposite sex. Hormones secreted by endocrine glands have long been known to be related to the chemical senses. Some women exhibit marked changes in olfactory thresholds during the menstrual cycle.

There are only a few scholarly studies of the chemical senses from a forensic and criminal perspective. There are numerous observations that chemical senses play an important role in the determination of conduct in certain forms of paraphilias leading to confrontations with the law (e.g., the excitement caused in certain men by vaginal odors), in necrophilia (desire to have sex with dead bodies) and cannibalism. The case of Jeffrey Dahmer (a serial homosexual killer involved in necrophilic and cannibalist practices who was found guilty in February 1992 and sentenced to spend 15 consecutive life sentences in prison) revived an interest in other historical cases. The book *Perfume* by the German writer Patrick Suskind, although fictional, is an excellent account of an individual whose behavior is governed by his olfactory sense.

Forensic neuropsychologists who work in civil (tort) law often encounter individuals who suffer total loss of smell as a result of a car accident in which the victim was hit from the rear of the car. (This is caused as the skull suffers a sudden forward acceleration where the brain, which normally "floats" within the skull, remains motionless and the olfactory nerves "snap" from the nose.)

19: OTHER HANDICAPPING CONDITIONS

AS INDICATED IN CHAPTER 2 ON THE CLINICAL NEUROPSYCHOLOGICAL EXAMination, mental health experts are required to have knowledge, expertise, and opinions on a vast array of disabling and disparate conditions. These include problems resulting from normal aging, alcoholism, amputations, arthritis, birth defects, blindness or various forms or visual impairment, brain damage, cerebral palsy, deafness and other hearing disorders, alcohol and drug-abuse problems, epilepsy, facial disfigurement, learning disabilities, mental and emotional disorders including a large variety of psychotic disorders, mental retardation, multiple neurological disorders including dementia, speech and language disorders, and stroke. The detailed discussion of each of these topics is beyond the scope of this introductory book. This chapter will focus on three of the most frequent conditions that are the focus of a forensic neuropsychological investigation: Amputations, motor disorders, speech disorders, and the evaluation of the non-English speaking individual.

AMPUTATIONS AND OTHER ORTHOPEDIC CONDITIONS

Amputations

Loss of limbs as a result of a tortious or criminal act may be the focus of an evaluation; sometimes amputations result from the defendant's own compulsions (see Exhibit 4.1, Love for Fireworks). In cases of personal injury, for example, the neuropsychologist may be asked an opinion about the extent to which the individual's loss disrupts, interferes with, or makes it impossible to function in his or her daily activities.

Although the term "amputation" refers to removal of any projection of the body, it primarily applies to removal of arms and legs or extremities. The hospital-based neuropsychologist is often involved with amputations resulting from vehicular or workplace accidents in which the removal of a limb is part of a life-saving treatment procedure or rehabilitation process. Automobile accidents account for approximatedly 50 percent of amputations. The court neuropsychologist, however, is likely to see amputations resulting from violence and/or the incapacity of individuals to take care of themselves (e.g., amputations that resulted from severe infections in a individual who does not seek medical treatment because he is rightly afraid that he circumstances surrouding an injury caused during the comission of a crime may be discovered during hospital admission).

There are many specific factors that render amputation necessary. These include:

☐ Trauma, in which crushing injuries or lacerations are so extensive that reconstruction is not possible (e.g., such as seen among mentally disordered, homeless individuals who often sleep in dangerous places such as seemingly abandoned railway tracks)

☐ Vascular disease involving cutting off of the blood supply with onset of gangrene (e.g., such as seen among poor people who do not seek medical attention for diabetes because of lack of money)

☐ Others, such as chronic infections of the bones, soft tissue injury, tumors (e.g., osteogenic sarcoma), and congenital malformations

The forensic neuropsychologist usually documents the circumstances and the extent of an amputation in a chart of the human body. As we have seen throughout this book, some defendants come to the court clinic as if out of a war. The circumstances of severe injuries and amputations often tend to reinforce the view of involvement in violent activity. Less frequently, the court neuropsychologist helps with the process of referral to the most appropriate vocational facilities.

Orthopedic Conditions

These comprise all anatomical and functional abnormalities of the musculo-skeletal system either at birth or due to later trauma. The forensic neuropsychologist may observe numerous acquired and congenital orthopedic conditions that result from environmental stress (violence) and neglect often resulting from ignorance and poverty, but also from denial of illness (such as occurring among people afflicted by drug abuse and alcoholism). These include birth injuries (such as torticollis), injuries resulting from physical assaults by the parents to the defendant when a young child (such as dislocated shoulders not properly set), other congenital abnormalities such as untreated *pes planus* (flat foot), *genu varum* (bowleg), or *genu valgum* (knock-knee) sometimes severely affecting the body image that the individual has of himself or herself.

MOTOR DISORDERS

Motor: A Term Designating Movement

Sometimes the court neuropsychologist needs to explain to the court the meaning of terms and mechanisms of action regarding movement. This is of the case as a result of the too simplistic view of things presented by the counsel or the prosecution.

The effector is the unit of analysis of any motor system:

☐ Skeletal muscles — e.g., those controlling the movement of the tongue

☐ Smooth muscles — e.g., that controlling the dilation or opening of blood vessels

☐ Glands — e.g., hypophysis or pituitary, testes

Movement can be viewed from at least four broad points of view.

☐ Our ability to walk, grab an object, lift a paper clip, move our eyes to follow a target, run, or communicate through body language or speech all are examples of motor functions which are voluntary and mediated predominantly, but not exclusively, by skeletal (voluntary) muscles. Sometimes the court neuropsychologist has to make a differential diagnosis between tics (not under the voluntary control) from voluntary actions. Once a defendant claimed that the result of her harassing calls (sometimes amounting to 200 calls a day) were caused by her self-diagnosed Tourette syndrome; in the latter, coprolalia is often present, the utterance of single obscene words, not entire narratives of obscene fantasies.

☐ The work of the heart, the need to breathe, the urge to urinate or defecate, thirst, hunger, sex, the emotions of fear, anger, etc. are only partially controlled by will and are mediated predominantly (but not exclusively) by the involuntary muscles under the control of the autonomic nervous system. Questions about lack of potency and libido such as in chronic drug abusers who are charged with sexual abuse and physical abuse of children is sometimes the province of the court neuropsychologist.

The concept of "motor" can be stretched to two additional systems:

☐ The nervous system also is intimately related to endocrine functions (through the neuroendocrine system) controlling the secretion of hormones. Sometimes, defendants inject steroids to cause excessive muscular development; steroids sometimes cause serious cognitive and mood disorders.

☐ Finally, it is now beginning to be understood that the nervous system also controls immunological functions through the neuroimmunological system (which is the basis for significance of supportive therapy in individuals afflicted by AIDS).

Extrapyramidal Syndromes

Extrapyramidal syndromes are neuropsychological signs and symptoms involving part of the cortico-spinal pathways (that is, from the cortex to the spinal cord) controlling movement. The basal ganglia comprise the corpus striatum and nuclei that are functionally associated with it. Disorders of the basal ganglia cause either a reduction in movement (akinesis or rigidity) or excess of movement (hyperkinesis). A forensic neuropsychologist needs to be aware of these disorders in order to establish the differential diagnosis of many disorders and conditions, or the presence of side effects of medications or illegal drugs in individuals who have been seen a physician in years.

Parkinsonism. This is a complex of signs and symptoms characterized by tremor, muscular rigidity, difficulty in initiating and stopping motor activity, and loss of postural reflexes. It is one of the most common of neurological disorders of the basal ganglia. It is defined as a symptom complex because sometimes Parkinsonism is the sole manifestation of a neurological disorder (this is called primary Parkinsonism, although the cause of the syndrome is often unknown). Sometimes, Parkinsonism is associated with other signs, symptoms and/or syndromes where the causes are known (e.g., the side effect of antipsychotic medication); these are called secondary Parkinsonism. A deficiency of striatal dopamine (a neurotransmitter) is common to all forms of Parkinsonism.

The signs and symptoms of primary Parkinsonism occur between the ages of 50 and 65. The clinical manifestations of primary Parkinsonism consist of the following:

☐ Lack of facial expression with diminished eye blinking (mask-like face; face of the poker player); however, presence of spasmodic winking when the forehead is tapped (Myerson's sign).

☐ Tremor of the distal segments of the limb at rest (called pin rolling of the fingers).

☐ Muscular rigidity readily evident on passive movement of a joint (cogwheel phenomenon rather than a smooth flowing motion).

☐ Psychomotor retardation; slowness in the initiation of movement; when attempts are made to walk, the patient is found "frozen to the ground."

☐ When pushed from in front or from behind, no attempt is made to stop the fall by stepping aside or by balancing movement of the arms.

☐ Postural abnormalities; tendency to let the head fall forward; lack of rhythmic movement of the upper limbs while walking.

Chorea. The onset of the Sydenham chorea occurs between the ages of 5 and 15. This neurological syndrome is important for the forensic neuropsychologist to bear in mind because the child (more frequently a male than a female) may be misdiagnosed as suffering from "attention-deficit" disorder while in school. The onset is often insidious and the first complaint is that the child is clumsy, constantly dropping things. When movement abnormalities are first noticed, the child is often described as restless, fidgety, and unable to keep still.

The choreic movements are quasi-purposive. Facial movements are almost always bilateral involving frowning, raising the eyebrows, pursing the lips, forced smiling, and sometimes bizarre movements of the mouth and tongue. The presence of involuntary movement of upper and lower limbs renders most purposive movement incoordinated. Individuals in the early stages of this progressive disease may try to hide choreic movement by pretending that the movement was purposive (e.g., fixing the shirt collar or the hair). In advanced stages, speech articulation disorder may be present; mastication and normal swallowing may also be involved; respiration sometimes is irregular. Hemiballismus is a violent movement often causing wide excursions of the limbs. While a defendant afflicted by choreas is in court, uniformed officers who need to enter in contact with the defendant may interpret hemiballismus as a threatening gesture.

Athetosis are slower, coarser movements than choreic movements. This condition is characterized by grimaces resembling caricatures of normal facial expressions. The head may be exaggeratedly rotated to the left or to the right during the occurrence of these grimaces. Hands may exhibit a forced flexion of the wrists. Both choreic and athetosis may be present at the same time; these are called choreic-athetosic movements.

The age of onset of symptoms of Huntington's chorea is from 30 to 45. Among the first symptoms are the presence of involuntary movements that are usually more rapid and jerky than in Sydenham's chorea. As the disease progresses, incapacitating ataxia of the upper limbs and of the gait frequently occur; disorders in speech articulation (disarthria) are also frequent. In the advanced stages of the disease, progressive dementia also occurs. There are case reports of spouses that have killed their loved ones suffering from the late manifestations of this devastating neurological disease. The neuropsychologist may be involved in the evaluation of the capacity of individuals to take care of their own affairs.

Tardive dyskinesia. The forensic neuropsychologist frequently examines individuals who are currently treated with antipsychotic medication. One risk factor of prolonged use of such medication is tardive dyskinesia (TD). Although the presence of tardive dyskinesia can be associated with age alone, the most frequent cause is use of antipsychotic drugs.

SPEECH, LANGUAGE, AND COMMUNICATION

In spite of their significance, speech and language is an area of relatively recent interest for forsensic scientists. This is primarily due to the complexity of speech and language as an object of scientific research and the difficulty of their objective study. There are many functions that intervene in speech production, speech recognition, and human communication; there are many factors that need to be disentangled. Even if one chooses to restrict communication to sound communication (humans also communicate by body language, signs, and writing) the task is formidable. As Sheppard (1983) has stated, "Apart from the identification of the speech area of the human cortex, the subject of mammalian vocal mechanisms does not even exist as far as most textbooks are concerned."

Human Speech

Humans developed speech by adapting a system originally designed for breathing and mastication. The main components of the mechanical elements involved in the sound production in humans are a source of air pressure, a set of vibrating elements, and a system of resonators and articulators.

- ☐ Air pressure is created by taking air into the lungs (inspiration) and expelling it (expiration). This is accomplished by the respiratory muscles, particularly the diaphragm, the intercostal muscles, and the abdominal muscles.
- ☐ The vibrating elements are the vocal folds within the larynx. Both are controlled by the laryngeal muscles. As air rushes through the widely open vocal cords, a white noise is generated. (A white noise is a sound composed of many sound frequencies.) This is the sound we hear while panting after vigorous exercise.
- ☐ The resonators and articulators are structures of the upper respiratory tract such as the pharynx, mouth, tongue, lips, sinuses, and related structures.

The sounds required in normal speech originate primarily in the vocal cords. When the vocal folds are closed, air accumulates under them; when they are open, a sound is emitted. The sounds required for human speech have a spectral composition varying between 100 to 7,000 Hz. The quality of the sound (its pitch) depends of how the vocal cords are opened (the vocal cords have several degrees of freedom) and the intensity of the air flow. The mouth is critical in the production of vowel sounds. The tongue, lips, teeth, hard palate, and soft palate are primarily involved in the production of consonants. A discipline called Psychoacoustics studies the physical composition of sounds as they are produced by the human phonation system.

In individuals whose vocal cords have been surgically removed, speech can be reconstructed. An artificial larynx (a battery-powered source of sound) is placed in the neck area under the jaw and the afflicted individual can still use the articulators to produce monotonic, but intelligible, speech. Sounds can be produced without the vocal folds as in whispering or whistling.

The Neural Control of Speech

Speech is produced by the orchestrated activity of muscles of the abdomen, chest, larynx, head, and neck. The motor neurons that control these muscles are distributed from the upper part of the spinal cord to the cerebral cortex.

☐ The muscles that control air pressure are innervated by motor neurons located in the upper levels of the spinal cord. The motor neurons that control the movements of the diaphragm originate in the cervical segments 3-5; those neurons controlling the intercostal muscles of the ribs in the thoracic segments 2-5; and those controlling the abdominal muscles in the thoracic segments 6-12.

☐ The muscles that control the larynx are innervated by the vagus (cranial nerve X) and accessory (cranial nerve XI). The laryngeal nerve supplies all the intrinsic muscles of the larynx except the cricothyroid. The laryngeal nerve is so essential to speech that functional loss due to infection or injury leaves the afflicted individual able to speak only in whispers.

☐ The muscles that control the resonators and articulators are innervated by motor neurons of the cranial nerves V, VI, VII, X, XI and XII.

The human phonation system is also innervated by sensory nerves. Propioceptive information of the position of the diverse elements of the speech production system is essential. An example of this is the difficulty in speaking we experience after returning from the dentist after local anesthesia has been applied to the mouth, spilling to the tongue and inner walls of the mouth. Another example of the importance of the propioceptive input is recognized by linguists who learn the correct pronunciation of vowel and consonant sound in many languages.

Higher Neural Centers Controlling Speech

Much has been learned about the localization of the higher neural centers controlling speech in the study of aphasias and other speech disorders.

☐ Aphasia is an acquired disturbance of language resulting from insult (e.g., trauma, vascular alteration, tumor) to specific areas of the cerebral cortex. There are many other speech disorders such as dysarthria and dysphonia

☐ Dysarthria is a disorder in the articulation of language.

☐ Dysphonia is a disturbance in vocalization.

Among the localizable forms of aphasia are Wernicke's aphasia, Broca's aphasia, and conduction aphasia.

Wernicke's aphasia is a speech deficit characterized by lack of language comprehension with relative sparing of the rate, rhythm, and melody of the verbal output. Sufferers of this speech disorder may incur logorrhea, i.e., excessive speech. The lesion involves the left posterior and superior portions of the temporal lobe, also known as Wernicke's area.

Broca's aphasia is a speech disorder in which the verbal output is severely impaired with preservation of language comprehension. The disorder varies widely from complete muteness to a deterioration of language in which simple grammatical structures (such as the exclusive use of nouns) are used (an inmate suffering from AIDS who recently suffered a stroke could say only the word four). Neural damage is localized in the motor association cortex in the frontal lobe including the posterior portion of the third frontal gyrus, also called Broca's area.

Wernicke's and Broca's area are linked anatomically by the arcuate fasciculus. Conduction aphasia is a speech disorder caused by lesions in the arcuate fasciculus often occurring after injury to the parietal and temporal lobes of the brain. In conduction aphasia, Broca's area, although intact, cannot receive information from Wernicke's area, which is also spared. Thus, language comprehension is fair and speech relatively fluent. However, speech alterations are uncovered when the sufferer of this disorder is challenged with tasks such as repeating words, reading aloud, etc. Writing might also be impaired, e.g., poor spelling, omission, reversal, or substitution of words.

Exhibit 19.1 (A Taste of Sex) illustrates the difficulties of performing a neuropsychological evaluation in individuals who suffer from severe communication problems. The defendant (and particularly his parents) were likely to feel that his was a "special case" that could not be evaluated according to guidelines drawn to evaluate "other defendants." Most likely, there are many mental health workers who feel that way too. Here, deafness in someone who does not speak English creates a dramatic scenario; the halo effect is irresistible. However, as the communication barrier tumbles, we do not find the stereotypical helpless individual; we find someone who was allowed to live, and later chose to live, by his own rules.

Another point that this case illustrates is the rewards of patience. An evalution that requires two professionals using two sign languages calls for a great deal of it. Sometimes one does not know where to focus one's attention; everything appears to be important. It is as if we must put our data-acquisition systems in a multi-channel mode. The appearance of the defendant is important; the dialogue between the defendant and the sign language interpreter is also important. We are further restricted in the professional use of our knowledge by the fact the defendant is exercising his rights not to discuss the events leading to his charges. In spite of these difficulties and restrictions, important lies are revealed. The young man told us that his friends wanted him to have a "taste of sex" (hence the title of the report) when in fact he had already fathered a child whom he later abandoned.

Then the case revealed important wider issues. From the defendant's mother's point of view, there appears to be a high motivation for him to continue exactly as he is. Part of the welfare money that the defendant received served the useful purpose of maintaining a needy relative abroad.

SPECIFIC DEVELOPMENTAL DISORDERS

The DSM system considers the existence of a subclass of disorders that are characterized by inadequate development of specific academic, language, speech and motor skills that are not linked to physical or neurological defects.

Academic Skills Disorders

According to the DSM system, the following conditions need to be recognized:

☐ The essential features of the Developmental Arithmetic Disorder is the marked impairment in the development of arithmetic skills. The DSM-IV indicates that this diagnosis is made only if the impairment interferes with academic achievement or daily living that requires the use of arithmetic skills. The Wechsler Adult Intelligence Scale, Revised (WAIS-R) contains a series of progressively more difficult arithmetic problems which is quite appropriate for the evaluation of arithmetic skills in adults; for adolescents in school age, additional testing may be required. There are many tests standardized for several age groups.

☐ Expressive Writing Disorder is an impairment in the development of expressive writing skills.

☐ A Developmental Reading Disorder is the marked impairment in the development of word recognition and reading comprehension.

The diagnostic criteria for all conditions described below state that the condition(s) are not explained by the presence of mental retardation, inadequate schooling, visual or hearing defects, or neurological disorders.

Language and Speech Disorders

Language — the most important of the human cognitive functions — has three different features: form, content, and use.

- ☐ The form of a language is the dictionary of words and the syntax which links words together in any language.

- ☐ The content of the language represents the ideas encoded in the spoken message.

- ☐ The use of a language is how people choose to respond to situations or contexts using verbal or non-verbal communication.

Certain neurological diseases can interfere with some or all three of these different features of language. Form, for example, can be affected by lesions of the cerebellum which alter the sequential programming of spoken words causing dysarthria. Broca's aphasia is caused by lesions of the brain in the area of the cortex where language is, to a certain extent, localized. The slurred speech that is observed in acute alcoholic intoxication or acute solvent inhalation is also an alteration of language's form.

The content of the language is disturbed by many neurological diseases that affect language and ideation. Alterations in content are observed in, for example in schizophrenia. The content of the language can be modified by neurotoxic agents as well. Carbon disulfide poisoning, for example, is known to produce psychosis; many hallucinogenic drugs (such as LSD) cause alterations in the content of language.

Alterations in the use of language are seen in many psychiatric illnesses. In autism (a severe psychiatric disorder primarily affecting children) for example, the individual suffering the condition does not communicate. People affected by various psychiatric disorders employ body language or drawing as a means of expression. An important component of the training of psychologists is the identification of messages disturbed people convey in such different channels of human communication.

Among defendants who face legal proceedings, abnormalities in speech are sometimes hard to distinguish from the "normal" manner in which some poorly-educated youngsters sometimes talk; this pattern of speech is characterized with numerous "fillers" and "verbal crutches" with no informational content (e.g., "you know," "like"). In addition, abnormalities in the production of speech including volume, pitch, stress, rate, and rhythm as sometimes appears in depressed people or shy people who are not used to verbally communicating with strangers. Finally, defendants who have a long history of confrontations with the law may show a relative absence of facial expression; his or her face does not give a cue to any emotions and feelings although the defendant appears to be able to experience them.

According to the DSM system, the following conditions need to be recognized:

☐ Developmental Articulation Disorder is failure to make correct articulation of speech sounds at the appropriate developmental age.

☐ Developmental Expressive Language Disorder is failure in the development and use of expressive language as measured by standardized tests.

☐ Developmental Receptive Language Disorder is failure in language comprehension.

The diagnostic criteria for all conditions described below state that the condition(s) are not explained by the presence of Mental Retardation, Pervasive Developmental Disorder, inadequate schooling, visual or hearing defects, or neurological disorders.

The DSM-IV's only entry on writing disorders concerns the "impairment" of writing. An experienced forensic psychologist may have opportunity to see inappropriate writing or writing in excess. Graphomania is the inordinate impulse to write. Sometimes individuals afflicted with delusional disorders are charged with harassment of individuals and less frequently of court personnel including judges and probation officers.

Motor Skills Disorders

According to the DSM system, the following conditions need to be recognized:

☐ Developmental Coordination Disorder, a condition characterized by a failure in the development of motor coordination that is not due to Mental Retardation or another physical or mental disorder.

☐ Specific Developmental Disorder Not Otherwise Specified, covering disorders of language, speech, academic and motor skills that do not meet the diagnostic criteria for other specific developmental disorders.

A neuropsychologistst is aware of the writing characteristics of people who suffer motor coordination disorders (seen while writing a sentence of their own, or upon dictation, in the Digit-Symbol subtests of the Wechsler Adult Intelligence Scale, the Bender Gestalt, in the Benton, etc). Grooved pegboards are sometimes used to assess incoordination of fine movements and tremor.

THE EVALUATION OF THE NON-ENGLISH SPEAKER

In the New York City courts, between 10 % and 15% of the defendants need to be examined in a language other than English. There are no general guidelines regarding the forensic neuropsychological examination of such individuals. The writer is a bilingual Spanish-English speaker and the first portion of this discussion refers to individuals tested in their native Spanish language.

- ☐ Although it appears to be a truism, knowledge of the defendant's language sometimes makes it possible to gather information that would be difficult if not impossible to gather otherwise. The circumstances under which sexual abuse of a child occurred in someone so charged who needs to be interviewed through an interpreter often does not clarify the events leading to the charges.

- ☐ Among uneducated individuals who are not aware of the seriousness of their charges (e.g., one who is an illegal alien who has been apprehended for international transporting of illegal drugs), knowledge of a common language may create the wrong impression of an opportunity for favoritism. Some of them have tried to "punish" the interviewer by not volunteering further information about themselves after the interviewer has refused to allow use of the office telephone (which is forbidden).

- ☐ The differential diagnosis of certain mental disorders is easier to ascertain if one is able to talk to the defendant in his or her native language. The differential diagnosis between certain forms of schizophrenia and mental retardation is a case in point; some defendants are erroneously classified as suffering from schizophrenia when in fact they exhibit mental retardation.

The following general remarks apply to the administration, scoring, and interpretation of the Wechsler Adult Intelligence Scale, one of the tests that is universally recognized as essential in the forensic assessment of the adult's cognitive skills.

- ☐ IQ testing is possible if appropriate translations are used. The matter of the proper standarization has never been solved. An intelligence test that has been standardized for Spanish-speaking individuals from Central America is unlikely to be valid for a New York born resident who speaks only Spanish.

- ☐ Performance tests are easier to administer and interpret than verbal tests; however, the characters of some of the performance tests (such as the King in the Picture Arrangement series) may not be recognized by the foreign born; a simple explanation that the King is an "important" individual is sometimes enough to cue an individual in finding the punch line in the explanation of the stories.

- ☐ Tests of general information intended to tap the individual's fund of general knowledge, whether obtained formally or informally, are most difficult. Sometimes a well-educated individual born abroad learns many important details of mainstream culture in the United States; in other cases, there are teenagers born in Manhattan do not know which direction one needs to travel going from Albany to Atlantic City.

- ☐ If the intention of administering the Vocabulary test is to ascertain the degree of premorbid intelligence, a Vocabulary in his or her native language is sometimes appropriate; if the purpose is to assess the degree of alienation in someone who has lived in New York for 15 years and has not learned English, a Vocabulary test in English may be appropriate.

□ The Wechsler's Similarities Test is easy to adapt for the non-English speaker; similarities can be used to assess ability to discriminate between essential and superficial likeness. This test calls for the ability to see relationships between things and ideas, and to categorize them into logical groups. It also measures the capacity to form conceptual units from verbal material and to express these concepts in words. Court translators in other languages who sometimes help with the evaluation and testing, often find no difficulties in finding equivalents in other languages.

□ In the Picture Completion Test, the defendant is required to discover and name the missing part of an incompletely drawn picture. This continues to be plagued by problems even for individuals born and educated in the United States. The suspension of the water container in the air is still for some more important than the water that is not pouring from the container.

□ Comprehension tests are most difficult to adapt in a foreign language; this is designed to tap common-sense reasoning and the ability to exercise social judgement in practical situations as well as the individual's exposure to "main-stream" culture. It is difficult to find equivalents to some of the proverbs and sayings.

The following test of the Wechsler Adult Scale of Intelligence usually presents no problems when administered in a foreign language:

□ Arithmetic (which is part of the Verbal IQ) requires the individual to solve numerical problems without the aid of pencil and paper. In the execution of this test, the individual needs to use basic arithmetic skills.

□ Block Design is a measure of the ability to analyse abstract figures visually and construct them from their component parts. It is essentially a measure of ability to handle spatial relationships.

□ Object Assembly requires the assembly of simple puzzles of a mannequin, a human profile, a human hand, and an elephant. Object Assembly taps the ability to recognize a picture of familiar objects from their separate parts, and to assemble the parts to make a correct picture of the whole object.

□ Digit Symbol requires looking at geometrical symbols placed under one-digit numbers and then copying the codes associated with the number as quickly as possible. This test requires a quick switch of attention and visual-motor speed. The author has administered this test without difficulty to individuals who never formally attended school.

□ **EXHIBIT 19.1**

A Taste of Sex

This evaluation was requested for Mr Rosario when he was in the community awaiting sentence. The defendant was an 18-year-old Hispanic male with 9th grade education in a special education school for the hearing-impaired. The evaluation was directed to the issues raised by the Probation Officer in charge of the case, namely: "The defendant and two co-defendants (also deaf-mutes) sodomized and raped a 15-year-old female. She was also a deaf-mute." Rosario was quoted as having "forced the complainant onto the bed, tore off her clothing, held her down and forced her to engage in vaginal intercourse." Rosario was then reported to have attempted to do the same with another victim, grabbing her but was unable to do so. The background documentation indicates that the defendant "again grabbed the first victim, held her down and forced her to have anal intercourse."

Mr Rosario met the diagnostic criteria for Pervasive Developmental Disorder Not Otherwise Specified as the following were present: A quantitative and qualitative impairment in the development of social interaction and of verbal and non-verbal communication skills; and markedly restricted repertoire of activities and interests. The defendant had been deaf since birth.

Born in Puerto Rico, the defendant was primarily reared and educated in English-speaking schools in New York City; however, members of his family spoke primarily Spanish at home and did not know English sign language which was the defendant's prevailing mode of communication. As a result, Mr Rosario had very limited ability to communicate with his family. The defendant's mother was described as being overprotective.

Mr Rosario's level of intellectual functioning appeared to be borderline; the defendant also had limited moral development and at times was unable to recognize why certain actions were "wrong," thus suggesting an antisocial personality. In addition, he appeared manipulative. The defendant was often restless and had a very poor control of his impulses.

As to the prognosis of diagnosed conditions, it was felt that many individuals afflicted by total deafness are able to live productive lives; however, because Mr Rosario had lived in an overprotective environment, he was generally resentful and experienced many antisocial personality traits; it was likely that in the future his antisocial tendencies might increase.

The prospect of his social rehabilitation was thought to be guarded to poor, as Mr Rosario appeared to have limited moral development including a poor regard for the truth; was not likely to have reflected on the events leading to his charges; may have had a longer history of conduct disorders that (as explained below) he tended to rationalize; had an inadequate level of intellectual functioning; seemed to have an inadequate control of his impulses; and functioned in an overprotective environment. There were some indications that early antisocial behavior occurred when the defendant was intoxicated by alcohol.

The quality of information was poor as the defendant appeared to have a poor regard for the truth. The Probation Officer in charge of the case indicated that the defendant was born on 12/8/72 and thus he was 18 years and 3 months old; however, the defendant indicated that "yesterday" (that is, 3/13/91) was the day on which he celebrated his birthday. It was suspected that by providing this information, the defendant may have been trying to persuade the evaluator that he was under age at the time of his conviction.

For the first two hours of the interview and psychological testing, the defendant explained that the events leading to his charges occurred only because the older men involved in the episode, wanted him "to have the taste of what sex is like" and that he had "never had sex before." However, toward the end of the evaluative session, when the evaluator was going over quickly standard questions about family life, the defendant revealed that when he was 15 years old, he fathered a child in Puerto Rico.

Many antisocial traits were revealed during probing about this child: Mr Rosario appeared to minimize his responsibility as a father because "it happened in Puerto Rico" (far away), when he was 15 years old (long ago), and he was drunk at the time (that is, for a reason, which was described as if it were out of his control). He also indicated that the "child was probably taken care of by his mother" as if the child was his girlfriend's "problem" and as if he were surprised when his role of a shared responsibility was called to his attention; the defendant did not appear to contribute to the welfare of the child; in fact, he did not know the whereabouts of the mother and the child.

Mr Rosario was very suspicious about providing details of the events leading to his charges; he indicated that, following the advice of his lawyer, he would refrain from discussing such events.

Mr Rosario stated that he was born with a congenital heart problem that required surgery immediately after his birth; he was born with congenital deafness. The defendant did not know whether his mother had rubella during pregnancy, a condition that often causes heart malformation and deafness. Mr Rosario stated that he was referred to a psychiatrist because of "emotional problems." He also indicated that in 1989 he was given sleep medication because he was unable to sleep.

Mr Rosario' parents were divorced. He lived with his mother (aged 43), two sisters, and a half brother.

Mr Rosario completed 9th grade in a special school for the hearing-impaired. The defendant was expelled from school after the incident that led to his current charges and was not attending school at the time.

The defendant had no work history; the background documentation indicates that the defendant's mother used part of his SSI (Social Security Income) money to support a daughter living in Puerto Rico.

In the background documentation, Mr Rosario was described as being overprotected by his mother; the defendant had no vocational goals and/or marketable skills. The defendant appeared to be frustrated about the fact that no members of his family spoke English or knew English sign language (which is quite different from the Spanish sign language he used to know).

Mr Rosario denied alcohol and/or illegal drug abuse; however, he said that he had had sexual relations with a woman aged 22 (he was 15 at the time) when he was drunk.

Because of the nature of his charges, Mr Rosario's sexual development was probed. Midway in the evaluative interview, the defendant stated that he could tell the "difference between boys and girls" at 4, first masturbated at 14, had his first sexual contact at 17 (as if early sexual behavior in Puerto Rico did not count; or as if the defendant were trying to overplay his role as passive "victim of circumstances" in which he only did what he did as a result of peer pressure).

The defendant was asked to explain the difference between a "consensual sexual relationship" and "rape", and the defendant could not explain the difference. The responses were hidden in a theatrical emotional outburst in which the defendant said "that is wrong!, that is wrong!" The defendant could not explain the difference between "sexual fantasies" and "acting out" on those fantasies. The defendant appeared to be terribly embarassed about being asked about his sexual behavior. He said that his mother forbade "dirty talk" at home and everything he learned about sex was learned on the streets.

Mr Rosario was a normal-appearing man (5'8", 135 lbs) who during the evaluative interview and testing appeared restless and very anxious. The sign language interpreter indicated that the defendant sometimes exhibited difficulties in communicating in sign language and while communicating the defendant exhibited signs of high emotionality and frustration. The defendant appeared to have a low tolerance for frustration. As explained below, the defendant appeared to receive correct visual information but he often misinterpreted the meaning of such information.

A screening battery of probes that included examination of posture, gait, whole-body balance, muscle strength, tremor at rest, intentional tremor, motor coordination, general appearance of the eyes, eye movements, and reaction of the eyes to light was performed and the results were all within normal limits.

From an extensive checklist of signs and/or symptoms possibly indicative of neurological or mental disorders, Mr Rosario was asked whether he had ever experienced them, and if so, to give examples. He denied ever having experienced these signs or symptoms. Paranoid ideation, delusions, and hallucinations were also denied.

Individual items of the WAIS-R were administered. His performance IQ was estimated to be about 81. This represents a borderline level of intellectual functioning.

During the administration of this test, the following was noted. The defendant was found to be very deficient in a test of general information; this appears to indicate that he is very isolated from "mainstream" culture. He indicated that at home he watched television without sound (because his family had not installed a device that allows sign-language communication for the hearing impaired).

The Picture Arrangement Test consists of a series of pictures which, when placed in the right sequence, tells a story, like a cartoon. Because the stories involved humans in various situations, this test is often used to assess so-called "social intelligence." The test requires the individual to evaluate the social relevance of pictured situations, to anticipate the consequences of actions, and to distinguish essential from irrelevant details. The subtest is sometimes considered a measure of planning ability. Many times, Mr Rosario failed to place the figures in correct order; often, was unable to explain what motivated the characters to behave the way they did.

As indicated above, Mr Rosario suffered from cognitive dysfunction which was related to his deafness; however, the defendant exhibited significant traits of adult antisocial behavior which he tended to minimize and/or dismiss.

☐ QUESTIONS FOR REVIEW AND DISCUSSION

△ Mr Rosario was educated primarily in the mainland, and his parents communicated poorly in English, yet the primary mode of instruction to which he was exposed was apparently English sign language. Consider what responsibility, if any, the schools had in forging communication links between Mr Rosario and his parents.

△ Mr Rosario seemed to dismiss his having fathered a child at an earlier age. Discuss the role of rationalization and of over-protective familial conditions in the development of antisocial traits in his case.

PART IV

FORGING CONCEPTUAL CHAINS AND CAUSAL LINKS

20: CAUSAL LINKS

THIS CHAPTER FOCUSES ON THE HEART OF THE FORENSIC INVESTIGATION, THE ascertainment of causal links - that is, links between offenses and brain disorders (in criminal law cases), or the ascertainment that brain damage has been the direct result of a tortious event (in civil law cases). The neuropsychologist who works in the courts, or acts as a expert counsel for the prosecution or the defense, offers a conceptualization of how events and offenses (murder) are or are not linked to the brain dysfunction, or a theory of how a tortious act (being hit by another car) is or is not linked to subsequent behavioral dysfuntion caused by brain trauma suffered during such an event. Needless to say, it is the jury who judges the merits of these and other arguments. These are some of the questions:

- ☐ Were the events leading to the charges an accident or were these events volitionally caused by the defendant?
- ☐ Are the events leading to the criminal charges likely to have happened as a result of faulty functioning of the defendant's brain or are the events only the result of a long history of narcissistic and antisocial personality traits?
- ☐ Is the victim of a violent crime unable to testify because he or she cannot remember events prior to devastating brain damage sustained during a criminal assault, or does the victim fear reprisal from the perpetrator of the assault?
- ☐ Are the personality "changes" that occurred after an occupational accident in which he or she suffered a closed head injury real, or had the worker exhibited these personality traits before the accident?

Textbooks of clinical neurology, psychiatry, psychology, and social work rarely address the art of establishing causal links for forensic purposes.

THE FORENSIC NEUROPSYCHOLOGIST

A forensic neuropsychologist is a professional who has the clinical and legal expertise to render an opinion not only of organic conditions affecting mind and behavior but a view of the evidence for the claimed or suspected link between diagnosed neuropsychological conditions and the offense, tortious events and handicapping outcomes. In this concluding chapter, we will see that the recognition that some behaviors have an organic basis is often helpful in establishing a link between such behavior and the offense during key phases of the legal proceedings; equally important is the recognition that often such a link cannot be established.

The vast majority of cases in which a psychological evaluation is requested by the court — a collective term vaguely designating judges, probation officers, the defendant themselves, or their lawyers — do not go to trial. As a result, the general public sees very little about how mental disorders and physical conditions are invoked during the key phases of the legal proceedings. In only a fragment of the cases in which organic conditions are invoked, and a neuropsychological evaluation is performed with expert written opinions submitted to the court, does the public get to hear about these procedures and activities.

As indicated in Chapter 1, a "mental" evaluation is often requested in various phases of the legal proceedings. We can refer to the two most important: Competence to stand trial and the insanity defense. The American system of law is based on the concept that anybody who is not competent to be brought to trial should not be. Technically, the examination to determine the individual's competence to face legal proceedings against him is one in which one needs to establish whether or not the defendant knows the charges brought to him, the roles of key court personnel such as that of the discrict attorney, the defense lawyer (counsel), the judge, and the jury. Such questions as whether the defendant understands what happens if the individual declares himself or herself innocent or guilty, and the consequences of having been found guilty as charged also need to be addressed.

The written opinion of such a team must contain a conclusion as to whether the defendant is or is not competent to face his or her legal proceedings. Until recently in New York State, the competence examination has been one performed by a team of psychiatrists; only in recent years, have licensed psychologists holding doctoral degrees been allowed to write an opinion concerning competence to stand trial. However, for a long time psychologists — and more recently neuropsychologists — have provided important objective evidence to help in that decision. Is the defendant mentally retarded? Is he demented? Does the defendant suffer profound memory problems as he claims? Does he suffer a visual perceptual disorder or is he malingering or faking one? Exhibit 8.1 illustrated a case of a defendant who underwent a presentence investigation after a series of competence examinations suggested by his serious mental illness. Exhibit 10.1 (The Car Tinkerer) is a report in which a defendant who undergoes a competence examination claims amnesia about the events leading to his charges.

Neuropsychologists have increasingly been called upon to render their expert opinion on matters of the insanity defense. As defined by Black (1983), insanity

> is a social and legal term rather than a medical one, and indicates a condition which renders the affected person unfit to enjoy liberty of action because of the unreliability of his behavior with concomitant danger to himself and others. The term is more or less synonymous with mental illness or psychosis. In law, the term is used to denote that degree of mental illness which negates the individual's legal responsibility or capacity.

As applied to law, insane is something that one is or is not. An academic psychologist, however, is normally trained to think along continua (e.g., not at all, likely not, likely 50% of the time, probably yes, definitely yes). A forensic neuropsychologist who successfully argues against such a link between the criminal offense and the defendant's state of mind during these events may maximize individual responsibility: During the offense, no mitigating circumstances were likely to be present; or during the event leading to the defendant's charges, there was evidence of no disease and/or condition in his or her brain likely to reduce criminal responsibility; and — most damaging — the defendant was found to have the ability to know and appreciate the nature and consequences of his conduct during the events leading to his charges and to know that such a conduct was wrong.

Another professional — based on the same or additional information — might argue the case for such a link, in fact, stating that during the critical time of the offense there were "mitigating circumstances" caused by a faulty functioning of the brain; or "reduced culpability" (diminished culpability or criminal responsibility) can be invoked; and (most beneficial for the defendant's case) that he had "absence of criminal intent" — that is, the defendant did not have Mens rea (criminal intent), indicating that he was found to be incapable of knowing and appreciating the nature and consequences of his conduct during the events leading to his charges and unable to know that such a conduct was wrong.

What is sometimes the main purpose of a clinical neuropsychologist working in the clinic or in private practice — namely, the identification of a neuropsychological disorder — for the forensic neuropyschologist is but only one of the many steps of a legal proceeding. If the forensic neuropsychologist acting for the prosecution successfully argues for the absence of a brain disorder, the matter of the link between the mind and behavior altered by a brain disorder is moot. If a professional acting for the defense is able to present convincing evidence of the presence of a neurological disease and/or condition, that mental health professional has won only half the battle; in criminal law, a persuasive causal link between the offense and the brain disorder still needs to be argued; in tort law, the link between the defendant's reckless driving and the plaintiff's head injury that left permanent handicapping conditions still needs to be demonstrated. But most importantly, the argument needs to be delivered so it would appear reasonable to a jury.

CLINICAL JUDGMENT IN THE ADVERSARY PROCESS

Clinically speaking, the link between organic mental disorders and offenses is a differential diagnosis in which the expert — based on all the information available on the individual, his or her history, the results of the physical examination, the information provided by special psychological and laboratory tests, and ruling out non-organic factors that can explain the signs and symptoms — zeroes in on specific organic mental disorders and conditions that caused the offense. A forensic neuropsychologist worth his or her salt, knows how to perform the differential diagnosis of a great number of psychiatric, neurological, and functional conditions, including the normal behavior of an individual acting on his own will.

Some of the frustration starts with basic information about the behavior of the individual, behavior that needs to be interpreted to understand the nature of the charges.

☐ Two people may interpret the same behavior differently. Charges are brought by laypersons with a layperson's understanding of the law and human behavior. For the defendant who had the urge to obey a call of nature to urinate in public can be interpreted by someone else as exposing one's genitals. Someone who "accidentally bumps" into someone else in the subway is interpreted by someone else as rubbing her buttocks.

☐ Although the vast majority of the criminal offenses are a reflection of behavior in which the individual does something, some charges result from the individual's failure to do something. In criminal law, cases in which the father is charged with endangering the welfare of the child because of his failure to report severe physical punishment of the child by his wife is a convenient example. In civil (tort) law, a typical case is failure to warn or to provide protective equipment or safety measures to the worker who is severely injured in the workplace.

☐ Self-selection of offenses attached to "suspects" who are physically or behaviorally unlikable or distasteful. The equation of "ugly" and "bad" has been perpetuated since time immemorial. Numerous folk stories around the world speak of the association between ugly and potential for unlawful behavior. Is it not true that the ugly person is the most likely to be picked up as a suspect? Inmates in detention centers appear to support these observations. Cesare Lombroso (1836-1909) may have arrived at the wrong conclusion, namely that the criminal is a physically unpleasant individual probably as a result of the physical appearance of unprivileged individuals found in Italian jails during the last century. Some individuals who exhibit gross physical defects sometimes go unnoticed as drug traffickers because they inspire sympathy more than suspicion. During the course of a forensic investigation, an individual showing a gross physical disfiguration may tell you: "Doc, what am I supposed to do? Nobody gives me work because of my looks." Behavior may also play a role in the tendency to pick certain individuals as suspicious. If you are a bore, your friends may just avoid you; but if you behave in the street as the schizophrenic sometimes does, then you may end up in jail. Defendants who suffer severe mental disorders such as schizophrenia may tell you that they "control" themselves when in public places, and they "let go" when in the privacy of their homes.

There is legal and psychological interpretation of behavior. Smith and Meyer (1987) give a good example of this dual interpretation.

A behavioral scientist, "Dr X," took a law school criminal law course. The class was considering the legal distinction between adultery and fornication. (In fornication neither of the participants is married to anyone, while in adultery one of the participants is married.) Dr X was called upon to explain the difference. "I am sorry, I do not know," he replied. "I've tried them both and I can't tell any difference at all."

The term *sodomy* as defined by law can mean both rectal penetration or even cunnilingus (oral stimulation of the vagina or clitoris). During a probe of sexual practices, one needs to ascertain the nature and specific details of the sexual acts involved.

☐ The final charges are not the ones originally brought. During a plea bargaining process for example, a manslaughter charge may be reduced to assault, a charge of sexual abuse changed to endangering the welfare of a child.

☐ The events leading to the offense sometimes cannot be reconstructed. In only a few cases, the events leading to the charges are videotaped; in the vast majority of cases, these events need to be reconstructed from the memories of human beings. It is often the case, that even when videotaped, the same event is interpreted as having a different meaning by experts representing opposing parties. Sometimes the defendant may not understand that the fact that he or she does not remember the events leading to the charges, does not render him or her less "guilty" (such as when offenses are committed by individuals who are intoxicated by alcohol and/or illegal drugs).

☐ Because of the nature of the mental disorder, sometimes the reconstruction of the events from the defendant's point of view is difficult. Sometimes the individual afflicted by an organic mental disorder exhibits confabulation (that is, the fabrication of facts or events in response to questions about situations or events that are not recalled because of memory impairment). Confabulation differs from lying in that the person is not consciously attempting to deceive. Confabulation is common in Organic Amnestic Disorder. Some others exhibit circumstantiality, a pattern of speech that is indirect and delayed in reaching the point because of unnecessary, tedious details and parenthetical remarks. The defendant's circumstantial replies or statements may be prolonged for many minutes; it is often felt that if the speaker is not interrupted and urged to get to the point, he would never get to it.

☐ Lack of regard for the truth. In successive sessions of supportive therapy, an inmate told this writer no less that four different versions of the events leading to his apprehension: That he was apprehended during a drug bust operation and he was only standing on the sidewalk; that he was waiting for a telephone call and was apprehended as he waited, but they found "nothing on him"; that he carried methadone, and that the drug was "legal" as he had it for its consumption on a Sunday; and that he was charged for "steering" (pointing where drugs are available) but that he was not true because he was just approaching a restaurant where he was going to have breakfast.

☐ Denial. We all sometimes reject what is too difficult to accept or too difficult to cope with. Denial occurs under such circumstances and escape from reality occurs. During the course of a forensic evaluation, one sometimes sees extremes: "I don't have a drug problem; I can stop whenever I want; I don't stop because I just do not want to; my stroke last year (the inmate is 21) has nothing to do with drugs;" or "I did not know that my wife was capable of doing such horrible things" (a defendant who was charged with endangering the welfare of a child and whose wife was charged with manslaughter for killing a child as a result of repetitive physical abuse).

☐ Rationalization. We all sometimes distort a little bit of reality to save face or to protect our self-esteem. Defendants referred to the forensic clinic, however, are sometimes masters in the art of rationalization. "I sell drugs because I need drugs;"or "my wife did not want to have sex with me anymore" (so, that is why he had sex with his son); or "she behaved seductively" (his five-year old daughter).

☐ Loss of sense of personal priorities. Individuals who are afflicted with mental disorders and are facing legal proceedings because of a criminal offense often lack a sense of what is and is not important. The following are just few examples: Drug addicts that say that they do not have money to see a physician and who volunteer a $200 drug habit. Much pathos — and sometimes ironic humor — is revealed in accounts of their sense of personal priorities. A man who was in prison for burglary may tell you that he was forced to rob to feed his family and to be sure that his kids had money to go to school. Minutes later he may tell you that he sometimes earned $15,000 to $20,000 a week as a professional jockey, but that he spent all the money on drugs.

☐ Jail talk. Some defendants develop a unique language to account for the events leading to charges in an effort to diminish personal responsibility. Sometimes, the most disturbing aspect is the realization that the defendant believes what he says: "I was in the wrong place at the wrong time and somebody was hurt"; "I did not mean to kill him. I shot at Albert and he (the dead victim) jumped in the middle and he was killed trying to stop me"; "He killed himself as he fell over my knife"; "I was addicted to the love that I had for that man"; or "My parents made me an addict" (as volunteered by a man of 45).

Other difficulties may be present. Due to the nature of the medical problem, it is sometimes difficult to determine whether a condition is organic or under willful control.

☐ The defendant may present a complex medical history, sometimes difficult to interpret. Consider the following case: Mr. Campbell is afflicted with numerous physical (neurological) problems causing chronic pain which in turn influences his affect (range of feelings) and cognition. However, psychological testing results failed to show the evidence of "brain damage" per se. The defendant describes episodes of "blackouts" that are said to to be petit mal epileptic episodes but are more likely to be dizziness spells as he claims he can control their onset or that they disappear if he smokes a cigarette. The last time he saw his doctor (two years ago), when he was treated for his leg gunshot injury, he did not consult with the professional regarding his "blackouts." It is not clear whether the defendant is malingering such episodes. The defendant gives the impression of someone coming out from a war. When he was nine years old he had a "serious accident" in which he damaged his right elbow (extensive scars were noted); at the same age, a "stray bullet" hit his elbow close to the area where he was injured during "the accident"; when he was 10, he was stabbed on the back probably injuring spinal nerves (scars were not examined because the defendant indicated they were close to his buttocks); at 15, he was shot in the head by someone who tried to "rob him" but there is no medical information indicating that the bullet actually penetrated the skull, injuring critical brain structures. Last year alone three major injuries resulted from three separate incidents of violence: He was bitten by a boy on the right side of his face during an argument whose nature the defendant did not clarify; another "stray" bullet hit his lower leg (the scar was examined); and he was cut with a sharp instrument on the right hand by "a friend" who wanted to steal his jacket (see also Exhibit 10.2, Christmas Celebration).

☐ The defendant, or the counsel, sometimes comes to the court invoking *ad hominen* scientific evidence, sometimes supported by impressive reports. Consider these examples: "I was afflicted by chronic fatigue syndrome; a reputable doctor has made such a diagnosis; I stole because I had poor self-esteem in those days." Or "Once a former director of the Tourette's society told me that I suffered from Tourette syndrome," which the defendant attempted to use as the explantion why he played obscene tapes over the phone to people he disliked. In one infamously historical case, the expert for the defense argued successfully the point that the defendant had the brain of a crocodile. A crocodile's cerebrum consists almost entirely of the "limbic brain." In humans, the limbic brain is covered by the neocortex, or "new brain." The argument used by the defense was that the accused lacked significant portions of the neocortex and that his behavior was thus controlled by the "limbic brain," making him a "crocodile man."

Clinical experience suggests that the vast majority of the offenses are not linked to organic mental disorders and conditions. It is true that many individuals charged with harrassment may suffer from delusional disorders, or delusions that are part of an organic personality disorder; it is also true that an individual who suffers from a delusional disorder may not know that there is anything wrong with him or her. Once I made the diagnosis of "adjustment disorder" in a female health professional who told me that she was shunned by a physician; a few days later, I was shown court papers indicating that the physician — under oath — indicated that he did not know her. It also appears to be true that a $200 a day drug abuser may claim that he "was forced to sell drugs" to support his drug habit. But sometimes it may also be true, that a defendant — who is charged with criminal sale of illegal drugs — may claim that he is a drug addict when in fact he is not; instead, drug addiction is invoked to elicit sympathy.

Conversely, the vast majorty of organic mental disorders and conditions do not lead to offenses. In the 1950s, the notion that certain crimes were committed by people who suffered from epileptic automatism was popular. A robot-like, killing machine created a powerful image in lay and professional audience alike. Many experts successfully argued a diminished responsibility or even innocence on account of these "facts." However, some of these backfired when "epilepsy" was equated with someone who loses control by force of the disease; many individuals afflicted by epilepsy and experts on this illness wrote extensively that the vast majority of epileptic sufferers were in fact law-abiding individuals.

The defendant often makes a rearrangement of proximal and remote causes. The defendant may offer a theory that "explains" the events leading to the charges, but the proximal, remote, and intervening causes (although all true) may actually have quite different links to the offense. Exhibit 20.1 (One for the Road) illustrates the case of a man who has been charged with vehicular manslaughter. In order to evaluate the prospect of the defendant's social rehabilitation, the following major areas of concern were identified: Alcohol abuse; recurrent depression; memory problems, most likely associated with a combination of factors such as early electro-shock therapy, depression, chronic alcohol abuse), normal aging; stress associated with loss of a loved one; adjustment disorder with exacerbation of depression causing the events leading to his charges; and antisocial personality traits. Of all of these, only alcohol abuse appeared to be most likely to be causally related to the events leading to his charges. Had he not drunk that night, the chances are that the victim may not have been killed. The defendant had been an alcohol abuser for many years and had had confrontations with the law — long before the death of his brother — because of his excessive alcohol use. Alcohol abuse is the proximal cause vis-à-vis the events leading to his charges.

Even when a mental disorder is present, the matter of criminal responsibility cannot be eliminated. In February 1992, a jury in Milwaukee concluded that Jeffrey Dahmer was probably insane but he was still found guilty as charged of murder. "One has to be crazy to do something like that (set a fire that caused several individuals to die); therefore, I am crazy."

The labels associated with many diagnostic categories may create powerful halo effects. Consider the following: "He is mentally retarded, therefore he is mentally incompetent to face the legal proceedings." (In fact, many individuals afflicted by mental retardation have good insight, are law-abiding citizens, and have a great respect for authority as they often depend on responsible adults.) "He suffered a terrible head injury that made him a killing machine" (looking at his personal history, one realizes that the defendant had a long history of antisocial personality disorder long before the head injury); "I am a good person incapable of hurting anyone" (the woman is a drug abuser who gave birth to a baby addicted to crack). Sometimes a lawyer for the defense may tell you that "court papers had already indicated that the defendant suffers from brain damage" (when in fact these "papers" are only a transcription of what the defendant said on his or her behalf). The prosecution and the defense often overemphasize these powerful preconceptions. One of the important roles of the neuropsychologist in court is to identify the powerful pressure that halo effects play on decisions about criminal responsibility and insanity defenses.

☐ **EXHIBIT 20.1**

One for the Road

Mr Casazza was interviewed and tested while still in custody, during a pre-pleading investigation. The defendant was a 63-year-old Caucasian male with a high school education. The evaluation was directed to the issues raised by the Probation Officer in charge of the case, namely that Mr Casazza had been charged with second degree Manslaughter and two counts of Vehicular Manslaughter. The defendant was allegedly driving while intoxicated; immediately after the accident, his BAC (Blood Alcohol Concentration) was 0.26 when he struck and killed a 29-year-old man. He reported not remembering what happened for approximately five to six hours on the night of the offense.

Mr Casazza was found to be suffering from Alcohol Abuse which was considered to be the primary diagnosis — above and beyond the diagnosis of Major Recurrent Depression to be described below. Alcohol abuse was the focus of his current behavioral problems, the main reason for his current problem with the law, and the focus of treatment intervention that was recommended. Major Depression, Recurrent, in partial remission, was also diagnosed. The defendant also showed antisocial personality traits since the time of adolescence; adult antisocial behavior in early adulthood leading to a five-year imprisonment; and presently, personality traits associated with aging.

Mr Casazza was given electro-shock therapy in early adulthood as a treatment for depression; he also suffered partial removal of his intestines as a result of a surgical operation for hernia.

His psychosocial stressors included being out of work due to a prolonged strike (Mr Casazza was a truck driver for a local newspaper when the union members were striking against this newspaper); his 54-year old brother was murdered shortly before the events leading to his charges; the defendant was currently suffering the stress of the charges against him (vehicular manslaughter) which he said he experienced as a "nightmare."

Before his incarceration, most likely the defendant showed moderate signs and symptoms and moderate difficulty in family and social functioning. These signs and symptoms had been exacerbated since the events leading to his current charges. Mild to moderate memory difficulties and intense guilt appeared to be genuine.

The prognosis of recurrent depression was considered to be guarded; it was felt that these episodes could become worse as the defendant aged and as a result of his incarceration. Although not clearly verbalized, it was also thought that the defendant could become suicidal while incarcerated.

While evaluating the prospect of social rehabilitation, the following major areas of concern were identified: Alcohol abuse; recurrent depression; memory problems most likely associated with a combination of factors such as early electro-shock therapy, depression, chronic alcohol abuse, and normal aging; stress associated with loss of a loved one; adjustment disorder with exacerbation of depression causing the events leading to the charges; and antisocial personality traits. Of all these, only alcohol abuse appeared to be most likely to be causally related to the events leading to his charges. The defendant had been an alcohol abuser for many years and had had confrontations with the law — long before the death of his brother — because of his excessive alcohol use.

Mr Casazza appeared to suggest that levels of alcohol in his blood — found to be elevated at the time of the event leading to his charges — had something to do with his intestinal operation. The defendant underwent surgery for intestinal hernia, during which portions of his intestines were removed. Once ingested, alcohol is directly absorbed by the gastrointestinal tract and is soon found in blood; the measured value of 0.26 of blood alcohol concentration found in the defendant's blood soon after the car crash, therefore, is likely to be a physiological consequence of a previously ingested amount of alcohol rather than an artifact caused by partial removal of his intestines.

The events leading to the charges were described as follows. The defendant claimed that he went to a house of a lady friend he knows carrying a bottle of wine as a present; during dinner, he said that he shared the bottle of wine with his host and in addition he drank a shot of rum. The event happened between the hours of 8 to 9 PM. The next thing the defendant claimed he remembers was the blue color of "safety horses" and perhaps shouts at about 2:00 AM while inside his crashed car. The next event said to be remembered was when he was already in the hospital waking up the following morning, when he said that he remembered overhearing a conversation to the effect that "there was no need to ask him anything now; he is going to be with us for a while."

The relevant medical history included the fact that, as indicated above, at an unspecified time in the past, the defendant underwent an operation to correct an intestinal hernia.

The defendant had a long psychiatric history. In the late 1940s Mr Casazza received a series of electroshock treatments to alleviate chronic depression. The defendant claimed that he suffered a marked memory loss after such treatment, and that his memory function was never totally recovered after such treatment. The defendant appeared to have suffered bouts of depression all his life. Important to note was that his depression did not disappear after electro-shock treatment or medication. In the 1950s he indicated he sometimes heard voices; in the 1980s he said he was once riding the subway and he left the train on 72nd street in New York City and called his wife because he did not know where he was; he said he asked her to come and pick him up.

Although at times he had been diagnosed as suffering from a "chronic schizophrenic reaction," his condition was more likely to have been a chronic schizo-affective disorder (that is, recurrent depression with erratic psychotic features). The defendant appeared to have taken at one time or another Miltown, Compazine, and Ritalin. These are medically prescribed drugs that are used for a variety of psychiatric and medical problems, including anxiety and depression. In the background documentation there was an indication that the defendant at times had a "gender identification problem" and that he "wished he were a woman." The defendant denied that he ever said that.

When a teenager, Mr Casazza was placed in a Youth Detention Center; the defendant claims that the charges were for running away from home. During the first interview, however, he indicated that a girl had become pregnant by him, but in further probings during the first and second interviews the defendant indicated that he "did not remember the details." In his early 20's, the defendant indicated that he spent about five years in a federal prison because of a crime involving storage of drugs in his own apartment. The defendant appeared to have a prior conviction for driving under the influence of alcohol in 1980.

Mr Casazza served in the Army in Texas in the late 1940s; after six months of service, he was released but he did not recall whether the discharge had anything to do with the onset of mental illness. However, soon after his release from the Army the defendant began his electro-shock treatment at a Veterans Administration hospital.

The defendant's father was born in the Jamaica and his mother in Venezuela; his mother, in her middle 80s, was described as sickly although very close to the defendant. Mr Casazza married and fathered six children, ranging in age from 12 to 16. Difficulties with his wife around 1970s were variously explained in the background documentation and by the defendant as: His wife left him; he left his wife; or that he had difficulties in adjusting to the thought that his wife had a child when he was in prison; he said that he accepted the child as his own. The defendant claims to have very good support from members of his family.

Mr Casazza completed his High School education. At the time of the events leading to his charges, Mr Casazza was employed by a newspaper organization to deliver newspapers. However, he had not been working for several months due to a strike. The defendant explained that, during the strike, he did not feel bored and/or anxious because of the lack of work — or that he did not drink more than usual — but, rather he was happy to have the chance of spending more time with his family.

Mr Casazza began drinking alcohol at the age of 12; the defendant mostly drank beer, wine, and rum. In 1977 he was ordered to attend Alcoholics Anonymous as a condition of keeping his job while working in a company he did not remember but said to be other than his present newspaper organization. At the time, he said he felt depressed, occasionally suffering from psychotic features. In 1980, as indicated above, he was charged with driving under the influence of alcohol. The defendant denied use of illegal drugs. He indicated that he was arrested for criminal possession of drugs when he kept drugs in his apartment "as a favor to a friend."

Mr Casazza was observed to be a well-developed individual (5'7", 155 lbs). As the defendant waited for the first and second interviews, he was reading a thick novel. He appeared melancholic and at times he was tearful when referring to the victim. ("He was only 29 years old, the father of children; I was told he was a very good man," he said). The structure and content of his speech was within normal limits; his communication skills were excellent. His eye contact was adequate.

A screening battery of probes that included examination of posture, gait, whole-body balance, muscle strength, tremor at rest, intentional tremor, motor coordination, general appearance of the eyes, eye movements and reaction of the eyes to light was performed and the following was noted: Poor whole-body coordination; and marked psychomotor retardation.

From an extensive checklist of signs and/or symptoms, possibly indicative of neurological or mental disorders, Mr Casazza was asked whether he had ever experienced them, and if so, to give examples. The following was volunteered: Forgetfulness; Mr Casazza indicated that at the time of his arrest he no longer bought umbrellas or expensive glasses because he lost these two items all the time; and depression, but not suicidal ideation (he said that he could not kill himself because he loves his family too much). Current paranoid ideation, delusions and hallucinations were denied.

The Wechsler Adult Intelligence Scale — Revised (WAIS-R) was administered. Mr Casazza's verbal IQ was found to be 93 and his performance IQ was 101; the overall test IQ was 96. These IQ levels represent a normal level of intellectual functioning.

His performance in the Wechsler was very erratic. His best performance was in vocabulary tests and tests of similarities, revealing a good command of word meaning and a good capacity to think in abstract terms (this capacity is often markedly reduced in individuals who suffer severe brain disorders). In tests requiring object manipulation, he was concentrated, motivated and methodical in the execution of the tasks. His worst performance was on a Digit Symbol test, performance that probably was a reflection of his marked psychomotor retardation. During a test of general information and digit recall, the defendant appeared to confabulate, that is, the defendant engaged in fabrication in response to questions about situations or events that are not recalled because of memory impairment. (It differs from lying in that the person is not consciously attempting to deceive.) However, this evaluator believed that the defendant was not truthful when he stated that the President of the United States was Johnson.

Mr Casazza was given the Embedded-Figures Test. He was shown outlines of common figures — such as a house, a knife, a fork, eyeglasses, etc. — superimposed on other outlines. People who suffer from subtle to severe forms of brain damage often fail to identify figures presented in such a fashion. There are four such plates, with ten figures on each plate amounting to 40 outlines. Mr Casazza correctly identified 25 out of the 40 outlines. In addition, there were few anomias — the inability to come up with the name of a figure one sees. There were no confabulations — an important sign of neurological or psychiatric disorder consisting of making up figures rarely seen by other people. The quantitative and qualitative features of Mr Casazza's performance are within normal limits for his age.

Mr Casazza was also given the Benton Visual Retention Test. The test involves the brief presentation of geometrical figures of increased complexity; the figures are then removed and Mr Casazza has to draw each one of them from memory on a piece of paper. This test is used to evaluate problems with recent-memory and/or concentration. The defendant made some errors only on the most difficult plates; this performance is within normal limits for an individual of his age.

☐ **QUESTIONS FOR REVIEW AND DISCUSSION**

Δ Historically, the individual is sometimes thought to be not accountable for his or her behavior because of the intervention of forces other than his or her free will. Contrast the tradition of supernatural determinism, which holds that human destiny is governed by the will of the gods, with factors within the brain that make our behavior legally accountable.

Δ Discuss science ad hoc, that is, theories, information, and data that is brought by the expert witness to explain why the individual behaved as he or she did. In particular, discuss cases of individuals suffering from epilepsy, and the links between epilepsy and criminal behavior, and epilepsy and the rights of the mentally ill.

21: EPILOGUE — HISTORY AND PROSPECTS

WE HAVE SEEN THROUGHOUT THIS BOOK THAT WHEN WORKING FOR THE COURTS or when acting as an expert witness, forensic scientists — including forensic neuropsychologists — are required to focus on single events — the offense — or single individuals (the defendant, the victim, the witness, etc). They reconstruct these events and evaluate these individuals by means of the available documentation and sometimes by means of well-accepted forensic procedures, information that is often derived from the observations of other forensic experts. In the last chapter, in particular, we also saw how difficult it is to link events leading to charges to behaviors that are known or suspected to be "organic," that is, biologically determined. I also emphasized that the unique contribution of the forensic neuropsychologist is to render an opinion as to whether the events leading to the defendant's charges can or cannot be explained by well-established facts in the neurosciences and clinical neuropsychology.

The intellectual activity and the use of knowledge and skills in this scientific part of inquiry, the process of observing facts and explaining these facts according to well-established scientific generalizations — sometimes called "laws" in disciplines such as physics — is no different from the activities of a professional working in the privacy of a research laboratory. In the adversary process of the courts, a report of his or her findings — or a deposition, frequently a videotaped statement — is written and formally submitted to the court by the expert witness.

Such a written opinion by the expert witness is read in the court by the conflicting parties involved in the adversary process; the written report circulates behind the scenes and is intensely scrutinized by experts and counsels of both parties. The expert cites available information that is likely to be later formally filed as "exhibits" in the court.

There is much posturing and retraction as a result of the perceived strengths of the arguments and opinions written by experts. A reputable scientist will sometimes appear in court ready to be challenged about his or her findings in front of the jury. This is the public process. This part of the adversary process is the sort of activity that sometimes appears on the front page of newspapers. Although the defense of a doctoral thesis before a committee of scholars may come to mind, needless to say, the public substantiation and defense of professional opinions in court, using a vocabulary that needs to be understood by lay people (the jury), is not exactly a part of the professional training of most mental health workers. The vast majority of mental health workers generally shun these public displays because of the inherent high degree of stress associated with them and because they can be potentially very damaging to one's reputation. By design, it is an aggressive process, in which not only the message but the character and integrity of the professional who brings that message to the court are targets.

There are few written speculations about how the public process of presenting and defending facts in the court — for example, the argument for or against the possibility that because of the presence of a neuropsychological disorder, the defendant was unable to know and appreciate the nature and consequences of his or her behavior and that such a behavior was wrong — enhances, or at least modifies, the corpus of the behavioral sciences, and ultimately creates the facts that are transmitted to future generations of scholars and professionals. One may argue the point that there is a slowly evolving process — that of incorporating facts and knowledge in the accepted corpus of many scientific and professional disciplines — that occurs as a sort of Darwinian process of natural selection and survival of the fittest. The past success or failure of these facts and this knowledge in court (mind you, not in ivory towers of colleges and universities; not in the scientific meetings; not in the reviewing process by editorial boards judging the merits of a scientific manuscript) plays an important role.

HISTORY

One needs to be reminded that, in the past, many disciplines purportedly to study the structure and function of the nervous system and the human mind were once considered "scientific" and are now discredited. A few were extensively used for forensic purposes, sometimes for extended periods of times. These have included phrenology (with its historical precedent, physiognomy and its heir, constitutional psychiatry) as comprehensive views of the interactions between body, mind and human behavior. It also has included hypnotism, polygraphy, and the use of "truth drugs" as employed in the truth-finding process. One feels that a lesson is to be learned in reviewing these once highly regarded disciplines that sometimes preoccupied the minds of most distiguished scientists; is forensic neuropsychology at risk of following a similar fate?

The truth-finding process as a "court procedure" has a complex, sometimes bloody, history, most of which cannot be reviewed here, however relevant. There are abundant historical and contemporary references to the use of a formalized process — centered in a device, a machine, or another contraption usually to produce pain and much personal suffering — by which people in a position of authority find a way "to know whether someone is truthful."

Some readers would certainly object to the thought of linking physical torture, brainwashing, and other forms of coercion to the supposedly honest, contemporary tools that are pain-free and used in the context of highly regulated professional activities of modern, ethical forensic investigators. There is no need to review all of the atrocities carried out by people who chased witches during medieval times, or the horrors of the Spanish Inquisition. One needs to be aware that as one reads this, in many parts of the world people are still being tortured — physically or otherwise, and for a perceived "just cause" (the cause of the oppressor).

The Eyes as the Windows of the Soul: Physiognomy

The link between physical characteristics of an individual and his or her "soul" or "character" has been widely recognized by writers, sculptors, and painters since antiquity. Classical painters and sculptors would freeze a bodily posture or a hand gesture giving an unambigous clue to the inner workings of the mind of the subject depicted in the portrait or sculpture. Physiognomy (the discovery of the disposition of the mind by the study of the lineaments of the body) was the subject of enquiry of the brightest minds. Aristotle (384-322 BC), Bacon (1214-1292), Bell (1774-1842), Darwin (1809-1892), and Lombroso (1836-1909) wrote extensively on the subject, often comparing the expression of emotions in animals and men. Charles Bell is often considered the founder of physiological psychology, the historical precedent of neuropsychology; he also wrote a book totally devoted to the expressive quality of the human hand! However, it is perhaps through the writings of Johan Kaspar

Lavater (1741-1801) that physiognomy became widely known. Physiognomy was once a widely recognized art of probing the mind and behavior and it can be said to be an important historical root to contemporary psychology.

As indicated in Chapter 3 (Appearances and Impressions) modern mental health workers still perform this art although few would ever know or admit its roots. We need to refer to physiognomy only in passing as it is the mother of phrenology, an obsolete theory that linked mental faculties to particular parts of the skull claiming that the shape of the skull is indicative of the predominance of a particular faculty. Supporters of phrenology — as we shall see next — had a more clearly defined agenda of linking their pseudo-science to the ascertainment of morality and possibly to criminology as we understand it today.

Head Bumps as Indicators of Human Character: Phrenology

Boring (1950) indicates that phrenology was a movement that helped to establish the concept that the brain is the "organ of mind," this at a time when the localization of the mind in the brain was much in doubt. Phrenology emerged as a result of the work by Franz Joseph Gall (1758-1828) who was primarily concerned with the anatomy of the head and brain. It is said that as a child Gall developed a theory that schoolmates with good memory had heads formed in characteristic shapes. As an adult, he continued his investigations with a segment of society that he found in jails and lunatic asylums. Early on, he proposed the concept that a "bump" on the head is a sure sign of acquisitiveness because he found this feature prominent among pickpockets. Later, phrenology was much in vogue in European salons and, as a topic of conversation of members of the upper class, it had a similar status as astrology and knowledge of one's horoscope has even today. In collaboration with Spurzheim (1776-1832), Gall published a book with a remarkably long title: *Anatomy and physiology of the nervous system in general and of the cerebellum in particular with observations over the possibility of recognizing many intellectual and moral dispositions in man and animals through the configuration of their heads.*

Boring pointed out the three major flaws of phrenology:

☐ Not even under the best circumstances does the exterior of the skull correspond to its interior and less to the internal features of the brain.

☐ Mind by itself cannot be analyzed into compartments or faculties, a requirement to perform phrenological analysis.

☐ Faculties of the mind had never been shown to be localized in the brain.

However, phrenology provided a comprehensive theory of mind supposedly based on a person's anatomical features (the pseudoscience), and a primitive technology and art of probing heads through which a "trained individual" was able to ascertain the examinee's "intellectual and moral faculties." Phrenology provided an advocacy for biological determination of moral characteristics of humans, an advocacy continued with the criminal anthropology of Cesare Lombroso well into the last decades of the 19th and 20th centuries, the constitutional psychiatry of Ernst Kretschmer (1888-1964) early in the 20th century, and William Sheldon (1898-1977), quite influential still in the mid 1950s and now almost forgotten. In *The Mismeasure of Man,* Stephen Gould (1981) provided a highly readable account of the historical development of these theories.

Modern readers tend to have an oversimplified knowledge of Cesare Lombroso. Lombroso was a first-class criminologist, and many of his unsound generalizations were derived from the scientific training common to European universities of his time. I have recently had an opportunity to examine a filmed copy of Lombroso's book *La Donna Delinquente* at the New York City Library and confess a sense of awe about his knowledge and scholarship. *La Donna Delinquente* argues the case after reviewing known "facts" (in reality, prejudices) about the female in the zoological world, the anatomy and biology of the female (accompanied by detailed pictures of vaginas from females of dubious morality), females' pity, compassion, and cruelty, their capacity for love, their moral sense, and their intelligence. The book concludes with an examination of "delinquency" by the females of the animal world and delinquency in "primitive cultures," ending with a history of prostitution. Lombroso was very much versed in the classics but he could not see himself immersed in a particular culture, sharing its ethical standards and prejudices. At the time, scholarship called for quoting everything known about one's subject, down to the Bible, the Greeks, and the Romans.

In addition, Lombroso makes surprisingly sophisticated use of quantitative techniques. His major shortcoming is that what he obviously meant to use as curious "illustrations" or "examples," were believed to be representative of larger scientific truths. Lombroso knew nothing about epidemiology, selection bias, and the limits of generalization imposed by the observation of biased samples.

The Royal Avenue to the Unconscious: Hypnotism

Hypnotism is related to animal magnetism and to the notion developed by Franz Anton Mesmer (1733-1815) in the late 18th century that there was "an invisible force permeating the universe which he could harness, accumulate in his body, and transmit to sick people with curative effects" (Laurence and Perry, 1988). James Braid (1795-1860) coined the term hypnosis in 1843 to draw attention to the behavior of the hypnotized person and nocturnal sleep (hypnos is Greek for sleep). Many claims have been made about the nature of this phenomenon. Early in the 20th century, studies conducted in the hypnosis laboratory at the University of Wisconsin finally established a link between hypnosis and suggestibility — a title of a book by Clark L Hull published in 1933. Hull, one of the foremost researchers in this area, eventually abandoned the field under the pressure of professors from the School of Medicine. Later, several electrophysiological studies conducted in the 1950s revealed nothing extraordinary about a state which looked no different from that of a person who is relaxed, alert, and with the eyes closed. By the 1960s and 1970s it was widely recognized by many that "hypnosis is a situation in which an individual is asked to set aside critical judgment, without abandoning it completely, and is asked to indulge in make-believe and fantasy" (Laurence and Perry, 1988). In their highly readable book *Hypnosis, Will and Memory: A Psycholegal History,* Laurence and Perry argue the point that hypnosis can be best understood in terms of the factors underlying the interaction between the hypnotist and the subject who is placed under hypnosis. They also write that "expectation, beliefs, and motivations are thus aspects of the hypnotic relationship that influence the hypnotized subject's ability to experience suggested phenomena whether it be amnesia, visual and auditory hallucinations, or hypermnesia."

Hypnotism has gained a well-deserved reputation in the clinic as an ancillary treatment of many conditions, most notably pain. However, an equal and unwarranted success was obtained in the use of hypnosis as an investigative process. Since the 1970s, police departments in the United States, Canada and Australia have established hypno-investigative units under the responsibility of police officers who, for the most part, received a 32-hour training in hypnosis. Needless to say, many of these free-lance professionals often lack a college education and subscribe to highly idiosyncratic views of underlying brain processes supposedly occurring during hypnosis. The concept that the human memory is nothing but a video tape recorder whose features could be played back during hypnosis, and that memory could be "freezed," "zoomed," and "enlarged" to be able to see in more detail — all metaphors borrowed from sport television — are many of the pseudo-scientific claims.

The book by Laurence and Perry (1988) is also valuable as it traces the historical development in which hypnosis was associated with power and dominance, and how concepts that were proven to be wrong time and again, managed to survive until today. The sad conclusion is that, through hypnosis one is able to gather no more information than if one were to hunt for evidence as part of the background investigative process. "Little wonder, then, that police forces during the 1970s were enticed by the possibility that hypnosis offered a time-saving alternative to the often time-consuming activity that they have trained to do best." In the United States, hypnosis — once considered to be the royal route to the unconscious — is rapidly disappearing as a technique for gathering evidence among crime suspects, crime victims, and witnesses to criminal offenses.

The Lie Detector: Polygraphy

As practiced in the United States, Canada, and other countries, polygraphy was once said to provide a truth-finding device and a scientific "proof" for deception. Cesare Lombroso, whom we left much discredited for his scientifically unsound anthropological views of common people and criminal behavior, comes to life again now as the first to have used a standardized physiological measure to determine the honesty of a criminal suspect. Lombroso also made important contributions to graphology, a discipline that is still widely used in questioned documents but less popular as an avenue to study the inner workings of the mind.

Polygraphy, as a technique to study deception, was extensively modified in the more than a century since it was first developed. In 1875, Lombroso made use of blood pressure and heart beat. In 1914, Vittorio Venussi first attempted to use changes in respiration to detect deception. William Marton is said to be the first individual who used several physiological measures — that included muscle tension, blood pressure, respiration, and galvanic skin response — at one point in time. (The galvanic skin response [GSR] is the change in the electrical resistance of the skin; GSR is thought to be under the control of the autonomic system, but the exact mechanism accounting for this change is a subject of debate.) In 1927, John Larson refined an instrument that allowed the simultaneous recording of various physiological measures, an instrument that was perfected in 1930 by Leonard Keeler, who reintroduced the use of galvanic skin response. The "Keeler Polygraph" is the grandfather of modern instrumentation.

The main theoretical assumption that polygraphs make is that "emotional arousal" is a unique physiological response indicative of secret knowledge and deception (e.g., the red hat on the bed of the victim that only the one who killed the victim is likely to know about or remember). One needs to have a cursory experience in a correctional facility to come to grips with the fact that one's notion of truth is not the same as one who is already incarcerated, facing 25 years to life in prison. It has long been known that individuals who suffer from antisocial personality disorder are less likely to be sensitive to the same emotionally-provoking situations encountered by individuals not so afflicted.

However, this would be only the case of "missing something that was expected to be there."

The most worrisome part is that — as a result of a polygraphic examination — a suspect or a defendant is sometimes found to be falsely reacting emotionally to an event for reasons that are sometimes very difficult to explain. Professional polygraphers sometimes claim that in up to 90% of the cases they can be sure when a given individual is lying or telling the truth (in fact, it is about 70% at most). The Congressional Office of Technology Assessment reviewed the literature on polygraphs and published its findings in 1983. The conclusion of that report is that polygraphy consistently fails to meet minimal standards for scientific research. The American Psychological Association made a similar formal proclamation. A good review, including the background, procedures, theoretical assumptions, and details of the polygraphic examination is found in the book by Smith and Meyer (1987) entitled *Law, Behavior and Mental Health: Policy and Practice.*

Truth Drugs

It has been known since ancient times that individuals under the influence of alcohol would reveal information about others and themselves that they would not while sober; *in vino veritas* - in wine, you shall find the truth — is a statement in which most of us are likely to believe. In the United States, "truth drugs" or "truth serum" have been in use since the 1920s in obtaining confessions. Scopolamine was originally used, but the term "truth drugs" is normally associated with sodium amytal and sodium pentathol. About a decade ago, there were accounts that other mind-altering drugs such as LSD were tried on unsuspecting volunteers to investigate the potential use of the drug as a "truth serum." As with hypnotism, it was soon realized that, on the one hand, an individual afflicted with a strong antisocial personality trait would continue to lie even when semi-conscious. On the other hand, individuals would engage in seemingly persuasive accounts of the "true events," accounts that were later found to be totally fictional. It is generally agreed that the use of the "truth drugs" presents many constitutional and ethical problems and is considered at best unreliable as court evidence.

In conclusion, used for forensic purposes, first physiognomy, phrenology, and hypnotism, and later the use of polygraphy and "truth drugs," share common characteristics. They represent fields of knowledge, expertise, and technologies that were proposed by sometimes highly reputable scholars and investigators, often as an honest-to-goodness attempt to gain knowledge of the inner workings of the brain and the human mind. But in many cases this knowledge and skill turned out to be no more valuable than trashable quackery, buried, rediscovered, and published time and again in the legal literature of successive generations. For research and clinical purposes, these techniques are still valuable additions to the enormous armamentarium already available to investigators in the behavioral sciences and clinical mental health workers.

PROSPECTS

To conclude, a brief reference will be made to two important issues that will certainly be the subject of future debates within the discipline of forensic neuropsychology itself and its potential for making a real contribution to the field of criminal law.

Undue Emphasis on Armamentarium

It is now hardly a matter of debate that the results of neuropsychological tests are an important component in the formulation of a legal opinion regarding the defendant's state of mind during the events leading to his or her charges. In fact, neuropsychological tests provide an identity and a proud common professional bond among all forensic neuropsychologists. But this undue emphasis on technology appears unwarranted. For instance, a recent book by Dywan, Kaplan and Pirozzolo (1991) appears to advocate the use of neuro-psychological tests, electrophysiological procedures, and hi-tech imaging techniques at the expense of — if not sometimes substituting for — most of the substantial legal issues involved in the course of the forensic neuropsychological evaluation.

Although recent publications have emphasized the importance of the comprehensive evaluations of multiple sources of information to make neuropsychological evaluations (Lezak, 1983; Shapiro, 1984; Sbordone, 1991), neuropsychological tests themselves continue to be the staple of the profession. Along with many other instruments, almost all neuropsychologists in the United States and Canada are familiar with these protocols: Wechsler's Adult Intelligence Scale (Revised), the Halstead-Reitan Barry, the Luria-Nebraska Battery, and the Minnesota Multiphasic Personality Inventory (MMPI and the revised MMPI-2). For clinical and forensic purposes, neuropsychologists routinely use these tests individually or in combination.

Often, forensic neuropsychologists need to be familiar — or seek the opinion of the experts — with the technical details of data-acquisition and the interpretation of the results of tests and laboratory and clinical procedures that are traditionally not "psychological" in nature. For example, during the review of background documentation, one needs to read laboratory reports dealing with the presence of alcohol and illegal drugs in hair, blood, urine, and other body fluids. At other times, the court neuropsychologist is provided with original pictures and written reports on imaging procedures such as CT (Computed Tomography), MRI (Magnetic Resonance Imaging), or, less frequently, PET (Positron Emission Tomography). A professional involved in a litigation in which the plaintiff is said to be suffering from peripheral nerve damage may need to be aware of the technical details of recordings of nerve conduction velocities (NCV). The identity of the perpetrator of telephone harassment may be found through the use of acoustical analysis of the human voice.

Neuropsychologists advocate and consciously help to perpetuate the use of neuropsychological tests — as administered by professionally-trained neuropsychologists — as essential for the future success of neuropsychology as a forensic discipline. However, as discussed earlier, hypnosis and polygraphy began to lose credibility in the court when the emphasis was turned to the technique itself and many "professionals" who were still using them lost perspective of the link of these techniques to the core medical or scientific disciplines within which they were born. The end result of this undue emphasis on techniques is that most neuropsychologists today have completely divorced themselves from hypnosis and polygraphy and, for legal purposes, consider them just short of quackery. It is interesting to note, that no recent comprehensive review of the field of neuropsychology and law (for example, that of Dywan et al. in 1991) even names these techniques.

The misconception that forensic neuropsychology is just supertechnology leads to two important conclusions: First, if one views the role of the neuropsychologist in court as limited to administering neuropsychological tests, then the legal significance of such neuropsychological findings vis-à-vis the defendant's charges needs to be interpeted to the jury by another professional (such as a forensic neuropathologist or a forensic neuropsychiatrist), thus negating the professional legal recognition that forensic neuropsychologists now seek. The neuropsychologist is relegated to the role of supertechnician. Second, batteries of specific neuropsychological tests become run the risk of being equated with the entire discipline of forensic neuropsychology. If this were the case, it is likely that — when used before criminal courts for forensic purposes — the now-valuable tools of the trade such as the Luria-Nebraska or the Helstead-Reitman will face being eventually discredited, just as hypnosis and polygraphy have become today.

The Science Underlying Forensic Neuropsychology

Criminal responsibility is a crucial concept in criminal law. But among the most important lessons to be learned from phrenology is that the brain itself is not the site of morality. It is very unlikely that the powerful techniques — such as imaging technologies now available — will one day reveal the process of how morally-guided behavior is created or where in the brain moral judgments are made. So, if neuropsychologists cannot translate facts of nervous system function into speculations about the rationality of an individual's behavior, how can the neurosciences make any useful contribution to criminal law?

The neurosciences are concerned with the review of basic facts about how we move, perceive, think, and remember. Knowledge derived from the gross observation of behavior under either field or experimental conditions, from the study of people afflicted by numerous disorders each due to different etiologies, to the study of facts about the activity at the cellular, and molecular level sometimes are invoked to explain these behaviors. One may want to lift the 6.5-pound (third) edition of *Principles of Neural Science* by Kandel, Schwartz, and Jessell (1991) and scan its pages just to have a tangible impression of the vast accumulation of facts about the brain and behavior.

But if one inspects the chapter in *Principles of Neural Science* where consciousness is explained, one is disappointed, as only stages of sleep and of coma defined clinically and electrophysiologically are reviewed. Conscience — that component of the human character usually discussed in closing chapters of classic scholarly psychology textbooks — is nowhere to be found. This is disappointing because neuropsychologists are often asked to address fundamental legal questions about whether during the events leading to the charges, the defendant knew and appreciated the nature and consequences of his behavior and whether his or her behavior is wrong (a value judgment). Where do we find neuropsychological guidelines to make such value judgments? Is it conceivable that when a neuropsychologist makes a judgment about criminal responsibility, he or she is really abandoning the tools of his or her trade, acting no differently from any other solid citizen? Is it conceivable that the answers to important questions about criminal responsibility lie in a realm having little to do with the facts of the neurosciences?

In each generation, the brightest minds have been haunted by the problem of the origin and nature of consciousness and moral judgment. In short, there are reputable contemporary experimental scientists who have argued that consciousness — meaning one's internal representation of physical reality, the awareness of one's own mental life, and ultimately the recognition of the laws that regulate human behavior — starts with an essential distinction between a "spiritual world" and a "physical world" — a dualism that originated in the philosophy of Descartes (1596-1650). Some others do not need to rely on these two different "worlds."

In 1991, Daniel C Dennett, director of the Center for Cognitive Studies at Tufts University, in his book *Consciousness Explained* integrated facts of psychology, neuroscience, computer sciences, and philosophy to try to answer how it is that we know that we are alive and aware of the external world and of the internal objects of one's deliberations. The main thesis of his book is that we traditionally have attemped to divorce ourselves from the fabric of the physical sciences — and because we see ourselves as something special — we tend to separate the events of our mind from the events of "physical reality." Dennett's is a physical interpretation of consciousness.

How "moral behavior" is imprinted in the human brain is not explained by Dennett, but he gives ample food for thought about how conscience (the substrate of morally-guided behavior) is likely to be built. Parenthetically, the French psychologist-philosopher Jean Piaget (1896-1980) wrote extensively on the origin of moral judgment in the child.

Since the times of the Greeks, philosophers have argued that the passions of the body are regulated by the mind, which has the power to control such passions. At some point, it appears that in matters of assessment of criminal responsibility we as neuropsychologists are asked to form an opinion as to whether the defendant was unable to control the force of his passions because of the weakness of his character. For a neuropsychologist, this is surprising and awkward, but this is the sort of question about which lawyers would like us to have an opinion. Unknown to most neuropsychologists who have been trained in the sciences, the historical root of the law is philosophy, a discipline that most scientists shun since it tends to be associated with unfounded speculation. But, historically, philosophers have written their speculations while being inspired by the scientific facts of the day. Dennett is a contemporary example of such a tradition. *Consciousness Explained* is also a very good introduction to the historical account of the alternative accounts on the development of consciousness in humans.

There is still much to be learned and neuropsychologists — instead of continuing to compete professionally with their archrivals, the neurologists and psychiatrists — might be better prepared to take the intellectual lead in the field of neuropsychology as a forensic science. An understanding of neuro-psychological substrates favoring the acquisition of conduct disorder and later antisocial behavior is essential. For instance, many experienced mental health professionals are aware of the fact that antisocial personality disorder is an individual's failure to recognize how one's behavior is shaped and controlled by society's rules and that certain behaviors are "right" and others are "wrong." Experts also know that if the child lacks an early exposure to commands that are obeyed or disobeyed — but not really understood — as an adult that individual may have difficulty in developing an internal locus in which his or her conduct is then regulated by these internalized commands. Is it conceivable that future research in neuropsychology will reveal that there are critical periods in which the human brain is capable of recognizing and internalizing such rules? Is it conceivable that neurochemical maturational mechanisms are essential to such a process? Scientific research at the interface between neuropsychology and criminal law has barely begun.

GLOSSARY OF TECHNICAL TERMS

Acute. Short-lived; of rapid onset and lasting a short time (e.g., acute symptom).

Adjustment disorder. It is a maladaptive reaction to identifiable psychological stressor(s) that occur within three months after onset of the stressor and has persisted for no longer than six months. The maladaptive nature of the reaction is indicated by impairment in the social, family, and occupational activities. The DSM-IV recognizes several types of Adjustment Disorders: with Anxious Mood, with Depressed Mood, with Disturbance of Conduct, with Mixed Disturbance of Emotions and Conduct, with Physical Complaints, with Withdrawal, with Work and Academic Inhibition, and Not Otherwise Specified.

Affect. A pattern of observable behaviors that is the expression of emotion, or a subjectively experienced feeling-state. Common examples of affect are euphoria, anger, and sadness. Affect is a behavior that varies over time, usually in response to changing emotional states, whereas mood refers to a pervasive and sustained emotion. A range of affect may be described as broad (normal), restricted (constricted), blunted, or flat.

Affective disorders. (See Mood Disorders).

Agitation. Restlessness; excitement (e.g., one of the many signs of delirium).

Agraphia. A form of aphasia often resulting from brain injury; a communication disorder characterized by the inability to write phrases, words, syllables, or even individual letters.

AIDS. Acquired Immunodeficiency Syndrome.

AIDS-dementia. Cognitive and mood disorders that are the sequela of brain infection with HIV. It differs from the Alzheimer's type of dementia in that it is associated with subcortical (basal ganglia) neurological signs.

Alzheimer's disease. A progressive neuropsychological presenile disorder associated with cerebral (primarily cortical) sclerosis. Prominent features are restlessness and disorientation with profound memory changes.

Amblyopia. Poor vision that is not caused by any organic defect in the refracting mechanism of the eye; term most frequently used to indicate visual deficits caused by a defect in the visual neural pathways or associated brain centers serving vision.

Anterograde amnesia. Loss of memory for the events after a traumatic event, often brain injury (See Retrograde amnesia).

Antisocial personality disorder. Replaces the term "sociopath" or "sociopathic personality." It is variously defined as pervasive behavioral disorder characterized by the inability to recognize "right" from "wrong," the tendency to violate community rules about personal property and rights, and lack of empathy for others. It is often preceded by conduct disorder in childhood.

Anxiety. Apprehension, tension, or uneasiness that stems from the anticipation of danger, which may be internal or external. Some definitions of anxiety distinguish it from fear by limiting it to anticipation of a danger whose source is largely unknown, where fear is the response to a consciously recognized and usually external threat or danger. The manifestations of anxiety and fear are the same and include motor tension, autonomic hyperactivity, apprehensive expectation, and vigilance and scanning. Anxiety may be focused on an object, situation, or activity, which is avoided (phobia) or may be unfocused (free-floating anxiety).

It may be experienced in discrete periods of sudden onset and may be accompanied by physical symptoms. If anxiety causes preoccupation with the fear or belief of having a disease, it is termed hypochondriasis.

Anxiety disorder. Persistent anxiety lasting at least one month.

Aphasia. Inability to speak, write, or understand the meaning of words due to brain damage.

Apraxia. Impairment in the ability to perform purposive, coordinate movements due to brain lesions but not associated with sensory dysfunction or motor paralysis.

Asthenia. Physical weakness, lack of energy or vitality.

Ataxia. Lack of coordination of intentional movements, general result from a dysfunction of the nervous system.

Athetosis. Slow, recurrent, apparently purposeless movement that follows lesions of the basal ganglia.

Attention. The ability to focus in a sustained manner on one activity. A disturbance in attention may be manifested by difficulty in finishing tasks that have been started, easy distractibility, or difficulty in concentrating on work.

Attention-deficit disorder. A childhood disorder characterized by inattention, impulsiveness, and hyperactivity.

Atypical psychosis. In the DSM-IV classification, a psychosis that does not meet the diagnostic criteria for the various standard types of psychosis.

Aura. Signs and/or symptoms that precede the onset of a mental disorder; term generally applied to symptoms that precede the onset of seizure (such as flashes of light, smells, etc.); also called prodromal symptoms.

Autism. Excessive form of egocentrism, narcissism, or inability to relate to other people (e.g., a child might treat adults as "pieces of furniture").

Automatism. Automatic acts that sometimes are observed among epileptics; in forensic neuropsychology, the counsel(s) for the defense sometimes argues that the events leading to the criminal charges were performed under conditions of automatism.

Autonomic nervous system. System of ganglia, nerves, and plexuses that innervate the viscera, heart, blood vessels, smooth muscles, and glands. It comprises the sympathetic and parasympathetic nervous system; it controls the mechanisms of drives and emotional expression.

Axis I disorder. In DSM-IV terminology, the presence of a major (generally psychotic) disorder such as schizophrenia, recurrent major depression, etc. When there are no signs or symptoms of a major psychiatric disorder, a special code designates that absence.

Axis II disorder. In the DSM-IV terminology, the presence of a personality disorder, generally a non-psychotic disorder.

Bereavement. Normal reaction to the death of a loved one; a full depressive syndrome is a normal reaction to such a loss.

Bipolar mood disorder. A mood disorder consisting of one or more Manic Episodes, followed by one or more Major Depressive Episodes.

Blocking. Interruption of a train of speech before a thought or idea has been completed. After a period of silence, which may last from a few seconds to a few minutes, the person indicates that he or she cannot recall what he or she has been saying or meant to say. Blocking should be judged to be present only if the person spontaneously describes losing his or her train of thought or if, upon questioning by an interviewer, gives that as the reason for pausing.

Body dismorphic disorder. The essential feature is preoccupation with some imagined defect(s) in the appearance of a normal-appearing person. Complaints usually involve facial flaws, appearance of feet and hands, asymmetries in the body, etc.

Body image (body schema). Mental representation of one's body that is gained through internal sensations, emotions, fantasies, posture, exercise, experience with external objects and the opinions of one's body voiced by significant others such as parents, friends, spouses, children, etc.

Borderline personality disorder. According to the DSM-IV, a pervasive pattern of instability of mood, interpersonal relationships, and self-image, beginning in early adulthood and present in a variety of contexts. These include: (1) a pattern of unstable and intense interpersonal relationships characterized by alternating between extremes of overidealization and devaluation; (2) impulsiveness in areas that are self-damaging, e.g., spending, sex, substance use, shoplifting, reckless driving, binge eating; (3) affective instability with marked shifts from baseline mood to depression, irritability, or anxiety, usually lasting a few hours and only rarely more than a few days; (4) inappropriate, intense anger or lack of control of anger, e.g., frequent displays of temper, constant anger, recurrent physical fights; (5) recurrent suicidal threats, gestures, or behavior, or self-mutilating behavior; (6) marked and persistent identity disturbance manifested by uncertainty about at least two of the following: self-image, sexual orientation, long-term goals or career choice, type of friends desired, preferred values; (7) chronic feelings of emptiness or boredom; and (8) frantic efforts to avoid real or imagined abandonment. Many drug polysubstance abusers suffer from this personality disorder.

Bradycardia. Slowness of the heart beat due to an organic condition; individuals who perform vigorous exercise on a regular basis may show bradycardia, associated to the effective working of an enlarged heart.

Bradykinesia. Slowness of movement due to an organic condition (especially the very old).

Brief reactive psychosis. The essential feature of this disorder is the sudden onset of signs and/or symptoms of mental disorder lasting a few hours or days, but no more than one month, with eventual full return to a premobid level of functioning.

Broca's aphasia. Aphasia associated with a lesion of the inferior frontal gyrus of the left cerebral hemisphere in right-handed individuals and characterized by an impairment of articulated or spoken speech.

Bulimia (hyperfagia). Eating disorder consisting of a increased appetite and desire for food sometimes seen among mentally disordered individuals.

Catatonic behavior. A form of behavior sometimes appearing in individuals suffering from schizophrenia. (1) Catatonic excitement is excited motor activity, apparently purposeless and not influenced by external stimuli; (2) Catatonic negativism is an apparently motiveless resistence to all instructions or attempts to be moved; when passive, the person may resist any effort to be moved; when active, he or she does the opposite of what is asked — for example, firmly clenching jaws when asked to open mouth. (3) Catatonic posturing is a voluntary assumption of an inappropriate or bizarre posture, usually held for long periods of time (e.g., stands with arms outstretched in the manner of Jesus on the cross). (4) Catatonic rigidity is the maintenance of a rigid posture against all efforts to be moved. (5) Catatonic stupor is a marked decrease in reactivity to the environment and reduction in spontaneous movements and activity, sometimes to the point of appearing to be unaware of one's surroundings; and (6) Catatonic waxy flexibility is said to occur when the limbs of the mentally disordered individual can be "molded" into any position, which is then maintained. When the limb is being moved, it feels to the examiner as if it were made of pliable wax.

Chorea. A neurological disorder characterized by irregular involuntary movement or spasms of the limbs and face.

Chronic. Permanent, established, and (sometimes) irreversible (e.g., a chronic symptom).

Circumstantiality. Term used to describe a pattern of speech that is indirect and delayed in reaching the point because of unnecessary, tedious details and parenthetical remarks. When the individual's circumstantial replies or statements are prolonged for many minutes, one may sometimes feel that if the speaker is not interrupted and urged to get to the point, he would never get to it.

Clanging. Speech in which sounds, rather than meaningful, conceptual relationships govern choice; it may include rhyming and punning. The term is generally applied only when it is a manifestation of a pathological condition; thus, it would not be used to describe the rhyming word play of children. Clanging is observed most commonly in Schizophrenia and Manic Episodes.

Coma. State of unconsciousness where most behaviors and reflexes are suspended.

Compulsion. (1) A state in which the individual feels as if he or she were behaving (or thinking) against his or her wishes. It is usually a repetitive and seemingly purposeful behavior that is in response to an obsession, or performed according to certain rules, or in a stereotyped fashion. The behavior is not an end in itself, but is designed to produce or prevent some future state of affairs; the activity, however, either is not connected in a realistc way with the state of affairs but is designed to produce or prevent, or may be clearly excessive. Example: A person feels compelled to wash his/her hands every time he/she shakes hands because of a fear of contaminanation, which he/she recognizes as excessive. (2) The "force" that compels that individual to act against his or her wishes. Compulsions are characteristic of Obsessive Compulsive Disorder.

Conduct disorder. A disturbance of conduct lasting at least six months, during which at least three of the following have been present: (1) has stolen without confrontation of a victim on more than one occassion (including forgery); (2) has run away from home overnight at least twice while living in parental or parental surrogate home (or once without returning); (3) often lies (other than to avoid physical or sexual abuse); (4) has deliberately engaged in fire-setting; (5) is often truant from school (for older person, absent from work); (6) has broken into someone else's house, building, or car; (7) has deliberately destroyed others' property (other than fire-setting); (8) has been physically cruel to animals; (9) has forced someone into sexual activity with him or her; (10) has used a weapon in more than one fight; (12) often initiates physical fights; (13) has stolen with confrontation of a victim (e.g., mugging, purse-snatching, extortion, armed robbery); (14) has been physically cruel to people. A Conduct Disorder can be further classified as Mild, Moderate, or Severe.

Confabulation. Fabrication of facts or events in response to questions about situations or events that are not recalled because of memory impairment. It differs from lying in that the person is not consciously attempting to deceive. Confabulation is common in Amnestic Disorder.

Congenital. Present at birth; not necessarily genetic.

Consolidation. A theory of learning that states that, even when a person is not in an active state of learning, the neurophysiological processes underlying learning continue to function.

Conversion disorder. A loss or alteration of physical functioning that suggests a physical disorder, but that is actually a direct expression of a psychological conflict or need. The disturbance is not under voluntary control, and it is not explained by any physical disorder (with this possibility having been excluded by appropriate examinations). Conversion symptoms are observed in Conversion Disorder and may occur in Schizophrenia.

Delirium tremens (DTs). A state that often occurs during alcohol withdrawal in individuals afflicted by alcoholism; it is characterized by tremors, anxiety, vivid hallucinations (of snakes, roaches, small people, etc.) and delusions.

Delusion. A false personal belief based on incorrect inference about external reality and firmly sustained in spite of what almost everyone else believes and in spite of what constitutes incontrovertible and obvious proof or evidence to the contrary. The belief is not one ordinarily accepted by other members of the person's culture or subculture (i.e., it is not an article of religious faith).

Denial. A defense mechanism in which the person fails to acknowledge some aspect of external reality that would be apparent to others.

Depersonalization. An alteration in the perception or experience of the self so that the feeling of one's own reality is temporarily lost. This is manifested in a sense of self-estrangement or unreality, which may include the feeling that one's extremities have changed in size, or a sense of seeming to perceive oneself from a distance (usually from above).

Depression. DSM-IV specifies the following criteria for Major Depressive Episode: (1) depressed mood (or irritable mood in children and adolescents) most of the day, nearly every day, as indicated by either subjective account or observation by others; (2) markedly diminished interest or pleasure in all, or almost all, activities most of the day, nearly every day (as indicated either by subjective account or observation by others of apathy most of the time); (3) significant weight loss or weight gain when not dieting (e.g., more than 5% of body weight in a month), or decrease or increase in appetite nearly every day (in children, consider failure to make expected weight gains); (4) insomnia or hypersomnia nearly every day; (5) psychomotor agitation or retardation nearly every day (observable by others, not merely subjective feelings of restlessness or being slowed down); (6) fatigue or loss of energy nearly every day; (7) feelings of worthlessness or excessive or inappropriate guilt (which may be delusional) nearly every day (not merely self-reproach or guilt about being sick); (8) diminished ability to think or concentrate, or indecisiveness, nearly every day (either by subjective account or as observed by others); (9) recurrent thoughts of death (not just fear of dying), recurrent suicidal ideation without a specific plan, or a suicide attempt or a specific plan for committing suicide. It cannot be established that an organic factor initiated and maintained the disturbance. The disturbance is not a normal reaction to the death of a loved one (which is called Uncomplicated Bereavement). A Major Depressive Episode can be classified as Mild, Moderate, Severe (with or without Psychotic Features), or in Partial or Full Remission.

Devaluation. A defense mechanism in which the person attributes exaggeratedly negative qualities to self or others.

Developmental disorders. The DSM-IV distinguishes between pervasive and specific developmental disorders. A pervasive developmental disorder is a quantitative and qualitative impairment in the development of social interaction and of verbal and non-verbal communication skills, associated with markedly restricted repertoire of activities and interests (it replaced the old concept of childhood autism). Among the specific developmental disorders recognized are academic, language and speech, and motor skills dysfunctions, with various subtypes.

Diplopia. Double vision, most frequently due to the lack of coordination of eye muscles.

Disinhibition syndrome. The lessening of cortical control of impulsive or vegetative function due to drugs and/or alcohol.

Disorientation. Confusion about the date or time of the day, where one is (place), or who one is (identity). Disorientation is characteristic of some Organic Mental Disorders, such as Delirium and Dementia.

Dissociative disorder. Type of mental disorder in which entire episodes of one's life are repressed as in amnesia, fugue and multiple personalities.

Distal. Away from the center of the body (i.e., hands, feet); the opposite of proximal.

Distractibility. Attention drawn too frequently to unimportant or irrelevant external stimuli. Example: While being interviewed, a subject's attention is repeatedly drawn to noise from an adjoining office, a book that is on a shelf, or the interviewer's school ring.

Dysarthria. Impairment in speech articulation caused by nervous system dysfunction.

Dyslexia. A reading disorder characterized by the inability to understand what one reads either silently or aloud.

Dysphagia. Inability to swallow.

Dysthymia. According to DSM-IV, a depressed mood (or sometimes an irritable mood in children and adolescents) for most of the day, more days than not, as indicated either by subjective account or observation by others, for at least two years (one year for children and adolescents). Presence, while depressed, of at least two of the following: (1) poor appetite or overeating; (2) insomnia; (3) low energy or fatigue; (4) low self-esteem; (5) poor concentration or difficulty making decisions; and (6) feelings of hopelessness. Dysthymia are further classified as primary or secondary type, with early or late onset.

Echolalia. Repetition (echoing) of the words or phrases of others. Typical echolalia tends to be repetitive and persistent. The echo is often uttered with a mocking, mumbling, or staccato intonation. Echolalia should not be confused with habitual repetition of questions, apparently to clarify the question and formulate its answer, as when a subject is asked, "When did you come to the hospital?" and replies "Come to the hospital? — Yesterday."

Encephalopathy. Any brain disease.

Engram. A postulated change in brain tissue that explains the retention of memories (biochemical changes, neural circuits, specific sites of the brain).

Exhibitionism. An impulse to show one's genitals, frequently unexpectedly, to an unsuspecting individual (occurs almost exclusively in men).

Factitious disorders. "Factitious" mean not real, not genuine or natural. These are disorders in which signs and symptoms are intentionally produced or feigned.

Fetal Alcohol Syndrome (FAS). A syndrome characterized by facial dismorphia and mental retardation associated with drinking alcohol during the early phases of pregnancy.

Flight of ideas. A nearly continuous flow of accelerated speech with abrupt changes from topic to topic, usually based on understandable associations, distracting stimuli, or plays on words. When severe, speech may be disorganized and incoherent.

Folie-à-deux. Simultaneous presence of the same mental syndrome in two people who are closely associated or are relatives (as in delusional disorders in mother and daughter).

Forensic. Pertaining to, or used in, legal proceedings.

Formal thought disorder (FTD). A disturbance in the form or thought as distinguished from the content of thought. The boundaries of the concept are not clear, and there is no consensus as to which disturbances in speech or thought are included in the concept. For this reason, "formal thought disorder" is not used as a specific descriptive term in DSM-IV. See loosening of associations, incoherence, poverty or content of speech, neologisms, perseverations, blocking, echolalia, clanging.

Frontal lobe "release" signs. Signs sometimes observed during lesions of the frontal lobes (snout reflex, compulsive masturbation).

Frotteurism. Recurrent intense sexual urges and sexually arousing fantasies involving touching and rubbing against a nonconsenting person.

Fugue state. A long term amnesia characterized by the individual leaving home and changing life style and identify (it must be distinguished from Antisocial Personality Disorder).

Gambling, pathological. An irresistible compulsion to gambling, often associated with devastasting effects on someone's personal and family life.

Gender identity disorder. Disorder characterized by the incongruence between one's biological sex and gender identity (sometimes appears in early childhood).

General paresis. A progressive form of neurological pathology generally due to syphilis of the nervous sytem, characterized by the presence of signs of brain pathology and psychosis.

Grand mal seizure. Epileptic seizure consisting of sudden loss of consciousness, tonic and clonic spasm, frothing at the mouth, and often urine incontinence.

Grandiosity. An inflated appraisal of one's worth, power, knowledge, importance, or identity. When extreme, grandiosity may be of delusional proportions. Example: A professor who frequently puts his students to sleep with his boring lectures is convinced that he is the most dynamic and exciting teacher at the university.

Hallucination. A sensory perception without external stimulation of the relevant sensory system. A hallucination has the immediate sense of reality of a true perception, although in some instances the source of the hallucination may be perceived as within the body (e.g., an auditory hallucination may be experienced as coming from within the head rather than through the ears). Hallucinations should be distinguished from illusions, in which an external stimulus is misperceived or misinterpreted, and from normal thought processes that are exceptionally vivid. Transient hallucinatory experiences are common without mental disorders.

Hematoma. A localized mass of blood that is confined within an organ, tissue, or space; the blood is usually clotted.

Hemiparesis. Slight paralysis affecting one side of the body.

Hemiplegia. Paralysis of one side of the body.

Histrionic personality. According to DSM-IV, this is a pervasive pattern of excessive emotionality and attention-seeking, beginning in early adulthood and present in a variety of contexts, as indicated by the following: (1) constantly seeks or demands reassurance, approval, or praise; (2) is inappropriately sexually seductive in appearance or behavior; (3) is overly concerned with physical attractiveness; (4) expresses emotion with inappropriate exaggeration, e.g., embraces casual acquaintances with excessive ardor, uncontrollable sobbing on minor sentimental occasions and/or has temper tantrums; (5) is uncomfortable in situations in which he or she is not the center of attention; (6) displays rapidly shifting and shallow expression of emotions; (7) is self-centered, with his/her actions directed toward obtaining immediate satisfaction, and has no tolerance for the frustration of delayed gratification; (8) has a style of speech that is excessively impressionistic and lacking in detail, e.g., when asked to describe his or her mother, can be no more specific than to say, "She was a beautiful person."

HIV. Human immunodeficiency virus.

Homonymous hemianopsia. Lateral loss of vision in the corresponding (right or left) lateral halves of the eyes.

Hypochondriasis. A morbid concern about one's health and/or exaggerated attention to any bodily sensations; a false notion that one is suffering from a disease.

Hypomania. A mild degree of mania.

Hypoxia. Decrease below normal levels of oxygen in air, blood, or tissue, short of anoxia (the lack of oxygen).

Hysteria. A group of mental disorders that have as a common feature the presence of psychogenic symptoms (hysterical amnesia, hysterical paralysis, etc.).

Ictal. Relating to or caused by a seizure (interictal: between seizures).

Idealization. A defense mechanism in which the person attributes exaggeratedly positive qualities to self or others.

Ideas of reference. An idea, held less firmly than a delusion, that events, objects, or other people in the person's immediate environment have a particular and unusual meaning specially for him or her.

Identity. The sense of self, providing a unity of personality over time. Prominent disturbances in identity or the sense of self are seen in Schizophrenia, Borderline Personality Disorders, and Identity Disorder.

Idiopathic. Denoting a disease of unknown cause (idiopathic epilepsy).

Illogical thinking. Thinking that contains obvious internal contradictions or in which conclusions are reached that are clearly erroneous, given the initial premises. It may be seen in people without mental disorder, particularly in situations in which they are distracted or fatigued. Illogical thinking has psychopathological significance only when it is marked, as in the examples noted below, and when it is not due to cultural or religious values or to an intellectual deficit. Markedly illogical thinking may lead to, or result from, a delusional belief, or may be observed in absence of a delusion.

Illusion. A false perception; a misperception of real external stimulus.

Inattention. Lack of attention or neglect. Applied to visual fields, it is failure to perceive a visual stimulus on one half of the visual field resulting to its consistent neglect (e.g., a clock is drawn with left half missing).

Incoherence. Speech that, for the most part, is not understandable, owing to any of the following: Lack of logical or meaningful connection between words, phrases, or sentences; excessive use of incomplete sentences; excessive irrelevancies or abrupt changes in subject matter; idiosyncratic word usage; distorted grammar. Mildly ungrammatical constructions of idiomatic usages characteristic of particular regional or ethnic backgroundss, lack or education, or low intelligence are not considered incoherence. The term is generally not applied when there is evidence that the disturbance in speech is due to aphasia.

Infarct. Area of necrosis due to lack of blood circulation.

Intellectualization. A defense mechanism in which the person engages in excessive abstract thinking to avoid experiencing disturbing feelings.

Intermittent explosive disorder. Several discrete episodes of loss of control of aggressive impulses resulting in serious assaultive acts or destruction of property. The degree of aggressiveness expressed during the episodes is grossly out of proportion to any precipitating psychosocial stressors. There are no signs of generalized impulsiveness or aggressiveness between the episodes. The episodes or loss of control do not occur during the course of a psychotic disorder, Organic Personality Syndrome, Antisocial or Borderline Personality Disorder, Conduct Disorder, or intoxication with a psychoactive substance.

Intracerebral. Within the brain.

Ipsilateral. On the same side, with reference to a given point.

Ischemia. Local anemia due to mechanical obstruction of the blood supply.

Jacksonian seizures. Seizure disorder characterized by the "march" of the attack from the distal to proximal parts of the body.

Kinesthesia. The perception of one's movement.

Kinetic. Pertaining to movement.

Long-term memory. Memory for the events of the distant past (one's youth); contrasted to Short-term memory (see).

Loosening of associations. Thinking characterized by speech in which ideas shift from one subject to another that is completely unrelated or only obliquely related to the first without the speaker's showing any awareness that the topics are unconnected. Statements that lack a meaningful relationship may be juxtaposed, or the person may shift idiosynratically from one frame of reference to another. When loosening of associations is severe, speech may be incoherent. The term is generally not applied when abrupt shifts in topics are associated with a nearly continuous flow of accelerated speech (as in flight of ideas). Loosening of associations may be seen in Schizophrenia, Manic Episodes, and other psychotic disorders.

Magical thinking. The person believes that his or her thoughts, words, or actions might, or will in some manner, cause or prevent a specific outcome in some way that defies the normal laws of cause and effect. Example: A man believed that if he said a specific prayer three times each night, his mother's death might be prevented indefinitely; a mother belived that if she had an angry thought, her child would become ill. Magical thinking is seen in children, in people in primitive cultures, people with poor education, and in Schizotypical Personality Disorder, Schizophrenia, and Obsessive Compulsive Disorder.

Malaise. A feeling of general discomfort and uneasiness.

Malingering. Feigning of illness.

Mania. A mental disorder characterized by emotional excitement, great psychomotor activity, rapid flow of ideas, exaltation, and unstable attention.

Manic-depressive disorder. A mood disorder characterized by the presence of manic and depressive symptoms, usually alternating every few days (also called Bipolar Disorder).

Masked fascies. Lack of facial expression often seen in Parkinsonism.

Meninges. Membranes covering the brain.

Meningioma. A tumor originating in the meninges, the membranes covering the brain.

Mental disorder. A clinically significant behavioral or psychological syndrome or pattern that occurs in a person and that is associated with present distress (a painful symptom) or disability (impairment in one or more important areas of functioning), or a significant increased risk of suffering death, pain, disability, or an important loss of freedom. In addition, this syndrome or pattern is not merely an expectable response to a particular event, e.g., the death of a loved one. Whatever its original cause, it must currently be considered a manifestation of a behavioral, psychological, or biological dysfunction in the person. Neither deviant behavior, e.g., political, religious, or sexual, nor conflicts that are primarily between the individual and society are mental disorders unless the deviance or conflict is a symptom of a dysfunction in the person as described above.

Migraine. Pain in the head, usually in one side.

Minimal brain damage. A term to indicate subtle psychological and behavioral manifestations due to brain dysfuction that are often detected by means of psychological tests.

Mood. A pervasive and sustained emotion that, in the extreme, markedly colors the person's perception of the world. Common examples of mood include depression, elation, anger and anxiety.

Mood-congruent psychotic features. Delusions or hallucinations the content of which is consistent with either a depressed or a manic mood. If the mood is depressed, the content of the delusions of hallucinations would involve themes of either personal inadequacy, guilt, disease, death, nihilism, or punishment that is deserved. If the mood is manic, the content of the delusions or hallucinations would involve themes of inflated worth, power, knowledge, or identity of special relationship to a deity or a famous person.

Mood-incongruent psychotic features. Delusions or hallucinations whose content is not consistent with either a depressed or a manic mood; in the case of depression, a delusion or hallucination whose content does not involve themes of either personal inadequacy, guilt, disease, death, nihilism, or deserved punishment; the case of mania, a delusion of hallucination whose content does not involve themes of either inflated worth, power, knowledge, or identity of special relationship to a deity or a famous person. Examples of such symptoms are persecutory delusions, thought insertion, thought broadcasting, and delusions of being controlled whose content has no apparent relationship to any of the themes listed above.

Multi-infarct dementia. Cognitive and mood deficits resulting from multiple infarcts of the brain as those occurring in boxing.

Multiple personality. Existence within the person of two or more distinct personalities, some of which may have distinct memories. The transition between personalities is sometimes sudden; personalities are sometimes aware of the others.

Mydriasis. Dilation of the pupils.

Myosis. Constriction of the pupils.

Narcissistic personality disorder. A pervasive pattern of grandiosity (in fantasy or behavior), lack of empathy, and hypersensitivity to the evaluation of others, beginning by early adulthood and present in a variety of contexts: (1) reacts to criticism with feelings of rage, shame, or humiliation (even if not expressed); (2) is interpersonally exploitive, i.e., takes advantage of others to achieve his or her own ends; (3) has a grandiose sense of self-importance, e.g., exaggerates achievements and talents, expects to be noticied as "special" without appropriate achievement; (4) believes that his or her own problems are unique and can be understood only by other special people; (5) is preoccupied with fantasies of unlimited success, power, brilliance, beauty, or ideal love; (6) has a sense of entitlement, i.e., an unreasonable expectation of especially favorable treatment, for example, by assuming that he or she does not have to wait in line when others must do so; (7) requires constant attention and admiration, e.g., keeps fishing for compliments; (8) lack of empathy, i.e., inability to recognize and experience how others feel, e.g., annoyance and surprise when a friend who is seriously ill cancels a date; (9) is preoccupied with feelings of envy.

Narcolepsy. A sudden, incontrollable disposition to sleep occurring at irregular, unexpected intervals.

Neologisms. New words invented by the subject, distortions of words, or standard words to which the subject has given new, highly idiosyncratic meaning. The judgment that the subject uses neologisms should be made cautiously and take into account his or her educational and cultural background.

Neurasthenia. An ill defined disorder characterized by easy fatigability.

Neuropathy. Any disorder affecting the nervous system (i.e., toxic neuropathy: a disorder of the nervous system caused to toxic agents).

Neurosis. A term indicating a psychological and/or behavioral disorder that is, in general, less severe than a psychotic disorder because the individual does not exhibit gross distortion of reality or disorganization of thought process. The main symptoms of neurosis is anxiety.

Neurotropic substances. Chemical compounds that display affinity for the nervous system.

Nystagmus. Rapid, repetitive movements of the eyes.

Obsessions. Recurrent, persistent, senseless ideas, thoughts, images, or impulses that are ego-dystonic, i.e., they are not experienced as voluntarily produced, but rather as ideas that invade consciousness.

Obsessive compulsive disorder. A personality disorder characterized by perfectionism and inflexibility; individuals afflicted by this disorder usually set unobtainable standards that actually interfere with the execution of the tasks set for themselves. They are aware of their relative status in relations of dominance and submission.

Organic mental disorder. Psychological and/or behavioral disorder that has its etiology in (medically verifiable) brain dysfunction.

Organicity. The presence of a personality trait and/or behavior that is caused by faulty brain function (i.e., perseveration, psychomotor retardation, various types of speech disorders).

Orientation. Awarenes of where one is in relation to time, place, and person.

Overvalued idea. An unreasonble and sustained belief or idea that is maintained with less than delusional intensity. It differs from an obsessional thought in that the person holding the overvalued idea does not recognize its absurdity and thus does not struggle against it. As with a delusion, the idea or belief is not one that is ordinarily accepted by other members of the person's culture or subculture.

Panic attacks. Discrete periods of sudden onset of intense apprehension, fearfulness, or terror, often associated with feelings of impending doom. During the attacks, there are such symptoms as dyspnea, palpitations, chest pain or discomfort, choking or smothering sensations, and fear of going crazy or losing control.

Panic disorder. Disorder characterized by the occurrence of spontaneous, episodic, and intense periods of anxiety usually lasting no more than an hour.

Paranoid ideation. Ideation, of less than delusional proportions, involving suspiciousness of the belief that one is being harassed, persecuted, or unfairly treated. In some instances the term is used when the clinician is unsure or whether the disturbances are actually delusional. Ideas of reference often involved paranoid ideation.

Paraphilia. Sexual disorder involving intense sexual urges or sexually arousing fantasies involving (1) nonhuman objects; (2) the suffering or humiliation of oneself or the other; and/or (3) children or nonconsenting adults. Paraphilias that are the focus of forensic investigation are exhibitionism, frotteurism, pedophilia, voyerism, and sexual sadism.

Peripheral nervous system. Portion of the nervous system consisting of the spinal and cranial nerves and peripheral ganglia.

Perseveration. Pathological signs consisting in repetition (i.e., while drawing a line of dots, continuing drawing till the edge of the page; in speech, persistent repetition of words, ideas, or subjects so that, once a person begins speaking about a particular subject or uses a particular word, that word continually recurs). Perseveration differs from the repetitive use of "stock words" or interjections such as "you know" or "like."

Personality. Deeply ingrained patterns of behavior, which include the way one relates to, perceives, and thinks about the environment and oneself. Personality traits are prominent aspects of personality, and do not imply pathology. Personality disorder implies inflexible and maladaptive patterns of sufficient severity to cause either significant impairment in adaptive functioning or subjective distress.

Petit mal seizures. Epileptic seizures consisting of absences and/or brief disruption of consciouness during which the individual loses contact with his or her environment.

Phobia. Persistent fear of a circumscribed stimulus or set of stimuli (object or situation). The most common simple phobias involved the fear of certain animals such as snakes, spiders, mice and so on. The fear of a specific object, activity, or situation results in a compelling desire to avoid the dreaded object, activity, or situation (the phobic stimulus). More commonly, the person does not actually avoid the feared situation or object, though he or she recognizes that the fear is unreasonable and unwarranted by the actual dangerousness of the object, activity, or situation. Some people with a phobia claim that their avoidance is rational because they anticipate overwhelming anxiety or some other strong emotion that is out of their control; they do not claim, however, that their anxiety is rationally justified.

Pica. Eating of non-nutritional subtances such as soil, paint, wood, etc.

Post-traumatic amnesia (PTA). Loss of memory that occurs after catastrophic events not necessarily associated with brain disorder.

Post-traumatic stress disorder (PTSD). The essential features of this disorder are (1) reexperience of a trauma through dreams or waking thoughts; (2) emotional numbing of other experiences and/or relationships because of the presence of these thoughts; and (3) mood disorders, particularly depression and complaints of lack of concentration.

Poverty of content of speech. The speech is adequate in amount but conveys little information because of vagueness, empty repetitions, or use of stereotyped or obscure phrases. Individuals sometimes provide enough information but require many words to do so.

Poverty of speech. Restriction in the amount of speech, so that spontaneous speech and replies to questions are brief and unelaborated. When the condition is severe, replies may be monosyllabic, and some questions may be unanswered.

Preclinical. Before the appearance of clinical signs or symptoms of disorders; psychological tests sometimes reveal subtle deficits that later on develop into readily observed signs or symptoms.

Presenile dementia. A type of cognitive and mood disorder observed in adulthood, before senium (old age).

Pressure of speech. Speech that is increased in amount, accelerated, and difficult or impossible to interrupt. Usually it is also loud and emphatic. Frequently the person talks without any social stimulation and may continue to talk even though no one is listening. Pressure of speech is most often seen in manic episodes, but may also occur in some cases of Organic Mental Disorders, Major Depression with psychomotor agitation, Schizophrenia, other psychotic disorders, and, occassionally, acute reactions to stress.

Prodrome. Early warning sign or symptoms.

Projection. A defense mechanism in which the person indirectly attributes his or her own unacknowledged feelings, impulses, or thoughts to others.

Prosody. Speech melody.

Pseudodementia. Cognitive dysfunction due to mood disorders, most frequently depression. The condition shows clinical features resembling a dementia that are not due to organic brain dysfunction or disease. Pseudodementia may occur in a Major Depressive Episode or may be seen in Factitious Disorder with Psychological Symptoms.

Psychomotor agitation. Excessive motor activity associated with a feeling of inner tension; the activity is usually nonproductive and repetitious. When the agitation is severe, it may be accompanied by shouting or loud complaining. The term should be used in a technical sense to refer only to states of tension or restlessness that are accompanied by observable excessive motor activity. Examples: Inability to sit still, pacing, wringling of hands, pulling at clothes.

Psychomotor retardation. General slowness in the speed of mental reactions that involve bodily movement or manipulation of parts of the body; thus, visible and generalized slowing down of physical reactions, movements, and speech.

Psychosis. A severe mental disorder characterized by loss of reality; individuals afflicted with psychosis incorrectly evaluate the accuracy of their perceptions and thought. The term psychotic does not apply to minor distortions of reality that involve matters of relative judgment. For example, a depressed person who understimates his achievements would not be described as psychotic, whereas one who believes he has caused a natural catastrophe would be so described. Direct evidence on psychotic behavior is the presence of either delusions or hallucinations (without insight into their pathological nature). The term psychotic is sometimes appropriate when a person's behavior is so grossly disorganized that a reasonable inference can be made that reality testing is markedly disturbed. Examples include markedly incoherent speech without apparent awareness by the person that the speech is not undestandable, and the agitated, inattentive, and disoriented behavior seen in Alcohol Withdrawal Delirium. In DSM-IV the psychotic disorders include Schizophrenia, Delusional Disorders, Psychotic Disorders Not Elsewhere Classified, some mental disorders caused by medical conditions, and some Mood Disorders.

Psychosocial stressors. Acute events and enduring circumstances that may cause an exarcerbation of a mental disorder (Axis IV in the DSM-IV classification system).

Rationalization. A mechanism in which the person devises reassuring or selfserving, but incorrect, explanations for his of her own or other's behavior.

Repression. A defense mechanism in which the person is unable to remember or to be cognitively aware of disturbing wishes, feelings, thoughts, or experiences.

Residual. The phase of an illness that occurs after remission of the florid symptoms or the full syndrome. Examples: The residual states of Autistic Disorder, Attention-Deficit Hyperactive Disorder, and Schizophrenia.

Retrograde amnesia. A form of memory disorder consisting in the inability to recall events before a given time (e.g., when a traumatic event occurred).

Schizoid personality. A pervasive pattern of indifference to social relationships and a restricted range of emotional experience and expression, beginning by early childhood and present in a variety of contexts as indicated by at least four of the following: (1) neither desires not enjoys close relationships, including being part of the family; (2) almost always chooses solitary activities; (3) rarely, if ever, claims or appears to experience strong emotions, such as anger or joy; (4) little if any desire to have sexual experiences with another person (age being taken into account); (5) is indifferent to praise or criticism by others; (6) has no close friends or confidants (or only one) other than first degree relatives; (7) displays constricted affect, e.g., is aloof, cold, rarely reciprocate gestures or facial expression, such as smiles or nods.

Schizophrenia. Presence of characteristic psychotic symptoms characterized by (1) delusions; (2) prominent hallucinations; (3) incoherence or marked loosening of associations; (4) catatonic behavior; (5) flat or grossly inappropriate affect. During the course of the disturbance, functioning in such areas as work, social relations, and self-care is markedly below the highest level achieved before onset of the disturbance. It cannot be established that an organic factor initiated and/or maintains the disturbance.

Seizure. A convulsion defined as an abrupt alteration in cortical electrical activity manifested clinically by a change in consciousness or by motor, sensory, or behavioral symptoms. Seizures (which may be due to a variety of causes) become important in the differential diagnosis of syncope.

Senile dementia. Cognitive and mood disorder associated with old age.

Short-term memory. Memory for recent events (i.e., series of numbers just recited).

Sign. An objective manifestation of a pathological condition. Signs are observed by the examiner rather than reported by the individual.

Sociopathic personality. Older term designating what is today called Antisocial Personality Disorder.

Sodomy. Technically, sexual intercourse through the anus. In the documentation of a legal process, sodomy may used to describe cunnilingus or fellatio.

Somatization. A defense mechanism in which the person becomes preoccupied with physical symptoms disproportionate to any actual physical disturbance.

Subclinical. Not observed during the normal course of the clinical observation and sometimes revealed through psychological testing.

Subcortical dementia. Cognitive deficits and mood disorders associated with dysfunction of the basal ganglia (i.e., Parkinson's dementia).

Suppression. A defense mechanism in which the person intentionally avoids thinking about disturbing problems, desires, feelings, or experiences.

Symptom. A manifestation of a pathological condition. Although in some uses of the term it is limited to subjective complaints, in common use "symptom" includes objective signs of pathological conditions as well.

Syndrome. A group of symptoms that occur together and that constitute a recognizable condition. "Syndrome" is less specific than "disorder" or "disease." The term *disease* generally implies a specific etiology or pathophysiologic process. In the DSM-IV most of the disorders enumerated are, in fact, syndromes.

Tic. A involuntary, sudden, rapid, recurrent, non-rhythmic, stereotyped, motor movement or vocalization. It is experienced as irresistible, but can be suppressed for varying lengths of time. All forms of tics are often exacerbated by stress and usually are markedly diminished during sleep. They may become attenuated during some absorbing activities, such as reading or sewing. Both motor and vocal tics may be classified as simple or complex. Simple motor tics are eye-blinking, neck-jerking, shoulder-shrugging, and facial grimacing. Common simple vocal tics include coughing, throat clearing, grunting, sniffing, snorting, and barking. Common complex motor tics include facial gestures, grooming behaviors, hitting or biting self, jumping, touching, stamping, and smelling an object. Common complex vocal tics include repeating words or phrases out of context, coprolalia (use of socially unacceptable words, frequently obscene), palilalia (repeating one's own sounds or words). and echolalia (repeating the last-heard sound, word, or phrase of another person, or a last-heard sound). Other complex tics include echokinesis.

Tinnitus. Ringing of the ears caused by damage in the nerves of the hearing organs/nerves.

Tourette syndrome. Characterized by multiple motor and vocal tics. The motor tics involve the head, and frequently other parts of the body such as torso and upper and lower limbs. The vocal tics may include clicks, grunts, yelps, barks, sniffs, coughs and words. Coprolalia is often present, a complex vocal tic involving the uttering of obsenities.

Transient ischemic attacks (TIA). A rapidly evolving and rapidly resolving neuropsychological disorder associated with the transient lack of blood irrigation to the brain.

Tremor. Shaking, an involuntary trembling movement (e.g., intention tremor, or shaking produced during the execution of a voluntary act).

APPENDIX A: PSYCHOMETRIC INSTRUMENTS

The following terms need to be understood in order to use this Appendix appropriately:

A **test item** is a question, a problem, a single item that elicits a response which can be measured (usually as "Yes" or "No," "correct" or "incorrect," "true" or "false." A psychological test may include many dozens, sometimes hundreds of individual items (e.g., MMPI).

A **test** is a standardized set of questions or tasks which are administered to an individual to assess the presence or absence of a particular skill or knowledge (concentration, memory, vocabulary, etc.).

The term **standard** has at least two meanings: (1) The test has been administered in the manner that it is recommended by the author(s) of the test (e.g., the same items, in the same sequence); (2) A test has been normalized, that is, administered to a statistically representative sample of a given population. A test is said to be standardized when its validity, reliability — and sometimes its sensitivity and specificity — is known in a quantitative manner. However, some well-known tests lack such rigorous standardization and test administrators rely on their "clinical experience" with the test (e.g., projective tests). During a court presentation, an expert witness may be confronted with questions about the validity and reliability of a given test.

A **test battery** is a group of related tests that are administered at one time. A battery of tests are usually aimed to assess large aspects of the individual's personality, cognitive functions, memory, etc. The Wechsler Adult Intelligence Scale is an example of a widely known test of intelligence allowing the estimation of the individual's IQ.

The reader may consult additional sources listed in Anastasi (1988), Lezak (1983), Valciukas (1991), and Wolman (1989).

Academic Skills. Tests aimed to assess spelling, reading, and arithmetic skills (e.g., Wide Range Achievement). Norms are available for two age levels: I (children from 5 to 11) and II (12 to 45). There are many variations of tests of academic skills.

Aphasia Screening Test. A set of tasks aimed at the evaluation of whether the individual suffers from impairments in language and/or other communication skills. In an aphasia test the individual is asked to name objects, read letters, numbers and words, perform arithmetic calculations, read and write sentences, pronounce words, identify specific parts of his or her body, and in the evaluator's body, determine right from left on his or her body and the evaluator's body. Scoring is usually the number of errors made in each group of tasks; some screening tests contain a weighing scheme proportional to the difficulty of the task (Russell, Neuringer, and Golstein, 1970).

Bender-Gestalt Test. Created by Dr. Loretta Bender (1897-1987) the test consists of the presentation and reproduction of nine cards containing drawings inspired in Gestalt theory of visual perception. In the correct reproduction of the figures, the relation between the component of the designs — e.g., a circle attached to a square — periodic groupings, overlapping of two figures, etc. must be recognized. Although this test requires drawing, the results do not heavily depend on motor abilities. Age and education are important factors. The test has been widely used in neuropsychology and in clinical neurotoxicology. The major drawback of the test is the scoring, which requires interpretation by the test administrator. There have been attempts to quantify the test (Lacks, 1984). Reports of results of the Bender Gestalt Test may contain expressions regarding quantitative and qualitative features of the reproductions. The following are the most common expressions: *Rotation* is a change in orientation of the major axis of the figure. *Overlapping difficulties* are problems in reproducing portions of the figures that should overlap. *Simplification* is an error in reproduction consisting in drawing a figure in a simplified or easier form. *Fragmentation* is the reproduction of the figures broken up into parts destroying the Gestalt; the figure is thus incomplete. *Retrogression* is said to occur when a more primitive gestalt is substituted for the stimulus. *Perseverations of Type A* comprise the inappropriate substitutions of the features of a preceding stimulus. Intra-design perseveration, or continuing to draw a figure beyond the limits called for by the stimulus, is termed *Perseveration of Type B*. *Collision* and/or *collision tendency* is the reproduction of a figure as touching or overlapping another figure (collision) or is drawn within 1/4 inch or less of another figure but does not touch (collision tendency). *Impotence* is the behavioral or verbal expression of inability to draw a figure correctly. Problems in the joining parts of figures together or getting adjacent parts of a figure to touch are termed *Closure Difficulty*. *Motor incoordination* is the presence of irregular (tremor-like) lines, especially with heavy pressure. *Angulation* difficulties are experienced in drawing the orientation of the major axis at proper angles. (This includes failure to reproduce angulation, angulations of the whole figure, variability in the angulation). *Cohesion* (size error) is the presence of isolated increase or decrease in size of figures.

Benton Facial Recognition Test. This is a screening test to assess subclinical manifestation of visual impairments. In one of the tasks the individual is presented with a photograph of a person's face, the target. The individual is then asked to recognize the target from among six photographs presented. The test is made more challenging by partially covering features of the target. The test contains the desirable features of being minimally dependent on linguistic skills and thus can be administered to individuals with little knowledge of English (Benton et al., 1983).

Benton Visual Retention Test (BVRT). This is a screening test to assess visual spatial perception and, in particular, visual memory. It is often used in the evaluation of memory functions that surface as a result of Organic Memory Syndrome. The individual is shown ten designs of increasing complexity, each for ten seconds; this is followed by either the immediate reproduction from memory of the designs by the subject or, after a delay period, before the individual is allowed to reproduce the patterns. Both the number of correct reproductions and the error scores are used to assess the functional status of the subject's visual memory. Some psychometric properties of the BVRT need to be emphasized. Although norms for certain populations are available in the literature, norms for blue collar workers and individuals of low educational and economic status have yet to be developed. Information on the effect of age and education on the quantitative characteristics of the individual's responses, characteristics which are important in the interpretation of the results, need also to be taken into consideration. The scoring procedure for the BVRT is time-consuming and quite elaborate. Commercially-available sets give little information on the test's validity and reliability. The report on standardization does not conform to modern psychometric thinking. For a review of memory tests used in the evaluation of the brain-damaged, see Lezak (1983). The presence of confabulations in the reproduction of test patterns during the administration of the BVRT can be readily noted. The examinee fills the gaps with patterns of his or her own invention just to avoid leaving the paper blank.

Block Design Test. This instrument assesses the ability to analyze abstract figures visually and construct them from their component parts; it is essentially a measure of ability to handle visual spatial relationships, an ability that sometimes is lost in individuals suffering gross and even subtle manifestations of brain disorder. The Block Design Test is also an important component for the screening of mentally-disordered individuals (particularly those suspected to be afflicted with schizophrenia). As a part of the Wechsler Adult Intelligence Scale, the test consists of the presentation of geometric bi-colored figures that need to be reproduced first with four cubes and later with nine cubes. Variations of this test are the Knox cubes (utilizing only four cubes) and Koh's Block Design (utilizing multicolored cubes), both of which are now rarely used.

Boston Naming Test. This test consists of 60 drawings of objects of decreasing familiarity (Bed, Pencil, Whistle, Comb, Saw; Trellis, Palette, Protractor, Abacus). If the individual does not recognize the object, he or she is presented with a cue of its use and a phonemic cue (the first syllable of the word). The test has been standarized for various age groups. Interpretation of results needs to be made with care for individuals who are not native-English speakers and who were born abroad.

Categories Test. This test is used as a screeing test (see) for brain damage. Although a part of the Halsted-Reitan Neuropsychological Test Battery, it is often administered by itself. The Categories Test assesses skill in the formation of concepts as it requires the discovery of underlying principles that link a group of four items of progressive difficulty. The individual must give a code name between 1 and 4 to the missing, or odd, element; the test administrator only indicates whether the examinee's selection is "right" or "wrong." The examinee is expected to adjust to the negative or positive feedback resulting from his or her selection. Perseveration in a selection strategy (inability to modify behavior as a result of feedback) is often seen in individuals of advanced age or who are suffering from brain disorders. It has been consistently reported in the literature that the results obtained in the Categories Test correlate highly with the overall results obtained from the administration of the entire Halstead-Reitan Neuropsychological Test Battery. It measures functions similar to those tapped with the Raven Progressive Matrices and the Wisconsin Sort Test.

Critical Flicker Frequency (CFF) Test. This test consists of a flickering light whose frequency can be manipulated. The CFF is the frequency at which the light is no longer perceived as flickering.

Dexterity Test. The ability to perform very delicate, coordinate movements with one's fingers is one important dimension of neuropsychological screening. A person with subtle brain disorder may have such ability impaired; some others — such as those suffering from alcohol-related hand tremors — may exhibit dysfunctions that can be observed at the clinical level but need to be documented quantitatively. There are essentially two tests widely used to assess motor dexterity: In the *Purdue Board*, the individual is instructed to insert metal round pegs in one of two rows of fitting holes; the test is performed with the dominant hand first, the nondominant hand second, and with both hands last. The score is the number of pegs inserted in 30 seconds. The *Grooved Pegboard* is more challenging since it requires the examinee to insert individual metal pegs into grooved holes with the preferred hand. This task is similar to that of inserting small keys into several keyholes. It has been standardized differently from the Purdue Board; in the Grooved Pegboard, the score is the time it takes to fill the board with all the pegs. Differences in scores between dominant and nondominant hand are important components of the analysis of results as they may indicate laterality of brain lesion (see also Finger Tapping and Grip Strength Test).

Digit Span Test. This test is an important screening component in many test batteries and mini-mental status evaluation. It consists of the repetition — first forwards, then backwards — of series of numbers of increasing lengths. Some examiners score separately the total number of digits that can be repeated forwards or backwards; in some tests, including the Wechsler Adult Intelligence Test, the score is the the total sum of digits correctly repeated forwards and backwards. It assesses concentration and short-term memory; it is highly affected by level of anxiety during testing.

Digit-Symbol Test. This test requires looking at geometrical symbols placed under one-digit numbers and then copying the codes associated with the number as quickly as possible, thus tapping both attention and visual-motor speed. As a screening test, it is one of the most widely used in neuropsychology. The computer-based symbol digit test, in which the examinee matches the number associated to a symbol, does not provide as much information as the traditional paper-and-pencil procedure, since in the latter the examinee must rely on hand-coordination, a skill that is substantially untapped in computer-based procedures.

Draw-a-Person. Goodenough's Draw-a-Man and the Draw-a-Person by the Machovers are important components of the psychological assessment staple, particularly in the assessment of children and/or severely disordered individuals. Goodenough's test was originally introduced and standardized in 1926 and was proposed as a quick way to assess child's intelligence by taking into consideration the amount of detail in the drawing. Machover's is a projective test proposed in 1948 for the assessment of the examinee's self- and body-image. The examinee (often a child), is asked to draw a person, and then a person of the opposite sex. The examinee is asked specific questions about the drawings such as sex, schooling, marital status, ambitions, and so forth.

Embedded Figures Test. This test was developed for the evaluation of adults suspected of chronic or acute exposure to neurotoxic agents in the environment or the workplace (Valciukas and Singer, 1982). The test is useful for the assessment of minimal brain damage or generalized brain dysfunction such as those occurring in the early stages of dementia. This type of test is inspired by the Gestalt theory of visual perception. Classical embedded figures tests were designed for patients suffering from serious traumatic brain injuries and are often not very challenging for workers whose brain functions might be affected but who were "normal" enough to be able to work (Valciukas, 1991).

Farnsworth-Musel 100 Hue Test. A test of color discrimination (Farnsworth, 1957).

Finger Tapping Test. This test measures the ability to tap or depress with one's index finger a lever attached to counter; the higher the tapping range, measured in periods of 10 seconds, the higher the score. It is part of the Halstead-Reitan Neuropsychological Test Battery. Performance with the nonpreferred hand is normally about 5 to 10 percent lower than the preferred hand. In the absence of any obvious orthopedic problems, information of a difference of 25 percent or more between the dominant and nondominant hand is important to ascertain laterality of a brain lesion (see also Dexterity Test and Grip Strength Test).

Grip Strength Test. This test essentially consists of measuring grip strength by means of a dynamometer. The examinee is given two, or sometimes three, trials with each hand; the score is the average strength with each hand. It is generally accepted that the strength of the nondominant hand is about 5% to 10% lower than the dominant hand. The difference in scores beween dominant and nondominant hand is an important component of the analysis of results as they may indicate laterality of brain lesion (see also Dexteriry Test and Finger Tapping Test). However, important factors such as orthopedic conditions suffered by individuals involved in car accidents need to be ruled out in the interpretation of results.

Halstead-Reitan Battery. This is one of the most widely used set of tests for the assessment of brain damage (Halstead, 1947; Reitan and Davison, 1974). The set consists of the following tests: Categories, critical frequency fusion (CFF), tactual performance, rhythm, recognition of speech sounds, finger tapping, and time sense. Some clinical psychologists add to this core set the trail making test, and tests for aphasia and agnosia. It is generally recommended that the Wechsler Adult Intelligence Scale and the MMPI (or MMPI-2) be administered along with the Halstead-Reitan battery. Thus defined, the complete administration of the Halstead-Reitan battery takes between six and eight hours.

Inkblot Test. See Rorschach Test.

Ishihara Test. This test is used for the screening of color blindness. It consists of separate plates in which figures and backgrounds are printed with dots varying only in hue and saturation. The results of the tests need to be interpreted with care because loss of discrimination between figure and background is progressively lost in advanced age. Other tests that are used to test color discrimination are the Farnsworth-Musel 100 hue test (Farnsworth, 1957) and the Lanthony D-15 desaturated panel (see following entry).

Lanthony D-15 Desaturated Panel. A test of color discrimination (Blain and Mengler, 1986).

Luria-Nebraska Battery. This battery is based on research performed by Luria (1966) and Luria and Majowski (1977). The battery consists of 269 items representing basic nervous system functions, such as motor, rhythm, tactile, visual, receptive and expressive, speech, writing, reading, arithmetic, memory, and intellectual process. The effort to standardize the content, administration, and scoring of this essentially qualitative battery has occurred only recently, so that its full impact on current clinical thinking and forensic work has yet to be evaluated. The major advantage of the Luria-Nebraska battery over its most obvious competitor (the Halstead-Reitan Test Battery) is that the former takes about two and a half hours to administer. Flexible use of test items is possible since they are considered as "units." Most batteries are built on the concept of "subtests" (e.g., the Wechsler Adult Intelligence Scale and the Halstead-Reitan). It is claimed that the "units" in the Luria-Nebraska test can be added or substracted without altering the essential nature of the test. No such claim has been made on "subtests" of the other two well-known batteries.

Millon Clinical Multiaxial Inventory (MCMI). This is a 175-item personality inventory test that requires the examinee to respond *true* or *false*. Although not as widely known and/or utilized as the MMPI or MMPI-2, it often appears in forensic neuropsychological reports. However, there is very little research on the usefulness of the MCMI in brain-damaged individuals.

Minnesota Multiphasetic Personality Inventory (MMPI, MMPI-2). The Minnesota Multiphasetic Personality Inventory (MMPI) was developed in 1937 (Hathaway and McKinley, 1942). To this date, there are over 9,000 publications on the MMPI, and it has been translated into most major foreign languages. The MMPI consists of 566 affirmative statements to which the examinee gives the response *True, False,* or *Cannot Say.* In the individual form of the test, the statements are printed on separate cards which the respondents sort into the three categories. Examples of the statements are: "I do not tire quickly"; "Most people will use somewhat unfair means to gain profit or an advantage rather than to lose it." A revised version of the MMPI (the MMPI-2) became available in 1989. The University of Minnesota Press added some scales and deleted questions which in the early version were found to be offensive. Like its predecessor, the MMPI-2 asks 567 *true-false* questions about feelings, symptoms, attitudes and beliefs. The MMPI-2 sample includes 2,600 subjects from Minneapolis, Cleveland, San Diego, Seattle, Norfolk, VA, Philadelphia, and Chapel Hill, NC, and from the surrounding rural areas. Minority representation reflects the 1980 US Census. In revising the test, its publishers initially hoped to develop a shorter test. Length was found to be an inconvenience in the early version. Abbreviation was not possible and in fact the MMPI-2 inserts an additional scale. However, the test items have been reordered in such a manner that, if a subject answers the first 370 items, the test administrator can still score all of the basic scales. Responses to individual items are classified on criterion-referenced "clinical scales," such as Hypochondriasis (Hs), Depression (D), and Hysteria (H). The test is now available for automatic computer interpretation. Further information about the MMPI appears with great frequency in many sources; a good guide to the immense literature is found in Anastasi (1988). A large number of so-called secondary or derivative scales have been developed from MMPI items. Those of major relevance in forensic psychology are the 20 "forensic" scales derived from the research of Megargee and Bohn (1979) on nearly

13,000 convicted offenders; the "overcontrolled hostility" scale (Megargee, Cook and Mendelsohn, 1967), which has been linked to habitually aggressive felons; and the MacAndrews (1965) Alcoholism Scale.

Projective Tests. These are tests used to uncover an examinee's attitude, motivations, defense mechanisms, and personality characteristics to his or her responding to unstructured, often ambiguous, stimuli. Examples of projective tests are the Rorschach (see), the Thematic Apperception Test (see), and the Draw-a-Person test (see). The use of projective techniques during the course of a forensic neuropsychological investigation poses numerous problems of administration, scoring, and interpretation, and they are shunned by many professionals. Some of the stories volunteered in the Thematic Apperception or Draw-a-Person Test are effectively used during court presentations (e.g., a drawing by a child suspected to be abused by her father).

Raven Progressive Matrices. This test was originally developed to measure a pervasive element in Spearman's theory of intelligence (factor G); however, the test soon became widely used as a test of intelligence. It consists of a set of matrices or arrangements of design elements forming a logical set, from which one unit of the set is removed. The examinee has to select the missing element from a menu of choices (Raven et al., 1986).

Reliability. Test reliability is the consistence of the scores obtained from the same person when examined with the same test on different occasions (Anastasi, 1988).

Rey Auditory Verbal Learning Test. The test consists of reading to the examinee a list of 15 words. After the list is read, the examinee is asked to recall as many words as possible, in any order. Some professionals read the list as many as five times, scoring the progressive efficiency in recalling. Others show a second (interfering) list of 15 words and ask the examinee to recall the first list. Still others introduce a delay between reading and recall, sometimes reading an interfering, irrelevant story (Lezak, 1983).

Rorschach Test. Although rarely used by professional neuropsychologists, this projective test continues to be used in clinical psychological evaluation in spite of its poor validity and reliability. The instrument was developed by Hermann Rorschach (1884-1922), a Swiss psychiatrist who used inkblots to study visual hallucinations in mentally-disordered patients. In his famous book *Psychodiagnostik,* Rorschach proposed a scoring system for the use of the test in the assessment of personality structure. That system has been refined substantially by John B. Exner and is now available in the form of a computer program from the Psychological Corporation.

Screening Test. This term is applied to an instrument that allows a two-fold classification of individuals: Inclusion or exclusion from a broad group (mentally disordered, organically disordered, etc.). However, screening tests do not permit further differentiation (or, more technically, differential diagnosis) within such discrete groups.

Seashore Rhythm Test. Time discrimination is sometimes affected by brain lesions. In this test the examinee is presented with tape recorded pairs of musical rhythms; the task consists in determining whether they are the same or different. Usually, it involves three sets of 10 test items.

Tactual Performance Test. Although the task is called "tactual," the test involves the use of proprioception (sense of balance, position, and movements of the limbs). Tactual and proprioception are sometimes lost as a result of brain damage but most frequently as a result of damage to the peripheral nervous system, such as occurring as result of occupational exposure to neurotoxic agents (notably, industrial solvents). In this test, the examinee — who is blindfolded — places ten blocks of different shapes into special shapes on a board. The examinee's task is to place each of the blocks into its respective shape on the boards.

Tangled Lines Test. Based on the clinical work of Rey (1964), this test taps the brain's normal ability to distinguish figures and grounds. This ability is generally lost as a result of brain damage. The examinee is presented with 16 horizontal superimposed lines forming a labyrinth. The examinee has to follow each line visually (that is, without the aid of hands), starting from the left indicating its ending to the right.

Thematic Apperception Test (TAT). This is a projective test (see) in which the examinee is shown pictures of people in different situations and is asked to tell a story about each picture, to indicate the characters of the story, the events that led to the present situation, and the possible outcomes. As it is true with many other projective techniques, the TAT poses numerous problems of administration, scoring, and interpretation, and the test is shunned by many neuropsychologists. In addition, defendants who appear in court-clinics are too suspicious and guarded to be able to volunteer free-flowing imagery. Even when these limitations are recognized, the following are the 14 pictures that, in the experience of that author, are likely to elicit useful information about the examinee and his or her circumstances; Person huddled near a couch with revolver; Young woman is standing with downcast head; Man averting woman; A middle-age woman standing on the threshold of a half-opened door; Grey-haired lady (left) and young man (right); Young woman sitting and older man with a pipe; Gray-haired man looking at a younger man sullenly staring into space; Adolescent and dim scene of a surgical operation; A young man lying on a couch and an elderly man is leaning; A young man and naked woman lying in bed; The silhoutte of a person against a bright window, with the rest of the picture black; A man is clutched from behind by three hands; Woman squeezing the throat of another woman by stairs; Person resting against a lamp post.

Token Test. This test is widely used to assess disorder in receptive language (language comprehension). The examinee is presented with a set of tokens and he or she is asked to execute tasks of increasing difficulty. In Part 1, in which only large squares and large circles of different colors are on the table, the examinee is asked simple commands such as "Touch the red circle" or "Touch the green square." In Part 2, in which large and small squares are on the table, the examinee is asked to "Touch the small yellow circle" or "Touch the large blue square." In Part 5, the most difficult, the examinee is asked to execute complex commands such as "Put the red circle on the green square" or "Pick up the blue circle or the red square" or "After picking up the green square, touch the white circle."

Trail Making. In the execution of this task, many regions of the brain are involved. The examinee is required to connect circles according to rules. In task A, the 25 circles are numbered from 1 to 25, and the examinee has to connect them in a sequence; in task B, circles are labeled with both letters and numbers and he or she has to connect them in alternate circles of numbers and letters (1-A-2-B-3-C, and so on).

Validation. The process by which the validity of a test is determined (part of the process of standardization).

Validity. Validity refers to what a test measures and how well it does so. Validity also concerns prediction of the examinee's actual behavior on the basis of his or her performance on a test which claims to be correlated with that behavior — e.g., whether scores on a test of scholastic aptitude predict later grade point average, whether a test for aggressivity predicts future aggressive behavior.

Vibratory Thresholds. Neurotoxic agents that affect the peripheral nervous system are sometimes associated with distal neuropathies, in which the sensations of hands and feet are numbed. The technique of determining vibratory thresholds is a recent development. It consists of the presentation of a vibrating rod at a known frequency; the examinee is asked to ascertain the intensity at which the vibratory sensation appears or disappears. In more elaborate arrangements, several stimulus frequences are used.

Wechsler Adult Intelligence Scale, Revised (WAIS-R). The Wechsler Appraisal of Adult Intelligence was created by David Wechsler (1896-1981). In the words of Matarazzo (1981), "probably the work of no other psychologist, including Freud or Pavlov, has so directly impinged upon the lives of so many people." Wechsler is known for three major contributions to the field of psychometry: (1) The development of a test which bears his name; (2) The substitution of a deviation quotient for Binet's and Stern's concept of mental age that related raw score to chronological age, the intellectual quotient or IQ, so that, in the computation of the deviation quotient, a group of the subject's age is taken as a reference for the appraisal of intelligence; (3) The clinical testing of multilingual populations. Much of Wechsler's career was spent at New York University and at Bellevue Hospital in New York City, where he was exposed to many different ethnic groups. Wechsler's battery is sometimes regarded not only as a test of intelligence but also as a comprehensive assessment of psychological profiles. The battery can be used for screening for brain damage and for various psychiatric disorders. It consists of 11 subtests: Information, vocabulary, picture completion, picture arrangement, similarities, digit span, object assembly, arithmetic reasoning, comprehension, digit symbol, and block design. Many professionals tend to discard those items which are heavily dependent on cultural and language factors, such as general information and vocabulary subsets. Some of the tasks may look silly for many healthy adults (e.g., the assembly of a puzzle consisting of a human body and another of a human hand). However, these puzzles are very difficult to complete for brain-damaged individuals (Matarazzo, 1972). The compoents of the WAIS-R are described in the following entries.

WAIS Verbal Tests. These comprise the Verbal Scale on the WAIS. *General Information* taps the examinee's fund of general knowledge, whether obtained formally or informally. Individuals who do well on this subtest usually are alert to the environment and have a good long-term memory for facts. Individuals who do not do well on this subtest usually are either not alert to the "mainstream" cultural environment or have no interest for facts dealing with such an environment. The *Digit Span Test* is used to assess multiple mental functions including the examinee's attention span and ability to concentrate. *Vocabulary* scores indicate the examinee's knowledge of word meaning and the ability to express these meanings verbally. *Arithmetic* requires the examinee to solve numerical problems without the aid of pencil and paper. In the execution of this test the examinee needs to use basic arithmetic skills. *Comprehension* taps common-sense reasoning and the ability to exercise social judgment in practical situations as well as the examinee's exposure to "mainstream" culture. *Similarities* is used to assess the ability to discriminate between essential and superficial likeness. This test calls for the ability to see relationships between things and ideas, and to categorize them into logical groups. It also measures the capacity to form conceptual units from verbal material and to express these concepts in words in the order specified by the instrument itself.

WAIS Performance Tests. These comprise the Performance Scale on the WAIS. In the *Picture Completion Test,* the examinee is required to discover and name the missing part of an incompletely drawn picture. *Picture Arrangement* consists of a series of pictures which, when placed in the right sequence, tells a little story, like a cartoon. Because the stories involved humans in various situations, this test is often used to assess so-called "social intelligence." The test requires the examinee to evaluate the social relevance of pictured situations, to anticipate the consequences of actions, and to distinguish essential from irrelevant details. This subtest is sometimes considered a measure of planning ability. *Block Design* is a measure of the ability to analyze abstract figures visually and construct them from their component parts. It is essentially a measure of ability to handle spatial relationships. *Object Assembly* requires the assembly of simple puzzles of a mannequin, a human profile, a human hand, and an elephant. Object Assembly taps the ability to recognize a picture of familiar objects from their separate parts, and to assemble the parts to make a picture of the whole object. *Digit Symbol* requires looking at geometrical symbols placed under one-digit numbers and then copying the codes associated with the number as quickly as possible. This test requires a quick switch of attention and visual-motor speed.

Wechsler Memory Scale (WMS). This test has been in existence since the middle 1940s; it was developed for the evaluation of people with severe neurological damage. Although the test is not challenging enough for individuals who are screened for possible subclinical manifestations of neuropsychologic disorders, this test is often cited in the clinical and forensic neuropsychological literature. The classical questions "How old are you?" or "Who is the president of the United States?" — the first questions on the WMS — are likely to be resented by individuals when formulated devoid of an appropriate context. The scale is not truly a memory test but a probe of a variety of cognitive functions.

APPENDIX B: ELECTROPHYSIOLOGICAL PROCEDURES

The forensic neuropsychological investigation has been traditionally dependent on electrophysiological procedures such as electroencephalography (EEG), electromyography (EMG), and nerve conduction velocities (NCV). Neuropsychologists and physiological psychologists receive training courses on stimulation and recording techniques and many become able electrophysiologists. Few have incorporated electrophysiological procedures to the "standard" battery of psychological tests.

Even if the court-based neuropsychologist may not need to perform these procedures, chances are that reports from other professionals (particularly neurologists who have written reports on behalf of their patients) contain technical details on a variety of electrophysiological procedures. Forensic neuropsychologis should be able to understand the form and substance of these reports.

In court, a neuropsychologist who uses classical psychometric batteries for the assessment of brain function may face questions about the validity, reliability, and sensitivilty of psychometric and electrophysiological procedures to assess brain dysfunction. Electrophysiological procedures have been extensively used in environmental and occupational neurotoxicology to assess the effects of neurotoxic agents on brain function.

BEAM (Brain Electrical Activity Mapping). This involves the mapping of the electrical activity of the brain and its display on a color computer monitor. This mapping technique was developed when it was obvious that long latency evoked potentials (Event Related Potentials or ERP) were sensitive to background variations of brain activity. Voltage frequencies detected at each electrode site are split in an equal-interval scale. Two codes are usually employed: (1) a "gray scale" code, where the values of each frequency range are assigned to different gradations of gray between white and black (or different intensities of a single color); and (2) a "pseudo color" scheme, where each range of frequency values is assigned to a separate color. BEAM scanning belongs both to the electrophysiological techniques being discussed in this section and to those reviewed in the next section on imaging. However, BEAM scanning does not compete with CT-, PET-, or NMR-scanning. It is essentially a much welcomed data-reduction technique in electroencephalographic and evoked potentials research. An expert working for the defense may produce BEAM reports as evidence of biologically-determined behavior. The forensic neuropsychologist is or should be aware of the facts and reported studies regarding correlations of BEAM and examinee's everyday behavior.

Electroencephalography (EEG). An electroencephalogram — EEG for short — is a permanent record of the spontaneous electrical activity of the brain; in the clinic, an electroencephalograph is the equipment used to obtain such a record. (The term "EEG" is often used interchangeably to designate the technique and the record derived from this technique). A polygraph is an apparatus used under clinical laboratory conditions when many other physiological measures are simultaneously recorded in addition to the EEG — e.g., heart beat, blood pressure, skin electrical conductance, breathing rate, eye movements, stimulus conditions present during the recording session, etc. Electroencephalography (that is, the technique for recording, analysis, and interpretation of human EEGs) was a well-developed clinical and research tool by the middle of the 1950s, and the principles of recording and interpretation have remained fairly unchanged. EEG is an essential component in the diagnosis of epilepsy and other seizure disorders. In the past, particularly when EEG was in its infancy, the presence of EEG abnormalities in individuals facing criminal legal proceedings, but who did not suffer from seizure disorders, sometimes were said to constitute a "biological" determination of their criminal behavior. EEG is essential in the definition of "brain death," in which the brain shows no EEG activity.

Electromyography. Term applied to a collection of techniques for the recording of the electrical activity of muscles. More appropriately, electromyography — or EMG techniques, as they are generally known — are electrophysiological techniques to determine the degree of intactness of the motor unit and its major components: Its cell body — located in the ventral horn of the spinal cord; its axon; the neuromuscular junction; and the muscle fibers innervated by that neuron. EMG techniques cannot easily be separated from electroneuronography, abbreviated ENG, the measurement of nerve conduction velocities. Electroneuromyography (or ENMG, for short) is a term that has been developed to accommodate the electrodiagnosis of the motor unit which involves both muscle and nerve activity. But the term EMG continues to be widely used in the neurotoxicological literature. (The term "EMG" is often used interchangeably to designate the technique and the record derived from this technique.) The electrical activity of the muscle is studied by inserting a recording electrode directly into the muscle. The electrode is a concentric needle consisting of a pointed steel cannula within which runs a fine silver, steel, or platinum wire that is fully insulated except for the tip. The bioelectrical potentials are then amplified and displayed on an oscilloscope for their visual analysis; amplifed potentials are very often sent to a loudspeaker for acoustical monitoring. The firing rate of normal or abnormal muscle activity is thus characterized acoustiscally. The needle electrode is inserted into the muscle on the basis of patient's neurological signs and symptoms. The electrophysiologist then explores systematically the muscle activity, observing the insertion activity, the activity of the relaxed muscle at the moment the needle is inserted, and firing rates. EMG is an invasive and painful procedure confined to the clinic. With the aid of EMG examination, a trained neurologist can ascertain whether a disease is likely to be affecting a motor neuron located in the spinal cord or peripheral nerves outside the vertebral column. Neurologists can also differentiate between whether the disease is typical of the lower motor unit (e.g., characteristic in flaccid paralysis) or typical of disease of the upper motor unit (i.e., where upper regions of the brain no longer exert their inhibitory action on lower regions of the spinal cord, creating a permanent contraction of the muscle). This differential diagnosis is important among individuals who claim nervous dysfunction resulting from occupational exposure to neurotoxic agents; the condition may be present but may not be related to occupational exposures.

Electrooculography. A technique for recording eye movement, in which voltage changes reflect proportional deviations, generally horizontal, of the eyes. The technique is used to study brain function abnormalities sometimes caused by absorption of occupational neurotoxic agents (see Glickman et al., 1984).

Evoked Potentials. Since the invention of electroencephalography by Berger in 1929, many investigators have used sensory stimulation to study resulting changes in the EEG recordings. These electrical changes became known as evoked potentials (EP). The term "evoked potential" has several meanings. In humans, it is the electrical response arising in the cerebral cortex as a result of a specific stimulation of a specific sensory system. Thus, visual, auditory and somatosensory stimulation will induce a visual evoked potential (VEP), an auditory evoked potential (AEP), or a somatosensory evoked potential (SEP). Evoked potentials can result from specific cognitive acts, in which case they are called event-related potentials or ERP. Evoked potentials can be recorded before a motor act is initiated; it is then termed the readiness potential. The forensic neuropsychologist may be involved in cases in which evoked potentials have been used to legally define blindness or deafness. Cases involving personal injury sometimes involve the presentation of evoked potential data to objectively document the extent of an alleged nervous system injury.

Nerve Conduction Velocity (NCV). NCVs are determined with the aid of the electromyograph. Three key features of the electrical response are recorded: The latency of the response, its amplitude, and the distance from the stimulating and recording electrode. The NCV is a measure obtained by dividing the latency by the distance between the two electrodes. Skin temperature can confuse the interpretation of findings. Nerve conduction velocity determinations have been extensively used to document changes in peripheral nervous system dysfunction associated with occupational and environmental exposure to toxic agents. Some examiners replace this invasive technique with the more acceptable determination of vibratory thresholds.

APPENDIX C: IMAGING TECHNIQUES

An imaging technique is one that allows the visualization of structural features of the nervous system or pharmacological processes resulting from the use of specially-treated chemical substances. Until recently, the location and extent of brain lesions were judged primarily on the basis of the neurological examination, the interpretation of signs and symptoms, and the use of imaging techniques of poor resolution such as X-ray.

In court, a neuropsychologist who uses classical psychometric batteries for the assessment of brain function may face questions about the validity, reliability, and sensitivity of psychometric and modern imaging procedures to assess brain dysfunction. During a hearing, for example, a forensic neuropsychologist may testify alongside a neurosurgeon who performed brain surgery on the defendant or victim in a criminal act or a neuroradiologist who performed and interpreted the results of an imaging procedure. Imaging procedures are beginning to be used in environmental and occupational neurotoxicology to assess the effects of neurotoxic agents on brain function.

Computer Tomography (CT). Tomography derives from the Greek "tomos" (a slice or a piece cut off) and "graphos" (to write, to represent). It is an imaging technique by means of which a single, cross-sectional plane of an organ (e.g., the brain) is outlined, eliminating the planes of other adjacent structures. Visually, a tomogram of the brain is a slice of someone's brain obtained *in vivo*. Computer-tomography (CT or CT scanning; the original term was "computer-axial tomography," or CAT) was specifically developed for the study of the structure of the whole body, not primarily for the brain. CT scanning is used to visualize gross alteration of the brain and associated nervous system structures. Brain malformations produced by organic mercury in children exposed to this neurotoxic agent *in utero* (Minamata disease), for example, can be visualized by CT scanning. But CT scanners cannot detect important and essential differences between the brain's gray matter (neural cells) and white matter (fibers). CT scans are also known as X-ray computed tomographs (XCT), to differentiate them from other imaging techniques based on different principles. Also called computerized axial tomography or computer-assisted tomography; the acronym for either is CAT.

Echoencephalography. The tragic sinking of the Titanic in 1912 motivated the search for better methods of locating icebergs. Echolocalization of objects was proposed about that time; but the effective use of sound echoes by sonar was not accomplished until around the time of World War II. Echoencephalography was short-lived as a brain imaging technique. It was first used in 1956 to detect shifts in the brain's midline structures. Morphologically, the brain is a fairly symmetrical structure. If the skull were transparent, looking at someone straight in the face, the left hemisphere of the brain would be the mirror image of the right. The midline of the brain is the site where both the left and right hemispheres are joined. Should a mass exert pressure on the right side, the acoustic picture of the midline will be seen as shifted to the left. Until the 1970s, echolocalization was used fairly effectively for that purpose. However, it faded away when improved imaging techniques, such as computer-assisted tomography (CAT), were shown to have superior image resolution capabilities. Ultrasound has long been successfully used in the imaging of unborn fetuses. This is an important research tool in teratology, where gross effects of neurotoxic agents in the unborn can sometimes be assessed. However, neurotoxicological studies in which the ultrasound image of the fetus is used are limited to case reports.

Magnetic Resonance Imaging (MRI). MRI scanners have often been described as dream machines. Unlike CT scanners and other X-ray based techniques, the MRI scanners can "see" through the thickest of bones. No contrasting material is required. Moreover, MRI scanners can differentiate between gray and white matter, a distinction that CT scanning cannot make. The imaging principle of MRI scanning is based on the magnetic properties of the element's nuclei containing an odd number of protons. These nuclei behave like tiny spinning magnets. The heart of the MR imager is a large superconducting magnet weighing about six tons. The magnet itself costs hundreds of thousands of dollars, representing about 30% of the systems's cost. When spinning magnets are placed inside the very strong magnetic field generated by the magnet, the vast majority of elemental nuclei line up in the direction of that field. The nuclei also wobble around the axis very much like spinning tops. Different nuclei wobble at different frequencies. A second magnetic field of alternating radio frequency — i.e., in the order of megaHertz — is then applied at right angles to the first. As a result of the addition of this alternating magnetic field to the steady one, some nuclei move into a new alignment. If the frequency of the alternating magnetic field matches that of the natural wobbling frequency, the nuclei are "in resonance." This phenomenon is similar to making a tuning fork "hum" by hitting it with a sound having the fork's natural resonance frequency. When the rapidly oscillating magnetic field is turned off, the resonating nuclei return to their original aligned position relative to the steady magnetic field. In the process of returning to their original aligned position they release energy, with decay characteristics for each element. The signal is detected by coils and processed by a computer. The computer performs a mathematical process called Fourier transformation aimed at analyzing the signal's distribution of frequencies and their relative strengths. A color code is then used to create a density map of the brain.

Positron Emission Tomography (PET). Pharmacological techniques taking advantage of a few isotopes that decay while emitting positrons have been available since the middle 1950s. But it is only since the middle 1980s that these techniques have been grouped under the common name of Positron Emission Tomography, also known by its acronym PET. The tracers most frequently used are carbon-11, nitrogen-13, oxygen-15, and fluorine-18. PET scanning involves four distinctive processes: Labelling of a selected compound — i.e., oxygen, glucose, fatty and amino acids, drugs, body fluids, gases, etc.; administering the compound by injection into the bloodstream; imaging of the regional distribution of positron activity in the brain as a function of decay time by means of special instrumentation; reconstructing the tomogram by means of a procedure such as the one described for CT. In PET scanning the image is that of the distribution of annihilating positron-emitting radionucleides. In PET scanning, as in many other scanning techniques, tissue "filtering" is also a factor to be considered. (Biological tissues "filter" the radiating energy by absorbing part of it; different tissues absorb different wavelengths.) In clinical studies, PET images for measuring oxygen and glucose consumption and protein synthesis are the most extensively used. PET scanning has been successfully used in the exploration of etiological factors of many brain disorders including psychiatric diseases (e.g., schizophrenia), neurological disorders (e.g., epilepsy and Alzheimer's disease), and cognitive function in healthy and mentally or emotionally disturbed individuals. PET is an invasive technique and subjects suffer considerable anxiety as a consequence of the necessary arterial and venous catheterization, the injection of the isotope and the actual process of scanning. Radiological studies of the brain, echolocalization, and CAT scanning on the other hand can, for all practical purposes, be considered noninvasive.

X-Ray Based Techniques. The invention of the X-ray by Roentgen (1895) was translated into practical use the very next year. In 1896, the first radiography of the skull was obtained. However, much to the disappointment of those who had hoped this technique would reveal new features of brain structure, no such visualization resulted. Among the basic documentation pertaining to a specific defendant or victim of crime, the forensic neuropsychologist may find X-ray reports, sometimes containing terse technical language.

REFERENCES AND SUGGESTIONS FOR FURTHER READING

☐ CHAPTER 1

Boring, EG (1950), A History of Experimental Psychology (2nd ed), New York: Appleton-Century-Croft

Campbell-Black, HC (1983), Black's Law Dictionary (Abridged 5th ed Publisher's Editorial Staff), St Paul, MN: West

DeSola, R (1988), Crime Dictionary, revised and expanded ed, New York: Facts on File Publications

Dywan, J, Kaplan, RD, and Pirozzolo, FJ (1991), Neuropsychology and the Law, New York: Springer Verlag

Grillot, HJ (1983), Introduction to Law and the Legal System (3rd ed), Boston: Houghton Mifflin

Hebb, DO (1949), The Organization of Behavior, New York: Wiley

Hutchins, RM, and Slesinger, D (1929), Legal psychology, Psychol Review 36: 13-26

Jenkins v The United States, 113 US App DC 300, 307 F2d 637 (1962)

Kandel, ER, Schwartz, JH, and Jessell, TM eds (1991), Principles of Neural Science (3rd ed), New York: Elsevier

Law Enforcement Assistant Administration, National Criminal Justice Information and Statistics Service (1976), Dictionary of Criminal Justice Data Terminology, Washington, DC: US Department of Justice

McMahon, EA, and Satz, P (1981), Clinical neuropsychology: Some forensic applications, in Handbook of Clinical Neuropsychology ed Susan B Filskov and Thomas J Boll New York: Wiley, 686-700

Morris, William E, Susan C Morris, Lisa Morris, et al v Chandler Exterminators, Court of Appeals, State of Georgia Case No 091A04000, Douglas County Superior Court Civil Action File No 88-5965-MM-242

Münsterberg, H (1908), On the Witness Stand, New York: Doubleday, Page

Neuropsychologia (1967), Tarrytown, NY: Pergamon

Sbordone, RJ (1991), Neuropsychology for the Attorney, Orlando, FL: Paul M Deutsch

Terman, LM (1931), Psychology and the law, Los Angeles Bar Association Bulletin 6: 142-153

Ziskin, J, and Faust, D (1988), Coping with Psychiatric and Psychological Testimony (3 Vols), Marina del Rey, CA: Law and Psychology Press

→ Additional Readings

Albert, ML (1984), Henry Hécaen, MD, Neurologist-neuropsychologist, Arch Neurol 41: 458-459

American Bar Association (1989), ABA Criminal Justice Mental Health Standards, Washington, DC: American Bar Association

American Psychiatric Association (1988), Diagnostic and Statistical Manual of Mental Disorders (Third ed, Revised), DSM-III-R, Washington, DC: American Psychiatric Association

American Psychiatric Association (1994), Diagnostic and Statistical Manual of Mental Disorders (4th ed), DSM-IV, Washington, DC: American Psychiatric Association

American Psychological Association (1981), Ethical Principles of Psychologists, American Psychologist 36: 633-638

Battersby, WS, Krieger, EP, Pollack, M, and Bender, MB (1953), Figure-ground discrimination and the abstract attitude in patients with cerebral neoplasms, AMA Arch Neurol Psychiat 70: 703-712

Bender, MB (1952), Disorders in Perception, Springfield, IL: Charles C Thomas

Bender, MB, and Teuber, HL (1947), Phenomenon of fluctuation, extinction and completion in visual perception, Arch Neurol Psychiat 55: 627-658

Bruce, D (1985), On the origin of the term neuropsychology, Neuropsychologia 23: 813-814

Costa, L, and Spreen, O (1985), Studies in Neuropsychology: Selected Papers of Arthur Benton, New York: Oxford Univ Press

Damasio, AR (1985), Norman Geshwind, Arch Neurol 42: 500-504

Douglas, JE, Burgess, AW, Burgess, AG, and Ressler, RK (1992), Crime Classification Manual, New York: Lexington Books

Ellis, AW, and Young, AW (1988), Human Cognitive Neuropsychology, Howe, UK: Erlbaum

Frye v United States 293 F 1013 (DC Cir 1923)

Gazzaniga, M (1984), Handbook of Cognitive Neuroscience, New York: Plenum

Gilandas, AJ, and Touyz, SW (1983), Forensic neuropsychology: A selective introduction, J Foren Sci 28(3): 713-723

Golden, CJ, and Strider, MA eds (1986), Forensic Neuropsychology, New York, NY: Plenum

Goldstein, G (1985), The history of clinical neuropsychology: The role of some American pioneers, Int J Neurosci 25: 273-275

Hale, M (1980), Human Science and Social Order: Hugo Münsterberg and the Origins of Applied Psychology, Philadelphia: Temple Univ Press

Hartlage, LC, and DeFilippis, NA (1983), History of Neuropsychogical Assessment, in Foundations of Clinical Neuropsychology, ed Charles J Golden and Peter J Vicente, New York: Plenum 1-23

Hécaen, H, and Albert, ML (1978), Human Neuropsychology, New York: Wiley

Keeton, WP (1984), Prosser and Keeton on the Law of Torts (5th ed), St Paul, MN: West

Lashley, K (1929), Brain Mechanisms and Intelligence, Chicago: Univ of Chicago Press

LeDoux, J, and Hirst, P eds (1986), Mind and the Brain: Dialogues in Cognitive Neuroscience, New York: Cambridge Univ Press

Luria, AR (1966), Higher Cortical Functions in Man, New York: Basic Books

McMahon, EA (1983), Forensic issues in clinical neuropsychology, in Foundations of Clinical Neuropsychology ed Charles J Golden and Peter J Vicente, New York: Plenum, 401-427

Meier, MJ (1992), Modern clinical neuropsychology in historical perspective, Am Psychologist 47(4): 550-558

Meyer, V (1961), Psychological effects of brain damage, in Handbook of Abnormal Psychology, ed HJ Eysenck, New York: Basic Books, 529-565

Milner, B (1964), Some effects of frontal lobectomy in man, in The Frontal Granular Cortex and Behavior, ed JM Waren and K Akert, New York: McGraw-Hill, 313-334

Milner, PM (1970), Physiological Psychology, New York: Holt, Rinehart & Winston

Mishkin, M. and Petri, HL (1984), Memories and habits: Some implications for the analysis of learning and retention, in Neuropsychology of Memory, ed LR Squire and N Butters, New York: Guilford, 287-296

Owens, H, Rosner, R, and Harmon, RB (1985), The judge's view of competence evaluations, Bull Am Acad Psychiat Law 13: 389-397

Reed, J (1985), The contributions of Ward Halstead, Ralph Reitan and their associates, Int J Neurosci 25: 289-293

Reitan, RM (1964), Psychological deficits resulting from cerebral lesions in man, in The Frontal Granular Cortex and Behavior, ed JM Warren and K Akert, New York: McGraw-Hill, 295-312

Robery, A (1965), Criteria for competency to stand trial: A checklist for psychiatrists, Am J Psychiat 122: 616-623

Robinson, PH (1984), Criminal Law Defense, (2 Vols) St Paul, MN: West

Smith, SR and Meyer, RG (1987), Law, Behavior and Mental Health: Policy and Practice, New York: New York Univ Press

Talland, GA (1966), Deranged Memory, San Diego, CA: Academic

Weinstein, S (1985), The influence of H-L Teuber and the psychological laboratory on the establishment and development of neuropsychology, J Neurosci 25: 277-288

☐ CHAPTER 2

→ Additional Readings

Bickerstaff, ED, and Spilane, JA (1989), Neurological Examination in Clinical Practice (5th ed), Boca Raton, FL: CRC Press

Collins, RT (1961), A Manual of Neurology and Psychiatry in Occupational Medicine, New York: Grüne & Stratton

Cummings, JL (1985), Clinical Neuropsychology, New York: Grüne & Stratton

Fiskov, SB, and Ball, TJ (1981), Handbook of Clinical Neuropsychology, New York: Wiley

Gilandas, A, Touys, S, Bermont, PJV, and Greenberg, HP (1984), Handbook of Neuropsychological Assessment, Orlando, FL: Grüne & Stratton

Golden, CJ (1978), Diagnosis and Rehabilitation in Clinical Neuropsychology, Springfield, IL: Charles C Thomas

Grant, I, and Adams, KM eds (1986), Neuropsychological Assessment of Neuropsychiatric Disorders, New York: Oxford Univ Press

Heilman, KM, and Valenstein, E eds (1985), Clinical Neuropsychology (2nd ed), New York: Oxford Univ Press

Kolb, B, and Whishaw, I Q (1985), Fundamentals of Human Neuropsychology (2nd ed), New York: WH Freeman and Company

Leestma, JE, and Kilpatrick, JB (1987), Forensic Neuropathology, New York: Raven

Martin, JB, and Reichlin, S (1987), Clinical Neuroendocrinology (2nd ed), Philadelphia: FA Davis Co

Mathers, LH (1985), The Peripheral Nervous System: Structure, Function and Clinical Correlations, Menlo Park, CA: Addison-Wesley

Pirozzolo, FJ (1989), New Developments in Neuropsychological Evaluation, Philadelphia: WB Saunders

Walsh, KW (1978), Neuropsychology: A Clinical Approach, New York: Churchill Livingstone

☐ CHAPTER 3

→ Additional Readings

Bremmer, J, and Roodenburg, H eds (1992), A Cultural History of Gesture, Ithaca, NY: Cornell Univ Press

Down, JLH (1866), Observations on an Ethnic Classification of Idiots, London Hospital Reports, 259-262

Evans, EC (1969), Physiognomics in the Ancient World, Philadelphia: Philosophical Society

Levinson, D (1987), A Guide to the Clinical Interview, Philadelphia: WB Saunders

Roebuck, JB (1967), Criminal Typology, Springfield, IL: Charles C Thomas

☐ CHAPTER 4

→ Additional Readings

Burgess, A (1962), A Clockwork Orange, New York: Norton

Cleckly, H (1976), The Mask of Sanity: An Attempt to Clarify Some Issues about the So-Called Psychopathic Personality, St Louis: CV Mosby

Gardner, H (1975), The Shattered Mind, New York: Knopf

Glasser, D ed (1974), Handbook of Criminology, Chicago: Rand -McNally

Inbau, FE, and Reid, JE (1967), Criminal Interrogations and Confessions, Baltimore: Williams & Wilkins

Levinson, D (1987), A Guide to the Clinical Interview, Philadelphia: WB Saunders

☐ CHAPTER 5

→ Additional Readings

Asbury, AK, and Johnson, PC (1978), Pathology of Peripheral Nerve, Philadelphia: WB Saunders

Bickerstaff, ED, and Spilane, JA (1989), Neurological Examination in Clinical Practice, (5th ed), Boca Raton, FL: CRC Press

Campbell-Black, HC (1983), Black's Law Dictionary: Definitions of the Terms and Phrases of American and English Jurisprudence, Ancient and Modern, St Paul, MN: West

Centofanti, C, and Smith, A (1979), The Single and Double Simultaneous Stimulation Test, Los Angeles, CA: Western Psychological Services

Collins, RT (1961), A Manual of Neurology and Psychiatry in Occupational Medicine, New York: Grüne & Stratton

DeJong, RN (1967), The Neurologic Examination, New York: Harper & Row

Dyck, PJ, Thomas, PK, and Lambert, EH eds (1975), Peripheral Neuropathy (2 Vols), Philadelphia: WB Saunders

Juntunen, J Ed (1982), Occupational neurology, Acta Neurol Scand Supp 92, Vol 66

Leestma, JE, and Kikpatrick, JB (1987), Forensic Neuropathology, New York: Raven

Martin, JB, and Reichlin, S (1987), Clinical Neuroendocrinology (2nd ed), Philadelphia: FA Davis Co

Mathers, LH (1985), The Peripheral Nervous System: Structure, Function and Clinical Correlations, Menlo Park, CA: Addison-Wesley

Mesumlam, M-M, (1985), Principles of Behavioral Neurology, New York: Wiley

Munetz, MR, and Benjamin, S (1988), How to examine patients using the abnormal involuntary movement scale, Hospital Comm Psychiat 39: 1172-1177

Ochoa, J (1980), Criteria for the assessment of polyneuropathy, in Experimental and Clinical Neurotoxicology, ed PS Spencer and HH Schaumburg, Baltimore: Williams & Wilkins, 681-707

Olson, WH, Brumback, RA, Gascon, G, and Iyer, V (1989), Handbook of Symptom-Oriented Neurology, Boca Raton, FL: CRC Press

Potvin, AR, and Tourtellotte, WW (1985), Quantitative Examination of Neurologic Functions, (2 Vols), Boca Raton, FL; CRC Press

Spencer, PS, and Schaumburg, HH eds (1980), Experimental and Clinical Neurotoxicology Baltimore: Williams & Wilkins

Sterman, AB, and Schaumburg, HH (1980), The neurological examination, in Experimental and Clinical Neurotoxicology, ed PS Spencer and HH Schaumburg, Baltimore: Williams & Wilkins, 675-680

Thomas, PK (1980), The peripheral nervous system as a target for toxic substances, in Experimental and Clinical Neurotoxicology, ed PS Spencer and HH Schaumburg, Baltimore: Williams & Wilkins, 35-47

Van Allen, MW, and Rodnitzky, RL (1981), Pictorial Manual of Neurological Tests: A Guide to the Performance and Interpretation of the Neurological Examination, Chicago: Year Book Medical Publishers

Vinkin, PJ, and Bruyn GW eds (1979), Handbook of Clinical Neurology, vols 36 and 37, Intoxications of the Nervous System, Part I and II, Amsterdam: North Holland

☐ CHAPTER 6

Campbell-Black, HC (1983), Black's Law Dictionary (Abridged 5th ed Publisher's Editorial Staff), St Paul, MN: West

→ Additional Readings

American Psychiatric Association, Task Force on DSM-IV (1993), DSM-IV Draft Criteria, Washington, DC: APA

American Psychiatric Association (1980), Diagnostic and Statistical Manual of Mental Disorders (3rd ed), revised, (DSM-III-R), Washington, DC: APA

Folstein, MF, Folstein, SE, and McHugh, PH (1975), Mini-mental state: A practical method for grading the cognitive state of patients for the clinician, J Psychiat Res, 12:189

Liu, IY, and Anthony, JC (1989), Using the mini-mental state examination to predict elderly subjects' completion of a follow-up interview, Am J Epidemiol 130(2): 416-422

Reiser, DE, and Schroeder, AK (1980), Patient Interviewing: The Human Dimension, Baltimore: Williams & Wilkins

Strub, RL, and Black, FW (1985), The Mental Status Examination in Neurology (2nd ed), Philadelphia: FA Davis Company

World Health Organization (1992), International Statistical Classification of Diseases and Related Health Problems, 10th ed (ICD-10), Geneva: World Health Organization

☐ CHAPTER 7

→ Additional Readings

American Psychiatric Association (1980), Diagnostic and Statistical Manual of Mental Disorders, (3rd ed), revised, (DSM-III-R), Washington, DC: APA

Olson, WH, Brumback, RA, Gascon, G, and Iyer, V (1989), Handbook of Symptom-Oriented Neurology, Boca Raton, FL: CRC Press

☐ CHAPTER 8

American Psychiatric Association (1980), Diagnostic and Statistical Manual of Mental Disorders, (3rd ed), revised, (DSM-III-R), Washington, DC: APA

American Psychiatric Association, Task Force on DSM-IV (1993), DSM-IV Draft Criteria, Washington, DC: APA

Dywan, J, Kaplan, RD, and Pirozzollo, FJ eds (1991), Neuropsychology and the Law, New York: Springer Verlag

Kaplan, HI, and Sadock, BJ (1991), Synopsis of Psychiatry, Behavioral Sciences, Clinical Psychiatry (6th ed), Baltimore: Williams & Wilkins

Pinel, P (1962), A Treatise on Insanity in which are Contained the Principles of a New Practical Nosology of Maniacal Disorder, translated from the French by DD Davis, New York: Hefner

Resnick, PJ (1984), The detection of malingered illness, Behav Sci Law 2:21-38

Sbordone, RJ (1991), Neuropsychology for the Attorney, Orlando, FL: Paul M Deutsch

Szasz, T (1961), The Myth of Mental Illness: Foundations of a Theory of Conduct, New York: Harper & Row

Szasz, T (1987), Insanity: The Idea and Its Consequences, New York: John Wiley

Valciukas, JA (1991), Foundations of Environmental and Occupational Neurotoxicology, New York: Van Nostrand Reinhold

World Health Organization (1992), International Statistical Classification of Diseases and Related Problems, 10th ed (ICD-10), Geneva: World Health Organization

→ Additional Readings

Abram, KM, and Teplin, LA (1991), Co-occurring disorders among mental ill jail detainees: Implications for public policy, Am Psychologist 46(10): 1036-1045

American Bar Association (1989), ABA Criminal Justice Mental Health Standards, Washington, DC: American Bar Association Justice Standards Committee

American Psychiatric Association (1974), Clinical Aspects of the Violent Individual, Washington, DC: American Psychiatric Association

Ausubel, DP (1971), Personality disorder is a disease, Am Psychologist 16: 59-74

Bloom, J (1989), The character of danger in psychiatry practice: Are the mentally ill dangerous? Bull Am Acad Psychiat Law 17: 241-254

Boorse, C (1975), On the distinction between disease and illness, Philosophy and Public Affairs 5: 49-68

Boorse, C (1976), What a theory of mental health should be? J Theory Soc Behavior 6: 61-84

Claridge, G (1985), Origins of Mental Illness, Oxford, UK: Blackwell

Cleckly, H (1976), The Mask of Sanity: An Attempt to Clarify Some Issues about the So-Called Psychopathic Personality, St Louis: CV Mosby Co

Coleman, D (1982), Can you tell if someone is lying to you? Psychol Today (August), 14-23

Daniel, A, Robins, A, Reid, J, and Wilfley, D (1988), Lifetime and six-month prevalence of psychiatric disorders among sentenced female offenders, Bull Am Acad Psychiat Law 16: 333-342

Deutsch, A (1949), The Mentally Ill in America: A History of the Care and Treatment from Colonial Times, (2nd ed), New York: Columbia Univ Press

Drob, SL, and Berger, RH (1987), The determination of malingering: A comprehensive clinical-forensic approach, J Psychiat and Law, Winter, 519-538

Ekman, P, and Frieson, WV (1974), Detecting deception from the body and face, J Personal Soc Psychol 29: 288-298

Ekman, P, and O'Sullivan, M (1991), Who can catch a liar?, Am Psychologist 46(9): 913-920

Eysenck, H (1977), Crime and Personality, London: Routledge and Kegan Paul

Gould, SJ (1981), The Mismeasure of Man, New York: WW Norton

Guze, S (1976), Criminality and Psychiatric Disorders, New York: Oxford Univ Press

Heaton, RK, Smith, HH, Lehman, R, and Voyt, A (1978), Prospects for faking believable deficits on neuropsychological testing, J Consulting Clin Psychol 46(5): 892-900

Jones, AB (1917), Malingering, London: Heineman Medical

Klassen, D, and O'Connor, W (1988), Crime, impatient admissions, and violence among male mental patients, Int J Law Psychiat 11: 305-312

Krakowski, M, Volavka, J, and Brizer, D (1986), Psychopathology and violence: A review of the literature, Comprehensive Psychiat 27: 131-148

MacDonald, J (1976), The simulation of mental diseases, in Psychiatry and the Criminal ed J MacDonald. Springfield, IL: Charles C Thomas 267-279

Monahan, J (1992), Mental disorder and violent behavior: Perceptions and evidence, Am Psychologist 47(4): 511-521

Monahan, J, and Steadman, H eds 1986), Mentally Disordered Offenders: Perspectives from Law & Social Science, New York: Plenum

Pollack, S, Gross, BH, and Winberger, LE (1982), Dimensions of malingering, in New Directions for Mental Health Services: The Mental Health Professional and the Legal System, ed B Gross and L Winberger, No 16 San Francisco: Jossey-Bass

Robins, LN (1966), Deviant Children Growing Up, Baltimore: Williams & Wilkins

Rogers, R ed (1988), Clinical Assessment of Malingering and Deception, New York: Guilford

Rosen, G (1986), Madness in Society: Chapters in the Historical Sociology of Mental Illness, Chicago: Univ of Chicago Press

Sarbin, T (1967), On the futility of the proposition that some people be labeled mentally ill, J Consulting Psychol 31: 447-453

Scheff, TJ ed (1967), Labeling Madness, Englewood Cliffs, NJ: Prentice-Hall

Silver, D, and Rosenbluth, M eds (1992), Handbook of Borderline Disorders, Madison, CT: International Universities Press

Sparr, L, and Pankaratz, LD (1983), Factitious post-traumatic stress disorder, Am J Psychiat 140: 1016-1019

Steadman, HJ, and Cocozza, JJ (1974), Careers of the Criminally Insane: Excessive Social Control of Deviance, Lexington, MA: Lexington Books

Thurrell, R, Halleck, S, and Johnson, A (1965), Psychosis in Prison, J Crim Law, Criminology and Police Science 4: 271-276

Toch, H (1977), Living in Prison, New York: Free Press

Wakefield, JC (1992), The concept of mental disorder: On the boundary between biological facts and social values, Am Psychologist 47(3): 373-388

Wessely, S, and Taylor, O (1991), Madness and crime: Criminology versus psychiatry, Crim Behav Mental Health 1: 193-228

☐ PART III

American Psychiatric Association (1980), Diagnostic and Statistical Manual of Mental Disorders, (3rd ed), revised, (DSM-III-R), Washington, DC: APA

Kandel, ER, Schartz, JH, and Jessell, TM (1991), Principles of Neural Science, New York: Elsevier

→ Additional Readings

Lishman, WA (1978), Organic Psychiatry: The Psychological Consequences of Cerebral Disorder, London: Blackwell Scientific Publishing

McFie, J (1975), Assessment of Organic Intellectual Impairment, New York: Academic

☐ CHAPTER 9

→ Additional Readings

Breuning, SE, and Poling, AD (1982), Drugs and Mental Retardation, Springfield, IL: Charles C Thomas

Brown, BS, and Courtless, TF (1974), The mentally retarded in penal and correctional facilities, Am J Psychiat 124: 1164-1166

Burd, L, and Martoff, JT (1989), Fetal alcohol syndrome: Diagnosis and syndromal variability, Physiol Behav 46: 39

Crocker, AC (1989), The causes of mental retardation, Pediat Ann 18: 623

Davis, E, and Fennoy, I (1990), Growth and development in infants of cocaine abusing mothers, Mental Retard 27: 213

Dosen, A (1989), Diagnosis and treatment of mental illness in mentally retarded children: A developmental model, Child Psychiat Hum Dev 20: 73

Kandel, ER, Schartz, JH, and Jessell, TM (1991), Principles of Neural Science, New York: Elsevier

Kaplan, HI, and Sadock, BJ (1991), Synopsis of Psychiatry, Behavioral Sciences, Clinical Psychiatry (6th ed), Baltimore: Williams & Wilkins

Landers, S (1990), Can jail protect a fetus of drug-addicted mother?, Am Psychol Assoc Monitor (April): 26-27

McFie, J (1975), Assessment of Organic Intellectual Impairment, New York: Academic

Oberl, I, Rousseau, F, Heitz, D, et al (1991), Instability of a 550-base pair DNA segment and abnormal methylation in fragile X syndrome, Science 252: 1097-1102

Palca, J (1992), Infection with selection: HIV in human infants, Science 255: 1069-1069

Pilowski, D, and Chambers, W eds (1986), Hallucinations in Children, Washington, DC: American Psychiatric Press

Robinson, HB, and Robinson, NM (1965), The Mentally Retarded Child, New York: McGraw-Hill

Schroeder, SR ed (1987), Toxic Substances and Mental Retardation: Neurobehavioral Toxicology and Teratology, Washington, DC: American Association on Mental Deficiency

☐ CHAPTER 10

American Psychiatric Association (1994), Diagnostic and Statistical Manual of Mental Disorders (4th ed), DSM-IV, Washington, DC: American Psychiatric Association

Kaplan, HI, and Sadock, BJ (1991), Synopsis of Psychiatry, Behavioral Sciences, Clinical Psychiatry (6th ed), Baltimore: Williams & Wilkins

Sbordone, RJ (1991), Neuropsychology for the Attorney, Orlando, FL: Paul M Deutsch

→ Additional Readings

Baddeley, AD (1976), A Psychology of Memory, New York: Basic Books

Barbizet, J (1970), Human Memory and Its Pathology, San Francisco, CA: WH Freeman

Binder, LM, and Pankratz, L (1987), Neuropsychological evidence of facticious memory complaint, J Clin Experimental Neuropsychol 9: 167-171

Christensen, A-L (1979), Luria's Neuropsychological Investigation, (2nd ed), Copenhagen: Ejnar Munksgaards

Dickson, LR, and Ranseen, JD (1990), An update on selected organic mental syndromes, Hosp Comm Psychiat 41: 290

Dudai, Y (1989), The Neurobiology of Memory: Concepts, Findings, Trends, New York: Oxford Univ Press

Fitzhugh, K, and Fitzhugh, L (1965), Effects of early and late onsets of cerebral dysfunction upon psychological performance, Percept Motor Skills 20: 1099-1100

Graf, P, Squire, LR, and Mandler, H (1984), The information that amnestic patients do not forget, J Exp Psychol: Learning Memory Cognition 10: 164-178

Greene, RL (1992), Human Memory: Paradigms and Paradoxes, Hillsdale, NJ: Lawrence Erlbaum

Horel, J (1978), The neuroanatomy of amnesia, Brain 101: 403-445

Hrdina, PD, and Singhal, RL (1981), Neuroendocrine Regulations and Altered Behavior, New York: Plenum

Jefferson, JW, and Marshall, JR (1981), Neuropsychiatric Features of Medical Disorders, New York: Plenum

Kopelman, MD (1987), Amnesia: Organic and psychogenic, Br J Psychiat 150: 428

Lishman, WA (1978), Organic Psychiatry: The Psychological Consequences of Cerebral Disorder, Philadelphia: Blackwell Scientific

Mark, VH, and Ervin, FR (1970), Violence and the Brain, New York: Harper & Row

Milner, B (1970), Memory and the Medial Temporal Regions of the Brain, in Biology of Memory ed KH Pribram and DE Broadbent, New York: Academic

Milner, B, Corkin, S, and Teuber, HL (1968), Further analysis of the hippocampal amnestic syndrome: 14-year follow study of HM, Neuropsychologia 6: 215-234

Monroe, R (1978), Brain Dysfunction in Aggressive Criminals, Cambridge, MA: DC Heath

Montagu, A (1973), Man and Aggression (2nd ed), New York: Oxford Univ Press

Moyer, KE (1971), The Physiology of Hostility, Chicago: Markham

Moyer, KE (1976), The Psychobiology of Aggression, New York: Harper & Row

Neisser, U, and Winograd, E (1989), Remembering Reconsidered: Ecological and Traditional Approaches to the Study of Memory, New York: Cambridge Univ Press

O'Keefe, J, and Nadel, L (1978), The Hippocampus as a Cognitive Map, London: Oxford Univ Press

Petrie, A (1952), Personality and the Frontal Lobes, London: Routledge & Kegan

Poon, LW ed (1986), Handbook for Clinical Memory Assessment of Older Adults, Washington, DC: American Psychological Association

Richardson-Klavehn, A, and Bjork, RA (1988), Measures of memory, Ann Rev Psychol 36: 475-543

Roberts, JKA (1984), Differential Diagnosis in Neuropsychiatry, New York: Wiley

Rosenzweig, MR, and Bennett, EL eds (1976), Neural Mechanisms of Learning and Memory, Cambridge, MA: MIT Press

Rundell, JR, and Wise, MG (1989), Causes of organic mood disorder, J Neuropsychiat Clin Neurosci 1: 398

Rylander, G (1939), Personality Changes after Operations on the Frontal Lobes, London: Oxford Univ Press

Schachter, DL (1992), Understanding implicit memory: A cognitive neuroscience approach, Am Psychologist 47(4): 559-569

Scoville, W, and Milner, B (1957), Loss of recent memory after bilateral hippocampal lesions, J Neurol Neurosurg Psychiat 20: 11

Small, J (1966), The organic dimensions of crime, Arch Gen Psychiat 15: 82-89

Spellacy, F (1978), Neuropsychological discrimination: Violent and non-violent men, J Clin Psychol 34(1): 49-52

Squire, LR (1987), Memory and the Brain, New York: Oxford Univ Pres

Squire, LR, and Butters, N eds (1984), Neuropsychology of Memory, New York: Guilford

Störring, G (1936), Gedächnisverlust durch Gasvergiftung, ein Mensch ohne Zeitgedächtnis, Arch für g Psychol 95: 436-511

Tulving, E (1983), Elements of Episodic Memory, Oxford, UK: Clarendon

Yanagihara, T, and Petersen, RC eds (1991), Memory Disorders: Research and Clinical Practice, New York: Marcel Dekker

☐ **CHAPTER 11**

→ **Additional Readings**

Alexander, MP (1984), Neurobehavioral consequences of closed head injury, Neurol and Neurosurgery, Update Series 20: 1-8

Bear, D, and Fedio, P (1977), Quantitative analysis of interictal behavior in temporal lobe epilepsy, Arch Neurol 34: 454-467

Benton, AL, Hamsher, KD, Varney, NR, and Spreen, O (1983), Contributions to Neuropsychology: A Clinical Manual, New York: Oxford Univ Press

Delgado-Escueta, AV, Mattson, RH, King, L, et al (1981), The nature of aggression during epileptic seizures, New Eng J Med 305(12): 711-716

Gastaut, H, and Broughton, R (1972), Epileptic Seizures, Springfield, IL: Charles C Thomas

Gunn, J, and Fenton, G (1971), Epilepsy, automatism and crime, Lancet 1: 1173-1176

Halstead, WC (1947), Brain and Intelligence: A Quantitative Study of Frontal Lobes, Chicago: Univ of Chicago Press

Hebb, D (1949), The Organization of Behavior: A Neuropsychological Theory, New York: Wiley

Jennett, WB (1975), Epilepsy After Blunt Head Injuries, (2nd ed), London: Heineman Medical

Jerison, H (1973), The Evolution of Brain and Intelligence, New York: Academic

Livingstone, S (1964), Epilepsy and murder, J Am Med Assoc 188: 172

Luria, AR (1966), Human Brain and Psychological Processes, New York: Harper & Row

Luria, AR (1980), Higher Cortical Functions in Man (2nd ed), New York: Basic Books

Malamud, N (1967), Psychiatric disorders with intracranial tumors of the limbic system, Arch Neurol 17: 113-123

Mednick, SA, et al eds (1992), Fetal Neural Development and Schizophrenia, New York: Cambridge Univ Press

Penfield, W, and Roberts, L (1959), Speech and Brain Mechanisms, Princeton: Princeton Univ Press

Pincus, JH (1981), Violence and epilepsy, New Eng J Med 305(12): 696-698

Russell, DS, and Rubinstein, LJ (1978), Pathology of Tumors of the Nervous System, Baltimore: Williams & Wilkins

Sbordone, RJ (1991), Neuropsychology for the Attorney, Orlando, FL: Paul M Deutsch

Shuman, SI (1977), Psychosurgery and the Medical Control of Violence, Detroit: Wayne State University

Smith, A (1962), Ambiguities in concepts and studies of brain damage and organicity, J Nerv Mental Dis 135: 311-326

Smith, A (1966a), Intellectual functions in patients with laterized frontal tumors, J Neurol Neurosurg Psychiat 29: 52-59

Smith, A (1966b), Verbal and non-verbal test performances of patients with acute lateralized brain lesions (tumors), J Nerv Ment Dis 141: 517-523

Smith, A (1981), Principles Underlying Human Brain Functions in Neuropsychological Sequelae of Different Neuropathological Processes, in Handbook of Clinical Neuropsychology ed Susan B Filskov and Thomas J Boll, New York: Wiley, 175-226

Suchenwirth, R (1979), Pocket Book of Clinical Neurology, Chicago: Year Book Medical Publishers

Teasdale, G, and Jennett, B (1974), Assessment of coma and impaired consciousness, Lancet 2: 81-84

Valenstein, ES (1980), The Psychosurgery Debate: Scientific, Legal and Ethical Perspectives, San Francisco: Freeman

☐ CHAPTER 12

→ Additional Readings

Alexander, MP (1984), Neurobehavioral consequences of closed head injuries, Neurol Neurosurg 20: 1-8

Barth, JT, Macciocchi, SN, Giordani, B, et al (1983), Neuropsychological sequelae of minor head injury, Neurosurgery, 15: 529-533

Benton, AL (1989), Historical Notes on the Postconcussion Syndrome, in Mild Head Injury, ed HS Levin, HS Eisinberg, and AL Benton, New York: Oxford Univ Press, 3-7

Benton, AL, Des Hamsher, K, Varney, NR, and Spreen O (1983), Contributions to Neuro-psychological Assessment: A Clinical Manual, New York: Oxford Univ Press

Binder, LA (1986), Persisting symptoms after mild head injury: A review of the post-concussive syndrome, J Clin Exp Neuropsychol 8(4): 323-346

Black, FW (1976), Constructional apraxia in patients with discrete missile wounds in the brain, Cortex 12: 212-220

Christensen, A Ed (1989), Neuropsychological Treatment after Brain Surgery, Boston: Kluwer Academic

Cooper, PR ed (1982), Head Injury, Baltimore: Williams & Wilkins

DiMaio, JM (1985), Gunshot Wounds: Practical Aspects of Firearms, Ballistics, and Forensic Techniques, New York: Elsevier

Earnes, P (1988), Behavior disorders after severe head injury: Their nature and causes and strategies for management, J Head Trauma Rehab 3(3): 1-6

Ginsberg, MD, Reivich, M, and Giandomenico, A (1976), Alterations of regional brain metabolism during focal ischemia, Neurol 26: 346

Goldstein, H (1942), Aftereffects of Brain Injuries in Man, New York: Grüne & Stratton

Goldstein, K (1936), The mental changes due to frontal lobe damage, J Psychol, Neurol Psychiat 17: 27-56

Gronwall, D, and Wrighston, P (1980), Duration of the post-traumatic amnesia after mild head injury, J Clin Neuropsych 2: 51-60

Gronwall, D, and Wrighston, P (1981), Memory and information processing after closed head injury, J Neurol Neurosurg Psychiat 44: 889-895

Head, H (1926), Aphasia and Kindred Disorders of Speech, Cambridge, UK: Cambridge Univ Press

Hebb, DO (1945), Man's frontal lobe: A critical review, Arch Neurol Psychiat 54: 10-24

Jennett, WB (1975), Epilepsy after Blunt Head Injuries, (2nd ed), London: Heineman

Kerr, P (1992), Centers for head injury accused of earning millions for neglect, The New York Times, March, A-1, D-4

Klonoff, H, and Robinson, G (1967), Epidemiology of head injuries in children: A pilot study, Canad Med Assoc J 96: 1308-1311

Klonoff, H, and Thompson, G (1969), Epidemiology of head injuries in adults: A pilot study, Canad Med Assoc J 100: 235-241

Larson, A (1970), Mental and nervous injury in workmen's compensation, Law Review 23: 1243-1263

Luria, AR (1950), Traumatic Aphasias, The Hague, the Netherlands: Mouton de Gruyter

Luria, AR (1963), Restoration of Function after Brain Injury, New York: Macmillan

McKinlay, WW (1981), The short-term outcome of severe blunt head injury as reported by relatives of the injured person, J Neurol, Neurosurg Psychiat 44: 527

McLean, Temkin, NR, Dikmen, S, and Wyler, AR (1983), The behavioral sequelae of head injury, J Clinic Neuropsych 5: 361-376

Miller, E (1979), The long-term consequences of head injury: A discussion of the evidence with special reference to the preparation of legal reports, Brit J Social Clin Psychol 18(1): 87-98

Miller, H (1966), Mental sequelae of head injury, Proc Royal Soc Med 59, page 257

Miller, H, and Stern, G (1985), The long term prognosis of severe head injury, Lancet 1: 225-229

Newcombe, F (1969), Missile Wounds of the Brain, London: Oxford Univ Press

New York Times (March 16, 1992)

Parker, RS (1990), Traumatic Brain Injury and Neuropsychological Impairment, New York: Springer Verlag

Rimel, RW, Giordani, B, Barth, JT, et al (1981), Disability caused by minor head injury, Neurosurgery 9: 221-228

Rosenthal, M, Griffith, ER, Bond, MR, and Miller, JD (1983), Rehabilitation of the Head-Injured Adult, Philadelphia: FA Davis

Rosner, R, and Schwartz, H eds (1987), Geriatric Psychiatry and the Law, New York: Plenum

Russell, EW, Neuringer, C, and Goldstein, G (1970), Assessment of Brain Damage: A Neuropsychological Key Approach, New York: Wiley-Interscience

Russell, WR, and Smith, A (1961a), Traumatic Aphasia, London: Oxford Univ Press

Russell, WR, and Smith, A (1961b), Post-traumatic amnesia in closed head injury, Arch Neurol 5: 4-17

Semmes, J, Weinstein, S, Gilbert, L, and Teuber, HL (1960), Somatosensory Changes After Penetrating Wounds in the Brain, Cambridge: Harvard Univ Press

Smith, A (1961), The duration of impaired consciousness as an index of severity in closed head injury: A review, Diseases of the Nervous System 2: 1-6

Teuber, HL, Battersby, WS, and Bender, MB (1960), Visual Field Defects After Penetrating Missile Wounds of the Brain, Cambridge, MA: Harvard Univ Press

Weinstein, S, and Teuber, HL (1957), Effects of penetrating brain injury on intelligence test scores, Science 125: 1036-1037

☐ CHAPTER 13

Alzheimer, A (1907), Über eine eigenartige Erkrankung der Hirninde, Allg Z Psychiatrie 64: 146-148

Anastasi, A (1988), Psychological Testing (6th ed), New York: Macmillan

Anger, WK, and Johnson, BJ (1985), Chemicals affecting behavior, in Neurotoxicity of Industrial and Commercial Chemicals, Vol 1 ed JL O'Donoghue, Boca Raton, FL: CRC Press, 51-148

Butler, RN (1975), Why Survive? Being Old in America, New York: Harper & Row

Calne, DB, Geer, EM, Eisen, A, and Spencer, P (1986), Hypothesis Alzheimer's disease, Parkinson's disease, and motoneuron disease: Abiotropic interaction between ageing and environment?, The Lancet, Nov 8, 1067-1070

Hamilton, A (1943), Exploring the Dangerous Trades, Boston: Little, Brown

Rosner, R, and Schwartz, H eds (1987), Geriatric Psychiatry and the Law, New York: Plenum

Selikoff, IJ, personal communication

Valciukas, JA (1991), Foundations of Environmental and Occupational Neurotoxicology, New York: Van Nostrand Reinhold

→ Additional Readings

Baltes, PB, and Schaie, KW (1974), Aging and IQ: The myth of the twilight years, Psychology Today 7: 35-40

Bayley, N, and Oden, M (1955), The maintenance of intellectual ability in gifted adults, J Geront 10: 91-107

Birren, JE (1964), The Psychology of Aging, Englewood Cliffs, NJ: Prentice Hall

Blessed, G, Tomlinson, BE, and Roth, M (1968), The association between quantitative measurements of dementia and of senile changes in the cerebral gray matter of elderly subjects, Br J Psychiat 114: 797-811

Bollerup, TR (1985), Prevalence of mental illness among 70-year olds domiciled in nine Copenhagen suburbs: The Glostrup survey, Acta Psychiat Scand 51: 327-339

Bolton, N, Britton, PG, and Savage, RD (1966), Some normative data on the WAIS and its indices in an aged population, J Clin Psychol 22: 184-188

Botwinick, J (1967), Cognitive Processes in Maturity and Old Age, New York: Springer Verlag

Botwinick, J (1978), Aging and Behavior, (2nd ed), New York: Springer Verlag

Brody, JA (1982), An epidemiologist views senile dementia: Facts and fragments, Am J Epidem, 115(2): 155-162

Brown, P, Cathala, F, and Gaddusek, DC (1979), Creutzfeldt-Jakob disease in France: III. Epidemiological study of 170 patients dying during the decade 1968-1977, Ann Neurol 6: 438-446

Caine, ED, Ebert, MH, and Weingartner, H (1977), An outline for analysis of dementia: The memory disorder of Huntington's disease, Neurology 27: 1087-1092

Caine, ED, Hunt, RD, Weingartner, H, and Ebert, MH (1978), Huntington's dementia: Clinical and neuropsychological features, Arch Gen Psychiat 35: 377-384

Crapper, DR, Krishnan, SS, and Quittkat, S (1976), Aluminum, neurofibrillary degeneration and Alzheimer's disease, Brain 88: 67-80

Dreibach, RH (1980), Hanbook of Poisoning, Los Altos, CA: Lange Medical Publications

French, LR, Schuman, LM, Mortiner, JA, et al (1985), A case-control study of dementia of the Alzheimer type, Am J Epidem 121(3): 414-421

Gajdusek, DC, and Zigas, V (1957), Degenerative disease of the central nervous system in New Guinea: The endemic occurrence of kuru in the native population, N Eng J Med, 257: 974-978

Goldman, R (1978), The social impact of the organic dementias of the aged, in Senile Dementia: A Biomedical Approach, ed K Nandy, New York: Elsevier, 3-17

Goodman-Gilman, A, Goodman, LS, and Gilman, A (1980), Goodman and Gilman's The Pharmacological Basis of Therapeutics, New York: Macmillan

Henderson, VW (1986), Non-genetic factors in Alzheimer's disease pathogenesis, Neurobiology of Aging 7(6): 585-587

Inglis, J (1957), An experimental study of learning and memory function in elderly psychiatric patients, J Ment Sci 103: 796-803

Inglis, J (1959), Learning, retention and conceptual use in elderly patients with memory disorder, J Abnorm Soc Psychol 59: 210-215

Jacoby, RJ, and Levy, R (1980), Computed tomography in the elderly: 2. Senile dementia: Diagnosis and functional impairment, Br J Psychiat 136: 256-269

Jarvik, LF, Ruth, V, and Matsuyama, SS (1980), Organic brain syndrome and aging: A six-year follow up of surviving twins, Arch Gen Psychiat 37: 280-286

Katzman, R, and Rowe, JW (1991), Principles of Geriatric Neurology, Philadelphia: FA Davis

Kendrick, DC, and Post, F (1967), Differences in cognitive status between healthy, psychiatrically ill, and diffusely brain damaged elderly subjects, Br J Psychiat 11: 75-81

Marx, JL (1989), Brain protein yields clues to Alzheimer's disease, Science, 243: 1664-1666

Marx, R (1988), Evidence uncovered for second Alzheimer's gene, Science 241: 1432-1433

Miller, E (1973), Short- and long-term memory in presenile dementia (Alzheimer's disease), Psychol Med 3: 221-224

Podlisny, MB, Lee, G, and Selkoe, DJ (1987), Gene dosage of the amyloid beta precursor protein in Alzheimer's disease, Science, 238: 669-671

Price, DL (1986), New Perspectives on Alzheimers' Disease, Ann Rev Neurosci, 9: 489-512

Rosner, R, Widerlight, M, and Schneider, M (1985), Geriatric felons examined at a forensic psychiatric clinic, J Foren Sc 30(3): 730-740

Rosner, R, Widerlight, M, Harmon, RB, and Cahn, DJC (1991), Geriatric offenders at a forensic psychiatric clinic, J Foren Sci 36(6): 1722-1731

Roth, M, and Hopkins, B (1953), Psychological test performance in patients over 60: I. Senile psychosis and the affective disorders of old age, J Ment Sci 99: 439-538

Rowe, JW, and Kahn, RL (1987), Human aging: Usual and successful, Science 237: 143-149

Salthouse, TA (1978), The role of memory in the age decline in digit symbol substitution performance, J Gerontol 33: 232-238

Schellenberg, GD, Bird, TD, Wijsman, EM, et al (1988), Absence of linkage of chromosome 21q21 markers to familial Alzheimer's disease, Science 241: 1507-1510

Scherr, PA, Albert, MS, Funkenstein, HH, et al (1988), Correlated of cognitive function in an elderly community population, Am J Epidemiol 128(5): 1084-1101

Schneidman, E (1989), The indian summer of life: A preliminary study of septuagenarians, American Psychologist, April, 684-694

Selkoe, DJ (1991), Amyloid protein and Alzheimer's disease, Scient Am 265(5): 68-78

Shalat, SL, Seltzer, B, Pidcock, C, and Baker, EL (1987), Risk factors for Alzheimers's disease: A case-control study, Neurology, 37(10): 1630-1633

Spencer, PS, and Schaumburg, HH eds (1980), Experimental and Clinical Neurotoxicology, Baltimore: Williams & Wilkins

St George-Hyslop, P, Tanzi, RE, Polinsky, RJ, et al (1987), Absence of duplication of chromosome 21 genes in familial and sporadic Alzheimer's disease, Science, 238: 664-666

Strong, R, Wood, G, and Burke, WJ (1988), Central Nervous System Disorder of Aging, New York: Raven

Tanzi, RE, Bird, ED, Lati, SA, and Neve, RL (1987), The amyloid beta protein is not duplicated in brains from patients with Alzheimer's disease, Science, 238: 666-669

US Department of Health, Education, and Welfare, Public Health Service (1977), Occupational Diseases: A Guide to their Recognition, Washington, DC: US Government Printing Office

Yankner, BA, Dawes, LR, Fisher, S, et al (1989), Neurotoxicity of a fragment of the amyloid precursor associated with Alzheimer's disease, Science 245: 417-420

Wold Health Organization (1985), Organic Solvents and the Central Nervous System, Copenhagen: World Health Organization

☐ CHAPTER 14

→ Additional Readings

Baer, JW (1989), Study of 60 patients with AIDS or AIDS-related complex requiring psychiatric hospitalization, Am J Psychiat 146: 1285

Drucker, E (1986), AIDS and addiction in New York City, Am J Drug Alcohol 12: 165-181

Eckholm, E (1992), AIDS, fatally steady in the US, accelerates worldwide, NY Times, Sun, June 28, Section E, p 5

Faulstich, ME (1987), Psychiatric aspects of AIDS, Am J Psychiat 144: 551-556

Fee, E, and Fox, DM eds (1992), AIDS: The Making of a Chronic Disease, Berkeley: Univ of California Press

Fenton, TW (1987), AIDS-related psychiatric disorder, Brit J Psychiatry 151: 579-588

Friedland, GH, and Klein, RS (1987), Transmission of the human immunodeficiency virus, N Eng J Med 317(18): 1125-1135

Gabuzda, DH, and Hirsch, DH (1987), Neurologic manifestations of infection with human immunodeficiency virus: Clinical features and pathogenesis, Ann Inter Med 107: 383-391

Grant, L, Atkinson, JH, and Hessenlink, JR (1987), Evidence of early central nervous system involvement in the acquired immunodeficiency syndrome (AIDS) and other human immunodeficiency virus (HIV) infection: Studies with neuropsychological testing and magnetic resonance imaging, Ann Inter Med 107: 828-836

Marotta, R, and Perry, S (1989), Early neuropsychological dysfunction caused by human immunodeficiency virus, J Neuropsychiat Clin Neurosci 1: 225

Margolick, D (1992), Tide of lawsuits portraits society plagued by AIDS, NY Times, Sun, Aug 23, p 1, cont p 28

McArthur, JC (1987), Neurological manifestations of AIDS, Medicine 66: 407-437

Navia, BA, and Price, RW (1986), Dementia complicating AIDS, Psychiatric Annals 16: 158-166

Perry, S, and Marotta, RF (1987), AIDS dementia: A review of the literature, Alzheimer Disease and Associated Disorders 1(4): 221-235

Poutinainen, E, Iivanainen, M, and Elovaara, I (1988), Cognitive changes as early signs of HIV infection, Acta Neurol Scand 78: 49

Price, RW, Brew, B, Sidtis, J, et al (1988), Brain in AIDS: Central nervous system HIV-I infection and AIDS-dementia complex, Science 239: 586-592

Rosenblum, RM, and Bredesen, DE eds (1988), AIDS and the Nervous System, New York: Raven

Simon, RI (1988), Ethical treatment of patients with AIDS, Psychiat Ann 18: 559

☐ CHAPTER 15

American Conference of Governmental and Industrial Hygienists, TLV[TM]: Threshold Limit Values and Biological Indices for 1985-86

Goodman-Gilman, A, Goodman, LS, and Gilman, A eds (1980), Goodman and Gilman's The Pharmacological Basis of Therapeutics, New York: Macmillan

Klaassen, CD, Amdur, MO, and Doull, J eds (1986), Casarett and Doull's Toxicology: The Basic Science of Poisons (3rd ed), New York: Macmillan

Ramazzini, B (1713), Diseases of Workers, New York: New York Academy of Medicine

Valciukas, JA (1991), Foundations of Environmental and Occupational Neurotoxicology, New York: Van Nostrand Reinhold

Zielhuis, RL, and Henderson, PT (1986), Definitions of monitoring activities and their relevance for the practice of occupational health, Int Arch Occup Environ Health 57: 249-257

→ Additional Readings

Bradbury, M (1979), The Concept of a Blood-Brain Barrier, New York: Wiley

Bandroft, J (1977), People who deliberately poison or injure themselves: Their problems and their contacts with helping agencies, Psychological Medicine 7(2): 289-303

Barnes, JM (1968), Percutaneous toxicity, in Modern Trends in Toxicology ed E Boyland and R Goulding, London: Butterworths, 18-38

Cooper JR, Bloom, FE, and Roth, RH (1986), The Biological Basis of Neuropharmacology, (5th ed), New York: Oxford Univ Press

Dreisbach, RH (1980), Handbook of Poisoning, (10th ed), Los Altos, CA: Lange Medical Publications

Ellenhorn, MJ, and Barceloux, DG (1990), Medical Toxicology: Diagnosis and Treatment of Human Poisoning, New York: Elsevier

Feldman, RS, and Quenzer, LF (1984), Fundamentals of Neuropsychopharmacology, Sunderland, Mass: Sinauer Associates

Felton, JS (1980), The occupational history: A neglected area in the clinical history, J Fam Practice July, 11 (1): 33-39

Goldman, RH, and Peters, JM (1981), The occupational and environmental health history, J Am Med Ass Dec 18, 246 (24): 2831-2836

Goldstein, GW, and Betz, AL (1986), The blood-brain barrier, Scient American Sept, 74-83

Hayes, AW (1984), Principles and Methods of Toxicology, (student ed), New York: Raven

Holden, M, and Sletten, I (1970), The patient as an information source, Clin Toxicol 3(2): 195-203

Kalow, W, Goedde, HW, and Agarwal, DP eds (1986), Ethnic Differences in Reactions to Drugs and Xenobiotics, New York: Alan R Liss

Lloyd, WE (1986), Safety Evaluation of Drugs and Chemicals, New York: Hemisphere

Suckling, AJ, Rumsky, MG, and Bradbury, MWB eds (1986), The Blood-Brain Barrier in Health and Disease, New York: VCH Publishers

☐ **CHAPTER 16**

Altman, LK (1988), Warning is issued on cocaine and sex, NY Times, Friday, June 3, D-1

Blanken, AJ, Adams, EH, and Durell, J (1987), Drug abuse: Implications and trends, Psychiat Med 3(3): 299-317

Keller, M (1979), A historical view of alcohol and alcoholism, Cancer Research 39: 2822-2829

Korsakoff, SS (1887), Disturbance of psychic function in alcoholic paralysis and its relation to the disturbance of the psychic sphere in multiple neuritis of non-alcoholic origin, Vestn Psichatrii 4 (Fasc 2)

National Institute on Alcohol Abuse and Alcoholism (1982), Occupational Alcoholism, Monograph 8, Washington, DC: US Govt Printing Office

National Institute on Drug Abuse (1987), Use of Selected Drugs among Hispanics: Mexican-Americans, Puerto-Ricans and Cuban-Americans, Rockville, MD: NIDA

National Institute on Drug Abuse (1991a), National Household Survey on Drug Abuse: Population Estimates 1990, Rockville, MD, (DHHS Publication No ADM 91-1732)

National Institute on Drug Abuse (1991b), National Household Survey on Drug Abuse: Main Findings 1990, Rockville, MD (DHHS Publication No ADM 91-1788)

National Institute on Drug Abuse (1991c), National Household Survey on Drug Abuse: Highlights 1990, Rockville, MD (DHHS Publication No ADM 91-1789)

National Institute on Drug Abuse (1991d), Drug Use among American High School Seniors, College Students and Young Adults, 1975-1990, Vol I, High School Seniors, Rockville, MD (DHHS Publication No ADM 91-1813)

National Institute on Drug Abuse (1991e), Drug Use among American High School Seniors, College Students and Young Adults, 1975-1990, Vol II, College Students and Young Adults, Rockville, MD (DHHS Publication No ADM 91-1835)

National Institute on Drug Abuse (1991f), Annual Emergency Room Data 1990, Data from Drug Abuse Warning Network (DAWN), Rockville, MD, (DHHS Publication No ADM 91-1839)

National Insitute on Drug Abuse (1991g), Annual Medical Examiner Data 1990, Data from Drug Abuse Warning Network (DAWN), Rockville, MD, (DHHS Publication No ADM 91-1840)

Ray, OS (1974), Drugs, Society, and Human Behavior, St Louis: Mosby

→ **Additional Readings**

Alapin, B (1973), Trichloroethylene addiction and its effects, Br J Addict 68: 331-335

American Psychiatric Association (1987), Diagnostic and Statistical Manual of Mental Disorders (3rd ed, revised), DSM-III-R, Washington, DC: APA

Brain, PF Ed (1986), Alcohol and Aggression, London: Dover

Bruckner, JV, and Peterson, RG (1981), Evaluation of toluene and acetone inhalant abuse, I Pharmacology and pharmacodynamics, Toxicol App Pharmacology 61: 27-38

Cho, AK (1990), Ice: A new dosage form of an old drug, Science 249: 631-634

Crabble, JC, and Harris, A eds (1991), The Genetic Basis of Alcohol and Drug Actions, New York: Plenum

Criteria Committee, National Council on Alcoholism (1972), Criteria for the diagnosis of alcoholism, Am J Psychiatry 120 (2): 127-135

DeFranco, C, Tarbox, AR, and McLaughlin, EJ (1985), Cognitive deficits as a function of years of alcohol abuse, Am J Drug Alcoh Abuse 11: 279-293

Gawin, FH (1991), Cocaine addiction: Psychology and neurophysiology, Science 251: 1580-1586

Gawin, FH, and Ellinwood, EH (1988), Cocaine and other stimulants: Actions, abuse and treatment, N Eng J Med 318: 1173-1182

Gay, GR, Inaba, DS, Sheppard, CW, et al (1975), Cocaine: History, epidemiology, human pharmacology and treatment: A perspective of a new debut for an old girl, Clin Toxicol 8(2): 149-178

Glasser, H, and Massengale, O (1962), Glue sniffing in children: Deliberate inhalation of vaporized plastic cements, J Am Med Ass 181: 300-303

Gonzalez, EG, and Downey, JA (1972), Polyneuropathy in a glue sniffer, Arch Phys Med Rehab July, 333-337

Grabski, DA (1962), Toluene sniffing producing cerebellar degeneration, Am J Psychiat 118: 461-462

Graham, JR (1987), The MMPI: A Practical Guide (2nd ed), New York: Oxford Univ Press.

Hart, JB, and Wallace, J (1975), The adverse effects of amphetamines, Clin Toxicol 8(2): 179-190

Hunt, LG, and Chambers, CD (1976), The Heroin Epidemics, New York: Spectrum

Institute of Medicine (1982), Marijuana and Health, Washington, DC: National Academy Press

Johnson, S, and Garzon, SR (1978), Alcohol and women, Am J Drug Alcoh Abuse 5: 107-122

Joint Committee of the American Bar Association and the American Medical Association on Narcotic Drugs (1961), Drug Addiction: Crime or Disease?, Bloomington: Indiana Univ Press

Juntunen, J (1982), Alcoholism in occupational neurology: Diagnostic difficulties with special reference to the neurological syndromes caused by exposure to organic solvents, Acta Neurol Scand 66(Supp 92): 89-108

Kaufman E (1982), The relationship of alcoholism abuse to the abuse of other drugs, Am J Drug Alcoh Abuse 9: 1-17

Kloc, JC, Boerner, U, and Becker, CE (1975), Coma, hyperthermia and bleeding associated with massive LSD overdose: A report of eight cases, Clin Toxicol 8(2): 191-203

Knox JW, and Nelson, JR (1966), Permanent encephalopathy from toluene inhalation, New Eng J Med 275: 1494-1486

Kolata, G (1988), Alcoholism or misbehavior? The Supreme Court is due to rule on whether alcoholism is a disease or character flaw, Psychology Today, April, 34-37

Kopin, IJ (1987), MPTP: An industrial chemical and contaminant of illicit narcotics stimulates a new era in research on Parkinson's disease, Environ Health Perspectives 75: 45-61

Korobkin, R, Ashbury, AK, Summer, AJ, and Nielsen, SL (1975), Glue-sniffing neuropathy, Arch Neurol 32: 158-162

Kosten, TR, Gawin, FH, Rousaville, BJ, and Kleber, HD (1986), Cocaine abusers among opioid addicts: Demographic and diagnostic factors in treatment, Am J Drug Alcoh Abuse 12: 1-16

Kozel, NJ, and Adams, EH (1986), Epidemiology of drug abuse: An overview Science 234: 970-234

Langston, JW, Tetrud, JW, and Irwin, I (1983), Chronic parkinsonism in humans due to a product of meperidin-analog synthesis, Science 219: 979-980

Learner, SE (1976), PCP revisited, Clin Toxicol 9(2): 339-348

Lings, S, Jensen, J, Christense, S, and Møller, JT (1984), Occupational accidents and alcohol, Int Arch Occup Environ Health 53: 531-329

Marchiafava, E (1933), The degeneration of the brain in chronic alcoholism, Proc R Soc Med 26: 1151

Markey, SP, Castagnoli, N, Trevor, AJ, and Kopin, IJ eds (1986), MPTP: A Neurotoxic Producing a Parkinsonian Syndrome, New York: Academic

Marlatt, A, and Miller, WR (1984), The Comprehensive Drinker Profile, Odessa, FL: Psychol Assessment Resources

Massengale, O, and Glasser, H (1963), Physical and psychological factors in glue sniffing, New Eng J Med 269: 1340-1344

Matsumura, M, Inoue, N, Onishi, A, Santa, T, and Goto, I (1972), Toxic polyneuropathy due to glue-sniffing, Clin Neurol 12: 290-296

Miller, WR (1976), Alcoholism scales and objective assessment methods: A review, Psychol Bull, 83: 649-674

Musto, DF (1991), Opium, cocaine and marijuana in American History, Scient Am 265(1): 40-47

Ng, SKC, Brust, JCM, Hauser, WA, and Susser, M (1990), Illicit drug use and the risk of new-onset seizures, Am J Epidemiol 132(1): 47-57

Parker, WA (1982), Alcohol-containing pharmaceuticals, Am J Drug Alcoh Abuse 9: 195-209

Parsons, OA (1977), Neuropsychologic deficits in alcoholics: Facts and fancies, Alcoholism 1: 51-56

Parsons, OA (1983), Premature aging, alcoholism, and recovery, in Alcohol and Aging: Advances in Research, ed WG Wood and MS Zlias, Boca Raton, FL: CRC Press

Peele, S (1984), The cultural context of psychological approaches to alcoholism: Can we control the effects of alcohol? Am Psychologist 12: 1337-1351

Pendery, ML, Malzman, IM, and West, LJ (1982), Controlled drinking for alcoholics? New findings and a reevaluation of a major affirmative study, Science 217: 169-175

Primavera, LH, and Pascal, R (1986), A comparison of male users and non-users of marijuana on the perceived harmfulness of drugs, Am J Drug Alcoh Abuse 12: 71-77

Rankin, JG ed (1975), Alcohol, Drugs, and Brain Damage, Toronto: Addiction Research Foundation of Ontario

Ridker, PM (1987), Toxic effects of herbal teas, Arch Env Health 42(2): 133-136

Rosett, HL, and Weiner, L (1984), Alcohol and the Fetus: A Clinical Perspective, New York: Oxford Univ Press

Sahenk, Z, Mendell, JR, Couri, D, and Nachtman, J (1978), Polyneuropathy from inhalation of NO2 cartridges through a whipped-cream dispenser, Neurology May 485-487

Shirabe, T, Tsuda, T, Terao, A, and Araki, S (1984), Toxic polyneuropathy due to glue sniffing: Report of two cases with a light and electron-microscopic study of the peripheral nerves and muscles, J Neurol Sc 21: 101-113

Smith, MC (1991), A Social History of the Minor Tranquilizers: The Quest for Small Comfort in the Age of Anxiety, New York: The Haworth Press, Inc.

Snyder, SH (1986), Drugs and the Brain, New York: Freeman

Snyder, SH, and D'Amato, RJ (1986), MPTP: A neurotoxic relevant to the pathophysiology of Parkinson's disease, Neurology 36: 250-258

Spears, RA (1986), The Slang and Jargon of Drugs and Drinks, Metuchen, NJ: Scarecrow

Strauss, RH (1987), Drugs and Performance in Sports, Philadelphia: WB Saunders

Susuki, T, Shimbo, S, Nishitani, H, et al (1974), Muscular atrophy due to glue sniffing, Int Arch Arbeitmed 33: 115-123

Tartar, RE (1975), Psychological deficit in chronic alcoholics: A review, Int J Addict 10: 327-368

Trice, HM, and Roman, PM (1979), Spirits and Demons at Work: Alcohol and other Drugs on the Job, Ithaca, NY: ILR Press, Cornell Univ

Wilkinson, A ed (1982), Cerebral Deficits in Alcoholism, Toronto: Addiction Research Foundation

Wyse, DG (1973), Deliberate inhalation of volatile hydrocarbons: A review, CMA Journal, 108: 71-74

☐ CHAPTER 17

Anger, WK, and Johnson, BJ (1985), Chemicals affecting behavior, in Neurotoxicity of Industrial and Commercial Chemicals, Vol 1 ed JL O'Donoghue, Boca Raton, FL: CRC Press, 51-148

Dreisbach, RH (1980), Handbook of Poisoning, (10th ed), Los Altos, CA: Lange Medical Publications

Fiddler, AT, Baker, EL, and Letz, RI (1987), Estimation of long-term exposure to mixed solvents from questionnaire data: A tool for epidemiological investigation, Br J Ind Med 44(2): 133-141

Goodman-Gilman, A, Goodman, LS, and Gilman, A eds (1980), Goodman and Gilman's The Pharmacological Basis of Therapeutics, New York: Macmillan

Gregerson, P, Angelo, B, Nielsen, TE, et al (1984), Neurotoxic effects of organic solvents in exposed workers: An occupational, neuropsychological, and neurological investigation, Am J Ind Med 5: 210-225

Hamilton, A (1943), Exploring the Dangerous Trades, Boston: Little, Brown

Klaassen, CD, Amdur, MO, and Doull, J (1986), Casarett and Doull's Toxicology: The Basic Science of Poisons (3rd ed), New York: Macmillan

Lipske, M (1986), Danger: Are you throwing poisons into the trash? Nat Wildlife, Aug-Sep, 20-23

Ørbæk, P, Risberg, J, Rosén, I, et al (1985), Effects of long-term exposure to solvents in the paint industry, Scand J Work Environ Health 11(Suppl 2): 1-28

US Department of Health, Education, and Welfare, Public Health Service (1977), Occupational Diseases: A Guide to their Recognition, Washington, DC: US Government Printing Office

Valciukas, JA (1991), Foundations of Environmental and Occupational Neurotoxicology, New York: Van Nostrand Reinhold

→ Additional Readings

Aitio, A, Riihimaki, V, and Vainio, H (1984), Biological Monitoring and Surveillance of Workers Exposed to Chemicals, New York: Hemisphere

Alapin, B (1973), Trichloroethylene addiction and its effects, Br J Addict 68: 331-335

Aldridge, WN (1986), The Biological Basis and Measurement of Thresholds, Ann Rev Pharmacol Toxicol 26: 39-58

American Conference of Governmental and Industrial Hygienists, TLV[TM]: Threshold Limit Values and Biological Indices for 1985-86

Arlien-Søborg, P (1991), Solvent Neurotoxicity, Boca Raton, FL: CRC Press

Arlien-Søborg, P, Bruhn, P, Gyldensted, C, and Melgaard, B (1979), Chronic painter's syndrome: Chronic toxic encephalopathy in house painters, Acta Neurol Scand 60: 149-156

Axelson, O, Hane, M, and Hogstedt, C (1976), A case-referent study on neuropsychiatric disorders amongst workers exposed to solvents, Scand J Work Env Health 2: 14-20

Baselt, RC (1988), Biological Monitoring Methods for Industrial Chemicals, (2nd ed), Littleton, MA: PSG Publishing

Berlin, A, Wolf, AH, and Hasegawa, Y eds (1979), The Use of Biological Specimens for the Assessment of Human Exposure to Environmental Pollutants, The Hague: Martinus Nijhoff

Berlin, A, Yodaiken, RE, and Henman, BA eds (1984), Assessment of Toxic Agents at the Workplace: Role of Ambient and Biological Monitoring ,The Hague: Martinus Nijhoff

Carson, R (1962), Silent Spring, Greenwich, CT: Fawcett Publications

Castleman, BI, and Ziem, GE (1988), Corporate influence on threshold limit values, Am J Ind Medicine,13: 531-559

Cherry, N, and Waldron, HA (1984), The prevalence of psychiatric morbidity in solvent workers in Britain, Int J Epidem, 13(2): 197-200

Cohen, GM ed (1986), Target Organ Toxicity (2 Vols) Boca Raton, FL: CRC Press

Cole, C (1976), Drugs in the workplace, Clin Toxicol 9(2): 185-197

Ecobichon, D ed (1982), Pesticides and Neurological Diseases, Boca Raton, FL: CRC Press

Hänninen, H, Antti-Poika, M, and Savolainen, P (1987), Psychological performance, toluene exposure and alcohol consumption in rotogravure printers, Int Arch Occup Environ Health 59: 475-483

Johnson, BL ed (1987), Prevention of Neurotoxic Illness in Working Populations, New York: Wiley

Juntunen, J (1982), Alcoholism in occupational neurology: Diagnostic difficulties with special reference to the neurological syndromes caused by exposure to organic solvents, Acta Neurol Scand 66(Supp 92): 89-108

Lauwerys, RR (1983), Industrial Chemical Exposure: Guidelines for Biological Monitoring, Davis, CA: Biomedical Publications

Lave, LB, and Upton, AC eds (1987), Toxic Chemicals, Health and the Environment, Baltimore: John Hopkins Univ Press

Lindstrøm, K (1981), Behavioral changes after long-term exposure to organic solvents and their mixtures, Scand J Work Env Health 7: (Supp. 4): 48-53

Lindstrøm, K (1982), Behavioral effects of long-term exposure to organic solvents, Acta Neurol Scand., 92: 131-141

Lings, S, Jensen, J, Christensen, S, and Møller, JT (1984), Occupational accidents and alcohol, Int Arch Occup Environ Health 53: 531-329

Lynch, JR (1985), Measurement of worker exposure, in Patty's Industrial Hygiene and Toxicology, Vol III, Theory and Rational for Industrial Hygiene Practice, 2nd ed, 3A, The Work Environment, ed LJ Cralley and LV Cralley, New York: Wiley, 569-615

Nappi, G, Homyliewicz, O, Fariello, RG, et al eds (1988), Neurodegenerative Disorders: The Role Played by Endotoxins and Xenobiotics, New York: Raven

Oehmen, FW (1980), Absorption, biotransformation and excretion of environmental chemicals, Clin Toxicol 17(1), 147-158

O'Flynn, RR (1988), Do organic solvents cause dementia?, Int J Geriatric Psych 3(1): 5-15

White, RF (1987), Differential diagnosis of probable Alzheimer's disease and solvent encephalopathy in older workers, Clin Neuropsycholist 1(2): 153-160

Williams, PL, and Burson, JL (1985), Industrial Toxicology: Safety and Health Applications in the Workplace, New York: Van Nostrand Reinhold Co

World Health Organization (1985), Chronic Effects of Organic Solvents on the Central Nervous System, Copenhagen: World Health Organization (Regional Office for Europe)

World Health Organization (1986), Principles and Methods for the Assessment of Neurotoxicity Associated with Exposure to Chemicals, Environmental Health Criteria 60, Geneva: World Health Organization

Zielhuis, RL (1984), Biological monitoring, In Assessment of Toxic Agents at the Workplace: Role of Ambient and Biological Monitoring A Berlin ed EE Eodaiken and BA Henman, 84-94

Zielhuis, RL, and Henderson, PT (1986), Definitions of monitoring activities and their relevance for the practice of occupational health, Int Arch Occup Environ Health, 57: 249-257

☐ **CHAPTER 18**

➔ **Vision**

Armington, JC (1974), The Electroretinogram, New York: Academic

Battersby, WS, Krieger, EP, Pollack, M, and Bender, MB (1953), Figure-ground discrimination and the abstract attitude in patients with cerebral neoplasms AMA Arch Neurol Psychiat 70: 703-712

Bender, MB (1952), Disorders in Perception, Springfield, IL: Charles C Thomas

Bender, MB, and Teuber, HL (1947), Phenomenon of fluctuation, extinction and completion in visual perception, Arch Neurol Psychiat 55: 627-658

Benton, CD, and Calhoun, FP (1953), The ocular effects of methyl alcohol poisoning: Report of a catastrophe involving 320 persons, Am J Ophthal 36: 1677-1685

Bizzi, E (1974), The coordination of eye-head movements, Scient Am 231: 100-106

Brandt, T, Wist, E, and Dichgans, J (1975), Foreground and background in dynamic spatial orientation, Perception and Psychophysics 17(5): 497-503

Brown, JW (1989), Neuropsychology of Visual Perception, Hillsdale, NJ: Erlbaum

Cooper, MN, Mitchell, GL, Bennett, IL, and Cary, FH (1952), Methyl alcohol poisoning: An account of the 1951 Atlanta epidemic, J Med Assoc Georgia 11: 48-51

Cornsweet, TM (1980), Visual Perception, New York: Academic

Davson, H (1980), Physiology of the Eye (4th ed), New York: Academic

Foulds, WS, Chisolm, IA, and Pettigrew, AR (1974), The toxic optic neuropathies, Brit J Opthalm, 58: 386

Fox, SL (1973), Industrial and Occupational Ophthalmology, Springfield, IL: Charles C Thomas

Frauenfelder, FT (1982), Drug-Induced Ocular Side Effects and Drug Interaction (2nd ed), Philadelphia: Lea and Febiger

Gehring, PJ (1971), The cataractogenic activity of chemical agents, CRC Critical Reviews in Toxicology 1(1): 93-118

Gouras, P (1985), Color vision, in Principles of Neurosciences ed ER Kandel and JH Schwartz New York: Elsevier, 384-395

Graham, CD ed (1965), Vision and Visual Perception, New York: Wiley

Grant, WM (1986), Toxicology of the Eye: Effects on the Eyes and Visual System from Chemicals, Drugs, Metals & Minerals, Plants, Toxins & Venoms, (3rd ed), Springfield, IL: Charles C Thomas

Hitchens (1986), Optical Radiation and Visual Health, Boca Raton, FL: CRC Press

Judd, DB, and Wyszecki, G (1975), Color in Business, Science, and Industry, (3rd ed), New York: Wiley

Livingstone, M, and Hubel, D (1988), Segregation of form, color, movement, and depth: Anatomy, physiology and perception, Science 240: 740-749

Nathans, J (1989), The genes for color vision, Scient Am, July, 42-49

Plestina, R, and Piukovic-Plestina, M (1978), Effects of anticholinesterase pesticides on the eye and on vision, CRC Crit Rev Toxicol 6(1): 1-23

Pritchard, RM (1961), Stabilized images on the retina, Scient Am 204: 72-78

Raitta, C, Teir, H, Tolone, M, et al (1981), Impaired color discrimination among viscose rayon workers exposed to carbon disulfide, J Occup Med 23: 189-192

Ratliff, F (1965), Mach Bands: Quantitative Studies on Neural Networks in the Retina, New York: Holden-Day

Reed, ES (1989), James J Gibson and the Psychology of Perception, New Haven, CT: Yale Univ Press

Richard, W (1971), The fortification illusions of migraines, Scient Am 224: 88-96

Smith, MB (1976), Handbook of Ocular Toxicity, Acton, MA: Publishing Sciences Group

Specchio, LM, Bellomo, R, Pozio, G, Dicuonzo, F, Assennato, G, Federeci, A, and Misciagna, G (1981), Smooth pursuit eye movements among storage battery workers, Clin Toxicol 18(11): 1269-1276

Spector, A (1970), Aging of the lens and cataract formation, in Aging and the Human Visual Functions, ed R Sekuler, D Kline, and R Dismukers, New York: Alan R Liss, 27-43

Sugimoto, K, Goto, S, and Hotta, R (1976), An epidemiological study on retinopathy due to carbon disulfide: CS2 exposure level and development of retinopathy, Int Arch Occup Environ Health 37: 1-8

Taylor, H (1980), The environment and the lens, Br J Opthal 64: 303-310

Teuber, H-L (1960), Perception, in Handbook of Physiology, Section I, Vol 3, Neurophysiology, J ed Field, HW Magoun, and VE Hall, Washington, DC: American Physiological Society, 1595-1668

Teuber, H-L, and Weinstein, S (1956), Ability to discover hidden figures after cerebral lesions, Arch Neurol Psychiat 76: 369-379

Teuber, H-L, Battersby, WS, and Bender, MB (1951), Performance of complex visual tasks after cerebral lesions, J Nerv Ment Dis 114: 413-419

Teuber, H-L, Battersby, WS, and Bender, MB (1960), Visual Defects after Penetrating Missile Wound of the Brain, Cambridge, UK: Cambridge Univ Press

Toates, FM (1972), Accommodation Function of the Human Eye, Physiol Rev 52: 828-863

Uhthoff, W (1911), Die augenstrungen bei vergiftungen, in Græfe-Saemisch Handbuch der Gesamten Augenheilkunde, II: 1-180, Leipzig: Engelman

van Heyningen, R (1976), What happens to the human lens in cataract, Scient Am 233: 70-81

Vigliani, EC (1950), Clinical observations on carbon disulfide intoxication in Italy, Ind Med Surg 19: 240-242

Walsh, FB, and Hoyt, WF (1969), Clinical Neuro-Ophthalmology, (3rd ed) Baltimore: Williams & Wilkins

Wertheimer, M (1912), Experimentelle Studies über das Sehen von Bewegung, Z Psychol, 61: 161-265

Wilmer, WH (1921), Effects of carbon monoxide upon the eye, Am J Ophthal 4: 73

Wurtman, RJ, Baum, MJ, and Potts, JT eds (1985), The Medical and Biological Effects of Light, Annals of the New York Academy of Science, Vol 453

Zigman, S, Datiles, M, and Torczynski, E (1979), Sunlight and human cataracts, Invest Ophthalm Vis Sci 18: 462-467

→ Auditory System

Berlin, CI ed (1984), Hearing Science, San Diego: College-Hill

Department of Labor, Occupational Health Administration (1981), Occupational Noise Exposure: Hearing Conservation Amendment, Federal Register, Friday, Jan 16, 4078-4179

Department of Labor, Occupational Health Administration (1983), Occupational Noise Exposure: Hearing Conservation Amendment, Federal Register, Tue March 8, 9738-9785

Hudspeth, AJ (1985), The cellular basis of hearing: The biophysics of hair cells, Science 230: 745-752

Hulse, SH, and Dooling, RJ (1989), Complex Acoustic Perception: The Comparative Psychology of Audition, Hillsdale, NJ: Erlbaum

Hybels, RL (1979), Drug toxicity of the inner ear, Med Clinics of North America 63 (2), March, 309-319

Kryter, KD (1985), The Effects of Noise on Man (2nd ed), New York: Academic

Marks, LE (1974), Sensory Processes, New York: Academic

Miller, JJ (1985), Handbook of Ototoxicity, Boca Raton, FL: CRC Press

Møller, AR (1975), Noise as a health hazard, Ambio 4 (1): 6-13

Prosen, CA, and Stebbins, WC (1980), Ototoxicity, in Experimental and Clinical Neurotoxicology, ed PS Spencer and HH Schaumburg, Baltimore: Williams & Wilkins, 62-76

Worthington, EL, Lunin, LF, Heath, M, and Catlin, FI (1973), Index-Handbook of Ototoxic Agents, Baltimore: Johns Hopkins Univ Press

→ Somatosensory System

Agate, NJ (1949), An outbreak of cases of Raynaud's phenomenon of occupational origin, Brit J Ind Med 4: 144-163

Cavanagh, JB (1973), Peripheral neuropathy caused by chemical agents, CRC Critical Reviews in Toxicology 2(1): 365-417

Halonen, P, Halonen, J-P, Lang, HA, and Karskela, V (1986), Vibratory perception thresholds in shipyard workers exposed to solvents, Acta Neurol Scand 73(6): 561-565

Hubbard, JI (1974), The Peripheral Nervous System, New York: Plenum

Katz, D (1925), Der Aufbau der Tastwelt, Leipzig: JA Barth

Marks, RM, Barton, SP, and Edwards, C eds (1987), The Physical Nature of the Skin, Boston: MTP Press

Mathers, LH (1985), The Peripheral Nervous System: Structure, Function and Clinical Correlations, Menlo Park, CA: Addison-Wesley

Maurissen, JOJ (1979), Effects of toxicants on the somatosensory system, Neurobeh Toxicol 1, Supp 1, 23-31

McCallum, RI (1971), Vibration syndrome, Brit J Ind Med, 28: 90-99

Schaumburg, HH, Spencer, PS, and Thomas, PK (1983), Disorders of Peripheral Nerves, Philadelphia: FA Davis

Seppäläinen, AM (1970), Nerve conduction in the vibration syndrome, Work-Environment-Health 7: 82-84

Taylor, W (1974), The Vibration Syndrome, London: Academic

Thomas, PK (1980), The peripheral nervous system as a target for toxic agents, in Experimental and Clinical Neurotoxicology ed PS Spencer and HH Schaumburg, Baltimore: Williams & Wilkins, 35-47

World Health Organization Study Group (1980), Peripheral Neuropathies, Technical Reports Series 654, Geneva: World Health Organization

→ Chemical Senses

Adams, RG, and Crabtree, N (1961), Anosmia in alkaline battery workers, Brit J Ind Med, 18: 216-221

Barrow, CS ed (1986), Toxicology of the Nasal Passages, Chemical Industry Institute of Toxicology Series, Washington, DC: Hemisphere

Buchan, RT (1974), Garlic breath odor, J Am Med Ass, 227: 559-560

Cain, WS (1974a), Contributions of the trigeminal nerve to perceived odor magnitude, Ann NY Acad Sc 237: 28-34

Cain, WS ed (1974b), Odors: Evaluation, Utilization and Control, Ann NY Academy of Sciences, Vol 237

Cain, WS (1974c), Scope and evaluation of odor counteraction and masking, An NY Acad Sc, 237: 427-439

Cain, WS (1977) Diffential sensitivity for smell: Noise at the nose, Science, 195: 796-798

Cain, WS (1979), To know with the nose: Keys to odor identification, Science, 203: 467-470

Cowart, BJ (1981), Development of taste perception in humans: Sensitivity and preference throughout the lifespan, Psychol Bull, 90: 43-73

Deane, M, et al (1978), Annoyance and health reactions to odor from refineries and other industries in Carson, California, Env Res, 15: 119-132

Doty, RL, Shaman, P, Appebaum, SL, et al (1984), Smell identification ability: Changes with age, Science 226: 1441-1443

Emmet, EA (1976), Parosmia and hyposmia induced by solvent exposure, Br J Ind Med, 33: 196-198

Engen, T (1972), The effect of expectation on judgment of odor, Acta Psychol (Australia), 36: 450-458

Finger, TE, and Silver, W eds (1987), Neurobiology of Taste and Smell, New York: Wiley-

Gilbert, AN, and Wysocki, CJ (1987), The Smell Survey: Results, National Geographic, Sept, 514-525

Henkin, RI (1967), Abnormalities of Olfaction and Taste in Various Disease States, In Chemical Senses and Nutrition, MR Kare and O Maller eds, Baltimore: John Hopkins Univ Press

Henkin, RI (1976), Taste in Man, in Scientific Foundations of Otolaryngology, ed D Harrison and R Hinchcliffe, London: Heineman Medical

Leonardos, G (1974), A critical review of regulations for the control of odors, J Air Poll Control Assoc, 24: 456-468

Naus, A (1975), Olphactoric Properties of Industrial Matters, Prague: Charles University

Pfaff, DW ed (1985), Taste, Olfaction, and the Central Nervous System: A Festschrift in Honor of Carl Pfaffman, New York: Rockefeller Univ Press

Sandmark, B, Broms, I, Löfgren, L, and Ohlson, CG (1989), Olfactory function in painters exposed to organic solvents, Scand J Work Env Health 15(1): 60-63

Schiffman, SS, et al (1976), Thresholds of food odors in the elderly, Exp Aging Res, 2: 389-398

Taniewski, M (1975), The sense of taste in some occupational exposures, Bull Inst Marit Trop Med, Gdynia 26: 329-336

Wood, RW (1978), Stimulus properties of inhaled substances, Env Health Perspect, 26: 69-76

Wright, RH (1982), The Sense of Smell, Boca Raton, FL: CRC Press

☐ CHAPTER 19

American Psychiatric Association (1994), Diagnostic and Statistical Manual of Mental Disorders (4th ed), DSM-IV, Washington, DC: American Psychiatric Association

Shepherd, GM (1983), Neurobiology, New York: Oxford Univ Press

→ Additional Readings

DelCastillo, J (1970), The influence of language upon symptomatology in foreign-born patients, Am J Psychiat 127: 242-244

Edgerton, RB, and Karno, M (1971), Mexican-American bilingualism and the perception of mental illness, Arch Gen Psychiatr 24: 286-290

Feyereisen, P, and de Lannoy, J-D (1991), Gestures and Speech: Psychological Investigations, New York: Cambridge Univ Press

Goldenson, RM ed (1978), Disability and Rehabilitation Handbook, New York: McGraw-Hill

Karmo, M (1966), The enigma of ethnicity in a psychiatric clinic, Arch Gen Psychiat 14: 516-520

Melzack, R (1992), Phantom limbs, Scient Am 266(4): 120-126

☐ CHAPTER 20

Campbell-Black, HC (1983), Black's Law Dictionary (Abridged 5th ed Publisher's Editorial Staff), St Paul, MN: West

Keeton, WP (1984), Prosser and Keeton on the Law of Torts (5th ed), St Paul, MN: West

Smith, SR, and Meyer, RG (1987), Law, Behavior, and Mental Health: Policy and Practice, New York: New York Univ Press

→ **Additional Readings**

American Psychiatric Association (1982), Statement on the Insanity Defense, Washington, DC: APA

American Psychiatric Association (1983), Guidelines for legislation on the psychiatric hospitalization of adults, Am J Psych 140: 672-679

American Psychiatric Association (1984), Issues in Forensic Psychiatry, Washington, DC: APA

American Psychological Association (1978), Report on the task force for on the role of psychology in the criminal justice system, American Psychologist 33: 1099-1113

Anderson (1990), Reality Isn't What It Used to Be, San Francisco: Harper & Row

Appelbaum, PS (1984), Hospitalization of the dangerous patient: Legal pressures and clinical responses, Bull Am Acad Psych Law 12: 323-329

Arenella, P (1977), The diminished capacity and diminished responsibility defenses: Two children of a doomed marriage, Columbia Law Review 77: 827-872

Beran, NJ, and Hotz, AM (1984), The behavior of mentally disordered criminals in civil mental hospitals, Hosp Comm Psychiat 35: 585-589

Blinder, M (1982), Psychiatry in the Everyday Practice of the Law: A Lawyer's Manual for Case Preparation and Trial, (2nd ed), Rochester, NY: Lawyer's Cooperative Publishing

Black, N (1988), Evolving legal standards for the admissibility of scientific evidence, Science 239: 1508-1512

Bonnie, RJ (1982), A Model Statute on the Insanity Defense, Charlottesville, VA: Univ of Virginia Press

Brakel, SJ, and Rock, RS (1971), The Mentally Disabled and the Law, Chicago: Univ of Chicago Press

Bresler, F (1988), Sex and the Law, London: Frederic Muller

Bromberg, W (1979), The Uses of Psychiatry in the Law: A Clinical View of Forensic Psychiatry, Westport, CT: Quorum Books

Brooks, A (1974), Law, Psychiatry and the Mental Health System, Boston: Little, Brown

Buckhout, R (1986), Personal values and expert testimony, Law Human Behav 10: 127-144

Burgess, A (1962), A Clockwork Orange, New York: Norton

Carter, RM (1978), Pre-sentence Report Handbook, Washington, DC: National Institute of Law Enforcement and Criminal Justice, Law Enforcement Assistant Administration, US Department of Justice

Cook, G ed (1980), The Role of the Forensic Psychologist, Springfield, IL: Charles C Thomas

Curran, WJ, McGarry, AL, and Petty, CS eds (1980), Modern Legal Medicine, Psychiatric and Forensic Sciences, Philadelphia: FA Davis Co

Curran, WJ, and Shapiro, ED (1970), Medicine and Forensic Sciences (2nd ed), Boston: Little, Brown

Dawes, RM, Faust, D, and Meehl, PE (1989), Clinical versus actuarial judgment, Science 243: 1668-1674

Dickey, W (1980), Incompetency and the non-dangerous mentally ill client, Crim Law Bull 16: 22-40

Dohrenwend, BP, Levav, I, Shrout, P, et al (1992), Socioeconomic status and psychiatric disorders: The causation-selection issue, Science 255: 946-959

Donaldson, K (1976), Insanity Inside Out, New York: Crown Publishers

Faust, D, and Ziskin, J (1988), The expert witness in psychology and psychiatry, Science 241: 31-35

Faust, D, and Ziskin, J (1989), Computer-assisted psychological evidence as legal evidence: Some day my prints will come, Computer in Human Behav 5: 23-36

Federal Rules of Evidence (1984), St Paul, MN: West

Goldstein, A (1967), The Insanity Defense, New Haven: Yale Univ Press

Groves, JE (1978), Taking care of the hateful patient, N England J Med 298: 883-887

Gunn, J, Robertson, G, et al (1978), Psychiatric Aspects of Imprisonment, New York: Academic

Guze, SB (1976), Criminality and Psychiatric Disorders, New York: Oxford Univ Press

Hagan, J (1985), Modern Criminology: Crime, Criminal Behavior, and its Control, New York: McGraw-Hill

Halleck, SL (1986), The Mentally Disordered Offender, Washington, DC: US Dept Health Human Services, Public Health Service, Alcohol, Drug Abuse and Mental Health Administration, National Institute of Health

Henderson, TW (1990), Toxic tort litigation: Medical and scientific principles in causation, Am J Epidemiol 132(1): S69-S78

Hermann, D (1983), The Insanity Defense, Springfield, IL: Charles C Thomas

Hoffman, M (1975), The medico-legal significance of pain and suffering, South Texas Law J 15: 279-288

Holden, C (1989), Science in court: Lawyers and scientists discuss how to improve the handling of expert testimony in damage suits involving toxic subtances, Science 243: 1658-1659

Huber, P (1991), Galileo's Revenge: Junk Science in the Courtroom, New York: Basic Books

Kassin, SM, Ellsworth, PC, and Smith, VL (1989), The general acceptance of psychological research on eyewitness testimony, Am Psychologist 44(8): 1089-1098

Laboratory of Community Psychiatry, Harvard Medical School (1974), Competency to Stand Trial and Mental Illness, New York: Jason Aronson

Levinson, RM, Briggs, RP, and Ratner, CH (1984), The impact of a change in commitment procedures on the character of involuntary psychiatric patients, J Foren Sci 29: 566-573

Loutzenhiser, L, and Amsel, E (1988), Causal reasoning among professionals: Comparing lawyers and psychologists, Canadian Psychology, 29, Abstract 478

Mayer, A (1982), The Crocodile Man: A Case of Brain Chemistry and Criminal Violence, Boston, MA: Houghton Mifflin

Melton, G, Petrila, J, Poythress, NG, and Slobogen, C (1987), Psychological Evaluation for the Courts, New York: Guilford

Miller, RD, and Maier, GJ (1987), Factors affecting the decision to prosecute mental patients for criminal behavior, Hospital Comm Psychiat 38(1): 50-55

Pallone, NJ (1990), Mental Disorder among Prisoners: Toward an Epidemiologic Inventory, New Brunswick, NJ: Transaction Books

Perr, IN (1991), Alleged brain damage, diminished capacity, mens rea, and misuse of medical concepts, J Forensic Sci 36(3): 722-727

Robertson, G (1988), Arrest patterns among mentally disordered offenders, Brit J Psychiat 153: 313-316

Ronsenhan, D (1973), On being sane in insane places, Science 179: 250-258

Simon, RJ (1967), Jury and the Defense of Insanity, Boston: Little, Brown

Steadman, HJ (1979), Beating a Rap? Defendants Found Incompetent to Stand Trial, Chicago: Univ of Chicago Press

Steadman, HJ, and Cocozza, J (1978), Selective reporting and the public's misconception of the criminally insane, Public Opinion Quarterly 41: 523-533

Steadman, HJ, Cocozza, JJ, and Melick, ME (1978), Explaining the increased arrest rate among mental patients: The changing clientele of state hospitals, Am J Psychiat 135: 816-820

Szasz, T (1963), Law, Liberty, and Psychiatry, New York: Macmillan

Szasz, T (1972), Ideology and Insanity, Garden City, NY: Doubleday

Yeudall, L, Fedora, O, Fedora, S, and Wardell, W (1981), Neurosocial perspective on the asessment and etiology of persistent criminality, Austral J Foren Sci 13(4): 131-159

Wells, GL, and Loftus, EF eds (1984), Eyewitness Testimony: Psychological Perspectives, New York: Cambridge Univ Press

Ziskin, J, and Faust, D (1988) Coping with Psychiatric and Psychological Testimony, 3rd ed, Marina del Rey, CA: Law and Psychology Press

☐ **CHAPTER 21**

Bell, Sir Charles (1806), The Anatomy and Philosophy of Expression as Connected to Fine Arts [Rare book]

Boring, EG (1950), A History of Experimental Psychology, New York: Appleton-Century-Crofts

Dennett, DC (1991), Conciousness Explained, Boston: Little, Brown

Dywan, J, Kaplan, RD, and Pirozzollo, FJ eds (1991), Neuropsychology and the Law, New York: Springer Verlag

Gould, SJ (1981), The Mismeasure of Man, New York: Norton

Kandel, ER, Schwartz, JH, and Jessell, TM, eds (1991), Principles of Neural Science (3rd ed), New York: Elsevier

Laurence, J-R, and Perry, C (1988), Hypnosis, Will and Memory: A Psycholegal History, New York: Guilford

Lavater, JK (1790), Aphorisms on Man, Boston, I Thomas & ET Andrews

Lavater, JK (1810), Essay on Physiognomy Designed to Promote the Knowledge and Love of Mankind, London: L Stockdale

Lezak, MD (1983), Neuropsychological Assessment (2nd ed), New York: Oxford Univ Press

Lombroso, C (1891), The Man of Genius, London: W Scott

Lombroso, C (1892), Les Applications de l'Anthropologie Criminel, Paris: F Alcan

Lombroso, C (1893), La Donna Delinquente: La Prostituta è la Donna Normale, Torino: Roux

Piaget, J (1932), The Moral Judgement of the Child, New York: Harcourt

Piaget, J (1954), The Construction of Reality in the Child, New York: Basic Books

Piaget, J (1976), The Grasp of Consciousness, Cambridge, MA: Harvard Univ Press

Sbordone, RJ (1991), Neuropsychology for the Attorney, Orlando, FL: Paul M Deutsch

Shapiro, DL (1984), Psychological Evaluation and Expert Testimony, New York: Van Nostrand Reinhold

Smith, SR, and Meyer, RG (1987), Law, Behavior and Mental Health: Policy and Practice, New York: New York Univ Press

Ziskin, J, and Faust, D (1988), Coping with Psychiatric and Psychological Testimony (3 Vols), Marina del Rey, CA: Law and Psychology Press

→ **Additional Readings**

Bentham, J (1789), Introduction to Principles and Morals and Legislation, London [Rare book collection]

Chapman, M (1988), Constructive Evolution: Origins and Development of Piaget's Thoughts, Cambridge, UK: Cambridge Univ Press

Delgado, JMR (1969), Physical Control of the Mind, New York: Harper & Row

Du Moulin, A (1549), De Diversa Hominum Natura: Prout a Veteribus Philosophia ex Corpurum Specifibus Reperta est, Cognosenda Liber, Lugunii Joanm Tornaesium

Evans, EC (1969), Physiognomics in the Ancient World, Philadelphia: Philosophical Society

Ferri, E (1897), Criminal Sociology, New York: Appleton

Foucalt, M (1965), Madness and Civilization: A History of Insanity in the Age of Reason (R Howard, Trans) New York: Pantheon

Fromm, E (1973), The Anatomy of Human Destructiveness, New York: Holt, Rinehart and Winston

Gazzaniga, MS (1985), The Social Brain: Discovering the Networks of the Mind, New York: Basic Books

Hume, D (1739), Treatise on Human Nature, London: John Noon

Koshland, DE (1992), Elephants, monstrosities, and the law, Science 255: 777

Locke, J (1690), Essay Concerning Human Understanding, London: Basset

Lombroso, C (1895), Grafology, Milano: U Hoepli

Lombroso, C (1907), Genio è Degenerazione: Nuovi Studie è Nuove Battaglie (2nd ed), Milano: Remo Sandro

Morison, A (1843), The Physiognomy of Mental Diseases, London: Longman

Redlich, RC (1951), Narcoanalysis and the truth, Am J Psychiatry 107: 586-593

Rennie, Y (1978), The Search for Criminal Man, Lexington, MA: Heath

Roebuck, JB (1967), Criminal Typology, Springfield, IL: Charles C Thomas

Science (1992), The insanity defense and mental illness (Letters to the editor; letters by WT Carpenter, M Sabshin, PR Marques and Barbara J Ballerman, with a response by DE Koshland), Science 256: 292-293

Sheldon, WH (1942), The Varieties of Temperament: A Psychology of Constitutional Differences, New York: Harper & Row

Sheldon, WH (1949), Varieties of Delinquent Youth: An Introduction to Constitutional Psychiatry, New York: Harper & Row

Skultans, V (1975), Madness and Morals: Ideas of Insanity in the Nineteenth Century, London: Routledge and Kegan Paul

Zimmern, H (1898), Criminal anthropology in Italy, Popular Science Monthly 52: 743-760

□ **APPENDIX A**

Amoore, JE, and Ollman, BG (1983), Practical kits for quantitatively evaluating the sense of smell, Rhinology 21: 49-54

Anastasi, A (1988), Psychological Testing (6th ed), New York: Macmillan

Anger, WK (1990), Worksite behavioral research: Results, sensitive methods, test batteries and the transition from laboratory data to human health, Neurotoxicol 11: 629-720

Axelrod, S, and Cohen, LD (1961), Senescence and imbedded figure performance in vision and touch, Percept Motor Skills 12: 283-288

Ayres, J, Templer, D, and Ruff, C (1975), The MMPI in the differential diagnosis of organicity v schizophrenia: Empirical findings and a somewhat different perspective J Clin Psychol 31: 685-686

Bender, L (1938), A Visual Motor Gestalt Test and Its Clinical Use, Research Monographs, No 3, New York: American Orthopsychiatric Association

Benton, AL, Hamster, KD, Varney, NR, and Spreen, O (1983), Contributions to Neuropsychological Assessment: A Clinical Manual, New York: Oxford Univ Press

Blain, L, and Mengler, D (1986), La dyschromatopsie chez des personnes exposés professionnellment aux solvants organiques, J Fr Ophthalmol 9(2): 127-133

Bowman, KJ (1982), A method for quantitative scoring of the Farnsworth panel D-15, Acta Ophthalm 60: 907-915

Bowman, KJ, Collins, MJ, and Henry, J (1984), The effect of age on the Panel D-15 and desaturated D-15: A quantitative evaluation, Doc Opthal Proc, Ser 38: 227-231

Cain, WS, and Gent, J (1986), Use of odor identification in clinical testing of olfaction, in Clinical Measures of Taste and Smell, ed HL Meiselman and RS Rivlin, New York: Macmillan, 170-186

Carlson, WS, Samueloff, S, Taylor, W, and Wasserman, DE (1979), Instrumentation for measurement of sensory loss in the fingertips, J Occup Med 21: 260-264

Cohn, NB, Dustman, RE, and Bradford, DC (1984), Age-related decrements in Stroop Color Test performance, J Clin Psychol 40: 1244-1250

Doppelt, JE, and Wallace, WL (1955), Standardization of the Wechsler Adult Intelligence Scale for older persons, J Abnor Soc Psychol 51: 312-330

Doty, RL (1983), The Smell Identification Kit, Philadelphia: Sensonics

Farnsworth, D (1957), The Farnsworth-Munsell 100 Hue Test for the Examination of Color Discrimination, Revised Manual, Baltimore: Munsell Color Co

Francois, J, and Verriest, G (1961), On acquired deficiency of color vision, with special references to its detection and classification by means of the tests of Farnsworth, Vis Res 1: 201-219

Gerr, F, Hershman, D, and Letz, R (1990), Vibrotactile threshold measurement for detecting neurotoxicity: Reliability and determination on age- and height-standardized normative values, Arch Environ Health 45: 148-154

Ghent, L (1956), Perception of overlapping and embedded figures by children of different ages, Am J Psychol 69: 576-587

Golden, CJ, Purish, AD, and Hammeke, TA (1985), Luria-Nebraska Neuropsychological Battery: Forms I and II, Los Angeles: Western Psychological Services

Graham, JR (1990), MMPI-2, Assessing Personality and Psychopathology, New York: Oxford Univ Press

Halstead, WC (1947), Brain and Intelligence, Chicago: Univ of Chicago Press

Hathaway, SR, and McKinley, JC (1942), A multiphasic personality schedule (Minnesota). III. The measurement of symptomatic depression, J Psychol 14: 73-84

Helve, J, and Krause, U (1972), The influence of age in the Panel D-15 colour test, Acta Ophthal 50: 896-900

Incagnoli, T, Goldstein, G, and Golden, CJ (1986), Clinical Applications of Neuropsychological Test Batteries, New York: Plenum

Lacks, P (1984), Bender Gestalt Screening for Brain Dysfunction, New York: Wiley

Lezak, MD (1983), Neuropsychological Assessment, 3rd ed, New York: Oxford Univ Press

Luria, AR (1966), Human Brain and Psychological Processes, New York: Harper & Row

Luria, AR, and Majowski, LV (1977), Basic approaches used in American and Soviet clinical neuropsychology, Am Psychol 32: 959-968

Matarazzo, JD (1972), Wechsler's Measurement and Appraisal of Human Intelligence (5th ed), Baltimore: Williams & Wilkins

Matarazzo, JS (1981), Obituary: David Wechsler (1896-1981), Am Psychol 36: 1542-1543

McManis, D (1974), Memory for designs performance of brain damaged and non brain damaged psychiatric patients, Percept Motor Skills 38: 847-852

Milner, B (1963), Effects of different brain lesions on card sorting, Arch Neurol 9: 90-100

Murray, HA (1943), Thematic Apperception Test Manual, Harvard College: President and Fellows of Harvard College

Orgel, S, and McDonald, R (1967), An evaluation of the Trail Making Test, J Consult Psychol 31(1): 77-79

Raven, L, et al (1986), A Compendium of American Normative and Validity Studies. Research Supplement No 3 to the Manual for Raven's Progressive Matrices and Vocabulary Scales, London: HK Lewis

Reitan, RM, and Davison, LA (1974), Clinical Neuropsychology: Clinical Status and Applications, New York: Winston/Wiley

Rey, A (1964), L'Examen Clinique in Psychologie, Paris: Presse Universitaires de France

Russell, EW, Neuringer, C, and Goldstein, G (1970), Assessment of Brain Damage: A Neuropsychological Key Approach, New York: Wiley-Interscience

Valciukas, JA (1991), Foundations of Environmental and Occupational Neurotoxicology, New York: Van Nostrand Reinhold

Valciukas, JA, and Singer, RM (1982), An embedded figures test in environmental and occupational neurotoxicology, Environ Res 28: 183-189

Wollman, BB (1989), Dictionary of Behavioral Science (2nd ed), San Diego: Academic

☐ APPENDIX B

Adelman, G ed (1987), Encyclopedia of Neuroscience, Boston: Birkhuser

Aminoff, MJ ed (1986), Electrodiagnosis in Clinical Neurology, New York: Churchill Livingstone

Araki, S, Murata, K, and Aono, H (1987), Central and peripheral nervous system dysfunction in workers exposed to lead, zinc and copper: A follow-up study of visual and somatosensory evoked potential, Int Arch Occup Environ, Healt 59: 177-187

Arezzo, JC, Simpson, R, and Brennan, NE (1985), Evoked potentials in the assessment of neurotoxicity in humans, Neurobeh Toxicol Teratol 7(4): 299-304

Armington, JC (1974), The Electroretinogram, New York: Academic

Babel, J, Stangos, N, Korol, S, and Spiritus, M (1977), Ocular Electrophysiology: A Clinical and Experimental Study of Electroretinogram, Electro-Oculogram, Visual Evoked Response, Stutgart: Georg Thieme Publishers

Basmajian, JV (1972), Electromyography comes of age, Science 176: 603-609

Bodis-Wollner, I ed (1982), Evoked Potentials, Annals of the New York Academy of Sciences Vol 388, June 18

Boring, EG (1950), A History of Experimental Psychology, New York: Appleton-Century-Crofts

Brazier, MAB (1984), A History of Neurophysiology in the 17th and 18th Centuries: From Concept to Experiment, New York: Raven

Brazier, MAB (1987), A History of Neurophysiology in the 19th Century, New York: Raven

Buchthal, F (1982), Human nerve potentials evoked by tactile stimuli, I: Maximum conduction and properties of compound potentials, Acta physiol Scand (Supp), 502: 5-18

Buchthal, F (1982), Human nerve potentials evoked by tactile stimuli, II Stimulus parameters and recruitment of components Acta physiol Scand (Supp): 502:19-32

Buchthal, F, and Rosenfalk, A (1966), Evoked action potential and conduction velocity in human sensory nerves, Brain Res, 3: 1-122

Callaway, E, Tueting, P, and Celesia, GG eds (1978), Event-Related Brain Potentials in Man, New York: Academic

Chalupa, B, Synkova, J, and Sevcik, M (1960), The assessment of electroencephalographic changes and memory disturbances in acute intoxications with industrial poisons, Brit J Ind Med, 17: 238-241

Chatrian, G-E (1986), Electrophysiology: Evaluation of brain death, in Electrodiagnosis in Clinical Neurology (2nd ed), ed MJ Aminoff, New York: Churchill Livingstone, 669-736

Chiappa, KH (1983), Evoked Potentials in Clinical Medicine, New York: Raven

DeJesus, PV, Hausmanowa-Petrusewicz, I, and Barchi, RL (1973), The effect of temperature on nerve conduction of human slow and fast nerve fibers Neurology (Minneap) 23: 1182-1189

Eccles, CU (1988), EEG correlates of neurotoxicity, Neurotox Teratol, 10(5): 423-428

Eisen, A, and Aminoff, MJ (1986), Somatosensory Evoked Potentials. In Electrodiagnosis in Clinical Neurology (2nd ed), ed MJ Aminoff, New York: Churchill Livingstone, 535-595

Evarts, EV, Shinoka, Y, and Wise, SP (1984), Neurophysiological Approaches to Higher Brain Function, New York: Wiley

Ewert, T, Beginn, U, Winneke, G, et al (1986), Sensory nerve conduction and visual and somatosensory evoked potentials in children exposed to lead, Nervenartz 57(8): 465-471

Feldman, RG, Hayes, MK, Younes, R, and Aldrich, RD (1977), Lead neuropathy in adults and children, Arch Neurol, 34: 481-488

Gilliatt, RW (1982), Electrophysiology of peripheral neuropathies: An overview, Muscle Nerve, 5: S108-116

Glickman, L, Valciukas, JA, Lilis, R, and Weisman, I (1984), Occupational lead exposure: Effects on saccadic eye movements, Int Arch Occup Env Health 54: 115-125

Halliday, AM (1982), Evoked Potentials in Clinical Testing, Bath: L Churchill Livingstone

Jabre, JF, and Hacken, ER (1983), EMG Manual Springfield, IL: Charles C Thomas

Johnson, BL (1980), Electrophysiological methods in neurotoxicity testing, in Experimental and Clinical Neurotoxicology, ed PS Spencer and HH Schaumburg, Baltimore: Williams & Wilkins, 726-742

Johnson, EW (1980), Practical Electromyography, Baltimore: Williams & Wilkins

Kooi, KA, Tucker, RP, and Marshall, RE (1978), Fundamentals of Electroencephalography (2nd ed), New York: Harper & Row

LeQuesne, PM (1978), Clinical expresson of neurotoxic injury and diagnostic use of electromyography, Env Health Persp 26: 89-95

Lopez da Silva, FH, and Storm Van Leeuwen, W eds (1986), Handbook of Electroencephalography and Clinical Neurophysiology, Amsterdam: Elsevier

Lowndes, HE ed (1987), Electrophysiology in Neurotoxicology (2 Vols), Boca Raton, FL: CRC Press

Metcalf, DR, and Holmes, JH (1969), EEG, psychological and neurological alterations in humans with organophosphorus exposure, Ann NY Acad Scie 160: 375-385

Ochoa, J (1980) Criteria for the assessment of polyneuropathy, in Experimental and Clinical Neurotoxicology, ed PS Spencer and HH Schaumburg, Baltimore: Williams & Wilkins 681-707

Ödkvist, LM, Larsby, B, Fredrickson, JMF, et al (1980), Vestibular and oculomotor disturbances caused by industrial solvents, J Otolaryn 9(1): 53-59

Oh, SJ (1984), Clinical Electromyography: Nerve Conduction Studies, Baltimore: University Park Press

Otto, DA (1986), The use of evoked potentials in neurotoxicity testing of workers, Seminars in Occup, Med 1(3): 175-183

Rosenman, KD, Valciukas, JA, Glickman, et al (1986) Sensitive indicators of inorganic mercury toxicity, Arch Env Res 41(4): 208-215

Seppäläinen AM (1984), Electrophysiological evaluation of central and peripheral neural effects of lead exposure Neurotoxicology 5(3): 43-52

Seppäläinen, AM, and Hernberg, S (1972), Sensitive techniques for detecting subclinical lead neuropathy, Brit J Ind Med 29: 443-449

World Health Organization (1986), Principles and Methods for the Assessment of Neurotoxicity Associated with Exposure to Chemicals, Geneva: World Health Organization

☐ APPENDIX C

Aichmer, F, Gerstenbrand, F, and Grévic, N (1989), Neuroimaging II, New York: VCH Publishers Inc

Andreasen, NC (1988), Brain imaging: Applications in Psychiatry, Science 239: 1381-1388

Andreasen, NC (1988), Evaluation of brain imaging techniques in mental illness, Ann Rev Med 39: 335

Andrew, ER (1984), A historical review of NMR and its clinical applications, Brit Med Bull 40: 115-119

Bigler, ED, Yeo, RA, and Turkheimer, E eds (1989), Neuropsychological Function and Brain Imaging, New York: Plenum

Birnholtz, JC, and Benacerraf, BR (1983), The development of the human fetal hearing, Science 222: 516-518

Duel, RK, Yue, GM, Sherman, WR, Shikner, DJ, and Ackerman, JJH (1985), Monitoring the time course of cerebral deoxyglucose metabolism by 31-P nuclear magnetic resonance spectroscopy Science 228: 1329-1331

Greenberg, J, Reivich, M, Alavi, A, et al (1981), Metabolic mapping of functional activity in human subjects with the (18F)-fluorodeoxyglucose technique, Science 212: 678-680

Gur, D, Good, WF, Wolfson, SK, Yonas, H, and Shabason, L (1982), In vivo mapping of local cerebral blood flow by xenon-enhanced computer tomography, Science 213: 1267-1268

Harms, ST, and Kramer, DM (1985), Fundamentals of Magnetic Resonance imaging, Critical Reviews in Diagnostic Imaging, Boca Raton, FL: CRC Press, 79-111

Heiss, W-D, and Phelps, ME eds (1983), Positron Emission Tomography of the Brain, New York: Springer Verlag

Hibbard, LS, McGlone, JS, Davis, DW, and Hawkins, RA (1987), Three dimensional representation and analysis of brain energy metabolism, Science 236: 1641-1646

Juntunen, J, Hernberg, S, Eistola, P, et al (1980), Exposure to industrial solvents and brain atrophy, Eur Neurol 19: 366

Marks, JL (1987), Imaging techniques passes muster, Science 238: 888-889

Maurer, K, and Dierks, T (1987), Functional imaging of the brain in psychiatry: Mapping of EEG and evoked potentials, Neurosurg Rev 10: 275

Mazziotta, JC, and Gilman, S (1992), Clinical Brain Imaging: Principles and Applications, Philadelphia: FA Davis

Oldendorf, WH (1980), The Quest for an Image of the Brain: Computerized Tomography in the Perspective of Past and Future, New York: Raven

Phelps, ME, and Mazziotta, JC (1985), Positron emission tomography: Human brain function and biochemistry, Science 228: 799-809

Radda, GK (1986), The use of NMR spectroscopy for the understanding of disease, Science 233: 640-645

Ramsey, RG (1987), Neuroradiology (2nd ed), Philadelphia: WB Saunders

Reichle, ME (1986), Neuroimaging, Trends in Neuroscience 9: 525-529

Robb, RA (1985), Three-Dimensional Biomedical Imaging (2 Vols), Boca Raton, FL: CRC Press

Valk, J (1987), MRI of the Brain, Head, Neck and Spine, Boston: Martinus Nijhoff

Wagner, HN, Burns, DH, Dannals, RF, et al (1983), Imaging dopamine receptors in the human brain by positron tomography, Science 221: 1264-1266

Williamson, PC, and Kaye, H (1989), EEG mapping applications in psychiatric disorders, Can J Psychiat 34: 680

INDEX OF TOPICS AND NAMES